RICHELIEU
AND HIS AGE

ASSERTION OF POWER
AND COLD WAR

by Carl J. Burckhardt

RICHELIEU AND HIS AGE
1. *His Rise to Power*

Bust of Richelieu

CARL J. BURCKHARDT

RICHELIEU
AND HIS AGE

VOLUME II

ASSERTION OF POWER
AND COLD WAR

TRANSLATED FROM THE GERMAN
BY BERNARD HOY

A HELEN AND KURT WOLFF BOOK
HARCOURT, BRACE & WORLD, INC.
NEW YORK

This Translation © *1970 by George Allen and Unwin Ltd*

Translated from the German
RICHELIEU, BEHAUPTUNG
DER MACHT UND KALTER KRIEG
© Georg D. W. Callwey, München, 1965

FOREWORD

In an earlier volume written some thirty years ago the author of the present work set out to describe Cardinal Richelieu as a political figure. That volume was conceived in purely biographical terms and the historical events of the period were considered from the point of view of Richelieu's personal activity in the first three decades of the seventeenth century. Since it was a biographical account it was necessarily of a more general and condensed nature, and it finished with the chapter entitled "The Day of the Dupes" (*la journée des dupes*), the event that marked the end of the long process of Richelieu's rise to power.

The means the Cardinal then employed in order to defend his power and deploy it in the interests of France were determined at every turn by the pressure of events, many of which had taken place long before his time. This section of Richelieu's career forms an integral part of European history as such, and the role he played and the influence he brought to bear on historical events during the last twelve years of his life cannot be expressed in biographical terms. No biographical method can encompass such diversity.

Unfortunately the great variety of individual investigations that French historians have culled from the immeasurable wealth of their source material, which includes their "little history" of the Cardinal and the King, are not readily adaptable for the non-French reader. These were written with the French reader in mind and no people of Europe is as well informed about its national history as the French. But in so far as France was also deeply involved in the affairs of Europe and of the world at large, it is perhaps both permissible and rewarding to attempt a detailed account of that involvement. Consequently the attempt has here been made to elucidate the underlying conditions governing Richelieu's life work, many of them rising out of historical situations that originated in the far distant past.

This second volume carries the action forward to the peace of Prague, the point marking the dramatic intensification of Richelieu's policies.

Situations that had already been dealt with in Volume I have in many cases been reconsidered in Volume II from different viewpoints and often in far greater detail.

C.J.B.

NOTE

A minimum of notes is given in this English translation. Greater detail and a complete list of references for the quotations may be found in Carl J. Burckhardt: *Richelieu*, Vol. IV (Registerband), Munich 1967.

CONTENTS

A*

CONTENTS

ILLUSTRATIONS

CHAPTER I

A GOVERNMENT PROGRAMME

Towards the end of the first, introductory volume of this monograph there is a description of the events known as the "great storm." Following the Day of the Dupes, which had been decisive for the whole of Richelieu's subsequent political career, the Cardinal continued to conduct defensive battles, in which his very survival was at stake, against the concerted opposition of his many enemies at home. All the forces of resistance to both his radical internal reforms and his national foreign policy, a policy which drove like a wedge between the opposing ideological fronts, were centred in Brussels around the person of Marie de' Medici, the Queen-Mother. The heir-apparent, Gaston d'Orléans, wavered between the tempting prospect held out to him of a throne with royal powers and the unimpeded enjoyment of the large donations that Louis XIII was constantly bestowing on him. The French resistance movement was strengthened by the contacts it was able to maintain in the Spanish Netherlands with Madrid, Vienna and London. Lorraine, whose independence was threatened by France, also afforded it every possible assistance. The French members of the Fronde, no matter what their allegiance, continued to enjoy Spanish support.

And all this despite the fact that the fearful experience of the Wars of Religion and, from 1618 onwards, the sight of the Holy Roman Empire bleeding from a thousand wounds had revealed to all concerned the dangers attendant on the fragmentation of great European territories into a host of sovereign states of feudal origin. Because Richelieu's every endeavour was directed towards the establishment of order and authority, his objective was approved on all sides and by many of the leading men of his day, not least by those who held distinctly liberal views. A particularly telling example of such approval is to be found in the fourth chapter of the first book of Hugo Grotius' *De iure belli ac pacis*. Grotius considered that Huguenot opposition within France was unjustified. In his *Carmen heroicum de capta Rupella*, which he composed after the fall of La Rochelle, he wrote: "Citizens, to have been conquered by this king and by such an army, this you need not be ashamed of." Indeed, the great Dutch Protestant went so far as to say that he considered Louis's war against the Huguenots to be a just war, because "the King was not doing violence to their religious freedom." This statement goes to the heart of the matter. An autonomous power with federal and republican leanings had long existed in France, preventing the French State from undertaking effective action outside its own borders. Once the great Huguenot strongholds had fallen and repressive measures had been applied with extreme severity in the South of France, particularly in the Cévennes, that power was broken. All that held the Protestants together now, after their collapse, was the invisible bond of faith. Their church was left without an organization; they suffered and hoped in passive allegiance and placed their faith in royal undertakings.

But Richelieu, unlike those who were to follow him, did not indulge in disastrous excesses. Instead, with the same astonishing composure that had characterized his attitude towards the Calvinists even before he entered the government, he remained true to the principles laid down in the Edict of Nantes. He considered that the Protestants should be spared religious intolerance. All he required of them was that they should take their places as disciplined and integrated subjects of the united monarchy.

The wisdom of the peace of Alais,[1] which marked the

---

[1] Cf. Vol. I, p. 329 ff.

end of the Huguenot wars, brought about an improvement in the attitude towards the monarchy, not only of the French Calvinists, but of Protestants in every part of Europe. And so as early as 1629, by means of this act of grace, Richelieu was already preparing the ground for the conclusion of Protestant alliances, England looming large in his calculations.

The Cardinal's far-sightedness and his impressive magnanimity, when magnanimity served his often far distant ends, appears especially creditable in this particular instance, because in the final phase of their struggle the Huguenots had entered into what amounted to an alliance with Spain, which clearly shows that Olivares was also prepared to seize upon every opportunity to inflict harm on his country's neighbour and was willing to depart from the Counter-Reformation "line" in order to do so. But more of this later in connection with Henri de Rohan, the Huguenot leader.

Time and again attempts have been made to prove that, contrary to the evidence of his Memoirs, the Cardinal did not pursue from the very beginning a consistent policy directed towards a few well-defined aims, but tended rather to act in terms of expedience in his early days, dealing pragmatically with each individual case. This view is contradicted by a number of factors which we shall be discussing. Quite the most important of these is the truly amazing speech, briefly mentioned in Volume I, which Louis XIII's First Minister delivered on January 13, 1629 in the presence of his sovereign, the Queen-Mother and Jean Suffren, the King's confessor. The main points of this speech need to be studied in relationship to one another. Rarely has a statesman addressed his Prince with such candour in the presence of witnesses. Richelieu's discourse embodied his ideas on both external and internal policy, it defended his work prior to 1629, it gave expression to the passionate eruption of his own personal claims and finally it gave, in the solemn tones of a spiritual adviser, a relentlessly critical and detailed analysis of the monarch's personal character.

Richelieu said in the presence of his King:

"The King is good, virtuous, discreet, courageous and intent on acquiring fame, but it is [equally] true to say that he is precipitate, suspicious, envious and susceptible to sudden antipathies and first impressions to the detriment of all and sundry; in short, he is subject to a certain diversity of mood and to various inclinations, which it will be easier for him to remedy than for me to recount, since I am so accustomed to praising his virtues to the world at large that I would scarcely be able to enumerate his defects. . . ."

Many of the following passages are to be found in the extant manuscript in Richelieu's own hand.

"We must accommodate the Duke of Orléans [Monsieur] in all things that are not harmful to the State but oppose him in all things that might prejudice the King's authority."

Richelieu then sounded a note of caution, lest Orléans should succeed to the throne.

"If this prince is treated honourably, he will never do anything to disturb the peace of the realm but will remain within the bounds of duty and [promote] the true interests of the State, for which he has such a natural affection that, even when he has had grievances, I have always noted the sound opinions he holds with regard to the public weal. The King must be like a father to him, he must be tolerant of his faults . . . and conceal them from everyone. In doing so, he will be doing himself no small service, since great harm comes to Princes who take pleasure in singling out the faults of the "great," for there are many who, in order to please them [the Princes], exaggerate those faults as much as they possibly can and subsequently, in order to escape the unpleasant consequences of their wild talk, commit a very special kind of treason by informing those whom they have slandered while attributing the slanders in their entirety to their master. It would be prudent of the King to refrain from passing any comment on the members of Monsieur's[1] entourage."

The Cardinal went on to say:

"If His Majesty were to try to silence all those who speak badly [of others] in his presence, which they will normally only do in order to elicit from him some [stinging] remark with which to pique their fellows, he would derive great benefit. . . . The history and my own experience of our times suggest to me that this has undoubtedly been the cause of many recent difficulties.

Nothing is more becoming in a Prince than to speak with constraint; he must imitate the queen bee, which has no sting."

He went further:

"His Majesty must avoid like death itself a certain tendency towards envy, which has prompted many a Prince to find it intolerable that his subjects should be dealing with affairs on his behalf that the ruler himself is neither willing nor able to deal with. . . . If this tendency is not overcome, then nobody will dare to make full use of his abilities, which is a dangerous state of affairs, since there are many occasions when, although it may not be possible to counter [political] ills by moderate and restrained means, it is easy to do so by strong and powerful measures, which, however, nobody will have the courage to take, since there are few who would risk courting their master's displeasure by serving him too well.

In this connection I wish to say quite openly that His Majesty must either decide to pursue the affairs of state with persistency and force or must delegate his authority to some other person, in order that he may act for him . . .; otherwise he will never be well served and his affairs will come to grief."

The Cardinal referred to the King's jealousy and mistrust

[1] Gaston d'Orléans, Monsieur, was the heir apparent until September 5, 1638, the day on which Louis XIV was born.

again and again. In the following excerpt the sun of Louis XIV can be seen rising.

"And in this respect it would seem that His Majesty is jealous of his own shadow, for, just as the stars have no other light save that which they receive from the sun, so too it is His Majesty who gives his creatures force; they shine only in his reflected light. . . ."

The King must realize that those who serve him "are as interested in safeguarding his person as he himself . . ., for if God were to remove him from this world, they would be exposed to all the hatred they have acquired by serving him so well."

How clearly this last statement described the Cardinal's own situation!

Yet again he warned his master of the danger, one to which he was particularly prone, of forming sudden antipathies. And then he began to give him advice on how to deal with the great nobles, which was of course tantamount to advice on internal policy.

"A good cuisine for the great!" he urged. And he went on to say:

". . . although it is one of the burdens it is also one of the prerogatives of royalty to have persons of this quality at its command . . . and if it is not possible to appease their inordinate appetites, then at least they must be shown a friendly face." Richelieu did not remain true to this principle. But in 1629 he was not yet in a position to reveal his real intentions.

There then followed an aphorism of indisputable validity:

"It is dangerous to forget the perils attendant on an evil that has been overcome, for if the memory is suppressed, one runs the risk of falling a victim to some similar evil." And from this point on the Cardinal began to refer indirectly to himself. He said:

"Princes who wish to receive true service must choose

ministers who are guided by reason alone and who spare no man [for subjective reasons]. . . . Many Princes, although strong in themselves, lack the strength to resist the representations that are made to them to the detriment of those who serve them best and to whom they owe greater protection.

This censure was of course levelled primarily at the King himself, for Richelieu immediately went on to say that men attach more importance to their personal prestige than to anything else in the world. He explained that a single adverse comment from the monarch could dash men's hopes and undermine their good will, while a cheering word or a sign of appreciation was better able to promote a sense of zeal in the service of the Crown than any gift, however rich. Again and again he told the King that in his judgements he should be far less severe. At the same time Richelieu himself grew more severe and more personal. He said:

"Many think, and not without reason, that His Majesty is naturally disinclined to apply himself to affairs of state and quickly tires of those which call for protracted effort. . . . If this is so, His Majesty must combat his aversion . . . for no man is intrepid enough to undertake to serve a Prince in some great enterprise, if he has cause to fear that he will tire of it before it is half finished. . . ."

And by now he had become quite vehement:

". . . The King pays so little attention to his affairs and disapproves so readily of the expedients proposed to him in order to ensure the success of those he does undertake that in future it may well prove difficult to serve him. The respect that is shown to him and the fear of offending his sensibilities stifle the very best intentions in the hearts and minds of his most capable servants. . . . There have been Princes who wanted the ends but not the means, which is to say that they wished their affairs to prosper but did not want to take the necessary steps to that end. . . .

"There still are Princes whose nature is such that, when their affairs go badly, they feel extremely dejected, develop a high regard for those able to apply remedies and resolve to conduct themselves in a manner conducive to such an end. But once the danger has passed they forget all about their good resolutions. . . . Such a failing is of no little consequence and His Majesty will please take care to avoid it.

"It is so very dangerous for the State when the application of the law is treated with indifference that I feel bound to observe that His Majesty appears to show a lack of firmness and zeal regarding the observance of his own laws, especially the edict forbidding duelling.

". . . His Majesty and His Majesty's council will have to answer for all those souls who perish in this diabolical way. . . ."

This is followed by a highly significant observation which enables us to approach the innermost secret of this great French statesman. It illumines his moral personality and it characterizes and explains the attitude of his contemporaries, who, although Christians, were nonetheless profoundly dedicated to the conception of the State.

Here is the passage:

"The sins Kings commit as Kings are different from those they commit as ordinary men. As men they are subject to all conditions it has pleased God to impose on the human race; as Kings they must make careful use of their power for the purposes for which it has been vested in them by the Almighty and, what is more, they must never abuse it. . . .

"Those who fail to invoke their authority to keep their State in due and proper order are also guilty before God. . . .

"If a King suffers the strong to oppress the weak with impunity in his kingdom . . ., if he allows men to disturb the peace of his realm . . ., he will surely perish; but equally a King who avoids damnation as a King will appear saintly as a man.

"A Christan can never forget a wrong or forgive an offence quickly enough, but a King, a governor or a magistrate can never punish them quickly enough when they concern the State.

"God did not wish to place vengeance in the hands of individuals, for under this pretext any man might have given free rein to his passions and disturbed the peace of the realm.

"But He did place it in the hands of Kings and magistrates, to be administered in accordance with His laws, since without examples and without punishments all manner of injustice and violence would be committed with impunity and to the detriment of public order.

"Man's ultimate salvation is achieved in the other world, and so it is not surprising that God should require individuals to leave to Him vengeance for wrongs, which He requites by His judgements in eternity.

"States do not survive this present world, their salvation is here and now or not at all, and so punishments necessary for their survival cannot be deferred but must be immediate.

"Moreover, justice must be administered dispassionately, and a Prince who dispensed it by persecuting those whom he disliked and excusing and exempting those fortunate enough to enjoy his favour, would have to give account of himself before the court of divine justice, which is superior to his own. . . .

"Since the Kings are God's representatives on earth, in that all blessings must flow from their hands, they cannot be too mindful of acquiring . . . a reputation for generosity . . . but they must do so, not by distributing favours, but by giving due regard to the merit and the services of individuals, for it is certain that there are very few who regard virtue as its own reward . . . and it is a precept of great Princes to reward those who serve their States worthily; it is an investment that will be repaid ten times over. . . ."

This last passage should be considered in the light of the criticisms which have been levelled at Richelieu on account of his "insatiability." It is also significant that, following this statement, the Cardinal should have sought to introduce a diversion. He said: "The Duke of Luynes often observed that the King's natural inclination was towards severity rather than lenience."

But he immediately added:

"I, for my part, have never found this to be the case, but the bad thing is that many believe it to be so, which imposes an obligation on His Majesty's servants to warn him, in order that he may dispose of this bad opinion, which, in effect, is without foundation."

And then came the brief, almost threatening remark:

"Kings should deal severely with all those who disturb the peace and violate the law within their kingdom, but they should not take pleasure in their severity."

With this thrust the Cardinal terminated his digression and turned once more to the question of just rewards, of rewards, that is, which could be justified on objective grounds. He said:

"His Majesty must try to master a certain tendency towards a [false] sense of goodness, which prompts many Princes to accede to all requests made to them in person, even though they be bad, and prevents them from saying anything they think will displease the other person, even though they be mistaken . . . .Those who do not know the King's nature attribute this tendency, which stems from pure goodness of heart, to weakness.

"A man must be strong by virtue of reason and not passion.

". . . Many, when fired by passion, speak and act with force and vigour, but when the fire has gone out of them, they let everything go. . . . The King will please take care to guard against this kind of failing.

"One of the things that greatly undermines His Majesty's authority is that people think he does not act on his own initiative, that he is more interested in trivialities than in great and important affairs and that the administration of the State leaves him indifferent.

"In order that this opinion may be dispelled it is desirable that His Majesty should show a keen interest in any event touching upon his own authority and should do so before any of his servants broach the subject with him. . . .

"Finally, His Majesty should speak frequently with one and all and should make it known that he is interested in all matters brought up for discussion which are of importance to the State.

"A great deal of good may come from the frankness, which my conscience and my passion for the monarchy have constrained me to use, in advising the King of what needs to be done in respect of his personal conduct, in order that he may become the greatest Prince in the world; but it could also be that nothing but harm will come of it, which would indubitably be the case if, as a result of this advice, His Majesty were henceforth to conceal his thoughts and feelings. . . . If he were to do so, they would prey upon his mind and cause him a thousand pains, from which he could only free himself by opening his heart and speaking of the things that oppressed him."

And then Richelieu spoke of himself. His words are sincere and moving, as is quite evident from their tenor:

"If it were as easy for me to cure my physical ills as to correct my spiritual faults, it would be a great consolation to me, for then I would not be obliged to implore Your Majesties to make allowance for my personal debility; my already depleted forces are daily reduced to such an extent that I am no longer able to endure the unbelievable strain imposed by the actions that have to be taken to ensure the safety of a great State, especially when this physical strain is accompanied by great deliberations, great anxieties and great spiritual afflictions."

This passage bears witness to the many burdens that weighed upon the Cardinal following the tremendous and protracted effort of his rise to power. It is as if a dam had broken, as if fatigue had lamed his powers of self-control and secrecy. This was a genuine outburst, nevertheless controlled by Richelieu's skill both as a judge of individual psychology and as a statesman.

Confession, calculation, church sermon, moral discourse—all these were present in his speech. And yet, as was inevitable, it still remained primarily political.

No interpretation could ever hope to come so close to the truth, to the essence, of Richelieu's personality or his monarch's, or to that of the relationship between servant and master, as this unique document. It is an outstanding portrait of a King.

But what did Richelieu have to say about internal policy in his speech? In the first place he insisted that Huguenot resistance must be broken once and for all. It was a matter of urgency that the strongholds of Castres, Nîmes, Montauban and the bases in Languedoc, Rouergue and Guyenne should be occupied. This part of the Cardinal's programme was of course realized within the year (see Vol. I, p. 212 ff.).

It took much longer, however, for the second point in his programme to be achieved. In this proposal Richelieu stressed the importance of razing to the ground all Huguenot strongholds save those situated on the French border, dominating river bridges or fords or adjacent to and thus capable of controlling rebellious towns. At the same time it was imperative that the border defences should be strengthened and that Commercy,[1] among others, should be occupied.

Richelieu then expressed wishes that, because they were never realized, make melancholy reading: the people should be relieved of some part of their burdens and the Paulette tax, which was due for renewal in the following year, should be allowed to lapse.

[1] Commercy: town in Lorraine situated on the Meuse between St Mihiel and Toul.

But he went on to outline plans that certainly were realized. Those groups that stood on their usurped rights and acted against the interests of the monarchy were to be kept down. Both great and small were to be coerced into absolute obedience to the Crown. Only capable people (i.e., people who shared the government's views and agreed with official policy) were to be appointed as bishops. The Crown lands were to be increased and enfeoffed estates bought back from their present owners.

And then came the most important aspect of Richelieu's whole programme: his vision of French foreign policy and the objectives it should pursue. First his *"ceterum censeo"*: the Spanish advances were to be halted, a requirement that imposed a two-fold obligation on France: the consolidation of her power both at home and abroad and the establishment of assault bases on all her borders, from which French armies might penetrate into any neighbouring country in order to defend it against Spanish oppression whenever the opportunity arose.

But if this was to be achieved, France had to increase her power at sea, for this would give her access to every country in the world. Metz was to be reinforced and if possible the French must advance as far as Strassburg, for Strassburg was to be the assault base for Germany. This last-named objective was to be pursued secretly and was on no account to be rushed into.

A citadel was to be built in Versoix,[1] the assault base for Switzerland, for the Swiss were a crude people who saw nothing beyond the ends of their noses. It was important that they should be impressed. Of course, no French patriot in his right mind would ever believe that the King was not deeply interested in preserving the Swiss alliance; since it was the Swiss who denied Germany access to Italy and since soldiering was their traditional profession, it was essential that

---

[1] Versoix was conquered by France in 1607 and was not incorporated into the Canton of Geneva until 1816.

France rather than her enemies should have the Swiss army at command. In this connection it remained necessary to acquire from the de Longuevilles the rights of sovereignty over Neuchâtel.

The marquisate of Saluzzo[1] was a further French objective, to be attained by entering into an agreement with the Duke of Savoy. This meant that the French would have to act at the precise moment when the ambivalent Duke happened to take up service again with the King and when it was also possible to help him acquire some sort of territorial gain in Italy. Failing this they would have to exploit any discord between the inhabitants of Saluzzo and their ruler and simply take the territory away from him. A strong fortress would then have to be built in order to safeguard this new acquisition.

Richelieu's aims in respect of both Lorraine and the Spanish Netherlands had already been formulated in 1629 but were not mentioned in this speech. Three years later, however, we find the following comment in a personal report which Richelieu submitted to the King:

"As far as Lorraine is concerned, for the time being we must dissemble . . . and, without binding ourselves, so arrange matters as to give them reason to believe that we do not intend to act against them."

And again:

"As soon as the Dutch have taken the field [i.e., as soon as the Spanish forces are tied down], we must send in 40,000 men to conquer Lorraine . . . and we must do so at the precise moment when our action is least expected."

In this same great exposition Richelieu stated his Italian policy: if France was to be respected in Italy it was absolutely essential that a force of thirty galleys be kept in the Mediterranean; this naval unit was to be placed under a different

---

[1] The Marquisate of Saluzzo had been occupied by Savoy during the French Wars of Religion.

command every three years, for then each new commander would be at pains to outdo his predecessor.

And finally: Franche-Comté must be wrested from the Spanish in the very near future.

By this time Richelieu's over-all plan was virtually complete. In the following pages we shall be considering both the factors that opposed the execution of this amazing project and the extent to which it was successfully implemented.

But for the moment let us consider just two of the postulates contained in this detailed statement of intent: the proposal that the great nobles be coerced into absolute obedience to the Crown and the submission that it was a matter of life and death for France to make herself strong at sea. These two policies were closely related to one another. For the continued existence of the feudal system in France was a factor that made it extremely difficult to organize French naval rearmament. In order to overcome this difficulty Richelieu was to wage his campaign against the feudal rights of sovereignty claimed by the great nobles to the bitter end.

CHAPTER II

THE NAVY AND NAVAL HARBOURS

One of the first departments mentioned by Richelieu in connection with rearmament was the navy. He had already subjected the problem of naval power to a systematic analysis before the commencement of his second term of office, and he proceeded to put his findings into practice as soon as he had the power to do so. He had two objectives in view: the creation of a fighting fleet and the construction of a merchant navy; the latter project of course presupposed the freedom of the seas.

Richelieu's first attempt to undermine feudal positions of power within the monarchy was directly connected with his work on naval reconstruction. This attempt was successful and resulted in Henri de Montmorency's being deprived of the office of Grand Admiral of France, which had been virtually hereditary in the Montmorency family. At the Cardinal's instigation Montmorency was required to place his office at the disposal of the Crown in return for 1,200,000 livres in compensation, whereupon the office of Grand Admiral of France was abolished. As soon as this crucial measure had been put into effect, the Cardinal did all he could to publicize its terms in order to expose the retiring Admiral as a man capable of accepting such a high indemnity. For a short period the King himself took over nominal command of both the navy and the merchant fleet. The relevant royal decree reads as follows:

"Through the retirement of Our Cousin, the Duke of Montmorency, from the Office of Grand Admiral of France,

Guyenne and Brittany, which now reverts to the Crown,
We find Ourselves obliged to make a new appointment. We
have decided that henceforth the title of Admiral of France,
Guyenne and Brittany shall be abolished for all time. We wish
nonetheless that the regulations, rights and privileges of the
Admiralty shall remain in force, in order that the person who
is placed in command of Our trade under Our authority shall
be better able to promote and develop it within Our kingdom."

The "short report" (*Succinte Narration*), the summary
composed in 1638 for submission to the King, mentioned
among other things the Cardinal's achievements in respect of
the navy. In that report Richelieu reproduced the same arguments regarding shipping which he had presented to the King
in the twenties. He regretted the general neglect of shipping
requirements in the past and stated that Louis XIII's predecessors had underestimated the importance of sea power, with
the result that Henry IV had ultimately found himself without
a single ship to his name. And from the *Political Testament*
we learn that England was too near, Spain with her colonies
was too strong and in the Mediterranean the Berbers pursued
a policy of intolerable piracy. Foreigners were at liberty to
disrupt the country's fishing industry, harm her trade, sink
her ships, drag their crews off to slavery, blockade the
estuaries of French rivers and make landings on French coasts,
while the King was powerless to intervene. It was an impossible
situation. France must have her own fleet of fighting ships,
if for no other reason than to prevent foreign powers from
coming to the aid of the Huguenots, although it was also
necessary that France herself should be in a position to bring
aid to those of her allies who could be reached by sea. Few
countries were so rich in the raw materials necessary for shipbuilding, in manufactured goods of wood and iron, in canvas
and ropes, and few countries had such splendid natural
harbours as France.

These general precepts had been taking shape in the

Cardinal's mind from 1624 onwards. The King was convinced by his adviser's arguments. What was required was a capable man to put the project into effect. And the only man with the drive and authority needed to carry out such a tremendous undertaking was Richelieu himself. A new title was created for him and he was appointed "Controller-General of Navigation and Trade." In this capacity, however, he did not at first have command of the marines.

Richelieu declared that he wished to receive no salary for his new office. But in point of fact he was granted full legal possession of all wrecks washed up on the French coasts and all incomes from anchorage rights, both sources of revenue to have effect from the first day of his appointment. The Cardinal announced that he would arrange for all such revenues to be used for naval purposes. According to a statement drawn up in the year 1636 of the amounts accruing from these rights, the total income for that year came to 131,702 livres. Further statements show that the year 1639 produced an income of 226,208 livres and 1642, the year of Richelieu's death, an income of 96,800 livres.

The Cardinal set to work at once. He required that forty warships, thirty galleys and ten galleons, a total of eighty ships in all, should be built or bought. This figure of eighty ships was to remain his maximum requirement. His correspondence, especially with the Dutch, shows how seriously he devoted himself to this undertaking right from the outset. To buy ships, to build ships, to cast cannon, to lay up stores of powder, to construct arsenals, to recruit and to train sailors and gunners, these were the aims he set himself. The King had told him that he wished to appoint him governor of a strongly fortified harbour town. Partly for reasons of family tradition Richelieu chose Le Havre and purchased the suzerainty of the town from Monsieur de Villars. But his opponents immediately put out that he had moved into this coastal stronghold in order to dominate the Seine estuary and place himself in an unassailable position. This kind of thing, they argued, only went to show that Richelieu was out to set himself up as a dictator. His next move would be to declare himself Constable and then Prince of Austrasia;[1] his very existence was a threat to the King, to the dynasty and to all Frenchmen. At this juncture Richelieu considered it advisable to turn to public opinion, to state his true aims and obtain the approbation of the leading personalities of the day.

As for Richelieu's family tradition and its influence on his choice of a fortified harbour town, the facts of the matter are as follows:

For a period of fifty years Richelieu's great-grandfather, Vice-Admiral Guyon Le Roy du Chillou, had fought the English at sea. He had fought the Spanish and the Turks. In 1499 he had taken part in the first naval battle of Lepanto and he had also built one of the most important naval harbours in France, Le Havre. This harbour, which was subsequently defended by the Cardinal's grandfather, François du Plessis, was then occupied by the English and finally retaken by Richelieu's father, François du Plessis. Thanks to his maternal uncle, Commodore Amador de La Porte, who knew the Mediterranean well, and to his elder brother, who had first-hand knowledge of the Brazilian province of Maranhão, Richelieu was already well versed in both maritime and colonial matters when still a very young man.

In September 1626 the Cardinal had suggested to his sovereign that an Assembly of Notables should be convened, which would, among other things, afford an opportunity of explaining both the reasons why and the way in which the new department of navigation was to be organized. Louis XIII also gave his assent to this project and on December 2nd the Assembly was opened in the Tuileries. This event too was primarily designed to aid the Cardinal in his struggle to strip

---

[1] A reference to the Austrasian "mayors of the palace," who assumed all effective power under the later Merovingian kings. One of them, Pepin the Short, made himself king, thus founding the Carolingian dynasty.

the nobility of their remaining feudal rights, for there was no single sphere in which this struggle was revealed quite so clearly or in which its justification on practical grounds was quite so strong as in the sphere of French shipping. Interestingly enough, however, naval affairs were touched upon only very briefly at the Assembly, chiefly out of consideration for the excitable condition of public opinion following Montmorency's dispossession. The Cardinal made a long speech of a very general and far-ranging nature on the financial estimates. He was preceded by the Keeper of the Seals, Michel de Marillac, and by Marshal Henri de Schomberg, then Superintendent of Finance.

Richelieu had asked Marillac to speak for him on naval affairs, since he himself, as the minister directly responsible, was unable to do so; he had set out his arguments in a memorandum and hoped that the Keeper of the Seals would find it possible to present them on his behalf. This memorandum has survived. In it we read:

"Until to-day we have suffered the ignominy of seeing our King, the foremost of all Christian rulers, weaker than the pettiest princes of Christendom in terms of naval power. His Majesty has recognized the great evils that may arise from this circumstance for his kingdom and his subjects and has resolved to set matters aright by making himself as strong at sea as he is on land. But for this resolution we would have to give up trading altogether. The King's subjects have not only been constantly deprived of their property but of their liberty [i.e., by pirates]; our neighbours have considered themselves justified in selling us their goods on their own terms and in taking ours at whatever price they chose to pay. These miseries will now cease, for His Majesty has decided to maintain thirty stout warships to keep the coasts clear, his subjects within lawful bounds and his neighbours mindful of the respect which is owing to so great a state.

"The annual cost of this force will be 1,500,000 livres."

Richelieu had added the following comment at the foot of this text:

"The Keeper of the Seals will decide whether it is desirable to mention the abolition of Montmorency's powers. This measure will result in an annual saving of 400,000 livres. He will also decide whether to mention that the King has deigned to decree that the Cardinal will henceforth command the fleet, for which duties he will claim no salary."

But Marillac made no use of this document. All he said was: "The King has abolished the offices of Constable and Grand Admiral and has deleted the salaries and expenses which these involved. The saving thus achieved amounts to at least 400,000 livres annually."

He made only a passing reference to Richelieu's disinterestedness.

In the minutes of the meeting we find the following passage:

"After the King had signalled to Monseigneur Cardinal Richelieu to begin his speech and the Cardinal had bowed to His Majesty and the Assembly of Notables he took his place with his head covered; he spoke with extraordinary grace and received the greatest applause from the Assembly."

In Richelieu's manuscript of his speech, the peroration closes with the following sentence: "I had intended to speak of the navy, but in view of what the Keeper of the Seals has already said on this subject I shall desist, for I have nothing to add to his remarks."

In his actual speech, however, he omitted this final sentence. This early incident casts a revealing light on the relationship between Richelieu and Marillac. It is also revealing to compare the facts as reported in the minutes of this conference with the report given by the Cardinal in his Memoirs. In the Memoirs we find the following passage:

"The great knowledge of the sea which he [the Cardinal]

had acquired prompted him to make various necessary, useful and honourable proposals before the Assembly of Notables that was held at that time, not so much to restore to the navy the respect it had previously enjoyed in France as to restore to France herself by means of the navy the glory that had once been hers. The Cardinal pointed out that the only reason why Spain was able to extend her dominion to the Levant and to obtain a regular income from her territories in the West was that she was powerful at sea, that it was thanks to its naval forces that the small citizen state of the United Provinces was able to oppose the mighty kingdom of Spain, and that England's importance was also due to her maritime prowess, but that France, who lacked all power at sea, could be insulted with impunity by her neighbours, who daily issued new laws and ordinances directed against French merchants, subjecting them to harsh penalties and unjust conditions, and plundered French ships and carried off their crews on the flimsiest of pretexts."

There is ample evidence to prove the truth of the assertion that the King of France was much weaker at sea than even the pettiest prince. To quote but one example: the Château d'If, built and fortified on the Isle d'If during the reign of Francis I, which was used as a state prison, had been seized by the Grand Duke Ferdinand of Tuscany, an ally of Spain, who asserted his power over the island with only four galleys at his command, as if in open defiance of France, for the gates of Marseille were less than two miles away.

One day Richelieu recounted the following incident to Louis XIII:

"When Your Majesty's defunct father, King Henry, instructed Monsieur de Liancourt to protest to the Grand Duke Ferdinand of Tuscany for having entered into a new relationship with Spain despite the alliance concluded between their two houses as a result of the King's marriage to Your Majesty's mother, the Queen, the Grand Duke, after listening patiently, gave a reply which said a very great deal in very few words and which Your Majesty and Your Majesty's successors should take to heart: 'If the King had had forty galleys in Marseille,' the prince said, 'I would not have done what I did.' "

The Grand Duke's remark dates from the time of Sully, who, as Henry IV's representative, had been exposed to ridicule in the eyes of the whole world by an English admiral. This admiral had forbidden Sully, the King's special ambassador and his closest friend, to enter English harbours while sailing under the French flag. The Duke was also denied the customary salute. In the circumstances Sully could only yield and was obliged to fly Dutch colours. As late as 1629, after the failure of Buckingham's attempt to relieve La Rochelle and the subsequent capitulation of the city, the English were still intent on denying to the French the right to sail the seas under their own flag. This sort of thing was not easily forgotten, least of all by Richelieu, whom Buckingham had called a "fresh-water admiral."

In 1625, before he was authorized to act in an official capacity in the sphere of shipping, Richelieu had a report drawn up that dealt with every aspect of the problems involved. He corrected the text himself and the document, which reveals some errors, also reveals all the elements of his later attitude to naval affairs. What we have here is evidently a rough draft for a royal decree. It reads as follows:

"In order to protect those of Our subjects who engage in trade in the Levant from the losses imposed on them by the pirates of the Barbary States and in order to preserve the prestige and dignity of the French Crown in the eyes of the world. We desire that henceforth forty warships shall be maintained in Our ports in good and proper order, ready to guard Our coasts both summer and winter. To this end We command Our Treasurer to provide forthwith the sum of 150,000 écus for the construction of thirty galleys. We instruct Our Controller-General of Artillery to furnish them with all necessary armaments; and We desire that an annual sum of 240,000 écus shall be placed at the disposal of the naval treasurers for the maintenance of the crews, both slaves and sailors, of the said galleys, whose captains shall each receive 6,000 écus to this end, while We Ourselves will maintain the fighting men. . . . To prevent the pirates from taking shelter in various of Our deserted harbours. . . . We desire that forts should be erected at various points . . . whose garrisons will control the sea approaches by means of artillery. Since the King of Spain has invaded the Valtelline, France can only come to the aid of Italy by way of Savoy and Piedmont or by sea. The use of the land route depends on the good will of a foreign Prince and is therefore unreliable. Moreover, it leads into Milanese territory, where the main Spanish force is concentrated; before We could bring help to the oppressed Italians We would have to combat the power of Spain in a locality where she would enjoy many [military] advantages. But there is still the sea route; and, if We were strong at sea, We would not only have free access to Italy, but could even prevent the Spanish forces there from obtaining help from Spain."

There then followed a passage in which the geography is not entirely clear:

"Since Spain lies on the Atlantic she cannot send reinforcements to Italy, which lies on the Gulf of Venice . . ., without crossing the Gulf of Lions and passing along the coast of Provence; on the 800-mile coastline between Spain and Genoa there are no harbours [that the Spanish can use] save those belonging to the King of France. It is clear, therefore, that forty galleys with fresh crews will be able to defeat eighty whose crews are fatigued after a long voyage, especially if, once Our harbours have been fortified, they are no longer able to land and take on food and water. From this it follows that they will either not come to Italy any more or will have to take to the open sea like the great sailing ships; but this they would find difficult for, since they would be carrying troops, they would be so heavily laden that they could not stay at sea for more than two days without taking on water; and if they were overtaken by a storm . . ., they would be in danger of foundering or of being forced to run for the coast of Provence or Barbary, where there are no ports but a large number of reefs on which they might be wrecked, and Moors, who are their enemies. Control of the sea route brings a further advantage: if the peoples of Naples and Sicily, who are harshly treated by their Spanish viceroys, knew that there was a French navy ready to bring them aid, they might decide to rebel. In short, all the Italian princes, whose attachment to Spain is prompted by fear rather than love, and even the Popes, once they realized that France offered a safeguard against Spanish oppression, might well decide to back French arms. But even if they were not prepared to do so, the King [of France] would still have free access to Italy and, unlike the occasion in the year——,[1] he could still drop anchor in various harbours. The Provence would pay for the erection of the forts, for the supply of ammunition and for the maintenance of the garrisons. The upkeep of the galleys could be paid for with the revenue received from the sugar and tobacco taxes."

A further memorandum from the year 1625, also inspired and revised by Richelieu, has been preserved. In it we read:

"In France it is customary to give the captains of the galleys 9,000 écus for the upkeep of their vessels; in return they must put to sea when ordered to do so and must provide for both sailors and fighting men.

"The King of Spain does things differently; he gives his captains 6,000 ducats, but they only have to serve for six months in each year, to feed their slaves and provide for their sailors. As far as troops are concerned, the galleys are manned

* The date is missing.

by infantry companies from the kingdoms of Sicily and Naples, who are deployed wherever there is need and are fed at the King's expense.

"To unite the Venetian and French forces by sea would be very difficult, if not impossible, for France and Venice are separated by a distance of at least 1500 miles, 800 miles of which are controlled by Spain, and a war fleet cannot stay at sea for more than nine or ten days without taking on water, which would always be an extremely difficult operation on coasts held by the enemy.

"Seamen are unsuitable for service on land, and especially so since the captains of the galleys delegate their command when they have to undertake an action on land. I consider, therefore, that it would be more to the purpose if the King were to have a thousand veterans trained for service at sea; in time, as they gained experience, these men would render great service.

"In our experience . . . there are great disadvantages . . . when the recruiting is left to the captains, and the King should be urgently requested to set up a corps of a thousand veterans, augmenting their pay, so that they can support themselves, and reserving for himself alone the right to disband them. And a register should be kept, listing the soldiers by name and place of origin and including their service records; they should be paid by a special paymaster to prevent false musters."

What was the basis of Richelieu's knowledge of the sea, which he acquired at such an early age? Historians have spoken of his atavism in this connection. The seafaring tradition runs in his family. Neither must we forget the relationship, of crucial importance in this respect, between Richelieu and Isaac de Razilly, whose estate bordered on Richelieu's own and whose knowledge of geography and overseas trade, gained from twenty-three years at sea, was to prove so valuable to the Cardinal. Razilly was a Knight of Malta who in 1623 commanded a warship and by 1624 a whole fleet; in 1626 he submitted to Richelieu an outstanding analysis of the French naval and colonial programme. He was also one of the one hundred members of the Company of New France, founded in 1627. In 1629 he defeated the pirates of Salé. In 1631 he forced the Sherif of Morocco to grant concessions similar to those from the Sublime Porte in force at the time. In 1632 he was appointed Viceroy of Canada, then the province of Acadia, which office he subsequently assigned to Champlain, while he himself took over the administration of French Guiana. Razilly had two brothers, François and Claude. In 1621 François had led ships of the King's fleet against La Rochelle, and Claude had taken part in the naval battle against the Huguenots on October 27, 1622. In 1628 he had defended the famous dike Richelieu had had erected across the harbour mouth at La Rochelle. He was later appointed Vice-Admiral of the Fleet. The frequent exchanges between the Bishop of Luçon and these three brothers will surely have been one of the essential factors determining his competence to deal with both shipping and commercial affairs. It was from the lips of Isaac de Razilly that Richelieu first heard expert criticism about conditions of French shipping.

But the power of the emerging French state both at sea and on land was still greatly undermined by the feudal system. It had long been recognized, especially under Henry IV, that the evil effects of this system were crippling France. At the beginning of the seventeenth century any daring and sudden attack by an enemy, any raid by pirates, was likely to succeed. And this was as true of the Mediterranean as it was of the Atlantic coasts. All seafaring peoples indulged in piracy, and in doing so received a considerable measure of support from their governments. The Spanish and the English, the Portuguese and the Dutch encouraged the pirates of the Barbary Coast in their actions against France. By the end of Henry IV's reign insecurity at sea had reached its peak.

Salagnac, Henry IV's envoy to Constantinople, once wrote to his sovereign: "The greatest losses suffered by Your Majesty's subjects are inflicted by the Berbers."

On another occasion he wrote: "It would be more honourable to risk an attack on North Africa than to endure such things; we should destroy Bizerta with cannon fire, then land and remain there until the Tunisians and Algerians have had enough."

Henry IV had been well aware of the necessity for building up the fleet. But on May 22, 1596, he wrote: "Our best ship carpenters have emigrated"; and on January 3, 1598: "How are we to pay for the building of a fleet?" ("With the proceeds from a tax on inns," replied a squadron commander.) Henry then found a partial solution to the problem by marrying[1] Marie de' Medici, the daughter of the biggest banker of his day. Before this princess had even set foot on French soil, part of her dowry had been invested in six galleys.

The naval allocations were far too small to maintain warships, so the government was obliged to charter ships as required while French warships lay about in the harbours in an unseaworthy condition. Paradoxically, at a time when literally no French ship was to be found at sea, a great number of captains and up to one hundred and twenty-five naval commissioners were registered on the naval staff.

"If I were Admiral of France," Sully had said, "I would create a royal power at sea such as would permit us to be very unpleasant neighbours to those English gentlemen."

In the budget for the year 1609 only 465,175 livres were allocated to the navy for its total requirements.

The office of Admiral of France had been created when, in the course of her territorial expansion, France had reached the Channel coast. The Admiral had been one of the high officers of the crown and equal in rank to the Constable.

Thus the position occupied by these high officers had been one of great importance, and initially it was in no way undermined by the consolidation of royal power. However, the authority invested in the Admiral of France extended only to

[1] Henry IV's first wife was Margaret of Valois, the sister of Charles IX. The marriage was dissolved in 1599.

the coasts of Picardy, Normandy, Poitou and Saintonge, i.e., to those maritime provinces which were subject to the Parlement of Paris. When Brittany, Provence and Guyenne were incorporated into France, they had each retained the right to an independent navy as part of their lawful privileges. In the case of the province of Languedoc, this right went back to the year 1361. But even at the beginning of the seventeenth century there were still four separate admiralties acting independently of one another, over and above which there were any number of local maritime rights and privileges dating from feudal times.

After Richelieu's death Admiral Brézé was to say that prior to his reforms it had been impossible to move naval forces from one province to another. This had been clearly demonstrated during the battle for La Rochelle, and also during the dispute arising out of the rivalry between the Duke of Montmorency and the Governor of Brittany. Time and again the monarchy had attempted to unite different admiralties in the person of a single commander. Joint commands of this kind were in fact established, but they seldom lasted very long, for when an incumbent died it was not always possible to appoint a single successor.

Henri II, Duc de Montmorency, was the first to make a really sustained attempt to co-ordinate French naval power. In 1612 he succeeded his uncle, Charles de Damville, in his dual function as Admiral of France and Brittany; it was this appointment which provoked the protest of the Governor of Brittany. Then, in 1613, Montmorency also took over the admiralty of Guyenne.

In fairness to Montmorency, it should be said that he concerned himself with the naval problem at great length. He realized that the task of recruiting men for service at sea must be pursued in a systematic manner. Until then the majority of naval officers serving in the Mediterranean had been recruited from Knights of Malta of Provençal origin. In the west of France, however, the nobility showed little inclination for naval service. Of the seventy-seven captains serving in the west in 1619, only very few were men of noble birth. The majority were the sons of merchants of high standing in Normandy or Brittany. Often one of these captains would embellish his bourgeois name by adding to it the title of some property owned by his family.

In a report drafted in 1617 Montmorency wrote that many brave men from merchant families had learned the sailor's profession in the face of danger and great hardships. In 1584 there had been fifty-four captains, while in 1619 there were seventy-seven. Montmorency constantly sought to raise their number, but the naval funds were so small that they barely covered the salaries of those already appointed.

On May 27th and August 5th and 17th, 1624, Montmorency issued orders to the effect that action should be taken against any captains, pilots and ship carpenters who showed signs of wishing to enter into foreign service. He also directed that the names of all men with knowledge of the sea or of shipbuilding should be kept on a register. The maritime police were already operating under the French Admiralty during the period of his command. No ship's captain was permitted to drop or weigh anchor off the French coasts without a permit issued by the naval authority. In principle all such permits should have been issued by the Admiral himself, but this principle was not observed by the provincial governors. Montmorency proceeded against persons contravening this regulation with great force. He published a decree stating that all those unable to produce a permit issued in his name would be treated as pirates. Since the Admiralty controlled the maritime police, it was able to keep a check both on normal trade and on smuggling, in fact on every Frenchman who put to sea. Even fishing on the high seas came under Admiralty supervision. And the Admiralty's authority extended not only to shipping at sea but to shipping on inland waterways as well. The programme of reforms for the merchant navy that Montmorency had submitted to the Assembly of Notables in 1617 was to remain the model for all of Richelieu's subsequent measures. At the time, Montmorency insisted that what was needed above all else was to take active steps to recruit new men, in order to foster a general interest among Frenchmen both in ships and in shipbuilding and to induce as many of the impoverished nobility as possible to enter the naval service. He recommended that the provision made in the ordinance of 1584 for the payment of a bounty to the builder of any ship exceeding three hundred tons should be reinstated. In 1617 Montmorency's suggestions were endorsed with spontaneous enthusiasm by the notables, who called for a new shipping code. The Admiral did his best to grant them their wish, but despite his persistent and energetic efforts he was unsuccessful. He had in fact already taken the initiative, three months before the Assembly of Notables was convened, with his ordinance of June 26, 1617, which was intended to solve the problem of the French flag. Boiteux writes as follows:

"In 1504 Louis XII, like various of his successors on later occasions, stated that the protectionist policy pursued by France's neighbours was ruining French sea trade."

Montmorency declared that, since other countries refused to recognize the French colours, France must henceforth refuse to recognize theirs. This stance was endorsed by the ship-owners of Le Havre, Dieppe and St Malo. A decree passed in the Royal Council on October 5, 1617, gave the force of law to this provision and an order was promulgated forbidding foreign ships to carry cargo from one French port to another. Shipments of this kind were to be made in French ships only.[1]

It was at this time that the great trading companies were being formed and Montmorency was their chief advocate. During Henry IV's brief reign, when trading privileges had

[1] This provision applied only to merchants from Flanders, Holland, Zeeland and England who were stationed in Rouen.

been dispensed with an all too liberal hand, he had acquired considerable experience in this sphere. Drawing on that experience he recommended that whenever a new company was formed there should always be a probationary period, that the company's trading record should be closely examined and that concessions should be restricted to periods of from two to three years. But he was not content merely to encourage and advise others. He himself actively fostered the two most important trading companies of his day, the "Montmorency East India Company," which was founded by his uncle, Charles de Damville, in 1611 and was reorganized in 1618, and the "Montmorency New France Company."

In point of fact a considerable number of projects to reform French shipping had already been devised by a wide variety of persons during Louis XIII's reign before Cardinal Richelieu took the problem in hand. As early as 1612 François du Noyer de Saint-Martin had suggested to the King that he should create a Royal Company of the Holy Sepulchre of Jerusalem. This Company was to consist of a corps of picked men, the Knights of St Louis, who would fight in the service of the King against the "infidel." The naval requirements envisaged for this undertaking were very considerable and far exceeded the demands made in later projects. Another scheme was submitted in 1615. Its author was René de Verdelay. His proposals were considered in 1621 and approved by Lesdiguières, Montmorency and several members of the Council; the King gave his assent in principle. The chief reason this plan was not then put into effect was Richelieu's consistently negative attitude towards any proposals that had met with Montmorency's approval. Montmorency—like the Duke of Guise, who commanded the Mediterranean fleet, like Albert de Gondi, Duc de Retz, who commanded the galleys, like the Count of Joigny—was viewed with suspicion by the Cardinal from the very outset, because he was far too independent, too well connected and too influential. In order to rid himself of such men Richelieu was prepared to go to any lengths. He would interest himself personally in police investigations instituted against them. As soon as the opportunity presented itself he extorted confessions from them and did not shrink from calling on informers to make incriminating depositions. And on the evidence of such documents he then persuaded the King to take harsh measures against them.

Montmorency was the Governor of Languedoc, while Charles de Lorraine, Duc de Guise, was the Governor of Provence. For the Duke of Guise, no less than for Montmorency, his office of governor was inseparable from what he held to be his prescriptive rights as an admiral. As early as 1515 a bastard of the house of Savoy had called himself "General of Provence and Admiral of the Levant." Guise enjoyed extensive powers under maritime law, including lucrative rights with regard to prize money, which had been confirmed by an ordinance of 1564. He defended himself stubbornly against Richelieu's designs, insisting on his own view that every sea must have its admiral and that the office of admiral was inseparable from the office of governor—for that was how things had always been under every King of France. A significant light is thrown on the tensions existing between these two provincial governors, both of whom enjoyed sovereign powers within their own territory, by the fact that Montmorency opposed the claims made by his neighbour and even asserted that Guise had no right of command at sea since he was not under oath, and consequently could not be in authority. The dispute between Guise and Montmorency was to continue over ten years. In actual fact, however, Guise had the same prescriptive right on his side as that which the unfortunate Montmorency was to invoke in his capacity as Governor, after he had been coerced into renouncing his accredited rights as Admiral of France, *vis-à-vis* the Controller-General of Navigation and Trade.

After Montmorency had been overthrown and put to death, Guise very soon discovered that Richelieu was an opponent of different mettle than the ill-fated Duke. Richelieu had seen

45

at once that, where Guise was concerned, he would achieve nothing by legal argument and immediately looked for an alternative solution.

First he sent a go-between to sound out Guise's wife as to whether Guise would also settle for money. Guise stated his requirements. He was prepared to accept either the office of a Grand Admiral of the Mediterranean or an indemnity of 900,000 livres. Richelieu reacted with a display of indignation and rejected his demands as extortionate. He would not advise the King to pay even a fraction of such a sum in order to acquire what was in fact a debatable right. Above all he dragged the negotiations out and waited for an opportunity to persuade Louis to decide in his favour. This opportunity did not arise until 1629 during the siege of Privas. Then Richelieu prevailed upon the monarch to sign an edict by which, in his capacity as Count of Provence, Forcalquier and the adjoining territories, he extended the jurisdiction of the Controller-General of Navigation to include the Mediterranean. But Richelieu had not yet reached his goal. The Parlement refused to ratify this edict. Richelieu nonetheless proceeded to act on its authority and sent to the seat of the admiralty in Toulon three resolutions of the Council of Ministers requiring that the terms of the edict be implemented. At this, Guise fell into a rage, declaring that he would have the bearers of these resolutions arrested and thrashed by his guards. But he thought better of it and instead lodged a complaint with the King against the "so-called Controller-General of Navigation." True, he paid nominal tribute to Richelieu's superior rank when the second galley in line in his fleet—the first was *La Réale*—was renamed *L'Amirale*. But he continued to pour scorn on the office of the Controller-General and asserted that, in contrast to this nebulous and purely honorary office, that of Commander of the Galleys was both real and tangible, for he was called upon to rid the Mediterranean of pirates and to repulse enemy attacks, and it was he who had the duty of safeguarding France and conserving Provence. By advancing such arguments Guise was of course putting the case for Gondi, who had wrangled with him in the past over naval matters. For, as has already been mentioned, Guise was not the only one to resist Richelieu after Montmorency's death. Gondi, the Commander of the Galleys, "His Majesty's Lieutenant General on Land and Sea in the Levant," also afforded stout resistance.

This naval function had been handed down from father to son in the Gondi family. They styled themselves "High Officers of the Crown" and claimed equality of rank with the Admiral. They also claimed rights which brought them special honours, not only within the whole of the kingdom of France, where their galleys were accorded the salute otherwise reserved for the great sailing ships, but also in Malta, where the Grand Master of the Order of Malta was obliged to offer his hand in greeting to the Commander of the Galleys when he landed on the island. Nor was this all. On the basis of a declaration of April 1562 they claimed the right to form battle fleets both in the Mediterranean and in the Atlantic whenever they saw fit, and in the event of their galleys joining forces with sailing ships they insisted that they should command the combined force. On board the galleys they decided all questions relating to pay and discipline, they were responsible for victualling and they even determined the amounts to be spent on equipping and operating their vessels. They had their own intendants, inspectors, treasurers and officers, they had their own budget, and they came directly under the Secretary of State responsible for French shipping in the Levant, who was required to advise them of the King's commands.

Although Guise and Gondi subsequently made common cause against Richelieu, there were three matters over which they were of course constantly quarrelling: the right to capture prizes, the exercise of naval law and the decision over the employment of galley slaves. With regard to the first of these points, the Parlement and the Council of Ministers decided against Charles de Guise and ruled that the Commander of the Galleys had exclusive rights. With regard to the second and third points, Gondi also received satisfaction.

The protracted nature of these controversies had already benefited Montmorency in his attempts to establish a central naval authority. But it was Richelieu who was to exploit this situation to its fullest extent, first against Guise and then, in a very energetic manner, against Gondi. And it was Gondi who was the first to realize that, "when this bell tolls," it was unwise "to feign deafness." He stopped resisting and began negotiating. The negotiations went on for a long time, but in 1635 Richelieu finally bought the command of the galleys and the marquisate of the Iles d'Or from Gondi for 560,000 livres. He then appointed in Gondi's place his own nephew, François de Vignerot, Monsieur Pont de Courlay, who was received in Aix on June 10, 1636, with all due ceremony. And with this Richelieu had at last extended his authority to both the Atlantic and the Mediterranean, to both galleys and sail.

But this was by no means the end of all resistance. Guise, a member of a reigning house, had complained to the King himself: "After failing to achieve his object by lawful means," he had written, "Richelieu is now using dishonest means and evil methods." He received no reply. And then it slowly dawned on him that he was fighting against a new force—the force of a new age. The Cardinal, meanwhile, was applying pressure in quite a different quarter. Riots had broken out in Provence in protest against a new system of taxation. For Richelieu it was no great matter to prove the Governor's complicity in these riots, and the Prince of Condé was immediately despatched with his dragoons to "pacify" the province. This prompted Guise to tread the dangerous path of revolt. But Richelieu's informers were alert and reported that the Duke's strongest citadel was his "main galley which was kept in constant readiness for attack." Of course there was no conclusive proof and it would in any case have been difficult to brand as traitor a man who had twice defeated the Huguenots and who had only recently defeated the Genoese. But there were other means. The King was informed that there were good grounds for suspecting that the Governor of Provence and Champagne had been involved in the Queen-Mother's flight to Brussels in 1631, whereupon Guise was summoned to appear before the King to vindicate himself, while Marshal Vitry[1] was appointed as the King's representative in Provence. At this juncture in his affairs Guise called to mind the fate which had befallen César de Vendôme in 1626 (cf. Vol. I), and through the intercession of his wife he obtained the King's permission to go first to Loreto and then to Rome. He had now "fled the country" and as far as Richelieu was concerned that was the end of the matter.

The King's representative, Vitry,. was granted no maritime rights whatsoever and Richelieu finally obtained the ratification of his own patents as Controller-General of Navigation from the Parlement of Aix. He had pursued his path with great tenacity and this path led him from naval to colonial affairs.

In his endeavours to concentrate power in the hands of the King, money had ultimately proved to be Richelieu's most effective weapon. This was also to be the case in the sphere of foreign policy. Acting on the advice of the Jesuits, Ventadour, a member of the ducal family of Lévis, had bought the viceroy-ship of Canada from Montmorency, but within the year he began to doubt the wisdom of his purchase and tried to extricate himself. Baron de Culey, a go-between, acted as dummy for Richelieu and offered Ventadour the modest sum of 100,000 livres in return for his high office. In the course of this transaction Richelieu's uncle, de La Porte, had voiced the opinion "that it would be more advantageous for the Controller-General to negotiate through a nobleman rather than as a Duke and Peer of France." But subsequently Richelieu, acting on Razilly's advice, approached Ventadour directly. Lauzon was then commissioned to arrange final terms and on

---

[1] Nicolas de l'Hospital, Baron (later Marquis) de Vitry, born 1572, was *capitaine des gardes du corps*. After the murder of the Marquis of Ancre he was made a Marshal of France and then, in 1632, Governor of Provence. In 1637 he fell from favour and was imprisoned in the Bastille, where he remained until 1644. Died 1645.

June 30, 1627, he was able to report to his principal: "Yesterday I executed your command; I have obtained the resignation of the Viceroy of Canada and I intend to deliver it to you in person."

And so Richelieu's methods were extended to the field of colonial affairs. But then his methods were always the same, both in great things and in small.

The following incident relating to the navy is also significant. There was another Controller-General of the Artillery, who was responsible for providing the navy with guns, powder, cannon balls and artillerymen. In 1627 Richelieu wrote to the Duke of Guise as follows:

"I am extremely displeased with the worthless powder which the Controller-General of Artillery has delivered to me. I am indignant over the cannon he has sent and even more so over the incompetent gunners. His mistakes are prodigious. If I were in this nobleman's place I would sooner be dead than guilty of such mistakes."

"This nobleman," however, was none other than the great and ageing Sully, who had been appointed to his office by Henry IV and who was determined to hand it on to his son. Indirect methods were called for. Richelieu obtained permission from the King to cast his own cannon and shortly afterwards he founded a commissariat that enabled him to purchase his own powder and so completely bypass the Controller-General of Artillery. This commissariat was directed by Richelieu's cousin, Le Meilleraye.

On June 24, 1633, Richelieu wrote: "This will be a great relief to Sully and will induce the old man to give up his office entirely." He gave it up and by way of recompense the King presented him with the Marshal's baton.

The pattern of feudal rights in France was a veritable maze. Every coast had its "High Officers of the Crown" who laid claim to maritime rights; many of them were chartered, many had been usurped during the Wars of Religion. As early as

February 1576 a proclamation had ordained that no person might appoint himself admiral of his domains or lay claim to admiralty rights of any kind. On the contrary, all persons were required to submit to the authority of the—then—Admiral of France.

In 1624 Richelieu had called for a detailed report on this extremely complex state of affairs. The author of the report was Leroux d'Infreville. The following facts were established:

"The Duke of Mantua was Monsieur de Saint-Valéry-sur-Somme; the Commander of Le Crotoy called himself 'Vice-Admiral of Picardy'; the Governor of Rue laid claim to Marquenterre; the Abbot of St Josse signed himself 'Admiral of Cuques and Tripié'; on the 'Sables' the admiral was the Marquis of Royan, in Bayonne the Count of Grammont, in Médoc the Duke of Epernon; all the above-named interfered in naval matters and issued leave passes."

In Richelieu's own diocese of Luçon the rights to administer naval justice, to operate the lookout service and to salvage were all claimed on prescriptive grounds.

Richelieu sent the following instruction to his executive officers: "I would be indebted to you if you would act against all those who call themselves 'hereditary admirals.' "

On December 13, 1629, he procured the publication of an edict forbidding all persons, on pain of severe penalties, to interfere in naval matters. This edict was directed against those "usurpers" who "obstructed the officers of the navy in the administration of naval justice."

The creation of efficient naval harbours was a task that was to occupy Richelieu throughout the whole of his life. In this sphere more than in any other he constantly encountered wellnigh insuperable difficulties. The port of Le Havre was particularly close to his heart, and in March 1632 he gave explicit directions for its development to the Archbishop of Bordeaux:

"Monsieur de Bordeaux will take soundings of the whole of Le Havre . . . in order to establish the amount of work already completed . . . and that still required to strengthen and embellish the citadel. He will also ascertain how much money has been spent in Le Havre, how much of this was provided by the King, how much was advanced by the Cardinal and how much still needs to be invested."

There then followed instructions regarding the supervision of the artillery, the powder magazines and—yet again—the citadel and the towers, to which the Cardinal added the characteristic comment that these buildings should not only be kept in good repair but in a state that would delight the eye of the beholder. As always Richelieu went into detail; he recommended that the saltpeter imported from Holland should be stored separately from the sulphur. The Archbishop of Bordeaux was instructed to inspect Pont-de-l'Arche and to effect the necessary improvements, after which he was to visit Brouage and the islands of Ré and Oléron.

But despite these repeated endeavours the Cardinal failed to produce satisfactory results. He spent enormous sums on the development of Le Havre only to find that it was constantly silting up. It was a long time before warships were able to use this harbour. Brest was also developed on Richelieu's initiative. His highest hopes were for Brest, which he always referred to as "mine." But here above all he met with insuperable local resistance and a total lack of understanding. Lack of funds also held up the development of this port. The harbour of Brest was not developed in the sense envisaged by the Cardinal until fifty years later. His plans for Brouage, which was to have linked the Atlantic and the Mediterranean, also remained abortive. Throughout the whole of his reign Louis XIII did not own a single harbour capable of giving adequate protection to a large fleet of ships.

But despite all the difficulties and reversals, and all the deficiencies to which these gave rise, we shall come to see just how decisively Richelieu's maritime achievements benefited the French cause from 1635 onwards during the "open war" with Spain.

Richelieu evolved his own system for dealing with maritime affairs. In respect of what he called "oceanic requirements," Launay, Razilly and Mantin provided him with detailed field reports with special reference to all matters bearing on the colonies. In Mediterranean affairs his specialists were Vireville and des Roches. Villemenon was put in charge of admiralty administration. In the sphere of shipping, as in every other department of government, Richelieu's régime saw the emergence of the specialist official. Godefroy and La Martellière dealt with all questions of maritime law. Richelieu expected the King's envoys abroad to have specialized knowledge of foreign trade. This produced a type of official which, although it disappeared from the scene after Richelieu's death, was in fact a precursor of the "commercial attachés" of a later age.

The Cardinal ordered frequent inspections of French coasts and harbours, especially inland harbours. However, Boiteux has pointed out that four technical advisers had been stationed in Rouen for this very purpose ever since 1616, when Montmorency was still Admiral of France.

One of Richelieu's chief sources of information, to which he turned with particular interest in regard to maritime matters, were the reports sent in by Father Joseph's missionaries. He read the works of Laffemas, Montchrétien, du Noyer de Saint-Martin and La Gomberdière with the same avid interest, and also studied the suggestions and memoranda on naval, trade and colonial affairs received by the Council of State since the turn of the century. Henry IV had founded a chamber of commerce, which was reorganized in 1616; Richelieu looked into its reports. All the documents received on the occasion of the Assembly of the Estates-General of 1614 and the Assembly of Notables of 1617 were examined by

Richelieu's secretaries, who produced abstracts of them. We have lists of documents on which Richelieu had marked in his own hand all the items requiring detailed analysis. For such analyses he employed men of widely differing political persuasions. He always read with pen in hand and corrected as he read. The annotated documents then formed the basis of the reports submitted to the King, but these were formulated to suit the King's personality and his frame of mind at any given moment. They also served as guidelines for Richelieu's ministerial colleagues and provided the factual content of their speeches and of the introductory remarks in edicts.

But there was much that escaped Richelieu. In many respects he remained a compiler. He often did violence to the facts by evaluating them purely in terms of the impression he wished to create in his memoranda, his Memoirs or his *Political Testament*, and he often sacrificed facts for the sake of a rhetorical and even a stylistic effect. It is also evident from the general tenor of his thinking on both naval and economic policy that he frequently applied his lightning intellect to the assimilation of other men's ideas, many of whom had lived before his time. In his *Political Testament* he openly admitted that the reason why he had for so long adopted a negative attitude to the Levantine trade centred on Marseille was that he had not gone into this question himself but had merely acquiesced in the opinion advanced by his advisers.

Summing up, what really interested Richelieu was the dynamic realization of policy. Theoretical or doctrinaire objections he simply thrust to one side. In his naval policy, as in his foreign policy, he was a tactician constantly on the lookout for opportunities, and with very few exceptions he exploited them to the full. Continuity in the realization of his general aims was his foremost concern. Pausing to reflect, to make wary enquiries—this was not for him. He constantly sought to override critical objections just as he constantly sought to assert the authority of the King and the State. Richelieu's driving force was his imagination, always racing ahead of his accomplishments; the things he did and the things he chose to leave undone all bore the stamp of his personality. We have already said that at the end of his life Richelieu's total achievement in the naval sphere fell far short of the goal he had set himself. Nonetheless, in his *Political Testament* he was able to write:

"If Your Majesty had been as weak [in the naval sphere] as your predecessors, you would not have reduced the combined Spanish fleets to ashes in 1638. That proud and arrogant nation would not have suffered such a great loss of prestige, not only in the eyes of all Italy, but in the eyes of all Christendom."

CHAPTER III

THE MONTMORENCYS

Among the noble names of France, the name of Montmorency, frequently mentioned in connection with naval affairs, was second only to that of the royal family itself. The unrelenting zeal with which Richelieu proceeded against this one dominant house affords the best possible example of the campaign he conducted against the great. Here his highly personal method is demonstrated with particular clarity and here too we gain an insight into certain aspects of his character. Most revealing, perhaps, is the way Richelieu tried to ensure that posterity would not blame him for the harsh outcome of events. Jacob Burckhardt once said of Richelieu that he "caught the nobles in their bouts."

In edicts published in 1602 and 1609, Henry IV had forbidden duelling on pain of death. These edicts applied not only to the challenger but also to the person accepting the challenge, and ultimately they were extended to include even seconds and witnesses.

In the *Mercure François* in the year 1606 we read:

"It seems incredible to have to report that in this day and age princes and Peers of France should be cutting one another's throats, that on account of some slight altercation men should be presenting themselves to do battle, and all because one had thrashed the other's groom or laid hold of his page and shaken him or criticized the amount of a tip."

The edicts were totally ignored. Henry IV had been extremely tolerant of duelling. He tended to look upon it as a training ground for personal courage and an expression of knightly honour, which, in a superficial and stereotyped sense, it actually was.

In 1623, however, the year before Richelieu joined the government, the above-mentioned edicts had been renewed, in response to what might well be called the pressure of public opinion, particularly bourgeois opinion. On that occasion the penalties were even heavier: provision was made for not only imposition of the death penalty on the guilty parties but also for confiscation of their property, which meant that their lawful heirs were also to be punished.

In 1619 Richelieu's elder brother, Henri, had been killed in a duel. The Cardinal's description of this event is informed by such a passionate desire for retaliation that we sense that but for his prelate's robe, he himself would have taken up the sword. Eighteen months after he had entered office yet another royal decree was published forbidding duels and affairs of honour. The remarkable thing about this decree is that, at Richelieu's instigation, and on psychological grounds, its terms were made more moderate than those of the earlier edicts. But the preamble contained the following remark: "The object of drafting a less severe decree is to prevent people from pressing us to pardon the guilty."

The Cardinal described the background to these events:

"Duels had become so commonplace in France that the streets of the towns were being used as fields of combat, and since the day was not long enough to encompass their madness, men fought one another by star and torch light. . . . If the edicts had been fully implemented, nobody would have been left to benefit from the examples set by the law."

In the late sixteenth and early seventeenth centuries, duels fought to decide affairs of honour were no longer regarded as a form of divine judgement. This serious background had disappeared. Duels were fought on the slightest provocation.

They had become a kind of sport, in which men felt duty-bound to demonstrate their prowess. Indeed, it was as if duelling had replaced jousting. Time and again throughout the course of historical events we are able to observe how a class that had fulfilled its function and was about to depart from the scene was seized by a mania for self-destruction. What we are faced with here is a sort of collective suicide—which in certain circumstances may well assume a spiritual form, but in the case of the old nobility emerging from the Middle Ages it assumed the absurd form of requiring men to test their physical courage with the naked sword. Since this duelling mania was hallowed by custom, it also constituted a socially acceptable means of enabling the individual to indulge a lust for murder, a lust that was extremely common at the end of the religious wars. In the early years of the century, soldiers who had been dismissed or had been swindled out of pay and booty roamed the countryside in marauding bands, burning and laying waste wherever they went. They were usually led by destitute nobles. To quote but one of countless examples—in 1604 the Baron d'Entragues and three of his sons were beheaded in Toulouse as highwaymen.

In 1599 Felix Platter, a citizen of Basle, reported that it was far less dangerous to journey through a virgin forest than to live in the streets of Paris.

The Venetian ambassador accredited to France from 1603 to 1605 noted:

"The worst of all is that, despite the harsh justice meted out to thieves and murderers, which is of such a kind that you must daily witness how men are hanged, quartered, broken on the wheel and tortured, all people ever talk about is robbery and murder, so that you well might say that in France this kind of justice fails in its purpose, which is to punish offenders as an example to others."

Duelling came under the same heading. In the year 1607 alone four thousand French noblemen and four thousand officers were killed in duels. During the civil war, when ordered society disintegrated, these gentlemen had learnt to procure for themselves what they considered to be their rights. On the slightest pretext they would call their friends together, take to their horses and lie in ambush for their opponents. To surprise an adversary, to kill him, even if he was unarmed, was not a thing they fought shy of. Nor was the Massacre of St Bartholomew an isolated incident.

Although the King did not indulge in such arbitrary actions himself, he was not strong enough to enforce the provisions of the law against those who contravened them. On October 28, 1597, in Angers, du Plessis-Mornay, a man who enjoyed great respect and who had been one of Henry IV's most faithful advisers during the dangerous early years of his rise to power, was attacked, thrown to the ground and nearly murdered by the young Marquis of St Phal on the pretext that du Plessis-Mornay had spoken slanderously of him to the King. Marshal Brissac immediately offered his nephew, St Phal, protection from the power of the State in his strongly fortified castle of Guerche, declaring that he would not deliver him up. The relatives of du Plessis-Mornay then took matters into their own hands and marched out at the head of three regiments in order to seize St Phal. At this point Henry IV undertook to obtain justice for the relatives of the assaulted man, but when the time came he was not prepared to cross the powerful Brissac. A court of honour consisting of the Constable and the Marshals of France was convened. Eventually the accused spent just one day in the Bastille. On January 13, 1599, he was conducted into the King's presence, where he said he was sorry for what he had done. And that was the end of the matter.

Apart from the royal house itself, the one house in France which appeared to be quite inviolable was the house of Montmorency. In his initial assault on this concept of inviolability Richelieu was to make use of the anti-duelling laws. But the first episode in the Cardinal's struggle against the "foremost Barons of Christendom"[1] was not as dramatically charged as his subsequent action against the head of this house. We shall come to see how patiently Louis XIII's adviser bided his time and watched over his prey and slowly spun the web in which he then trapped this glittering scion of an ancient house. Many attempts have been made to explain these events in the psychological terms of a love-hate relationship, but here too the really crucial consideration was probably an impartial one. Richelieu wished to eradicate both the form and the diversity of medieval privileges so clearly discernible in the colourful hierarchy of the French nobility.

François de Bouteville-Montmorency

Count François de Bouteville-Montmorency, who was born in 1600, was the first object of Richelieu's concern. He was considered the best swordsman of the century and his fame on this account had carried far beyond the borders of France. At the age of twenty-seven he had already fought twenty-two duels. Once, when challenged by a young blood, Président de Chevry is said to have replied: "If you want to pick a fight, go and pluck de Bouteville's beard, he'll soon tame your ardour."

In his last duel this invincible young swordsman had slain Count Torigny. He had then escaped across the Flemish border and sought asylum with the Infanta Isabella Clara Eugenia.[2]

Guy d'Harcourt, Baron de Beuvron, was the cousin of Count Torigny, who had been the son of Eléonore d'Orléans-Longueville. Travelling in disguise, he also crossed the border with the intention of avenging his kinsman. But in the hotel in Brussels where he took rooms, he was recognized and kept under close surveillance both day and night. Louis XIII wrote a personal letter to the Infanta asking her to take all possible measures to prevent a further duel and to reconcile the two

---

[1] The phrase formed part of the title of the Montmorency family.

[2] Isabella Clara Eugenia of Austria (1566–1633), daughter of Philip II and Elisabeth of Valois, married to Albert of Austria, Stadholder of the Netherlands.

adversaries. De Bouteville then swore an oath that he would on no account fight a duel on the soil of the country that had afforded him asylum.

The Marquis of Spinola,[1] a man of great distinction, was asked to bring about a reconciliation. He invited de Bouteville-Montmorency, Harcourt-Beuvron and de Bouteville's friend, des Chapelles, to his house, requesting also the presence at this meeting of the French ambassador and various Court officials. His attempt at mediation seemed at first to succeed, for the two young adversaries shook hands and embraced. But immediately afterwards Harcourt-Beuvron informed first des Chapelles and then de Bouteville-Montmorency himself that he would never be satisfied until he stood facing them sword in hand. It was now the Infanta's turn to write to Louis XIII to solicit clemency for her guest. She did not obtain it. De Bouteville, who was greatly angered by Louis's refusal, boasted that although he would not duel in Flanders, he would certainly do so in France, and in Paris at that, in the heart of the capital in broad daylight, in the Place Royale.

And so it was. On May 12, 1627, in the Place Royale, three pairs of swordsmen faced each other: de Bouteville crossed swords with Harcourt, des Chapelles with the Baron de Bussy, and de Bouteville's page, La Berthe, with Bussy's page Chocquet. The engagement remained undecided, but des Chapelles killed Bussy. Thus was the King's authority openly defied.

Beuvron and the two pages fled to England. De Bouteville and des Chapelles took the stagecoach for Lorraine. But in Vitry-le-Brûlé,[2] a few kilometres from Bar-le-Duc and just short of the border, they were arrested by Captain Gordes of the Royal Guard, brought back to Paris, taken to the Bastille and from there to the Conciergerie.

Richelieu noted:

---

[1] Ambrosio Spinola, Marqués de Los Balbases (1571–1630).

[2] Vitry-le-Brûlé, 4 km from Vitry-le-François, is now called Vitry-en-Perthois (Marne).

"His Majesty called the Parlement to the Louvre and commanded it to proceed most scrupulously with the trial, but he allowed the relatives and friends of the accused to call on the judges."

These events have to be considered against the general background of the period, for the method Richelieu employed in his dealings with the King is much more obvious when viewed in context. This "incident" was to occupy the Cardinal for the rest of his life. Even in his Memoirs he devoted no less than fifteen pages to it. But the final outcome of the proceedings was to be decided by a single sentence Richelieu had written to the King:

"Either the duels must be done away with, or Your Majesty's edicts."

In his Memoirs the Cardinal described some of the events which bore on the trial:

"Monsieur le Prince [the Prince of Condé] and Madame his wife [the sister of Henri, Duc de Montmorency], the Duke himself and many others took the most urgent steps to move the King to clemency. But the King, fearing lest by sparing their lives he should cause the death of a great many others and so offend God, could scarcely grant this request."

There then followed a noteworthy passage:

"The Cardinal was inwardly torn. To those of noble heart it was impossible not to feel compassion for de Bouteville-Montmorency, for his youth and courage were deserving of great pity. All did their utmost for him. People who excel in some capacity, even though they abuse it, are usually admired and loved on that account by a great number of people."

He went on:

"He stood in a close relationship to most of the great men of the land. It was argued that, if he were saved, all would be indebted. The services rendered by his father and his father's brother, who, although Catholic, had remained loyal to Henry IV even when he was a Huguenot, were considerable. . . . De Bouteville had his horse killed beneath him at Saint-Jean-d'Angély,[1] he was buried by a mine during the battle of Royan,[2] he fought bravely in the suburb of Ville-Bourbon at Montauban and in the naval battle of Pertuis-Breton he showed the same courage at sea as he had shown on land.[3] It seemed that there could be no more appropriate occasion for demonstrating the King's clemency, the King who [and here, unobtrusively inserted, came the sting] had so often been offended by the absolute disdain shown for his authority."

Then, without any transition, Richelieu reverted to his apologia:

"It must be said that de Bouteville had never once contravened the social code of honour and had not consciously violated human rights, for he was never cruel to those he vanquished. It might also be thought that this absolute craze for duelling was a mental disease, which was now at its peak but would be cured by the maturity that comes with age."

And then:

"As a private individual the Cardinal was deeply pained by the outcome of the trial and felt strongly inclined to persuade the King to pardon de Bouteville, but he was restrained by the consideration that to spare this gentleman . . . was to condemn the cream of the French nobility [in future]."

He went on to say:

"The Cardinal realized that it was impossible to spare his life without giving full licence to duels and to every kind of offence"

and added

[1] Siege and conquest of St Jean-d'Angély, June 3–23, 1621.
[2] Conquest of Royan, May 11, 1622.
[3] Naval battle against Soubise (a Rohan) in Pertuis-Breton, September 16, 1625.

"There was also a danger that those who had tried to save de Bouteville would be inclined to ascribe an act of clemency to their own influence and not to the King's kindness, and that de Bouteville himself would feel more indebted to his helpers than to his sovereign . . ."

And finally:

"As a result of all these considerations the Cardinal's judgement was, as it were, suspended, which prevented him from following his own wishes in this affair, especially in view of the fact that, whereas clemency is of the essence of a Prince, justice is of the essence of a State, whose welfare is of greater moment than the welfare of individuals."

It has to be considered that the Cardinal wrote the many pages from which these quotes are taken at a time when his activity of twenty years as a statesman had had worldwide repercussions—and he wrote them at such length for inclusion in his Memoirs that were destined for posterity.

But even more remarkable accounts of these events have been preserved for us, above all the "written opinion" submitted to the King by Richelieu before sentence was passed. This text, informed and motivated by its author's passionate desire for a particular outcome, meant so much to the Cardinal that he constantly returned to it in later years.

In the seventeenth century it was customary, when composing such documents, to set out the pros and cons of the case in hand in a symmetrical pattern. The Cardinal exploited this convention to his own advantage.

He opened his report by disclaiming all desire to act as judge. His sole object was to state the issues involved. And so he wrote:

"After hearing the evidence, Your Majesty, who surpass us in judgement as you surpass us in power, will yourself take the decision which best serves the interests of the State."

By setting up the "interests of the State" as the principal

HENRI II.

Duc de Montmorenci, Maréchal de Fr.

Né le 30 Avril 1595. Décapité à Toulouse le 30 Octob. 1632.

1. Henri II, Duke of Montmorency, Marshall of France, beheaded 1632

2.   Marie, Duchess of Chevreuse

criterion in this matter, Richelieu had already shown his royal reader the direction in which his judgement was to be guided. But having made this crucial statement he immediately reduced its dynamic impact by going on to say:

"Whatever the decision may be, Your Majesty can only benefit from the errors of the accused; for either the punishment you impose will demonstrate the power of royal justice and command for it general respect and dread, or else the clemency you display will prompt general acknowledgement and admiration of royal mercy."

But then the pendulum swung straight back again to its original position:

"There can be no doubt but that they deserve to die. It is also certain that their lives cannot be spared without endangering the lives of many others.

"It is difficult to save [the two accused] without in fact permitting what the law forbids, thus giving full licence to duels, augmenting the evil by granting impunity and exposing Your Majesty's authority and the justice of the State to disdain. . . . What we are faced with is not a simple transgression of the edicts but their systematic violation and a public declaration of intent to abuse royal authority and trample the laws underfoot, respect for which is the sole foundation of States. . . . Every single quarrel which has arisen at Court over the past six years was instigated or caused by the two accused. They have constantly assumed the role of paid gladiators and have transformed this occupation, the sole object of which is the destruction of human life, into a veritable art form. Whereas heretofore duels were employed solely as a means of redressing personal offences, it would seem that these two gentlemen have used them simply as a means of demonstrating their skill in public, particularly on this last occasion, when they abused the dignity of your presence, the edicts of the land and the majesty of the law by putting on this bloody tragedy, the consequences of which must be disastrous to the State, in the heart of Paris, in the Place Royale, in full view of the Court, the Parlement and all France. Tacitus has said that the most effective way of strengthening the law is by punishing persons whose social rank is as exalted as their crimes are grave. . . . To punish petty crimes is a mark of cruelty rather than of justice; it commands hatred for a Prince and not respect. And if only persons of low birth are punished, the great nobles will scoff at such punishments and assume that they have been legislated for the unfortunate and not the guilty."

This is a point to be noted. This is the voice of a new age, one heightened by rhetoric, it is true, but a certain social impulse makes its presence felt. And this voice continued to assert itself, for now we are told:

"In the present case Your Majesty is faced with the following facts: the prisoners belong to the most illustrious families in the land. One of them has spurned the edicts twenty-two times, which means that he has deserved to lose his life as often as he has set it at hazard."

On this philippic note Richelieu might well have closed his testimony. But the King, rendered extremely insecure by the experiences of his childhood and youth, was nowhere more vulnerable than in matters in which his authority was questioned. At this point in his reading he would already have passed judgement. And at this point Richelieu thought of himself and of the power wielded by the class he was attacking. He thought of the judgement of posterity. Since the Renaissance, the rage for personal renown and posthumous fame had become as powerful a spur as the traditional chivalric concepts of honour and standing—a rage that had been weakened in the Middle Ages through belief in an after-life and in the vanity of worldly display, and which in our day is again on the wane, though for quite different reasons. And so the Cardinal proceeded to the defence of the accused in a manner virtually identical with the one he used in his Memoirs.

Here we read *inter alia*:

"The whole of France is speaking for the accused. The great nobles, to whom de Bouteville is related, argue that if his life is spared the honour of their houses will also be preserved. . . .[1] The services which de Bouteville's father and his uncles . . . rendered in extremely difficult times were not inconsiderable. It was thanks to their magnanimity that Senlis was saved and thanks to the successful defence of that town that the League was destroyed."

Richelieu then turned to the psychological argument exactly as he was to do in his Memoirs, stressing that "this relentless craze for duelling" was a "mental disease" that age would cure.

Having said all this, however, he immediately cancelled it out again by the following sentence: "But all these arguments, even when they are reinforced by Your Majesty's natural goodness, can only appear moving, but not convincing."

And then he considered the King's feelings:

"The strictest Princes have wished they were unable to write, whenever it was a question of signing the death warrants of persons who had turned against King and country. . . . There is no greater act than that of a Prince who, being offended, inclines to clemency, and who, having the power to punish, contents himself with his ability to do so. . . . If it is true that this nobleman's faults have their origin in a disease, then prison would be the appropriate penalty, because if the penalty for malefactors is the scaffold, for madmen it should be prison."

This was of course a genuine alternative, which was here being mentioned for the first time. Did Richelieu mean this proposal to be taken seriously? He went on to elucidate it:

"The relatives [of the accused] would be satisfied, for the dishonour threatening their houses would be averted. . . . The

[1] Execution by the sword was a dishonourable death.

Parlement would have no reasonable grounds for complaint, since it would not be a question of pardoning the accused but merely commuting their sentence."

This document, which is both highly informative and, because of its ambivalence and suggestive power, highly sinister, closes at this point. If we do not read between the lines, it would appear that, after justly considering the pros and cons of the case, the Cardinal was advocating imprisonment. But on closer scrutiny of these casuistical dialectics, we discover a single overriding desire: to ensure that mercy, which the court, the great nobles and the whole class of those accustomed to the dispensation of justice according to rank quite generally assumed would be extended, was in fact denied. And this denial was to be achieved by the one argument that was calculated, as we have already emphasized, to have the greatest effect on Louis XIII: "Your Majesty's authority is at stake." The pressure brought to bear upon the King was extreme, considering his own family code of honour and the youth and merits of the accused.

Every conceivable attempt was made to influence Louis. De Bouteville's wife threw herself at his feet when he was leaving church after mass. But the King walked on and gave no answer to her entreaties. To the members of his entourage he said that he felt sorry for the woman but that in this instance he must and would enforce obedience. The Bishop of Nantes, a confidant of Richelieu's, who had visited the prisoners in the Bastille, brought letters to the Cardinal from the two accused. Richelieu asked how they had come by their writing materials, to which the Bishop replied that he himself had provided them with pen, ink and paper. The Cardinal then informed the Bishop that he was unable to intercede on the prisoners' behalf, since he had collaborated on the drafting of the edict prohibiting duelling.

He later wrote in his Memoirs:

"The King considered and carefully weighed the evidence;

68

but the first group of arguments proved the stronger. The King's love for his State was greater than his compassion for these two gentlemen. After the Parlement had judged and condemned them, the sentence was duly carried out."

This was followed by a very significant passage, in which Richelieu abandoned his customary caution:

"But it must be said that the court was unjust to the King in two respects: first, by condemning only the two prisoners and acquitting the dead man [Bussy, who fell in the duel], and that simply because his mother is the wife of the Président de Mesmes; and second, by confiscating only one third of the property of the executed men instead of their whole fortune, as required by law."[1]

After delivering further attacks on the Parlement, the Cardinal suddenly lapsed into the customary seventeenth-century eulogy of the deceased and closed his account:

"By their conduct at the end, they lent nobility to the ignoble death imposed upon them; never had these two gentlemen shown more steadfastness, less perturbation, more force of character or more magnanimity."

The execution took place on June 22, 1627. On June 24th Richelieu wrote to de Bouteville's cousin, the Governor of Languedoc and head of the family, Henri II, Duc de Montmorency:

"The misfortune that has befallen Monsieur de Bouteville prompts me to write to you and to assure you that nobody is more sensible than I to the grief you feel at the loss of so close a kinsman. No words of mine can describe the hardship this

[1] This passage on the behaviour of the Parlement would seem to indicate what the Cardinal's real opinion was. However, many historians hold the view that Richelieu really did try to prevail upon the King to commute the sentence to one of imprisonment. They argue that on this occasion Louis XIII was showing just how independent he could be. This argument is expounded in Louis Batiffol's book, *Richelieu et le Roi Louis XIII*, Paris 1934.

extreme decision imposed on the King, but the condemned man had so often lapsed in respect of this offence, which offers a direct threat to the King's authority, that His Majesty felt that if this inveterate evil was to be removed, it must be removed root and branch, and that consequently he must allow justice to take its course and accept responsibility in the eyes of God and the world. In all other matters, which do not involve the welfare of the State, you will undoubtedly receive tokens of His Majesty's good will towards you. As for myself, I would ask you to place your trust in the love to which my future actions will testify and which will show you more clearly than words that I am, as far as is humanly possible, your affectionate and sincere servant."

We possess other statements of this kind—for example, the letter written by Richelieu on June 24, 1627, in which he expressed his condolences to Charles Duc d'Angoulême, the son of Charles IX and Marie Touchet, and related to the Montmorencys by marriage. In it he said:

"I have written to the Duke of Montmorency and told him that there is nothing I would not do for him. I beg you to assure the Countess of Bouteville that in future I shall take all measures calculated to contribute to her welfare. I sympathize with her more than I can say."

If we compare this last assurance with the outburst of rage that overcame Richelieu when the law court refused to confiscate the whole of de Bouteville's property and which still possessed him when he came to write his Memoirs for posterity, a certain scepticism is indicated.

In this connection, we may recall that in the course of the perilous Lyon crisis (see Vol. I), Richelieu received protection from the Duke of Montmorency.

When de Bouteville was put to death, his wife was expecting a child, which was born on January 7, 1628. This child grew up to become the Marshal of Luxemburg and, as a cousin and disciple of the great Condé, one of the most successful army commanders ever to serve the French Crown.

The End of Henri II, Duc de Montmorency

If we wish to pursue, from its first inception to its violent end, the gradual destruction of the special position enjoyed by Henri de Montmorency, the head of the Montmorency family, if we are to grasp its wider implications and its grave consequences, we have first to go back and establish its direct causes. Thus considerable light will be cast on the gradual elimination of medieval authorities, a process not completed until the nineteenth century.

Henri was his name and Henry IV had been his godfather. This King had always addressed him as "my son" and throughout his reign had given him frequent indications of his paternal affection.

Ever since the tenth century the Montmorencys, who originally came from the Ile-de-France, had produced leaders who had always been soldiers or soldier-statesmen.

Montmorency was seventeen when, in 1612, Louis XIII appointed him Admiral of France and eighteen when he was made Governor of Languedoc. As early as 1619 he was invested with the Order of the Holy Ghost. A chronicler of the times once called him the best-loved and the most lovable of the great nobles, and on another occasion the "idol of the Court, of the provinces, of the army and of the whole nation." His name reflected the entire course of French history from its earliest days. He seemed to symbolize the serenity and valour attributed to the knightly heroes of the romances of chivalry and at every opportunity he displayed them on the stage of history which could boast few such dazzling protagonists.

At the beginning of Louis XIII's reign, when power was in the hands of the Queen-Mother's favourites, Montmorency, who was then twenty-five, distinguished himself in the Wars of Religion. Through his marriage to Marie de' Medici's

Roman-born niece, Felicia Orsini, Montmorency was closely related to the Queen-Mother (cf. Vol. I, p. 194), who spared no effort to win him over to her own circle and to her own policies. But Montmorency followed his father's advice and remained true to the anointed King of France. Not even the initial suspicions of the young monarch and his entourage were able to deter him from his allegiance.

In the Huguenot wars one Protestant fortress after the other fell before him, his intervention at the sieges of Montauban and Montpellier was decisive and he was wounded at Montpellier.

In these hard-fought battles the province of Languedoc, which he had governed since 1613, was one of the major theatres of war. Thus Montmorency was constantly involved in a series of battles, which came to an end in 1622 only to break out again in 1625. By then he was in command of a fleet of ships chartered from Holland and England with Dutch and English crews. The captains of these naval units had been ordered by their governments not to attack the Protestants, whom they were to regard as their brothers. Montmorency's opponent was an experienced seaman, Benjamin de Soubise, the younger brother of Henri de Rohan. No sooner had Montmorency arranged for a number of the warships under his command to be manned by all-French crews than he sought out the enemy, drove him into the *"Fosse des Loix"* and obliged him to remain there until the tide turned and his ships stuck on the sand.[1]

The battle was hard, the enemy severely mauled, and, as

[1] Saint-Luc, La Rochefoucauld and Toiras occupied the island of Ré. Soubise remained at the rear of his battalions with five or six horse. As soon as he saw that the engagement was likely to turn against him he quickly withdrew and just succeeded in reaching a sloop, which carried him to the island of Oléron. Acting on the assumption that the Huguenots would be unable to refloat their ships even when the tide returned, Montmorency had decided to occupy Chef-de-Bois and so cut the line of communication between La Rochelle and Oléron, which would enable him to starve out Soubise in the midst of his own troops. In the early hours of September 16th he was amazed to see that with the rising of the tide and the aid of a stiff offshore breeze, Soubise was again able to manœuvre his ships and was preparing to attack. Montmorency lost no time and succeeded in gaining the wind.

Richelieu reported in his Memoirs, only the onset of night enabled him to carry out his withdrawal manœuvre. When dawn broke and the tide returned, the Duke gave pursuit and succeeded in capturing eight of the enemy ships. The remainder of Soubise's force made good its escape and reached the island of Oléron.

Following the occupation of the islands of Ré and Oléron, Montmorency supplied the royal army with ammunition from his own stores to the value of 100,000 thalers. When told that he was being over-generous he said, and rightly so, "I am not here to make money but to win honour."

La Rochelle fell and shortly afterwards the young Duke defeated his next opponent, Henri de Rohan, in Languedoc. After Rohan's defeat Montmorency was the first to advocate an amnesty for the Huguenots.

From that point onwards, as we have already seen, Louis XIII, urged on by Richelieu, concentrated once more on his enemies abroad. Montmorency went to the Italian front. On July 10, 1630, in the Piedmont campaign, he won the crucial victory of Veillane by one of the most glorious feats of arms in the course of the whole war. And no sooner had he left the field of battle than he committed his troops to the mountains in order to link up with Marshal de La Force, whose rearguard had been subjected to a surprise attack by Doria, the commander of the Imperial troops.

Here Montmorency's élan was demonstrated to the full. At the head of the cavalry unit *Gendarmes du Roi*, he broke through the enemy lines. Alone he jumped a wide ditch and forced his way through to Doria, whom he twice wounded with his sword. When the other riders had caught up with him, he launched an attack on the enemy cavalry, who were speeding to the aid of the Genoese. Again he broke through and attacked a German battalion head-on. Failing to observe that scarcely a man had succeeded in keeping up with the fast-riding Duke, the enemy took to their heels. Seven hundred men of the Imperial army were killed and six hundred taken prisoner, including Doria. The Duke of Piedmont had followed the engagement from the safety of a lofty and strongly fortified position, which he had had the wisdom not to leave. After this encounter Louis XIII wrote to the victor: "I feel as indebted to you as it is possible for a King to be." He appointed the thirty-four-year-old Montmorency Marshal of France. But the Duke's luck had begun to turn after October 1626, when Richelieu as the newly appointed Controller-General of Navigation and Trade deprived him of the office of Admiral of France.

The King had never treated Montmorency as one of his subjects but always as a friend and kinsman. As for Richelieu, he constantly asserted that the Duke was the man he admired most at Court and on whose support he most confidently counted. The part played by the Duke during Louis XIII's serious illness in Lyon, the measures he took at that time to protect the Cardinal, who was under terrible threats, show his supreme indifference to the personal affronts he had received. A single request from the sick King, whose life was despaired of, had sufficed for Montmorency to extend his aid and protection to the Cardinal, whereby he himself incurred the active displeasure of the hostile majority. Not even the fact that Richelieu, despite the desperate situation in which he then found himself, was still trying to curtail the powers of his helper, could deter him.

Montmorency, born in 1595 in Chantilly, was ten years younger than Richelieu. He was the son and grandson of a Constable of France. As Governor of Languedoc he presided over "the most pleasant Court in Christendom," which was "far more free and gay than the royal Court." Wherever he was—whether in his fortified castle of Pézenas with its seven towers overlooking the river Hérault as it meandered through the fertile lands to the Mediterranean, or at his house in Grange-des-Prés with its vast gardens, or in his palace in Montpellier, everywhere the people loved him. His decisiveness, his courage and above all his kindness were praised by one and all.

Our enquiry into the naval question has already shown us

that to describe Montmorency as a madcap and a daredevil, as Richelieu did in an attempt to belittle his intended victim, is to describe only one part of the man. And that is not good enough. In the organizational sphere Montmorency displayed initiative, consistency and considerable powers of original thought.

The following lines were written to the Duke by Richelieu after 1631:

". . . I beg you to believe that the affection which I feel for you will be of such a kind as to preclude all possibility of change on my part, since it is prompted by the good qualities which I have observed in you and which give me reason to hope that you will always remain true to yourself."

But shortly after Montmorency had accorded the Cardinal his crucial support at Lyon, the party of Orléans and the Queen-Mother, who had been the losers in that affair, discovered the Duke's Achilles' heel. It seemed to Montmorency no more than fitting that he should be invested with the rank of Constable,[1] which had become virtually hereditary in his family. But this particular office, which was the perfect embodiment of feudal powers, Richelieu was determined to abolish once and for all.

The last Constable but one had been the Duke of Luynes. The last had been François de Bonne, Duc de Lesdiguières. Lesdiguières, a Huguenot who was later converted, had distinguished himself in the Wars of Religion, fighting with Henry of Navarre against the Duke of Savoy and later as an ally of the latter against the Spanish. But when Lesdiguières died in Valence in 1626, Louis XIII, acting on Richelieu's advice, did not renew the office of Constable. This high

---

[1] Constable (*connétable*), count of the stable, derives from the late Latin *comestabulus*, which in turn derives from *comes stabuli*—literally, companion of the stable. In the early days of the French monarchy the Constable was the chief officer in the King's Household and took precedence over all other dignitaries. He subsequently became Commander-in-Chief of the French armies. But in the seventeenth century this high office was sacrificed by Richelieu to the cause of absolutism.

military appointment, as old as France herself, died out in Louis XIII's reign and was not revived until the reign of Napoleon I.

Everybody was at pains to persuade Montmorency that the Cardinal's revolutionary method consisted in abolishing prescriptive rights and dissolving the traditional authority that the nobles had succeeded in building up over the centuries, in order to take both rights and authority for himself and unite them in his own hands. Now Montmorency had hoped, especially in view of the repeated and almost servile protestations of affection which the King's Minister had made to him, that this powerful man might yet procure for him the one position he regarded as his inviolable birthright. But this hope was not fulfilled. The members of the Orléans faction at Court argued that the only way Montmorency could oppose the Cardinal's intrusion on his rights was by trying to mediate between the King and his close relatives, although the success of any such attempt would of course depend on whether Louis's foreign policy had drawn closer to that pursued by the Queen-Mother and Orléans. But if a reconciliation were brought about between these parties, Richelieu's position would be untenable. In 1619 the Duke of Epernon had succeeded in releasing Marie de' Medici from her exile in Blois and had persuaded her to come to terms with Louis XIII (cf. Vol. I). What an Epernon had achieved in 1619, a Montmorency could surely achieve in 1631. And if he did, the Constable's sword must surely be his. On this occasion Montmorency succumbed to the blandishments of Orléans and his followers. The fate of Marie de' Medici, who lived in exile in Brussels, touched him, as it touched many of his contemporaries, very deeply. It was also a subject his own wife was constantly broaching. But the means he employed in order to gain his ends were destined to enable the Cardinal to prepare for Montmorency, who until then had been considered inviolable, the fate that had long formed part of his plans. Montmorency was convinced that a reconciliation between the various members of the royal family could only be brought about if Orléans's power were increased so that he might negotiate with the King from a position of strength. A soldier by both nature and profession, Montmorency opted for military measures. From early in 1632 onwards Orléans, operating from Brussels, had inundated France with revolutionary propaganda in the form of lampoons. He had then joined forces with the army commanded by the Spanish General Gonzalo de Córdoba and subsequently pressed on with a small force into Lorraine and thence into Languedoc, for Montmorency's province was to serve as a base for the operations planned by the "first agnate." But Orléans had miscalculated. He had hoped to recruit partisans from the discontented French provincial nobility, but very few came forth. He had counted on the active intervention of Charles IV of Lorraine and of the Duke of Savoy, but both failed him. Above all Montmorency had expected the Huguenots to rise. But they followed the instructions of their leader, Henri de Rohan, and continued to observe the provisions of the peace of Alais. Orléans asked Wallenstein, Montecucculi and Mérode, the victor of Mantua, for support, but he asked in vain. Only three hundred French nobles joined his ranks. Both the Imperialists and the Spanish allowed the opportunity to slip. The Cardinal-Infante, the Viceroy of Catalonia and the Duke of Feria also forsook him, while Bouillon remained within the walls of Sedan without making a move. The result was that the heir-apparent found himself in Languedoc with an initial following of just eight hundred men and with Montmorency his only effective support. Gaston refused to listen when the Duke advised him not to act until he could dispose of adequate military means.

Both before these events and also when the action was already under way, Richelieu approached the Duke through mutual friends of many years' standing in order to impress on him the hopelessness of his undertaking. His messages were couched in the clearest possible terms and, after advising

Montmorency on extremely cogent grounds, indeed imploring him, to return to the strict path of duty, he informed him that if he should draw his sword against his sovereign his life would be forfeit. He left him in no doubt about this.

In all subsequent reports on this episode in the struggle for power in France, an incident is mentioned that casts light on Montmorency's personal situation. The Duke was talking one day with his wife, who lay ill in bed. A lady-in-waiting was also present. Montmorency spoke heatedly of the difficult situation in which he found himself. His wife countered most of the arguments he advanced, and then the young and perhaps unwilling listener heard the Duke make the following remark: "Very well, Madame, it shall be as you wish. I shall do it in order to satisfy your ambition, but remember that it will cost me my life." And when Marie de' Medici's niece tried to answer him, Montmorency brought the conversation to an end: "We shall discuss the matter no further. The decision has been made. I will not be the one who regrets it in the end." All the listener heard after this were the sighs of her mistress, who trembled at her own victory.

Montmorency, however, was already regretting his decision. He had committed himself to an undertaking that for a man of honour could end only in victory or death. Other men would have tried to escape abroad. He kept the word he had given to the heir-apparent.

Then, far too early, before Montmorency had even been able to complete his preparations, Gaston appeared at the head of an army, consisting for the most part of mercenaries picked up by him in the neighbourhood of Trier. Montmorency had managed to secure the support of the towns of Lodève, Albi, Uzès, Alais, Béziers, St Pont, Lunel and various others; but the larger towns—such as Nîmes, whose population was predominantly Protestant, Narbonne, Montpellier, Carcassonne and Toulouse—refused to follow him. The King's army, under Marshal de La Force, was already approaching via Pont-Saint-Esprit, and Orléans was retreating in its path.

Marshal Schomberg was moving across upper Languedoc in order to encircle both Gaston and Montmorency, whose total force now numbered some seven thousand men. Richelieu considered it necessary that Louis XIII should appear in person near the scene of the impending engagement. He himself repaired to Lyon. Yet again he sent a mediator to Montmorency, but without success. The Archbishop of Narbonne, a personal friend of the misguided Governor, also tried to persuade him to negotiate. But by that time the Duke must already have been driven to complete despair by the royal proclamation issued in Cosne and dated August 23rd, in which, on the grounds of *lèse-majesté*, he had been declared an enemy of the State and deprived of all his offices and titles. His entire property was to be confiscated and the Parlement of Toulouse had been directed to proceed against him on a charge of high treason. In fact, once Richelieu had ascertained that with the exception of a single province the whole of France had remained loyal to the King, he no longer wished to negotiate.

Meanwhile Schomberg advanced with caution, indeed with great consideration, against the probable heir to the throne. He too had to think of the future and before mounting his attack he sent a certain Cavoie into the enemy camp to negotiate a settlement, which, in the light of past experience, it was quite certain that Orléans would accept. Montmorency, on the other hand, as Dupleix has told us, held his adversaries in contempt and placed his faith in his own valour. "Negotiations come after the battle," was the reply he gave to the Marshal's emissary.

The action, which lasted no more than thirty minutes and cost one hundred lives, took place at Castelnaudary on September 1, 1632. The same élan that had once carried the Duke to triumph at Veillane now carried him to perdition. He rode a light, fast Arab grey, decked out in accordance with ancient custom, with yellow, blue and purple feathers, which waved and fluttered in splendid array. He had approached to within thirty paces of the enemy camp when the musketry opened up on him with a powerful volley of fire that stopped twelve of his followers in their tracks. Montmorency himself was wounded in the neck. Angrily he set his horse at a wide ditch and, clearing it, forced his way into the enemy echelons where, even in the seventh row, he still contrived to kill several men. Two captains of the *chevau-légers*, Beauregard and Laurière, tried to bar his path. With a pistol shot the Duke shattered Beauregard's left arm, but with his right hand the wounded man shot Montmorency in the mouth from close range, breaking his teeth and splitting his cheek from mouth to ear. Still Montmorency found the strength to unseat Baron de Laurière. But by now the Duke's horse was staggering. Laurière, regaining his feet, thrust his sword into the Arab's flank. The noble animal collapsed, rose once more and then crashed to the ground in his death agony, pinning his rider. "Here, here, Montmorency!" the Duke cried as he lay crushed under his horse. He was bleeding from seventeen wounds. But his own men brought him no help, and the nobles of the King's army, who loved and admired him, looked away. "Let him die," they said. But finally, after he had asked Sainte-Marie and Boutillon not to abandon him but to fetch a priest and to give his ring to the Duchess as a token of remembrance, Sainte-Marie untied the leather thongs which were throttling him, removed the cuirass from his breast and carried him on his shoulders into a nearby hut, where Schomberg's chaplain heard his confession and a surgeon bandaged his wounds. He was then taken to the village of Castelnaudary. The chronicler reports that the people were moved to great sorrow and wept and lamented as Montmorency was carried into the little town on an improvised stretcher, followed by seven men of the Royal Guard.

After Montmorency's capture the two opposing armies separated. Schomberg wrote to the King: "I have never before taken part in an engagement so short in which so many persons of rank were killed, wounded or captured."

This was the end of yet another revolt inspired by Orléans and the Queen-Mother. For what then followed was no more than a police action and the trial. The battle, which had scarcely begun, was already over.

On September 7th Richelieu wrote to Marshal de La Force:

"Now that Monsieur de Montmorency has been taken prisoner, the outlook for those who cannot bear to see France prosper is bad."

And on September 10th the Cardinal, who left nothing to chance, wrote to Schomberg:

"It is rumoured here that he is dead and because the news of his capture, which proved true, was allowed to circulate for three days before being confirmed by you, people believe [the rumour], especially in view of the number of his wounds and the location of some of them. As soon as the King has been informed of either the decease or the recovery of Monsieur de Montmorency he will decide what further measures are to be taken."

For as long as the prisoner's recovery seemed improbable, Richelieu spoke in terms of lifelong imprisonment. But soon a courier arrived with a laconic report from Schomberg to the effect that Monsieur de Montmorency would not be succumbing to his wounds.

Orléans' subsequent behaviour is not strictly relevant in this context, but it should be mentioned that he did what he could to save Montmorency. He sent Monsieur de Brionne to beg in all humility that Louis XIII might exercise his clemency. For a long time Brionne was not received and when he was finally admitted to the King's presence he was sent away again without an answer. When the Prince and Princess of Condé appealed on her brother's behalf and submitted a document to the King containing a reprieve which only needed signing, Louis XIII replied:

"Cousin, you know that my duty to the kingdom must take precedence over all other considerations; that is the reason why I am unable to give any undertaking in this case."

To the Princess he wrote:

"What you have told me of your feelings concerning your brother's dereliction makes me more wretched than I can say; but this fault is so grievous and of such consequence to the welfare of my State that I assume you too will understand when I say that in this case I am unable to give any undertaking without creating a serious precedent."

But then what could he have promised at that time? His letter to the Prince and Princess of Condé was written on September 16, 1632. Three days before, the Keeper of the Seals had told the Duchess of Chevreuse that, if Montmorency were to recover, the King was determined to have him beheaded.

Meanwhile Schomberg had taken his prisoner to the small town of Lectoure. He feared that the inhabitants of Castelnaudary or Toulouse might try to set him free. But even in Lectoure, where the castle was built on a rock, he tarried only for as long as it took to administer a little beef broth to his severely wounded prisoner, who was suffering from extreme exhaustion. A certain "first president," Montrabé, one of Richelieu's dependents, had informed the Cardinal that the members of the city council of Toulouse, the so-called *capitouls*, were determined to rescue the Duke, and Richelieu immediately notified Schomberg to this effect. During the journey from Toulouse to Letoure, a distance of some twenty miles, Montmorency was so feeble that he was expected to die at any moment. At one of the places where they stopped for a brief rest, the prisoner was laid in a room in which one wall was covered by a tapestry. The surgeon, who had presumably been briefed by the owner of the house, told his patient that behind the tapestry was a secret door leading straight out into the open at a side of the house that was unguarded. The chronicler reports: "The seventeen wounds made flight impossible."

Even in Lectoure, despite constant blood-letting, the Duke felt much improved, thanks to his powerful constitution. One of the guards, who had been bribed by the mistress of the castle, undertook to make all necessary arrangements for the Duke's escape. He would bring silk ropes. Once they had climbed down these ropes they would find themselves in the farmyard. The prisoner could then slip out through a hole in the wall where the Marchioness would be waiting for him with twenty mounted men. But the plot was discovered, the guards were hanged and the prisoner kept under even sharper watch than before.

If, contrary to his usual practice, Orléans had decided not to come to terms on this occasion, there would have been only one course open to him: to flee the country by crossing the Pyrenees and entering Spain. His supporters maintained that he negotiated only in order to save the lives of his loyal followers. And it was the Duchess of Montmorency, one of the principal instigators of the revolt, who most insistently urged him to submit.

The first set of conditions proposed by Gaston were rejected by the King. Orléans' representative, Brionne, was then instructed to inform Louis that the heir-apparent accepted full responsibility for the revolt. But on the very day when Brionne was given an audience, Richelieu had handed Louis XIII a detailed memorandum, drafted in Beaucaire on September 17th, urging Louis to show no mercy to the Governor of Languedoc. Montmorency's fate had already been decided before the negotiations began.

In the first volume of his Memoirs, the Cardinal went back to the events of the year 1614. By comparison with the many respectful statements he had made about the unfortunate Montmorency's forbears during the long period when the Duke had been held in high esteem, the observations Richelieu set down in his Memoirs clearly constitute an attempt to dim the glory and enduring fame of a whole house. He wrote:

"At that time the Constable, Henri I, Duc de Montmorency, died of old age. He was the most handsome and able horseman and the best warrior of his day and was said to possess a sound judgement, although he was no man of letters and was scarcely able to write his own name. In the interests of self-preservation, he was obliged to resist the Guises' persecutions of his house by entering into an alliance with the Huguenots of Languedoc, although in point of fact, as a servant of the King, he should have been fighting them. However, he did not allow them to predominate, but preserved a balance of power that permitted him to continue the war and so provided him with a pretext for remaining constantly under arms. In order to remove him without dishonour from his province, where he had lived almost as a sovereign, the King, Henry the Great, appointed him Constable of France, an office that three of his ancestors had held before him. . . ."

We have already seen that in the memorandum Richelieu drafted in 1627 on the de Bouteville affair he still lauded Henri de Montmorency's great ancestors. But in 1632—by which time he had discovered that historical arguments weighed heavily with the King—he completely reversed his former practice and penned what was virtually a diatribe against the house of Montmorency:

"But, since he was determined to take his ancestors as his example, it is not to be wondered at that he should have shown, in all manner of malicious ways, that it was not only their lands that the two last Constables in his family had passed on to him but also their blood; in trying to destroy the monarchy he was following in their footsteps. He was taught from the cradle to squint, to make him resemble the Constable, although the more discerning would have us believe that if he were really to resemble his father, he would need to be one-eyed. . . . His grandfather was no less disastrous to the State, for during . . . the long period in which he enjoyed royal favour, he did more harm than our worst enemies during the century before and the century after [his lifetime].

"Under Francis I he was responsible for the loss of the Duchy of Milan; he concluded that offensive truce with the Piedmontese; he persuaded the King, in return for a bribe, to permit Charles V to march through French territory; and he refused aid to the rebels in Ghent because he was in league with Queen Eleanor and the Duchess of Etampes, with whom he committed all manner of treason.

"It is true that he forced the pass of Susa [this at least Richelieu could not deny, but having conceded the achievement he immediately belittled it] which was defended by Cesare of Naples, a soldier of fortune with the rank of colonel . . . ; but under Henry II, Francis [II] and Charles [IX] we were made to pay dearly for his services, for just the one battle of St Quentin, which was lost through his fault alone, cost the King more than three hundred fortified positions. . . .

"He had Marshal Brissac, one of the best army commanders of his day and one of the King's most faithful servants, removed from Court, simply because he envied him his ability.

"It was always suspected that his oldest son, Marshal Montmorency, was in league with his Châtillon cousins, and the Queen [Catherine de' Medici, who was then Regent] was sufficiently persuaded of his involvement in all those disorders that she was obliged to imprison him to ensure the safe return from Poland of King Henry III.

"And the Constable, Henry II's father [Henry I], was not above suspicion, even when he was doing his best for the State, for when he lost his life in winning the battle of St Denis, the following couplet was circulated throughout the whole of Christendom:

Impavidus pugnat nolens pugnare, suosque
Dum non vult victos vincere, victor obit."

This is not an edifying text. It reveals a trait in Richelieu which can also be gathered from a certain expression of his mouth. In the many letters he wrote to members of the Montmorency family, irrespective of whether he was expressing his sympathy or communicating factual information, there was often a hint of servility. For that servility the Cardinal was taking his revenge. And yet, the really basic reason underlying his action had little to do with such feelings. Here, as in all things, his ultimate motive was a determination to concentrate power in the hands of the King. The myth of exalted birth, which had been operative since the days of antiquity, had to be destroyed.

The negotiations between the King and Orléans were opened on September 26th in Béziers, the town to which Orléans had withdrawn. The Secretaries of State Bullion and des Fossés acted on behalf of the King. Free pardons were granted to those who were in Monsieur's entourage at the time of the revolt. This act of clemency did not embrace Montmorency or those of Orléans's followers who had remained in Brussels—Le Coigneux, Monsigot and La Vieuville. When Orléans tried to intercede on the Duke's behalf, he was told that this was a matter which only the King could decide. But to Marshal Châtillon, who personally implored him to exercise his mercy, the King said: "I would not be a King if I possessed the feelings of a private person."

At this time Louis was in Montpellier. He had not yet forgiven his brother and did not wish to meet him. Gaston, for his part, was staying in Lyon when the news reached him that Montmorency's trial was about to begin. He immediately instructed a certain Comte de La Vopot to go to Louis as his representative. "I would have you speak respectfully and submissively to the King on my behalf, but I would also have you say that this [the Montmorency trial] is the most important thing in the world for me. My honour and my reputation are both at stake. There will be no future happiness for me unless

His Majesty should decide to grant me this one favour." A week later Orléans also wrote to his brother and to the Cardinal in order to plead his friend's case and to remind them of the great services rendered by Montmorency in the past. These letters were dated October 30th.

The Court left Montpellier on October 4th and after a two-day journey via Mèze and Pézenas arrived in Béziers. The articles of the agreements between the King and his brother, drafted by Richelieu, had been signed on September 29th. When Richelieu read the letter Orléans had written to the King on Montmorency's behalf, he said to his sovereign:

"Monsieur is pleading for the life of the Duke of Montmorency. Would it be better to pardon his crimes or not? There are strong reasons for an act of clemency. If he is to break off his relations with Lorraine and Spain, Monsieur needs a decent pretext—that is, a pardon for the rebel. Without this act of clemency Monsieur cannot honourably return to the path of duty. Whatever the nature of the undertaking he was required to give, he would be forced to flee to Spain at the earliest possible moment. There he would sow the seeds of a new war, for the Spanish would provide him with the means to promote a further rising in France. If we push Monsieur to the wall . . . then those who have the honour of serving Your Majesty will be accused of harshness [against Montmorency]. They will not be secure for a moment, for Monsieur's followers will regard the downfall of the King's advisers as their only hope of salvation."

As Richelieu spoke the King may well have imagined the murdered Cardinal stretched out before him, for had not Orléans declared that ". . . if the unhappy Montmorency is condemned to death, there are twenty noblemen who are determined to cut down Richelieu."

"Words, words," was Richelieu's reply when told of this. But the King feared for his chief minister. If anything were to happen to Richelieu, then the crushing weight of political responsibility would fall on his shoulders.

"But if Monsieur returns to the path of allegiance," the Cardinal continued, "if he honestly decides to support Your Majesty's great projects abroad, then there is nothing we could not undertake against the Spanish, against this nation which is naturally hostile to us, which is opposed to the person of our King and the government of our country."

Just as he had pleaded for de Bouteville, so Richelieu pleaded for Montmorency, without of course intending that the King should seriously consider the possibility of clemency. In no time at all he had abandoned the defence and was presenting the case for the prosecution. But in order to give an impression of moderation and ensure that the responsibility for the decision should be borne by the King alone, he spoke as if he were developing the opinions of others:

"Those who hold that Montmorency must be punished as an example to others have a strong case." (The King was childless, his health was said to be bad and Monsieur was, of course, the heir to the throne.) "Unless those who place themselves at the disposal of the heir-presumptive are strongly dealt with, it could well be that if the monarch were to fall ill, even slightly, many of the more opportunist nobles would go over to the heir-presumptive. But if the Duke receives the punishment he deserves, then even if Your Majesty were to suffer a serious illness, nobody would consider it sufficiently dangerous to warrant risking his future. For everyone will go in mortal dread of the punishment he must consider certain should the King recover."

These benevolent spirits, whom Richelieu had summoned up to be his spokesmen, then invoked the tenor of the times in support of their opinion:

"Should the crimes committed on Monsieur's behalf go unpunished, there can be no doubt but that the great nobles will gladly risk their good fortune and their wealth in the hope of prospering at the expense of both the King and of the State. In such cases dispossession is meaningless unless accompanied by the death penalty, for as soon as Monsieur mounted the throne he would be able to return any offices, money and property that had been lost in this way."

And then His Eminence, who knew every single facet of the King's personality, hit upon one of his most effective formulas:

"The great nobles would consider that to hazard their fortune on Monsieur's account would be to invest it at exorbitant rates of interest with no capital risk."

The Cardinal's attitude had changed considerably since 1629, when he had written that "If this prince [Orléans] is treated honourably, he will never do anything to disturb the peace of the realm." In the meantime there had been Lyon and the Day of the Dupes.

Much later, when he undertook to characterize all the French army commanders in gnomic form, Richelieu was to say of Henri de Montmorency: "A strong heart, a weak head, in the end disloyal."

In the remaining days of his life the condemned man learnt that the whole of his property had been confiscated, whereupon he submitted his one and only request to the King—that he might be permitted to dispose of the contents of two small rooms and a closet. His request was granted. The Duke then bequeathed to Richelieu various extremely beautiful pieces— articles of furniture fashioned by leading cabinet-makers and an oil painting of the death of St Sebastian by Carracci. Richelieu had once admired the painting and the furniture, and the Duke now apologized for not having given these works to him at the time. The contents of the second room he left to his sister, the Princess of Condé, and the contents of the closet went to his niece, Mademoiselle de Bourbon.

On October 30th, the day on which Gaston had addressed his petition to the King, Montmorency was executed in the courtyard of the town hall of Toulouse in a ceremony of macabre splendour. He went to his death, as was only to be expected, with the bearing that has always distinguished men of his stamp.

Many years later his widow confessed to Orléans's daughter, the "Grande Mademoiselle," that for the rest of her life she had suffered agonies of remorse for having encouraged her husband to embark on the enterprise. It had taken years of strict penance before she had been able to forgive Richelieu, although she had never felt animosity towards Orléans. "He has shown me such kindness," she added, "that I always include him in my prayers."

Louis XIII said on his death-bed that during the whole of that wretched journey to Toulouse, which he had undertaken against his will, it had been his intention to spare Montmorency's life, but that he had allowed himself to be persuaded by the countless "reasons of state" which had been presented to him. The whole affair had left him with a grievous sense of regret, although he had always suppressed it. How sad was the fate of Kings who, because they were shown only the dark side of things, were induced to suspect their closest relatives and their best friends, men whom they themselves had believed loyal and true, and to pursue a policy guided by political phantoms, which in actual fact merely served the interests of a third party.

CHAPTER IV

THE REPERCUSSIONS OF
THE EXECUTION OF MONTMORENCY

Time and again throughout history the lowly are raised and the mighty are humbled. This was an observation Richelieu was to make on many occasions.

Although he is usually depicted as the strong man who took the initiative in humiliating and weakening the great nobles and who had the fortifications of cities, towns and castles razed to the ground in order to break the resistance of both nobles and Protestants, it is quite evident that Richelieu was in fact no more than the energetic executor of centralizing tendencies that had been present long before he himself began to direct French national policy.

At a time when freedom of political action was the prerogative of only a small number of persons who, whatever their nationality, all belonged to one exclusive caste, decisive events were influenced, significantly and specifically, by the tension of highly personal relationships. Within the historical sphere ideas are often much more important than facts, and in our modern age of equality it is difficult to grasp the importance once attributed to the rank of certain exalted families and consciously accepted at every level of contemporary society.

The members of the European aristocracy felt themselves threatened by Montmorency's death, which they blamed on Richelieu. The execution of a man who to his own class represented the perfect embodiment of all that they stood for, was a sensational event; it had repercussions throughout the whole of Europe and in France itself gave rise to a crisis that threatened to overwhelm the Cardinal.

Looking back at this point, we can see how much had happened within the Cardinal's immediate sphere in the two years since the Day of the Dupes. To recapitulate: the fall of the Marillacs in the course of the "great storm"; the tremendous and for many contemporaries scandalous struggle between the King and the Queen-Mother; the flight of the Queen into exile; constant conspiracies between Brussels, where the exiled party had taken refuge, and London, where Marie's daughter Queen Henrietta had espoused her Florentine mother's cause. Marie's negotiations with her son-in-law, the King of Spain, had become known, and it was all but certain that the reigning Queen, Anne of Austria, had been involved in these treasonable activities. It was rumoured that Madrid had tried to persuade the Emperor to attack Toul and Langres, and it was known that in Nancy moves were afoot to establish a coalition between the Holy Roman Emperor, the King of Spain, the Duke of Lorraine and possibly the Duke of Savoy. There had been the brief engagement at Castelnaudary, the outcome of which had frustrated, for a short time at least, any plans the rebellious but weak heir-presumptive, Gaston d'Orléans, might have had in mind. But with Gaston d'Orléans we come up against major considerations of foreign policy, which need to be considered against a wider background.

For the time being let us consider the events around the Cardinal which arose from Montmorency's execution, in which Court intrigue played a particularly significant part.

Marie de Chevreuse

With the mention of the word "intrigue," it is time to turn our attention once more to a woman we have encountered and will encounter many times in the course of this history: the Duchess of Chevreuse, who caused Richelieu more difficulty and annoyance, in both the long and the short run, than many of the powerful and influential men of his day. In Chapter XIII of the first volume of this study we have dealt in detail with this tempestuous woman, primarily within the context of her activities in England but also in connection with the part she played in the downfall of the young Count of Chalais. We have seen her as Luynes's wife, and then, after her second marriage to the Duke of Chevreuse, as a member of a reigning house. But whether she had love affairs with foreign monarchs or was casting her spell on their most influential advisers, whether she was leading the French opposition leaders on, exploiting the influence she had in Lorraine or introducing elements of confusion into the already confused relations between Madrid, London and Brussels, we have seen that in the most hazardous undertakings involving the utmost danger she was always able to extricate herself by her imperturbable self-assurance. She had a constant need of men, whom she exploited for her own ends and promptly discarded once she had finished with them, which was usually quickly. When in 1679 she neared death, she had the certain knowledge that few women of her time had exercised an influence on world affairs comparable to her own.

Even Richelieu was fascinated—of that there can be no doubt—first by the extremely clever reports she had sent to him as his agent in England and then, after her return, by her person.

In his Memoirs the Cardinal said of her:

"She was the ruin of the Queen, whose naturally healthy outlook was corrupted by the example she set; she controlled the Queen's heart, she ruined her, she made her turn away from the King and from her duties, she estranged the royal couple."

Madame de Motteville, who had seen the Duchess daily over long periods, described the Queen's situation as follows:

"It was the Queen's misfortune that the King, her husband, did not really love her, and consequently she felt obliged to place her affections elsewhere and to give her heart to ladies who sadly abused such a favour. Instead of urging the Queen, in the early years of her marriage, to try to please her husband and so win his love, they strove to draw her farther and farther away from him, in order that they themselves might possess her the more securely."

Marie de Chevreuse, the former Marie de Luynes, was the central figure in the strange clique surrounding Anne of Austria, the daughter of Philip III of the Spanish Hapsburg line. They were highly unsuitable company for the young Queen whose husband neglected her. To the circle belonged Mademoiselle de Verneuil, a natural daughter of Henry IV, whom Tallemant des Réaux described as "one of the greatest madcaps at Court," Antoinette de Luynes, sister of the favourite and wife of a certain Barthélemy du Vernet; and finally Marguerite de Lorraine, the forty-three-year-old widow of the late Prince of Conti, of whom Marsillac had said (in a letter to Richelieu written on April 29, 1622) that she was "the matchmaker behind every love affair."

Marie de Chevreuse was always attracted by bad company, but she seemed immune to its bad effects. In the spring of 1622, as a result of Marie's recklessness, the Queen suffered an accident and lost the child that would have ensured the succession. Louis XIII then decided to remove the Duchess from Court. (The correspondence between the King and his wife relating to this incident has been preserved.)

After Marie's first husband, Luynes, had died and she had married the Duke of Chevreuse, a Guise of the reigning house of Lorraine, it became much more difficult to proceed against her.

The Guises

The house of Guise, which had played such an important part in the history of the French monarchy, went back to Claude de Lorraine, a son of René of Lorraine and Bar. At the beginning of the sixteenth century Claude had undertaken to serve in France and had been granted the Duchy of Guise by Francis I in recognition of his services.

His heirs were to become powerful leaders of the Catholic party. The eldest son of Claude de Lorraine and Antoinette de Bourbon, François de Lorraine, the second Duke of Guise, was one of the most eminent of the French army commanders in the wars against Charles V of Spain. His successful defence of the fortress of Metz against the Emperor was of crucial importance for the further course of world history. But of his many great deeds as a general, the greatest by far was the re-conquest of Calais, the port England had held since 1347.

Francis II, whose wife, Mary Stuart, was the daughter of James V of Scotland and of Marie de Lorraine, appointed the Duke of Guise and his younger brother, the Cardinal de Lorraine, to key positions in the government as soon as he succeeded to the throne. Upon the death of Francis II, whose mother, Catherine de' Medici, was declared Regent for the duration of Charles IX's minority, Guise joined forces with his former rival, the Constable Montmorency, and Marshal Saint André to form the "triumvirate." Their object was to frustrate the Queen-Mother's policy of reconciliation between Catholics and Huguenots. This aim and the triumvirate's bad financial policy provoked violent resistance. Now, for the first time, the Bourbons came out in open opposition to the Guises. An armed clash between Catholics and Huguenots near Vassy in 1562 marked the beginning of the Wars of Religion. François de Guise had been present at this battle, and he played an important part in the wars thereafter, conquering Rouen in 1562 and then going on to win the battle of Dreux, but during the siege of Orléans he was murdered by a Protestant, Jean Poltrot de Méré.

The marriage between François de Guise and Princess Anne of the house of Este produced a son, Henri, whose anti-Huguenot tendencies hardened into total enmity when his father was murdered. As a military leader he was his father's equal. After distinguishing himself both in the Turkish wars and later, in 1569, at the battles of Jarnac and Poitiers, he helped to plan and direct the Massacre of St Bartholomew, in which he was motivated above all by his hatred of Admiral Coligny. He supervised the Admiral's murder in person. Because Henry III of Valois was held in general contempt as a weak King, Guise's popularity was allowed to rise unchecked, especially in Paris. It was he who founded the Holy League, which was based on an alliance with Spain. The hopes he entertained at that time of succeeding Henry III as King of France were well founded. In 1587 he defeated a German army at Vimory and a Huguenot army at Auneau. Although forbidden to do so by Henry III, he entered Paris in triumph. Henry was besieged by rebels in the Louvre and it was Guise himself who rescued him from his plight and helped him to flee the capital. But Guise remained in Paris. A temporary reconciliation was brought about between the King and the Duke, and then the tables were turned. Ignoring all warnings, the Duke travelled to Blois to the assembly of the Estates-General. On December 23, 1588, relying on the notorious indecisiveness of the King and on the position of power he himself held, Guise left the assembly room and quite unconcernedly went to visit the King at the latter's request in his private chamber. But his lack of concern was to prove his undoing. Led by an officer of the Royal Guard, eight musketeers burst out of an adjoining room with daggers drawn and murdered him. The following day the Duke's corpse was burnt together with that of his brother, who had also been murdered. If Henri de Guise had gained possession of the Crown, France's relations with Spain and the Holy Roman Empire would have developed along quite different lines and the Counter-Reformation would have followed an entirely different course.

Henri de Guise and his wife, Catherine of Cleves, had fourteen children, seven of whom survived. But with them the French branch of the house of Lorraine entered into a

3. Front view of the Château Rueil and its Gardens

4.   Front Entrance of the Château Richelieu

decline. The oldest son was of feeble intelligence. The second was a reckless Renaissance prince who, like de Bouteville-Montmorency, was famed for his duelling. Called Claude after his great-grandfather, he bore the title of a Prince of Joinville, but in 1612, when the King awarded him the small Duchy of Chevreuse, he adopted this new title instead. Until then the Guises had enjoyed the rank accorded to members of a foreign ruling house, but once the French Parlement had ratified his title, Claude de Guise, Duc de Chevreuse, was bound by oath to the King of France.

In 1620 Rucellai had written to the Duke: "The zeal which you have displayed on His Majesty's behalf has firmly established you in his esteem. . . . You may rest assured that henceforth you will enjoy greater privileges than others."

Tallemant considered that it would be difficult to find a more level-headed man than Chevreuse. Gaston d'Orléans, on the other hand, called him "unreliable, indolent and soft." But Gaston's poor opinion of Chevreuse may have been due to the fact that, despite the pressure exerted by his wife, Marie de Chevreuse, he refused to join the party of the rebellious prince. In the Turkish wars Chevreuse not only proved his worth, he distinguished himself. And when there were neither Turks nor Huguenots for him to destroy, he engaged in affairs of honour with such great Court dancers as Schomberg, Termes, Sommerive, St Luc and Pompignan. He was a great ladies' man. Was it just coincidence that so many of the women he chose to pursue were the mistresses of Henry IV? Although he had been a close friend of the King's ever since the latter's conversion, when he tried to approach the Countess of Moret Henry banished him, first to England and then to a remote castle in France. Subsequently, after his return to favour, he turned his attentions to the Marchioness of Verneuil. One evening in the Marais, the fashionable quarter of town, when he was pursuing this very popular lady, he came close to killing the Duke of Bellegarde. Stung to genuine anger, the King seriously considered having him executed, but Guise had found refuge in the arms of the wife of the Governor of Le Havre, the influential Madame de Villars. Next he became the lover of Angélique Paulet, the famed singer, and shortly afterwards of the widow of Marshal Fervaques, who placed the whole of her fortune at his disposal. But in Marie de Rohan, then the wife of the Duke of Luynes, he met his match. He saw her often in the house of his sister, the Princess of Conti. Everyone knew that they were lovers, except Marie's husband. Rucellai wrote to Chevreuse towards the end of Luynes's life: "I have read your letter out to Monsieur de Luynes; he is gratified to receive your assurances of friendship and service and wishes to inform you of his own friendship and esteem." (See Vol. I).

One day Louis XIII started dropping hints to Luynes about his wife's conduct. But that sort of thing was against the code, and Bassompierre, who felt himself duty bound to enlighten his sovereign on such matters, explained to Louis that it was a sin to sow discontent between a man and his wife.

On December 21, 1621, Luynes died and from that day on Chevreuse and Marie appeared together quite openly. They were inseparable. But when Marie was banished from Court, Claude de Chevreuse happened to be on a pilgrimage to Notre-Dame-de-Liesse near Laon in the company of Messieurs de Liancourt, Blainville, Zamet and Fontenay-Mareuil. On this happy journey of pious intent he received news of his lover's disgrace. She had despatched an express courier to inform him that if she was to be rescued from her intolerable situation, there was only one thing to be done: he must marry her and be quick about it, for then she would be able to arrange matters so as to regain her position at court.

Claude de Chevreuse was embarrassed and annoyed. He candidly asked his companions for their advice. All were against the marriage. Fontenay-Mareuil has given a very lively description of this incident in his Memoirs. The Duke's fellow pilgrims pointed out to him that he would be exposing himself to a great deal of unpleasantness and would be undermining his own position. The King would feel slighted by this marriage. Chevreuse acquiesced in all their arguments and informed the Duchess that he was unable to comply with her wishes.

After commanding that the incorrigible Marie de Luynes was to vanish from his wife's sight, Louis XIII had proceeded with courtesy, indeed with great consideration, so that Marie found it quite an easy matter to play for time.

Upon his return Claude de Chevreuse, fortified by the opinions of his friends and by the certain knowledge that his unequivocal reply had arrived in Paris ahead of him, visited his disgraced lover and was instantly lost. Marie told him that, in accordance with Court etiquette, she would be writing to the King to obtain his approval for her new marriage. Chevreuse was powerless to prevent her from doing so.

As was so often the case, Louis XIII fell into a violent but ultimately impotent rage. With Louis, moral arguments always prevailed and so he was told that conscience required that two people who had already compromised themselves to such an extent in public should not be prevented from legalizing and sanctifying their relationship. At the same time it was hinted that at some later date it would always be possible to find ways and means to annul this union.

Fearful that Chevreuse might still change his mind, Marie de Rohan made the wedding arrangements in great haste and the ceremony was performed in the presence of a very small circle on April 20, 1622, four months after Luynes's death.

When he informed Richelieu of these events, Marillac wrote: "The King feels extremely hurt by the behaviour of the Constable's wife and Monsieur de Chevreuse. He now hates them both." But the King was faced with a fait accompli.

The marriage contract has been preserved.

On April 21st the newlyweds arrived at the castle of Lésigny-en-Brie, which had been built by Luynes. Marillac commented: "The blissful lovers are praising God in the chapel of Lésigny and taking possession of the house which the late

Duke of Luynes unwittingly prepared for them. The Court is highly amused."

Shortly afterwards Chevreuse took his wife to Dampierre Castle, which lay close to Paris, in order to "do her the honours of his Duchy."

Though the activities of this intriguer at the Court of Louis XIII may at first sight appear irrelevant, on closer scrutiny they help us to understand Richelieu's life.

Time and again the Cardinal tried to make use of the influence the Duchess wielded over Anne of Austria and Gaston d'Orléans. In this he never succeeded. According to the perspicacious La Rochefoucauld, Richelieu was not long in doubt as to the nature of the feelings Marie entertained for him following the death of Chalais (see Vol. I).

After the bloody outcome of the various plots, the Duchess was always able to cover up her tracks. She assumed in any case that no one would dare to accuse her, and she also knew that it would scarcely be possible to produce really incriminating evidence against her. But even so her customary practice was to quit the country in good time, travelling in disguise. She would cross the border into Lorraine where she set the tone and continued to sow the seeds of discord. We shall be reporting on these visits in greater detail in connection with the whole question of Lorraine (see Vol. III). Marie appeared in Brussels, in Spain and also in England, a country that appealed to her and where we have already seen her at work following the marriage of Henrietta of France. She was involved in hair-raising escapes, in the course of which she performed quite astonishing athletic feats. But as soon as she felt that the atmosphere in Paris had cleared, she would return with all possible speed, convinced as always that she was needed, and devote herself yet again to the task of winning influential men, a task she pursued in the fullest sense and without sparing herself in any way. In Paris she was completely in her element, and her visits abroad remained for her a kind of exile. At Court she expressed and spread opinions so outrageous that in the end their very extravagance discredited them.

She would tell anyone who was prepared to listen that the King was a weakling and a halfwit unfit for rule, and she declared it to be a national disgrace that a rogue like Richelieu should be at the helm. However, this state of affairs was not enough to persuade her to quit the field. After Castelnaudary and the death of Montmorency, she stayed with Anne of Austria. She was convinced that this time Richelieu had overstepped his limits and was nearing his end.

In the closing months of the year 1632—at the time of Gustavus Adolphus' death at Lützen—Cardinal Richelieu undertook one of the strangest journeys of his life.

On October 30th Montmorency's head had fallen and on the very next day the King set out from Toulouse to return to Paris. On November 1st we find him in Montauban and on November 5th he wrote to Richelieu from Brive-la-Gaillarde: "I wish to tell you that I miss you enormously; it seems more than two months since you left me. All that I can say, while awaiting your return, is that I shall love you until death." Then on November 12th in Saint Marcel, near Argenton-sur-Creuse, the King learnt of his brother's flight to Lorraine. On November 20th he arrived in Versailles with an escort of three hundred dragoons, where he received news of the death of Schomberg, who had been carried off by a stroke in his fifty-second year.

It was Richelieu's intention to travel in the company of the reigning Queen from Montpellier via Bordeaux, to show her the port of Brouage, of which he was Governor, then to break their journey in La Rochelle and finally to do her the honours of the town of Richelieu, where he was about to build his palace, the residence that was to perpetuate his name, in the strictly symmetrical spirit of seventeenth-century architecture.

On November 10th the Queen and her retinue were in Lectoure. Suddenly Madame de Chevreuse approached

Mon Cousin ( ) on ma dit aujourdhuy,
que vous aurés pris resolution de
vous anbarquer sur vn vesseau pour
estre au conbat, Je vous conjure
au non de Dieu de changer la que
vous aués prise, , et de ne vous
mettre point en lieu ou vous puisiés
courre aucune fortune, Je vous en
prie encornes vnerfois denevous mettre
en lieu ou vous puisiés courre, Je
tiendray le mesme soin que vous,
aurés de vous comme si cettoit de moy
mesme que vous lussies, cest le plus
grand temoygnage daffon que vous
me puisies que danoir soin de vous

car vous savez que je vous ay
dit plusieurs fois que si je vous
avois perdu il me sembleroit estre
perdu moymesme je vous prie et
commande pour la troisieme fois de ne
vous point ambarquer sur aucun
vesseau le jour du combat et de ne
vous mettre en lieu ou vous puisies
courire fortune, je mattans que vous
le feres pour lamour de moy, je finiro
an priant dieu quil vous tienne an
Ste garde LOUIS

a Calen ce xxvij me may
1628

Richelieu and said to him: "Tell us something of the disclosure which Monsieur de Montmorency made to the King through Launay." To this the Cardinal replied: "Launay reported on various matters; I do not know what it is you wish me to tell you." "He told him to report," replied the Duchess, thoroughly enjoying her sensational news, "that Orléans' marriage to the Princess Marguerite de Lorraine had already been solemnized. I am only telling you this lest you should imagine that we are not informed about those matters which you conceal from us."

Who could have betrayed the secret? Richelieu knew at once: Châteauneuf, the faithful Châteauneuf, who only a few months earlier, on March 11, 1632, had acted as his tool in presiding over the special court that had condemned Marshal Marillac to death. Châteauneuf had succeeded Michel Marillac as the Keeper of the Seals. Meanwhile, however, there had been an important new development. Châteauneuf, on whom both the King and Richelieu relied, had become so enslaved by the Duchess of Chevreuse that she was able to write to him: "I command you to obey me, not only in order that you may satisfy your passion, in case you should feel driven to do so, but also in order that you may satisfy my desire, which is to exercise absolute control over your will." She always drew her victims into the Spanish camp, which served the interests of the Queen-Mother and Orléans. She received emissaries from England, Lorraine and the Netherlands. She felt so sure of herself that she openly inveighed against the Cardinal and treated him unsparingly. By having Montmorency executed he had—or so she thought—alienated one and all, not only the Court, but the Parlements as well, indeed the whole of French public opinion.

But that was not the end of the Cardinal's troubles. Anne of Austria, attended by a large retinue, was returning to Paris by a different route from that taken by the King. It was not only because he wished to show her the town of Richelieu and to inspect Brouage that the Cardinal had joined the Queen's party. He also found it more congenial to travel by water whenever possible. But he soon realized that he was made the scapegoat for all that had happened, and that despite his escort and his bodyguards his life would be constantly threatened in this company. This weighed heavily on his mind and his health deteriorated from day to day. From the very beginning of the journey he was treated without courtesy and even subjected to insults: when he entered a room people laughed in the corners. Châteauneuf, the Duchess' pawn, began to assume great airs. Richelieu, they were all convinced, was a dying man. Suffering from "fiendish kidney pains" he sailed past the fertile banks of the Garonne, following Anne of Austria's ship in his own light little galleon. Arrangements had been made for the party to break its journey in the truly regal castle of Cadillac, which lay on the north bank of the river and was the residence of Jean-Louis de Nogaret de La Valette, Duc d'Epernon. In this house the Cardinal was likely to feel singularly ill at ease.

Richelieu's ship dropped anchor in sight of the castle. He landed but no one was there to receive him. The Queen's retinue was so great that the carriage intended for the Cardinal had been commandeered by ladies of the Court. The sick man was left to negotiate the escarpment and the steep road leading up to the palace on foot. On learning of this breakdown in the reception arrangements, which had in fact been engineered by a group of the Queen's courtiers, Epernon hurried off in his capacity as host to meet his sombre guest but was unable to persuade him to enter his carriage. And so the seventy-eight-year-old Governor of Guyenne found himself obliged to accompany the Cardinal on foot to the rooms prepared for him. No sooner had he arrived than Richelieu was anxious to depart. He felt hemmed in. True, his personal following, designed for his safety, comprised twelve hundred men of the King's Horse, a number of men-at-arms and *chevaux-légers*, in addition to his own bodyguards. But something sinister was in the air. The Duke had arranged for the men of the

King's Horse to be camped on the other side of the Garonne. And as for his bodyguards, without whom the Cardinal never budged an inch, here too the Duke had taken appropriate measures. There had not been a single room left for them in the castle and they had been housed elsewhere. Their commander, Monsieur de Cahusac, was obliged to pass the night in the blacksmith's house. Richelieu concentrated his most reliable men in his own room and in the antechamber, and at the crack of dawn he was on his way again. Apart from some meat broth prepared for him by his personal cook he had nothing to eat or drink. This was doubtless a wise precaution, for Epernon was old enough to be acquainted with the Renaissance customs practised at the Valois Court.

Before the waters of the Garonne had risen with the tide, the Cardinal was on board his galleon. He reached Bordeaux without succumbing to his ailments, but once there he went down with a severe attack of fever.

Meanwhile the Queen and her Court had arrived in the city of great wines, and Epernon followed. The old Governor presented himself daily at Richelieu's sick-bed or, as was assumed with certainty and with undisguised pleasure, at the death-bed of the hated man. "I have not come to molest you but to enquire after your health," he would say to the Cardinal. None the less, he was accompanied on every visit by two hundred armed men of his own force. Richelieu's person was threatened. It seems that there was a plot afoot to seize him and hold him prisoner in the Château Trompette and that it was not carried out only because the plotters fully expected the dreaded Cardinal to die at any moment.

The doctors diagnosed Richelieu's condition as a severe abscess at the anus accompanied by total retention of urine. The much tormented patient did not do his unwelcome visitor the favour of telling him the exact nature of his illness, but he did inform the King, either directly or through Bouthillier, of every detail in order to allay his anxiety; during that time the monarch revealed a genuine and heartfelt concern for the

Cardinal. The Cardinal's opponents, however, claimed that he had simulated this illness throughout the whole length of his journey in order to escape assassination.

In Bordeaux a doctor catheterized Richelieu with a hollowed taper. "He has now removed all the urine from my bladder, which was killing me, and I feel an inexpressible relief. I hope that this will free the King from his anxiety," Richelieu wrote to the devoted Secretary of State.

Meanwhile, the Queen's Court continued its journey. Châteauneuf, whom the Cardinal had promoted after Marillac's downfall, was like a man possessed. Caught up in his lady's web, he lived only for the moment when the great Minister would die and he, as he fondly imagined, would replace him. He paid no attention at all to the sick man. All he ever did was to send an emissary from time to time in the hope of receiving the bad news he so ardently longed for. One of these messengers, La Porte, arrived at night and gained immediate access to the Cardinal, pleading that he had important letters to deliver from both the Queen and the Duchess. He found Richelieu sitting in a high chair between two beds, while the doctor treated the abscess that was causing him such torment. He took the letters from La Porte, read them cursorily and then subjected him to what was virtually a cross-examination: did the Keeper of the Seals have frequent discussions with the Queen? Did he often visit the Duchess? La Porte was evasive, pleading ignorance of such matters. Richelieu detained him to question him further. Meanwhile Châteauneuf had grown impatient and sent a second messenger after La Porte. The two men met midway between Bordeaux and Surgères, just eight miles short of La Rochelle, where Queen Anne and her Court had broken their journey. "How long has he still to go? Will it soon be over?" the second emissary asked the first. But the answer he received was not encouraging. No sooner had La Porte arrived in Surgères than he was received by Châteauneuf: "Well?" he asked. As the messenger made his report, the ambitious Châteauneuf's face darkened and immediately afterwards he hurried off to the Queen and her ladies. There was general consternation.

Anne of Austria made her triumphant entry into the former Huguenot fortress of La Rochelle. But her gracious smile masked a secret fear.

The Keeper of the Seals had gone very far. His infatuation had made him so foolishly sure of himself that he had completely neglected the sick man but for sending his spies to observe him. While the Queen was in Bordeaux, he had arranged a ball in her honour almost next door to the house where Richelieu lay seriously ill, and at the ball he himself had danced like a young blood. And Marie de Chevreuse, playing on the Cardinal's hypersensitive nature, had tried to wound and torment him by passing on some of Châteauneuf's spiteful comments about him.

On November 26th Charpentier reported to Bouthillier:

"The Cardinal asks that the King be requested to send a message to Cardinal de La Valette to the following effect: 'I wish to thank you for having stayed with my cousin, Cardinal Richelieu, and for not having deserted him throughout the entire course of his illness; I do this because I wish to show my especial esteem to all who, like yourself, love him truly and without hypocrisy.' "

Louis de Nogaret de La Valette, a bishop and an army commander who received his Cardinal's hat in 1621, was the son of the avaricious and power-seeking old Gascon who had been Richelieu's dangerous host at the castle of Cadillac. But he was a very different man from his father. He belonged to the new generation and approved of Richelieu's policies. He had already seen action on many a battlefield and was to continue to render exemplary service in the future. Cardinal de la Valette, in this also unlike his two brothers,[1] was at all

---

[1] The Duke of Epernon had three sons: Henri and Bernard, who inherited the ducal title in turn, and Louis the youngest son, who became Cardinal de La Vallette. Louis was born in 1593 in Angoulême and died of a fever in Rivoli on September 28, 1639. Cf. Vol. III, chapter on peasant revolts.

times loyal both to his King and to the King's First Minister. He admired Richelieu profoundly. We shall be meeting him again in his capacity as joint commander, with Bernhard of Saxe-Weimar, of the French armies.

In the year 1632—the year of the executions, as it came to be known—the King spent the month of December partly in Versailles and partly in Saint-Germain. On December 14th he received his wife in Versailles. She arrived long before Richelieu, who was obliged to complete his journey wrapped in silk robes and carried on a litter. It was not until January 3, 1633, that the King and his First Minister were reunited after their long separation. During the whole of Richelieu's journey back to Paris, Louis XIII had subjected him to a barrage of letters, which betrayed a real longing for the Cardinal. And the first meeting between the two lasted for a full three hours without witnesses. But the very next day the King was off to Dourdan again to inspect the eastern frontier, for the outcome of Gaston's latest escapade was still uncertain.

"I must confess," Louis XIII wrote to the Cardinal from St-Germain-en-Laye on February 4th, "that there are two things that anger me tremendously and often disturb my sleep: the insolence of the Parlement and the mockery which certain persons well known to you vent on both our persons." Shortly afterwards he sent a coded letter, which contained the following passage:

"I have just heard from a very reliable source (which I will reveal to you later) that a worker has arrived from England and has visited the lady stonemason in Jouarre. . . . If she does not tell you about this visit herself you will know for certain that she is treacherous and is simply making game of us both."

The lady stonemason was the Duchess of Chevreuse, the English worker Lord Montagu, a cold and haughty aristocrat of prepossessing appearance who was entirely at home in the world of political calculation. He spoke and wrote French extremely well, had great joie de vivre and few prejudices. He had been involved in every one of Marie de Chevreuse' enterprises when she was in England. He knew her intimately, was a confidant of Queen Henrietta's and had been a close friend of Buckingham's until his assassination. This, then, was the "worker" from Britain.

The three-hour conversation between Richelieu and his sovereign produced immediate results: on February 25th the Keeper of the Seals, Châteauneuf, was arrested in Saint Germain, the seals were taken from him and handed over to Président Séguier, who became his successor. A follower and willing tool of the Duchess, François de Rochechouart, Chevalier d' Jars, who had played an active part in the Duchess' Orléans plot and had seemed quite safe thanks to the favour he enjoyed with Anne of Austria, was sentenced to death but received what was literally a last-minute reprieve—after he had already mounted the scaffold. Like Châteauneuf's removal from office and arrest, this action against Rochechouart was taken on the King's own initiative. It was his personal decision. In this whole affair Richelieu had remained in the background, although it was primarily on his account that the King had taken these measures. Louis's attachment to his First Minister had reached its height in the first half of the thirties.

The Châteauneuf affair had now been settled. But where the Duchess was concerned the situation was more complex.

Charles IV, Duke of Lorraine, was arming against France, the French heir-apparent had contracted a secret marriage with his sister and it was feared that the Duke, who was a prince of the Holy Roman Empire, might at any moment appeal to the Emperor for help and throw the frontiers open to the Imperial army. Further, England was working against French interests in Nancy.

At this juncture the King's party took up again the original idea of conciliating the dangerous Duchess by offering her an opportunity to play the role of a successful mediator, thus fulfilling the ambition of her life. It was decided to send her on a highly confidential mission to her cousin, the Duke of

Lorraine. The object of this mission, to persuade Charles to lay down his arms, did not in fact appeal to the Duchess, since it ran entirely counter to her own aims. But the thrill of the game—the joy of staking and winning—led her to undertake this mission for the Cardinal and she persuaded Charles IV to agree, temporarily at least, to reduce his army and enter into negotiations. We shall hear more of this later. The Duchess then returned to Paris. But despite her success the King did not want her to remain close to his wife or close to the centre of power. And so he asked her patient and pleasure-seeking husband to conduct her to the castle of Couzières, a residence of the Rohan family near Tours, and to ensure that she stayed there. But Marie de Chevreuse remained in closest contact with the King, through the intermediary of English agents and of Monsieur de Brion, Orléans's equerry and one of the young noblemen currently ravished by the versatile Duchess. It goes without saying that our old friend La Porte also played his part in forwarding the correspondence of this indefatigable lady, as did Marsillac, the son of the Duke of La Rochefoucauld and a man whose harsh experience of the world in early life was the preface to the great wisdom he later revealed as the author of the *Maxims*. And there were others besides. The specialist historians who have written biographies of this great "card-shuffler," who gave no peace to either Louis XIII or Richelieu as long as they lived, have listed a whole company of devoted accomplices, ranging from a rich burgher of Tours to an erudite scholar and taking in the sons of gentry on the way.

We shall be meeting this beautiful intriguer at various junctures and have to assess her importance according to the criteria of her own time. Her activities and her influence were indissolubly linked with Gaston d'Orléans, who entered the limelight time and again. We have already dealt with Gaston in some detail in connection with the execution of the Count of Chalais, the first of the sensational actions taken by Richelieu against the existing social order.

Before we go on to deal with Richelieu's subsequent domestic struggles and the means he employed to resolve them, before we assess the large-scale foreign policy the Cardinal instituted after the Day of the Dupes and try to establish its world-wide causes, many of which had their roots in the distant past, before we discuss the immense hatred that gathered against the great statesman and consider the steps taken by his opponents, we must first concern ourselves with the circumstances of his personal life. In doing so we must remember that this extremely lonely man was also a very vulnerable man, for this influenced everything he ever did and explains the severity of the measures he took against his adversaries.

CHAPTER V

THE CIRCUMSTANCES OF
RICHELIEU'S PERSONAL LIFE

There exist a whole series of portraits of Cardinal Richelieu painted by Philippe de Champaigne, a Brussels-born artist who has often been described as a realist. But the concept of realism fails to do justice to Champaigne's work unless it is applied with far more discrimination than usual. Of these paintings the most expressive is doubtless the portrait in London, which dispenses entirely with the décor normally demanded by contemporary taste in representative art and simply presents Richelieu's face in three different views, two profiles and one full-face. In this portrait Champaigne not only succeeded in expressing his subject's penetrating intellect and unbending will power, he also contrived to indicate in the facial characteristics Richelieu's mental anguish and physical suffering. From other portraits, too, we know the creator of this work, one of the greatest and most uncompromising artists ever to fathom the innermost nature of a human being and represent it undistorted by any mask or pose. His portrait of Marshal Turenne in the Munich Gallery, which is characterized by great restraint and precision, his moving study in Geneva of a nun of Port-Royal, his paintings of Louis XIII and his self-portrait in the Louvre—all succeed in arresting the truth imprinted in human physiognomy in a way achieved by only a very few painters. It is highly significant that the Cardinal should have been a patron of this painter. Champaigne was a profoundly serious man informed by the spirit of Jansenism, as familiar with the unfathomable depths of human nature as Shakespeare, Racine or Pascal, and able to sense the underlying problems of those who must play their parts on the splendid stage of world affairs. In this particular instance a strange affinity seems to have existed between an outstanding master of the painter's art and an equally distinguished master of the art of politics. It would almost seem that these two men had been engaged in a conversation that might have been conceived by Walter Savage Landor as one of his *Imaginary Conversations* (see Vol. I, frontispiece).

In Richelieu's *Maxims of State and Political Fragments* there are many highly informative passages apparently written as if the Cardinal were observing himself from a long way off, as if he were setting himself up as an independent observer and judge and were assessing himself, Armand du Plessis, not as a living person but as a man transformed into a historical figure by his struggles with the exacting demands of public service. There we read:

"I knew that although my mental powers were equal to the task facing me, it was out of all proportion to my physical frailty. I was able to observe the truth of this fact daily. I confided in a few of my closest friends. Together we sought remedies. . . . But, quite apart from the sentiments instilled in me by the love I have always borne both the State and the monarch, I knew that at Court, as in War, the man who retreats in the face of the enemy runs the risk of being pursued and often utterly destroyed. . . . I knew that calumny is never silent and will have recourse to fabrications when truth is unable to furnish her with valid criticisms. And so I concluded that I was like a soldier who, having been ordered to defend an indefensible position, freely does so, knowing that he must perish, because he places his honour above his life."

Of those statesmen who have exercised a decisive influence on the development of a whole era, very few only have furnished us with a detailed and continuous commentary on their life such as Richelieu did. And there are very few about whom their contemporaries have given such detailed testimony.

Richelieu was a sick man throughout the whole of his life. In 1608 he had suffered from ague and in 1611 he wrote that he was plagued by fever and for months had been unable to get about save in a sedan chair. In the same year he wrote to the Superior-General of the Carthusian Order to thank him for sending him a stone from the stomach of an ibex, which was then in great demand as a remedy. From 1621 onwards he made continual reference to his headaches, which had afflicted him since childhood but were then becoming intolerable.

None the less, during the siege of La Rochelle he endured severe physical hardships. A year later he rode at the head of an army that crossed the Alps. From June 1630 onwards, however, his general physical debility obliged him to make all his journeys on a litter, on board ship or in a spacious sedan chair. In 1632, as we have already seen, he suffered from a painful abscess at the anus and was unable to pass urine. His recovery was so slow that he was prevented from rejoining the King until January 3, 1633, in Rochefort-en-Yvelines. In May 1634 he was again said to be suffering from complete exhaustion and received treatment for a severe haemorrhoidal condition. In a letter to Bouthillier he said that he was being consumed by an inner fire. Shortly afterwards he fell victim to the same critical condition that had assailed him in Bordeaux. On this occasion even his litter was of no avail, for he could neither sit nor lie down. He wrote to the King: "If heretofore I have passed for a genuine diamond, I now regard myself as a diamond of Alençon, which . . . is as fragile as glass." In the final stage of this illness the infection produced a very painful eruption of festering boils all over his body.

Some of the doctors attending him considered his ailments as nervous in origin. Many of his entourage said he was hypersensitive to an alarming degree. He always found it very difficult to accept bad news, and when there was bad news—

especially when somebody had made adverse remarks about him—he asked to be told about it as gently as possible. On the extremely rare occasions when he lost the thread of his argument, he also lost all control over his facial expression. If a word, or even a gesture, displeased him, his features could change in an instant. He was always close to tears. Marie de' Medici said of him, "He cries at will," and she likened him to the crocodile. Richelieu reproached himself for this weakness. In their reports, foreign ambassadors referred to his tormented expression. In moments of absolute despair he would some-times retire to bed in the middle of the day, and this usually brought him relief. But after such an episode he is said to have looked like one turned to cold stone. When threatening events burst upon him, he would first alternate between despair, indeed paralysis, and a frenzy of activity; then he would suddenly focus his powers and decide upon a clear-cut course of action. The boldness and the penetrating power of his will often erupted from an underlying mood of melancholy.[1] As early as 1611 Henri du Plessis had spoken of his brother's fits of depression. The Bishop of Lavaur, Abra de Raconis, said of him: "His was a dark nature, he was full of black gall."

There were days when nobody dared speak to the Cardinal. Tradition has it that nearly every month, for two or three days on end, he would lock himself up in his room with a doctor and a servant. His outbursts of anger are said to have been uncontrolled. Several independent witnesses have testified to the fact that he sometimes screamed and howled until foam came to his lips, that on occasion he would even crawl under a bed and his servants would have the greatest difficulty persuading him to come out again. Of the countless reports we have concerning the Cardinal's more intimate idiosyncrasies, many come from his valet, Olivier. But no

---

[1] His mother was given to melancholy. His brother Alfonse, the Cardinal of Lyon, was mentally deranged, and his sister, the wife of Urbain de Maillé, Marquis de Brézé, died insane.

matter what their source, although these reports certainly bear witness to the extent to which the Cardinal was observed, they are far less reliable in their varying accounts of what was observed. The very fact that they were committed to paper means that one report may well have been copied from another. It would be inadvisable to attach too much importance to them as they stand. If, however, we consider them in the light of the contradictions they reveal, we may perhaps be able to form a valid judgement.

Richelieu was constantly surrounded by doctors. The physician for internal diseases came high on the list of his retainers, only the noblemen in his service ranking higher. He received a salary of 900 livres. By contrast, the apothecary and the surgeon received 150 livres; they were "artisans." Richelieu's physician in ordinary, an academician by the name of François Citoys, had taken his doctorate in Montpellier in 1596. He had been medical adviser to the Cardinal since 1609 and was one of his personal servants, although he did not appear on his household list until 1635. Richelieu always addressed him as "my little doctor" and tended to treat him with benevolent irony, for he was quite convinced that he knew more about medicine than any member of the medical faculty. He once declared that all medicines were a swindle. And yet, when the King was ill, the advice Richelieu gave to his doctors would not have shamed a specialist. At times his jokes about medical science make one think of Molière. But he certainly did not scorn medicines where he himself was concerned. In a single year the money he spent on "mixtures" amounted to 2816 livres and 9 sols. In 1635, the year when France openly entered the war, the sum of 1401 livres and 14 sols is mentioned as the amount spent on seventy-five different medicines, all of which were intended for the Cardinal himself. Richelieu knew that his countless enemies followed his illnesses with diabolical glee. The most spiteful and tenacious of his political opponents, Mathieu de Morgues, addressed him in a pamphlet in this way:

"How should you remember what is written in the Book of God, when you yourself have lost all knowledge of His teachings—even though Nature presents them to you daily in the form of your afflictions and the many medicines you take, and reminds you of what you are and what you are not. Unlike the Shah of Persia, you need no slave to shout in your ear every morning: 'Remember that you are mortal!' The headaches, the adulterated blood, the raging fever that never leaves you, the syringes, the lancets, the sitz baths are quite enough to show you that you are mortal and that you possess your brief span of life only on miserable conditions."

The doctors tormented Richelieu. They were constantly bleeding him. In his day bloodletting had become a mania.[1] Citoys was one of its most passionate advocates and also a great believer in strong purgations. Laxatives and enemas were administered almost daily, and this despite the fact that he lived a very frugal and careful life. He usually ate alone in his room and did not partake of the generous hospitality extended to his many guests. He made every effort to follow a healthy regimen.

Richelieu's Working Methods and Daily Schedule

The Cardinal considered that audiences were a waste of time. Unfortunately those charged with the task of ensuring that he was able to concentrate on his work in peace and quiet contributed in no small measure to his unpopularity because of the clumsy way in which they dealt with interruptions. In this respect Richelieu himself said: "Because of my bad health I was unable to receive everybody, as I would have liked." Foreign ambassadors often reported that they had gone to Chaillot without being admitted.

[1] It is said that in the thirties one seven-year-old child of noble birth, who was suffering from bronchitis, was bled thirteen times in fourteen days. Another child was subjected to the same procedure eight times for a cold, and an eighty-year-old doctor, who had an inflammation of the lungs, was bled sixteen times over a period of ten days.

When the King heard of complaints about the unsuitable way in which the Cardinal's appointments were handled, he instructed one of his own chamberlains to devote himself exclusively to the task. Bassompierre, a spontaneous and somewhat boisterous person, received a royal reprimand when he entered Richelieu's antechamber and asked in a booming voice: "Will he be on show today?"

We have many accounts of how Richelieu spent his day. At 11.00 A.M., after he had completed his morning's work, he went out into the garden whenever possible, and returned to the garden both after lunch, which he took at noon, and after his evening meal. These walks in the park were always undertaken in the company of friends and on the strict understanding that business matters were not to be discussed. His confessor, the Abbé Mulot, a man well known for his wit, would sometimes try to make him laugh. The group taking part in these walks was known as "His Eminence's little clique." But it was not only with these chosen few that Richelieu indulged in jokes. When Bassompierre, a womaniser throughout his life, turned pious in his old age, Richelieu sent him a rosary expressing the hope that it might help him gain the indulgence he surely needed. He asked Bassompierre to pray the first Hail Mary for him, since this was usually the devout one, and concluded by congratulating him on having learnt to esteem the grace of his Creator as highly as he had once esteemed the grace of His creatures.

Richelieu usually retired at eleven o'clock at night. He would then kneel in prayer for about half an hour. But from two until five in the morning he worked in bed, and at nine he started again and worked consecutively until it was time for his morning walk. He went to confession and Communion every Sunday, celebrating Mass only on great feast days and on the festivals in honour of the Blessed Virgin. This was normal practice for a seventeenth-century prelate. Even Bossuet did not say Mass every day or even every Sunday.

Richelieu's confessor, his almoner, his chamberlain, his

officers-at-arms and his servants were unanimous in praising his devoutness as a celebrant. Father Joseph spoke of his "exemplary devotion." From time to time Richelieu would hear a sermon in his private room. At Easter he retreated into a monastery if this was at all possible.

Richelieu applied to Rome for permission to take part in royal councils at which criminal cases involving the death penalty would be heard. Bérulle interceded on his behalf and in February 1625 he brought Richelieu a *breve* from the Curia granting his request.

In 1624, when the thirty-nine-year-old Cardinal accepted his second office under the Crown, he tried to obtain a dispensation that would absolve him from the necessity of reading the breviary. Urban VIII had already refused a similar request from the Bishop of Orléans and his initial reaction was to refer to this precedent. But when he saw the speed of Richelieu's rise to power he relented and gave him a verbal dispensation.

Considering that Richelieu was a sick man, the amount of work he got through in the course of each day was astounding. Quite apart from his official duties, which he performed with meticulous thoroughness, he also carried on a whole host of other seemingly unrelated activities. But in every sphere he achieved significant results—whether it was arranging for a conference to determine the prime meridian, or rounding out his magnificent library with works on geography, philosophy, medicine and psychology, whether he was applying himself to the great political "leverage" of the theatre, or working out the guidelines for a college of political science which was to train men for high government service, or whether he was establishing the Académie Française. In whatever he did he revealed a dual personality. He, the most hated man of his time, consistently charmed his close associates. His great rhetorical powers and his astonishing gift for language have been mentioned by countless numbers of his contemporaries. His mastery of Latin, Spanish, Italian and Greek was equal to his mastery of French. Everyone praised the natural grace of his delivery and his ability to reply spontaneously to a speech, an interpellation, an attack or a question. One day in Rueil Monsieur de Serizay, the director of the Académie Française, delivered a prepared speech as the head of a delegation, and Richelieu gave an extempore reply that was said to have been "as light as air and yet both dignified and sincere, in a word: enchanting." But the fluency of his rhetoric, the force of his arguments and their irrefutable soundness had already been praised on an earlier occasion—at the Assembly of Notables of 1626. It was said at the time that when he spoke, the resolutions he put forward had seemed to those present like laws and oracles.

His opponents reproached him for his arrogance and his mocking tone, and even his admirers conceded that he was moody. His fits of temper were sparked by trivial incidents. In their reports foreign ambassadors spoke of his "fiery, dry and wrathful nature." One description mentions "the pinched nostrils, his furrowed brow, his trembling lips going white." But in a letter to the Bishop of Bordeaux in 1632, Richelieu claimed "my rages are calculated."

Others said of him: "He does not do what he says, he does not say what he does, he keeps none of his promises." And his habitual impatience was regarded as an intolerable fault. But he himself countered this last charge when he said that what drove him to distraction was "the French tendency to drag everything out," the *longueurs de France*, which consisted of the "frivolity of one group, the negligence of another and the lack of scruple of the great majority." He was censured for undertaking too much, for wanting to get things done in too much of a hurry. He was even called a foolhardy *hasardeur*. But all such censures were effectively disposed of by Secretary of State Brienne, who said: "I know from my late father that Cardinal Richelieu was an extremely skilful negotiator, that he possessed great foresight, rarely made a mistake and, when he did, was very quick to correct it."

Theories, abstractions and programmes he rejected. He was

extremely suspicious of what he called "*capacités pédantesques*." In seventeenth-century usage the *pédant* was the exact opposite of the *honnête homme* or the "man of the world," and "man of the world" had none of the slighting connotations it has today. Among other things an *honnête homme*, unlike a pedant, would never offend against good taste by indulging in speculative theories or abstractions.

Another thing that annoyed the Cardinal was the practice of referring to precedents. To him this was, like all other purely formal arguments, acceptable only as a tactical weapon and then only to a strictly limited extent. The conservatives were of course accustomed to acting on the basis of examples drawn from the past. In this connection Richelieu said: "The past bears no reference to the present; the relationship between times, places and persons is always an entirely different one." He thought little of so-called "great reforms." Instead, he dealt with things as they came, bending them to his will. But the means he used to attain his ends changed from one occasion to another. To his mind the practice of invoking mere ideals as reasons for action was always highly suspect. Fully at home in the ways of the world, he remarked that "In an old monarchy, in which abuses have become habitual, disorder makes a not un-useful contribution to the order of the State." He was an opponent of large deliberative assemblies, regarding them simply as a means of influencing public opinion. He based his view on the fact that intelligent men were far rarer than mediocrities, so in large assemblies the mediocre majority must necessarily overwhelm the intelligent minority. In the conduct of government he held that all decrees must be fully practicable. He insisted that every advantage be exploited to the full, since in politics the course of events is determined by the need of the moment rather than preconceived plans.

In view of the many indirect hints, the subterfuges and the dialectical nature of the arguments in Richelieu's diplomatic correspondence, it is interesting to note that, like Bismarck, he has been censured for his occasional practice of suddenly springing his secret purposes on the world at large. He himself maintained that he always acted on the principle of stating quite openly what he wanted, that for a man of his age, who always went straight for his objective, detours were unnecessary. But we must not take this too literally either. Often, when it suited his purpose, he would indulge in sudden candour, but on other occasions he trod very secret paths indeed. Besides, what a man says is what he says, not what he is, especially when the man is such a subtle, masterful manipulator.

He considered that all decisions must be made in the light of reason, never on impulse. And in point of fact, despite his *crises*, his sufferings and his hasty temper, he always kept a cool head, and within the larger context of his grand design, he always remained intensely cautious, and this made him wary of his own nervous reactions. He said that everything he ever decided in anger had turned out badly. To all negotiators he recommended that they cultivate flexibility and imperturbability, which he himself possessed to such a high degree. In this connection he remarked: "I place the will on a level with reason. . . . A man must have a man's character and do everything by reason." He constantly impressed upon his associates the immense value of secrecy, and one of his most famous sayings—often quoted as a statement of his working methods—directly contradicts his occasional use of candour: Secrecy is the very soul of all important undertakings.

Richelieu regarded human frailty as one of the fundamental conditions of life. As a moralist he was quite as harsh as La Rochefoucauld. He is said to have been the author of the maxim "Men are slow to forgive favours and quick to forget punishments".[1]

Richelieu punished often and he punished hard. Yet time and again he protested against needless harshness. On March 12, 1629 he wrote to Marshal d'Effiat:

[1] Madame Violette Trefusus has in her possession in the castle of St Loup a handwritten volume entitled *Aphorismes de Monsieur le Cardinal*, in which some correspond almost word for word to those of La Rochefoucauld.

"Caution and patience are necessary. Authority need only be exercised in the most extreme cases."

And on another occasion he was to say that harshness is always dangerous.

In May 1631 he wrote to the King in connection with the intrigues of Gaston d'Orléans:

". . . it is better that men should return to the path of duty of their own accord than that we should force them to do so."

Few historical figures have been the subject of such contradictory assessments on the part of their contemporaries. If we disregard the polemical utterances of his political opponents, which were inspired by hatred, the majority of the statements made about the Cardinal may be subsumed into the following antithesis:

"Majesty," "charm," "gentleness," "amiability"—and then: "One still trembles in his presence."

A certain de La Roche once said to the Cardinal: "I confess that the incomparable sight of your person impresses me so greatly that I am bereft of speech in your presence."

In his memoirs Pontis mentions the uncanny effect the Cardinal always produced when he suddenly broke off a conversation with the conventional formula *"serviteur très humble"* (your humble servant). These words were the signal for an immediate withdrawal from his presence.

Tallemant des Réaux, who took great pleasure in enumerating the real or apparent weaknesses of one and all, nevertheless said of Richelieu that all who approached him with love he requited with love. The members of his personal entourage were very attached to him and his servants seldom changed. He kept one of his household servants, a certain Desbournais, for seventeen years.

He treated his followers generously and interested himself in their personal needs. He never failed to advance the cause of persons, even of whole families, who had helped him and his relatives in the past, especially in the difficult years of his childhood and early youth. We shall also see that he furthered the interests of members of his own family.

There are two points to be noted here. The first is Richelieu's capacity for personal loyalty and gratitude, and the other is the tremendous drive displayed by the French at that time, especially members of the bourgeoisie and the nobility, to improve the fortunes of their houses. The social order of the day was firmly rooted in a hierarchical system, and although the upper stratum was subject to constant change—with many of the great aristocrats overthrown and ruined and many of the nobility impoverished, their places being taken by aspiring members of the bourgeoisie—the ties that bound the individual to his family remained unbroken and he was held responsible for its success or decline. These conditions, so far removed from those of our own classless society, must always be borne in mind if we are to understand an era in which they were widespread.

The Social Hierarchy

The age of a family, its origin, were not of crucial importance. Some of the oldest families of France eked out an impoverished existence on estates that were little more than smallholdings. A family's position in the social order was assessed in a very different light according to who carried out the assessment—the Court, the Parlement[1] class or public opinion.

The Court's assessments fluctuated in much the same way as stock-exchange prices today; the only criteria known to the Parlement class were those of property and influence, while

[1] Not to be confused with the modern parliament. Under the Ancien Régime the French Parlement (which was also called Parloir, Parlatorium and, after 1239, Parlamentum) was the highest court of the land and remained so until the French Revolution. At first the members were jurists (and by the end of the thirteenth century jurists versed in Roman law) and the great nobles resident at the royal Courts, but from the fifteenth century onwards they were joined by the Peers of France. Under Charles V seats in the Parlement could be bought or inherited, and from the reign of Francis I onwards it was practically impossible for a member to be

public opinion concerned itself only with the princes of royal households, the few powerful ducal families and the economically powerful members of the new nobility. Nor were these assessments determined by an institutionalized and generally accepted order of merit, but rather by the random element of fashion.

The things people paid attention to were the standard of living, the style, the manner, the taste and even the accent of those they were judging. Their achievements, and especially their military exploits, were duly noted and quickly forgotten. To hold a position in government administration or in the diplomatic service was still considered undignified. Almost without exception those raised to the nobility by letters patent protested against the claims made by the hereditary nobles, while the hereditary nobles were embittered in their turn over the practice of creating new titles. The two sides were brought together to some extent, however, by marriages contracted for money on one hand and position on the other. In the seventeenth century the desire for social advancement was more active in France than in England. The French bourgeoisie struggled to cross the class frontier separating them from the nobility. They gave their sons as complete an education as was then possible, in order to prepare them for public office. In provinces ravaged by the civil wars, more and more of the property of the nobles was passing into the hands of the bourgeoisie. And after only a brief interval the civil and religious wars were followed in 1635 by war abroad. In 1636 there was a general exodus of the old noble families from the ravaged province of Burgundy. These were then replaced by members of the emerging Parlement class who, with their

deposed. This meant of course that the Parlement was politically influential and its influence was greatly enhanced by the fact that all decrees enacted by the sovereign had to be ratified by the Parlement before they became law. This right of ratification was, however, subject to limitation by a *"lit de justice,"* which meant that if the King appeared in the Parlement in person, he could, in his capacity as supreme judge override all objections and enforce the ratification of any decree. In the course of time similar Parlements were instituted in the provinces. Since 1771, however, the Parlement of Paris has asserted its pre-eminence.

organizational and business ability, entrenched themselves more and more firmly until, by the time of the French Revolution, they had become the real landowning class.

While the members of the various Parlements, the so-called *noblesse de robe*, were establishing themselves in the country, a new class was also emerging in the towns, consisting of moneyed people—bankers and so-called *traitants*, who were bound by the terms of a treaty concluded with the King. This entitled them to purchase the right to raise levies or taxes on behalf of the Crown. These *traitants* were the tax farmers of whom Boileau said, *"Sache quelle province enrichit les traitants."*

It should be borne in mind that through his forbears Richelieu was linked with each of the classes of the old social order. On his father's side he was descended from the old provincial nobility (see Vol. I, p. 15). The du Plessis family were landowning gentry who had improved their social standing by marriage. Périnne de Clérembault had brought Geoffroi du Plessis the estate of Richelieu, which lay between Touraine and Poitou, as her marriage portion. In 1542 Louis I du Plessis had married Françoise de Rochechouart, Richelieu's grandmother; she was a daughter of one of the leading houses of France, which had been particularly prominent under Louis XII and Francis I. The Cardinal also had royal blood in his veins, for a François du Plessis had married Anne Le Roi, the granddaughter of two princesses of the house of Dreux, who were descended from Louis the Fat.

On his mother's side, however, Richelieu was connected with the bourgeoisie, for his mother's father had been a lawyer and her grandfather an apothecary.

The problem of the privileged classes occupied Richelieu throughout his life. In a comprehensive report on the subject drafted for the King's information, he declared that the nobility were to be regarded as the main artery of the State and as an indispensable element in the task of reconstructing and preserving the French community. This is a subject to which we shall be returning.

Richelieu's critics have never stopped censuring him for enriching himself at the expense of the State and living in such an extravagant style on public funds. But he held that the need for display, the need to impress, was an essential prerequisite for a man who held power and who used power. And in this he was no more than a child of his time. Even during his exile in Avignon, when he was crippled with debts and was obliged to seek loans from various people, including his confessor, Father Mulot, he wrote to his brother regarding a gift he wished to make: ". . . I can only say that I would like to have at my disposal an object worthy of my rank."

Here rank was evaluated, and most accurately, taking into account the rank he was striving for in the future. More than any other man Richelieu gave the lie to the notion that great personalities must be indifferent to conventional gestures. Here too his maxim applies: "Cohesion and completeness are the ultimate measure of the perfection of all things."

On another occasion Richelieu wrote:

"Great minds . . . will normally think only of great designs, but it is altogether necessary that they should constrain and humble themselves to deal with the most trivial, for from small beginnings great disorders may easily arise, and many momentous decisions owe their inception to considerations that appeared to be of no moment."

His opponents found fault with his love of display and the vast scope of his projects in time and space—and then complained of his pettiness.

In the modern sense of the word, Richelieu was not an individualist. In everything he did he acted as the representative of his house. Tallemant des Réaux wrote that his rage for grandeur reached its apogee in the demands for more power and glory for his family. In fact, whether he was demanding "proper respect" for the members of his family or showing the utmost sensibility to questions of royal or national prestige, the principle was the same: power must be

5. Mohammed the Conqueror

6. Ferdinand II, Emperor of Germany

made visible. On the occasion of the reception for the Duke of Parma, Richelieu sent the following note to the Secretary of State:

"The stage that has been built for the ballet destroys the over-all impression of the great hall of the Louvre and must be removed. I would ask you to do all that is necessary to ensure that the Duke's reception is in keeping with the dignity of the monarchy."

When Marie de' Medici was dying in Cologne, although Richelieu himself lay in Tarascon wracked with pain, he sent a nobleman to the Queen-Mother with 100,000 livres, in order that her house might be kept in a style befitting a former Queen of France. Even before her death he had reckoned the cost of bringing her body back to France in state and giving her a royal funeral.

Spendthrift he was and yet, like his sovereign, he had a sense of economy, although this did not stop him from reproaching Louis for being penny wise. Louis XIII considered it unseemly for a nobleman to be a "royal servant." Besides, noblemen at Court were expensive. And here Richelieu always opposed his King. To his mind such an attitude was a relic of feudal thought, which held that the King was merely the "first among equals." On the contrary, he argued, the King's true grandeur could only be made manifest if his pages were the "sons of Dukes and Marquises." In his *Political Testament* Richelieu spent one whole chapter deploring the lack of awe-inspiring splendour at Louis's Court. The description of an ideal Court which then follows anticipated the Court of Louis XIV.

In the *Political Testament* we read:

"Although the whole world knows that no King has ever raised the dignity of his State to greater heights than Your Majesty, it is also undeniably true that no King has ever allowed the splendour of his Court to sink so low."

And then:

"Foreigners who have come to France in my lifetime have often expressed surprise at finding such a mighty State and such a neglected Court. . . . Everything is in disorder, from the kitchens to the royal chamber. In your father's lifetime the officers of the Crown and all the great nobles of the realm dined at the royal tables, but in your own day it has seemed as if they had been designed to cater for . . . simple *chevaux-légers* and men-at-arms; and the service has been so bad that, far from vying with one another for admission [to your tables], many of them have been fastidious enough to shun them. . . . Foreign visitors have often complained that they were served by scullions and not, as at other royal Courts, by gentlemen. The royal household needs order and cleanliness; it needs splendid furniture, and all the more so since it is by outward appearances that strangers recognize a Prince's greatness. . . . At present anyone is at liberty to enter the royal chamber, and this is not only harmful to Your Majesty's prestige, it also endangers your royal person."

Finally he reproached his ruler for not keeping a stud of show horses for festive occasions, while at the same time spending more money on his stables than other Courts where there was no such deficiency. This criticism continues for pages. Baroque pageantry!

Richelieu's Standard of Living—His Income and Expenditure

Just how much did Richelieu spend on his own account at the height of his career and where did the money come from? Let us take the year 1638 as an example. In this year the Cardinal's total expenditure was 1,257,172 livres and 5 sols, while his total income was 1,413,500 livres, 13 sols and 4 deniers. Richelieu's life was marked by vicissitudes, and so too was his financial situation. On June 6, 1610, when he was still Bishop of Luçon, he wrote to Madame de Bourges:

"Since I am rather ambitious . . . I would like to create a greater impression." And he asked his friend, who was trying to further his cause in Paris, how much two large and beautiful silver salvers would cost; he was prepared to pay five hundred talers; more than that he could not afford. He went on to say: "I am a poor devil [*je suis gueux*] and, as you know, I am unable to create an impression of wealth. None the less, once I possess a few beautiful silver plates my position will be much improved." He finished his letter with the words: "And so now you see the misery of a poor monk who is obliged to sell his furniture."

During his first period of office Richelieu did not appear impressive. Only the few who were very close to him recognized his great mental powers. The chroniclers and historians of the period scarcely mentioned him. He was not noticed. And yet even then his whole object was not only power, but the appearance of power as well. Incidentally, the poverty he complained of to Madame de Bourges was only relative, and by the time he re-entered the King's service in 1624 he was receiving an annual income of over 25,000 livres. After the death of his brother Henri in 1619, he drew almost the same amount from the property he inherited, although he had protracted legal battles with his relatives before it was finally settled on him. His brother was killed in a duel (cf. Vol. I), and Richelieu by 1629 was obliged to keep thirty men-at-arms because his own life was constantly in danger. There had already been many threats to murder him. Twelve months before his Ministry began he had negotiated several major property transactions. He bought the castle of Limours for 400,000 livres, which he subsequently sold at a profit to the Duke of Orléans. In 1623 he also bought the castle and estate of Montlhéry for 24,850 livres. Expenditure of this order was quite beyond his personal means, but by then he already had various ecclesiastical livings, which constituted his chief source of income.

In 1617 he had become the Prior of Coussay, near Mirebeau;

in 1618, upon the death of Arthur d'Epinay Saint-Luc, he received the abbacy of Redon, and in 1623 the abbacy of Pontlevoy, which he ceded to his nephew Pierre de Bérulle in 1629; in 1627 he received the abbacy of Ham, in 1629 that of Vauleroy, near Reims, and in 1630 he became Abbot of Cluny, Marmoutier, Saint-Benoît and La Chaise-Dieu, and later Abbot of Saint-Lucien, Ricquier and Saint-Arnoul at Metz. In 1624 his receipts from ecclesiastical benefices totalled 25,000 livres; in 1640, 500,000 écus (*sic*). His income was further augmented by his personal properties, which ultimately provided 150,000 écus annually, and his pensions, which brought in 100,000 écus; the Governorship of Brittany yielded a similar amount, while monasteries and chapter houses supplied a further 100,000. We already know from our enquiry into Richelieu's activities as Controller-General of Navigation, a function he assumed almost immediately after his Ministry began, that from this source alone he received the very considerable sum of 100,000 livres annually. In the year we are using as example, 1638, it rose to 203,280 livres. Given all this, Richelieu was in a position to behave magnanimously. Consequently, he did not accept the special pension of 20,000 écus offered him by the King, and he also declined the offer of further abbacies.

Richelieu often used the "Admiralty Council" as a cover for his personal affairs. His uncle, de La Porte, was its president and the Bouthilliers, father and son, who were his closest confidants, were both members.

Richelieu had a current account with "Tallemant and Rambouillet." An entry made in this account on October 1, 1639, reveals that he had drawn 51,581 livres and 5 sols, which he needed for his household expenses.

In 1639 his personal expenditure was particularly high. In that year he approved the plans for the three-storey house that he was having built in Sauzon, and the estimated cost of 55,000 livres, which he undertook to pay within two years. Exact details of the large sums that he was transferring at that time to the notary Pierre Parque, in the Châtelet in Paris, are given by Deloche. In the same year Richelieu authorized the construction works in Brouage and the alterations and repairs in Rueil and Paris. In the Palais Cardinal, Jacques Lemercier built the great theatre hall, and in Rueil the architect Thirio completed the stables and a number of pavilions. In order to extend both his park and his palace in Paris, Richelieu bought up the adjoining houses, which included the Chapeau-Rouge. He also bought the Hôtel des Trois-Pucelles for 35,400 livres. The personal interest he took in the Sorbonne placed a further strain on his budget. A carriageway was needed. For this purpose the Cardinal purchased land from the Collège des Trésoriers and he also acquired a building site belonging to the Collège d'Harcourt. His principal notary was Pierre Parque, in whose registers and files the full story of Richelieu's economic affairs has been recorded. The most valuable document in the Pierre Parque archive is the deed of donation presenting the Palais Cardinal to the King.

In his later years Richelieu's income exceeded by twenty per cent the one enjoyed by the Prince of Orange, who was then reckoned the richest sovereign in all Europe.

From the reports of the Venetian envoys, we learn that the banking house of Godefroy had drawn up a list of Richelieu's real estate, including the following properties:

The Duchy of Richelieu, the estates of Chillou, Château-neuf, Mousson, Beauregard, La Chapelle, Bellouis, Mirebeau, the Duchy of Fronsac together with Barail du Bec, the principality of Mortagne, the County of Cosnac, the Barony of Barbezieux, Rueil, the Marquisate of Graville and the County of Beaufort. This list omits both his estate in Normandy, which yielded 50,000 livres a year, and various farms that together yielded a further 60,000 livres. According to the Godefroy records, the total annual income from the properties listed, most of which were royal gifts, was 175,858 livres, and Richelieu's constant transactions added greatly to this sum.

In his extremely detailed book on Richelieu's household, Maximin Deloche has regretted the fact that our knowledge of Richelieu's accounts is incomplete. What is quite certain, however, is that in the midst of a great financial catastrophe, when France was destitute and Europe engulfed in war, Richelieu (and without employing the dubious methods favoured by his successor, Mazarin) was able to acquire possessions and incomes that demonstrated to one and all the respect he considered due the grandeur of the State, the glory of the monarchy and the glory of his own person.

His household was a miniature state, a kind of testing ground for economic, administrative, financial and even military questions. Here, as elsewhere, unity and discipline were the qualities on which Richelieu insisted. He was the absolute ruler. Whenever possible he drew his staff from backgrounds and localities that were well known to him. Richelieu believed in biological selection, in specific hereditary traits. Although his knowledge of mankind had made him a pessimist, he trusted his "own people"; he ruled over them justly and strictly, but he also cared for them and always tried to safeguard their future.

When ready money accumulated in his coffers the Cardinal would invest it in some object of value. In this way he acquired many pictures and statues in Italy. He was an admirer of Philippe de Champaigne and commissioned him to create the decorations for the Palais Cardinal in Paris. He had valuable furniture made and collected Gobelins. Craftsmen were constantly working for him. His household would have done credit to any of the great provincial governors. There were the noblemen in his service, his bodyguards, his thirty-six pages, his orchestra, his actors and finally his staff, his "people," from the chief steward down to the humblest lackey, from the head cook to the scullions, the kitchen-maids and the cleaning women. Criticism of such blatant luxury was always severe. The previously mentioned pamphleteer Mathieu de Morgues attacked Richelieu for his great wealth in a lampoon that was disseminated throughout the whole of Paris. In it we read:

"Your little estate, which was subject to the Barony on whose borders it lay, you have turned into a Duchy. And then you appropriated all the surrounding land, even the territory of the gentleman whose vassal you once were."

De Morgues also accused the Cardinal of no longer knowing who he was, being simultaneously Cardinal, First Minister, Grand Admiral, Constable, Chancellor, Keeper of the Seals, Superintendent of Finance, Controller-General of Artillery, Foreign Minister, Duke and Peer of France, governor of thirty fortresses, abbot of innumerable abbeys, commander of a private army and so enamoured of titles that he was obliged to condense his remaining functions into a simple et cetera. The pamphleteer then went on to describe the dreams that must, he assumed, plague the Cardinal at night.

"The people who have slept in your room say that you have worse nightmares than Apollodorus, who thought the Furies had torn out his heart and were dancing in the light of the fire around the pot in which he was being roasted. You know what the Scriptures say about the conscience seared with a hot iron. Your conscience has been so seared. It is not possible that your heart should have remained unmarked, since you have wounded the heart of the King, the heart of the Queen-Mother, who was your own patron and benefactress, the heart of the King's wife and of the King's brother, the hearts of the princes and of the great nobles of the realm and of two Marshals of France, the hearts of people of every degree, whom you have exposed to the torments of war, famine and the plague. You, who are working for the downfall of Europe, have infected the whole of Europe; you have infected the Church of God, whose ruin you bring on by the help you give her enemies! In many places religion has disappeared.

"How could all this fail to destroy your peace of mind?

And how should it be possible for you to preserve your tranquillity when you are constantly tormented by the four devils: ambition, greed, vengefulness and—as we have recently heard said—lust!"

For a priest to be accused of scandalous conduct was a slander that could be relied upon to appeal to the people. But the accusation that Richelieu had enriched himself at the expense of the oppressed people was to prove even more provocative. Although ceremonial splendour was still able to provide an impressive, exciting and popular spectacle and although the rise to power and the ascendancy of the great French houses was still admired as if it were a marvel of nature, public opinion was becoming more and more conscious of the gross discrepancy between this glittering show and its setting of dire misery. The fact that a turn of the wheel of fortune might bring many great houses to ruin no longer appeared as retributive justice. The same houses had enjoyed power too long. From time to time individuals from their own ranks, occasionally from a lower stratum, forged their ascent through them, carrying their kindred along. Like the dominants in the music of the period, they became dominants in their turn. Exalted by the style of lordly magnificence, they shone forth in their new position—often only briefly—under constant threat of great danger, and vanished again, some into nothingness, living on only in the conflicting estimations of posterity.

Richelieu's Family

Richelieu's typically Latin attachment to his own family was always predominant and grew towards the end of his life. His younger sister, Nicole, born in 1587, was always the object of his tender and heartfelt care. He had married her to Urbain de Maillé-Brézé, a man of high birth whom he then favoured, and despite many disappointments he advanced him over a long period. Maillé was ten years younger than his wife. By 1620 he was already a member of the Queen-Mother's *garde du corps*. The palace he built for himself was financed by a loan from Richelieu. He was to prove a great builder. His ascent was rapid, and he was soon commanding the Royal Guard. He was then made a Marshal of France and entrusted with important missions, such as the one to Gustavus Adolphus in 1632. In the same year he was made Governor of Calais. Later, when he was placed in command of an army in Germany, he enjoyed the same rank as Marshal de La Force. He was present at the relief of Heidelberg and he took part in the reconquest of Speyer and somewhat later he fought the Spaniards in Belgium successfully. But his failure at Louvain caused Richelieu to give vent to the long-simmering anger he had suppressed till then. The harshness with which Maillé-Brézé treated his wife had been a constant worry to the Cardinal. For years the Marshal had had an illicit relationship with a woman of provincial origin, to whom he was sexually enslaved. She was the wife of a gun-loader of his named Desvois, and had borne the Marshal several children. Richelieu reacted to the Louvain incident by withdrawing Maillé-Brézé from the governorship of Saumur. But having done so, he immediately began to advance his brother-in-law again, for Maillé-Brézé could only contribute to the family prestige if he held high positions and influential offices. In 1636 Maillé-Brézé shared the command of an army in Picardy with Chaulnes and the Count of Soissons, and of an army in Holland with Châtillon. He was also appointed Governor of Anjou and of the town and castle of Angers, in order to augment his income. In 1638 he was put at the head of the Luxemburg army, but when he heard that he was to share the command with de La Force and Châtillon he left his troops and withdrew to Angers. His ascent continued unabated, even as late as 1641. Together with the Prince of Condé he commanded the army in Roussillon, and in Champagne he shared the command with Châtillon and in Picardy with La

Meilleraye. He was present at the fall of Lens and Bapaume. Finally he became Viceroy of Catalonia, in which capacity, as we shall see, he was to suffer his most severe setback.

For years Richelieu did all in his power to prevent his brother-in-law from neglecting and even mistreating his wife. She was a hapless woman, completely dependent on her brother. Like Cardinal Alphonse-Louis du Plessis-Richelieu, Archbishop of Aix and Lyon and Grand Almoner of France, she finally went mad. Obsessed with the idea that her buttocks were made of glass, she refused to sit down. For a soldier such as Maillé-Brézé, this state of his wife was highly irritating, and he reacted with disgust and impatience when she insistently complained that the back of her hand was frozen and tried to cure it by pouring up to five hundred drops of resin oil a day onto what she firmly believed was a frost-bitten spot. In 1635, at the age of forty-eight, she was finally released from her suffering.

She had two children. Armand, her son and the family heir, possessed his uncle's highest qualities: strength of will, resolution and the unerring aim of a hawk, all this, however, unalloyed by pathological excitability or physical weakness. Richelieu's nephew had an iron constitution. The Cardinal brought him up within his own personal circle, and as a result the boy was thoroughly prepared for his short but impressive career as the nation's foremost naval hero. We shall encounter him later, aboard the battleship *Grand Saint Louis* at the battle of Orbetello, where at the height of his achievement he came to an early death. By that time he had already succeeded Richelieu as Controller-General of Navigation. But he outlived his god-father by only four years. Richelieu bequeathed him his duchy, the peerage of Fronsac and Caumont with all the appurtenances, the property and Marquisate of Graville, the County of Beaufort-en-Vallée, the Barony of Fresnes in Anjou, the manor farm of Poits in Normandy, together with 300,000 livres, which had been deposited in the castle of Saumur, to enable him to acquire further noble estates. But

Jean-Armand, Marquis de Brézé, Duc de Fronsac and Caumont, Marquis de Graville, Comte de Beaufort-en-Vallée and Baron de Fresnes, was not his uncle's most favoured beneficiary. All the male heirs received their portion, in some cases at the expense of the distaff side.

Armand-Brézé's sister, Claire-Clémence de Maillé-Brézé, was one such neglected relative, despite the fact that she had attained a higher rank than any other member of the family. At her uncle's bidding she had married a prince of the royal house, the Duke of Enghien, when she was only thirteen years of age. The dowry that Richelieu provided for her then was all she ever received from him, for when he died she got nothing. Her disappointed husband never forgave her for this. Like her mother's, her married life was wretched. At the time of her marriage she had been unable to read or write and was sent to a convent to make good this deficiency. Emotionally she was still a complete child and her husband regarded her as a thorough nuisance. For Richelieu this connection was one of the high points on his path to greatness, and he could scarcely wait for the children of the marriage to be born. Here we meet with a strange trait in this imperious man: he gave this much too young wife a large doll's house inhabited by six dolls—a woman in childbed, a wet nurse, an infant, a nurse, a midwife, and a grandmother.

Together with the Duchess of Enghien, Madame de Rambouillet—who later became the exemplar for the *précieuses*—Madame de Bouteville-Montmorency and various other ladies amused themselves with his symbolic plaything for evenings on end. They undressed the dolls one day and dressed them again the next, they fed them and gave them their medicine. As for the Duchess of Enghien, the blissful owner of this idyllic toy, it was only with the greatest difficulty that she was persuaded not to bathe the beautifully fashioned figures her uncle had had made for her. This little episode illustrates the Cardinal's peculiar talent for conceiving and implementing essentially feminine means for attaining his psychological ends, a talent he was to employ time and again in his relationship with the King.

The husband of Claire-Clémence became Louis II, Prince of Condé and Duke of Bourbon. He was of course "the great Condé," who in 1643, one year after Richelieu's death, when he himself was only twenty-two, defeated the Spanish at Rocroi. This crucial victory destroyed Spanish power for many years to come, and so realized one of Richelieu's lifelong aims. Condé was the son of Charlotte de Montmorency, the sister of the ill-fated Duke Henri, whose martial virtues, handed down through the generations since Carolingian times, re-emerged in his nephew. In the year of Condé's great victory, Claire-Clémence gave birth to a son, Henri-Jules, who later married Anne, daughter of the Count Palatine, Edward of Simmern. The last representative of the house of Condé was the Duke of Enghien who was executed by Napoleon I.

The great Condé himself was a man of exceptional mental alertness, participating in all the problems of his day. Although he fulfilled one of Richelieu's lifelong aims at Rocroi, he opposed his other aim, absolutism and centralization, with every means at his disposal. During the Fronde under Mazarin, Claire-Clémence, who had been a disappointment to Richelieu, showed her true mettle at her husband's side.

Richelieu's older sister, Françoise, who was born in 1578, also died young. She married a certain René de Vignerot, Monsieur Pont de Courlay. Her son, François de Vignerot, later the Marquis Pont de Courlay, became Governor of the town and citadel of Le Havre. After being made a Knight of the King's Orders in 1633, he was appointed Commander of the Galleys, a high and responsible office, for which he proved totally unfit. In due course he was obliged to surrender it to Armand de Maillé-Brézé.

Richelieu also showered the kinsmen on his mother's side, the La Portes, with offices; they were nearly all mediocrities, but Pont de Courlay was utterly incompetent. Pont de Courlay's sister, on the other hand, Marie-Madeleine, the wife of Antoine de Beauvoir du Roure, Monsieur de Combalet, was an extremely gifted woman. In 1638, after the death of her husband, she was given the title of Duchess of Aiguillon on her own account. Richelieu thought more highly of her than of any other member of his family. She was childless, and, having lost her husband early in life, she made her home with her uncle and devoted herself entirely to caring for him until his death. She had his absolute confidence and shared both his interests and his innermost thoughts. It was of course inevitable that this close relationship, this singular case of perfect intimacy, should have been subjected to diverse interpretations.

Marriage Customs of the Nobility

If we are to understand the great influence wielded by the women of the upper classes in seventeenth-century France, we must remember that in their society marriage was not a union of two individuals, as it was to become in the bourgeois society of a later era, but an alliance between two houses, a political and economic transaction. It was not a question of personal wishes but of family interests. The wife retained her family identity; in everything she did she acted as a representative of her house and signed all documents in her maiden name.

If a son wished to marry without his parents' consent, he had to wait until he was thirty; a daughter had to wait until she was twenty-five. But with the parents' consent a son could marry at the age of fourteen and a daughter at the age of twelve. Twelve-year-old wives were by no means rare. Once, when a Rohan married a Sully, the parents of the girl were asked: "Has this child been baptized?" She was only eleven, so the marriage required a dispensation. From their seventh year onwards children could become engaged. Many marriages were contracted by proxy, the partners never having even seen one another. The head of the house was all-powerful. Alliances with rich and influential families were frequently achieved by kidnapping or seduction. Men would ride out and overpower a castle or a house in a town and abduct some rich heiress, who would then be imprisoned and forced into marriage.

In May 1638 a certain Madame Ferrier, née Isabaud de Guiraud, wrote to Richelieu and begged him in the name of her late husband, who had been in the Cardinal's service, to take steps to rescue her daughter, who had been forcibly abducted by a certain d'Oradour from her house on the Rue du Temple in the heart of Paris between nine and ten o'clock one evening. On May 8, 1638 the Cardinal sent the following note to the abductor:

"Since brief follies are always the best, I would advise you upon receipt of this letter to release Mademoiselle Ferrier and return her unharmed to her mother. I tell you clearly that if you do not do so, and choose instead to ignore my counsel, and if you do not do all within your power to make good your error, I for my part will leave nothing undone to ensure that you receive the punishment you deserve."

Before the Council of Trent, marriages were contracted without a church ceremony. All that was needed was a formal agreement between the two families. It was almost impossible to withdraw a promise of marriage once it had been given. Marshal de Vitry, held as a state prisoner in the Bastille, sent a message to Richelieu offering to place his daughter at the Cardinal's disposal, so that he might marry her off as he saw fit, provided he would be freed. Chancellor Séguier also offered his daughters to Richelieu in exchange for the Cardinal's favour. Richelieu actually arranged a marriage between one of these girls and a kinsman of his, a little hunchback by the name of Monsieur de Coislin. He allowed Séguier to choose a husband for his other daughter himself. The Count d'Harcourt undertook to marry any female relative of Richelieu's the latter cared to suggest. Gramont received a note from the Cardinal saying: "I had promised you

Mademoiselle de Pontchâteau and now find I can no longer give her to you. Please forgive me. May I ask you to accept Mademoiselle du Plessis-Givray in her place." Gramont replied that the choice was a matter of indifference to him.

After the introduction of church weddings, papal annulments became quite common. Childless marriages could be dissolved. A man who discovered his wife in the act of adultery could expect severe punishment if he took his revenge on her directly, but he could have her locked up in a convent, in which case her property was usually confiscated. This was quite a simple matter and the grounds on which a husband might take this step were not terribly exacting. The insane were allowed to marry during lucid intervals, as were the mentally deficient, provided they were not entirely witless. But marriages *in extremis*—that is, marriage to a dying person—were forbidden.

After 1600, illegitimate children were no longer regarded as members of the nobility. In the Middle Ages the position of the bastard sons of great houses had been virtually the same as that of children born in wedlock. Even in the seventeenth century, however, an illegitimate son could be legitimized by a royal dispensation. Between 1610 and 1643 the following were legitimized and thereby raised to the nobility: Gabriel and Christophe de Chabanes (sons of the Marquis of Gontaud-Biron), François de Polignac, Jean de Montalembert, André de Mailly and Hannibal de La Trémoille. Sometimes the mother's name was mentioned in the deeds, sometimes it was not. The law itself was strict, but its application was extremely liberal. This is quite evident from the fact that Guy de Lusignan, Monsieur de Saint-Gelais, was legitimized as the son of Urbain de Lusignan, the Bishop of Comminges, and of Catherine de La Nazière.

Although polygamy was punishable by death on the gallows, both adultery and the issue of adulterous relationships were tolerated. In an edition of the *Courrier Véritable* from the year 1632 we read: "Relations between marriage partners have become extremely cool now that it is no longer customary for husband and wife to make mutual confession of their faults; instead they are simply intent on deceiving each other. There would be good cause to fear lest the country be depopulated but for the fact that the daughters of the Third Estate, and above all the wives of our vintners, continue to bring their twelve children into the world." For a man to love his wife was considered unsophisticated and rather ridiculous. D'Andilly said that his own marriage was very happy, but added, "How unlike the usual marriage, which only joins property to property."

There were marriage bureaux supplying detailed information concerning the marriage portion and financial situation of eligible children of noble families. A Marshal of France married one of Henry IV's former mistresses, who had already borne several children to Cardinal de Guise. The Constable Lesdiguières solved his financial difficulties by marrying a certain Marie Vignan, widow of a rich cloth merchant of Grenoble whom she had murdered. She had borne the Constable two children while her husband was still alive, and Lesdiguières did not hesitate to have both children legitimized.

Many more instances might be mentioned. These scandals, which have been widely reported in memoirs and letters, have achieved considerable notoriety, and literary monuments have been erected to the great courtesans such as Ninon de Lenclos and Marion de Lormes. It may be safely assumed, however, that all these events took place against a general background of stability, which was unchronicled at the time and so has not been handed down to us.

Penalties were severe only in respect of incestuous or unnatural relationships, although here too custom was more lenient than written regulations.

We mention all this in order to cast some light on the habits of the upper class, which was the only social group exercising authority in politics and military affairs.

It still possessed a great deal of vitality and a great deal of ability. It was for this reason that Richelieu always espoused the cause of the provincial nobility, from whose lower ranks he himself had emerged. As we have already seen, he defended their rights time and again, and he had such a clear conception of their duties that he recommended to the King that any who failed to observe the injunction "noblesse oblige" should be stripped of their rank. And yet all of the Cardinal's observations on this particular subject were informed by a sense of resignation. He knew that the rise of the bourgeoisie was not to be halted. Because of the wealth trade had brought them and the education and knowledge they had acquired, members of the Third Estate were constantly rising to high office and thus obtaining titles for their families. These newly appointed nobles were intermarrying with the hereditary nobles and, by a process of imitation and identification, were assimilating qualities that derived from the old knightly code of honour.

Richelieu begins his comprehensive discourses on this subject with the statement that the nobility must be regarded as the "central nerve" of the State and as an indispensable element in the task of reconstructing and preserving the French community. But in this context, he meant the provincial nobility and not the great houses.

Of his own class he said, "For some time now it has been greatly humiliated by the large number of officials who have risen up at its expense. . . ." How strange that Richelieu, who had advocated this new development, should have expressed uneasiness about the result.

He continued:

"The provincial nobility needs to be protected from intimidation by such people. The opulence and arrogance of the favoured class aggravates the neediness of the other, whose only wealth lies in its courage, which moves its members to dedicate their lives to the service of the King, from whom the new administrative class draws its whole substance."

145

And further:

"To take the life of persons who daily risk their life for the sake of honour [that is, to have them executed in certain circumstances] is far less harsh than to take their honour and leave them their life, which then becomes a constant torment."

As a guide to the stratification of French society in Richelieu's time, it is worth noting that at the Estates-General of 1614 the various national groups were represented as follows: 144 members of the clergy, 130 nobles, 188 representatives of the Third Estate.

As far as tax exemption was concerned, a privilege from which only the Third Estate was excluded, in 1634 one still made a distinction between those families who had already been titled in 1559 and those ennobled since then. This was the only tangible exception to the general indifference felt towards the concept of genealogical *ancienneté*.

This indifference is clearly illustrated by the following incident: When the Duke of Nevers, of the Italian house of Gonzaga, declared that, although he was well aware of the respect due to the Queen-Mother, the whole world knew that his family had been of princely estate long before the Medici had risen from the ranks of the bourgeoisie, his statement was felt to be scandalous, tactless and un-French.

There were no hard and fast genealogical barriers to be surmounted; France differed in this respect from most Central European nations, where such barriers were zealously maintained. Men set out on the road to high position in a society that was still flexible. As we have already said, the only members of society who were firmly established in the public esteem were the "great nobles," many of whom Richelieu had set out to destroy—partly from political necessity and partly from his own unconscious feelings for them, in which admiration vied with dislike. From the violent elimination of members of some of the greatest houses to the fostering of difficulties that were reducing them to penury, Richelieu

146

employed many effective weapons in his battle against the nobility. We have already considered various cases that illustrate this very clearly. In the measures he took to safeguard the property he himself had so speedily acquired, he followed his customary practice of collaborating with men personally close to him, bound by moral obligations and a relationship of absolute trust.

Intimates

Richelieu's private financial transactions were managed by his own steward and secretary, Le Masle. Le Masle did not have an easy time of it. Richelieu was always urging him on with the words, "Income is the thing to worry about, not expenditure."

Le Masle was known as the "*Prieur des Roches*." As choral director of Notre-Dame, he was also director of the "little schools" of Paris and administered their scholarship fund. He was the author of a directive requiring, under threat of dismissal, that the masters and mistresses of these schools should enrol Protestant children and instruct them in the catechism, language and literature in exactly the same way as their Catholic fellows. On July 6, 1633, Le Masle stated: "These little ones called 'Reformed' must be treated with the same humanity and kindness as the others."

We know from Richelieu's accounts that Le Masle received a salary of 2,000 livres. He and Richelieu were inseparable. In the library of the Sorbonne a portrait of Le Masle hung next to a portrait of Richelieu. In 1646 Le Masle presented a large library to the University of Paris, supplementing the library founded by Richelieu.

An interesting piece of information about Le Masle appeared in a book published in 1639. We read there: "The whole city [Paris] is under the command of a single head; at the present time this is the Abbé des Roches, the choral director of the Cathedral of Notre-Dame; he has under his command fifteen captains, fifteen lieutenants, fifteen ensigns and thirty sergeants." If we consider the enormous number of political pamphlets written by Le Masle, it is astonishing to think that this prior and school-director should at the same time have found it possible to perform such an important police function.

Another of Richelieu's collaborators was the indefatigable Charpentier. We find documents in his hand dating from February 1609. He entered the Cardinal's service when the latter was Bishop of Luçon and remained with him until he died. Charpentier's ability to imitate Richelieu's handwriting to perfection has posed a problem for later researchers. He used his skill mainly when etiquette required a personal reply from the Cardinal. The difference between the two handwritings can, however, be established by graphologists. Charpentier also acquired a number of other people's handwritings. He too is listed as receiving a salary of 2,000 livres. His official title was: "Advisory Secretary to the King, to the Royal Household and to the Crown of France. Secretary to Cardinal Richelieu." In his will Richelieu said of Charpentier: "I have never known a better, more loyal or more honest servant."

Charpentier had a cousin by the name of Cheret (or Cherré or Cheré), who entered the Cardinal's service in 1630 and remained with him until his death. Tallemant des Réaux said of him: "Cheret was a poor young lad from Nogent-le-Rotrou," who was assigned to the Cardinal. At first the Cardinal was pleased with him, but later he dismissed him. In the Bastille, guards had found on a prisoner four letters of Cheret's, in which he complained of being kept in harsh slavery by the Cardinal. After taxing him with his ingratitude, Richelieu is supposed to have said: "You are a rogue. I never wish to see you again." Tallemant goes on to report that at the urgent request of Richelieu's niece, the Duchess of Aiguillon, Cheret was reinstated; he was put on night duty, drafting the Cardinal's "night letters."

Tallemant also said: The Cardinal had a chief secretary

named Charpentier, who was slightly more mannerly than Rossignol. Rossignol came from Albi and entered the Cardinal's service in 1627, when he was thirty-seven. He worked in the code section and was an expert in that field. The Prince of Condé, who had led the King's troops against the Huguenots in Languedoc, credited the fall of Réalmont to Rossignol; he had decoded an intercepted letter from the town authorities to those in Montauban. Tallemant, on the other hand, was more sceptical of Rossignol's specialist knowledge, declaring that Richelieu had extolled his infallibility simply for propaganda purposes. Actually, he said, Rossignol was a vain, petty and ridiculous little man. The fact that Mazarin retained his services would appear to contradict this characterization.

A man called Cébéret also worked for the Cardinal, but only for a short period. It is known that he was engaged on theological questions and was later employed in the administration of the Cardinal's library. From 1624 to 1625 we find him as a member of the staff of the French embassy in Venice.

The person in charge of shipping and naval affairs in Richelieu's personal secretariat was a man by the name of Martin. And finally there was his personal physician, Citoys, who lent a hand when confidential texts were to be drafted.

A number of men of rank occasionally collaborated with the Cardinal's personal secretariat by drafting a special letter or despatch, report or memorandum. These men were: Henri de Sourdis, Archbishop of Bordeaux, the Bishop of Chartres, Cardinal de La Valette, the Jesuit Father Coton, the Bishops of Nantes and Mende and finally Abra de Raconis, who was preacher to the King, a doctor of theology and Bishop of Lavaur, to whom we are indebted for his handwritten records of many of Richelieu's conversations.

In his Memoirs Father Garras related a significant incident in which the Cardinal appears in a sympathetic light: Father Coton had been absent from Rueil for a considerable period, and at the time of his return the Cardinal happened to be in conversation with two English diplomats. But as soon as he heard the name Coton he jumped up and, without a word of explanation to his foreign guests, hurried off to embrace him.

All the helpers and executive workers whom we have been describing here were intimates, men who lived in the Cardinal's house.

The Civil Service—and Close Associates of Higher Rank

In many ways, conditions in the state civil service built up by Richelieu were not so very different from those in his own household. Nearly all of the officials were well known to him, nearly all belonged to his personal circle. First among them was Léon Bouthillier, the Secretary of State for foreign affairs, who later became Comte de Chavigny. He was the son of Claude Bouthillier. In 1632, when he was only twenty-four years old, he was appointed Secretary of State, assuming his father's functions, which he then carried out for eleven years until the death of Louis XIII. The King called him "Monsieur le Jeune."

Who were these Bouthilliers? According to Saint-Simon, Richelieu's maternal grandfather, La Porte, had an office clerk in whom he placed particular confidence and whom he helped to become an advocate. This was Denis Bouthillier. When La Porte died, he left his practice to Bouthillier and asked him to care for his grandchildren as if they were his own. This Bouthillier did most conscientiously. His son Claude shared the tie of close childhood friendship with the future Cardinal and the two began their careers under the Regent Marie de' Medici.

The Cardinal was to demonstrate his capacity for both gratitude and vindictiveness time and again. In the case of the Bouthilliers his gratitude was lifelong. After Richelieu's father died, Denis Bouthillier had done a great deal for his widow and children, and Richelieu repaid the debt a hundredfold. Léon, the grandson of the original benefactor, owed everything to the Cardinal. But he was worthy of his advancement and of the trust placed in him; he was industrious and level-headed, he had a ready wit and a highly developed sense of tact and self-discipline. When Claude Bouthillier reminded Richelieu of a promise he had given him with regard to Léon, he quoted two comments, one verbal, the other written, which Richelieu had made about the boy. The verbal comment, going back two years, had been:

"This young man is developing very well; two years from now he will be capable of taking over your office."

In his written comment Richelieu said:

"Incidentally, I have seen your heir; he is quite grown up now, a whole man, modest and at the same time bold; his answers are to the point; in a word, he is even more a man of the world than his father." This last quip was no more than friendly banter. The chief emphasis was on the impression Léon made, which Richelieu described as *modestement hardi*, a phrase implying the sterner qualities of *honnêteté*, integrity and reliability.

There was one occasion, however, when this same *honnêteté* made Léon Bouthillier appear suspect to a representative of Protestant England. Leicester wrote of him as follows:

". . . he is as hard to be found as a mouse in a barne; he lyes sometimes at bathing houses and sometimes in other places, and is so much a man of pleasure, as it is a wonder to many that the great Apollo of this State will put so many and so great businesses into his hand; . . ."

The fact of the matter is that Richelieu treated the Count of Chavigny as if he were his own son, and was very tolerant of any mistakes he made. Tallemant, whose psychological explanations reveal a constant preoccupation with sexual gossip, hinted at an intimate relationship between Richelieu and Chavigny's mother, Marie, a member of the Bragelonne family. But the true motives for the Cardinal's attachment to the representatives of three generations of Bouthilliers were not to be found in the circles Tallemant frequented.

In 1632 came the great defeat of the party of the *Dévots* and the end of both Marillacs, one going to prison, one to execution; and then d'Effiat died. Richelieu was now able to fill two key positions with men from his own party: his childhood friend Claude Bouthillier and Claude de Bullion assumed joint responsibility for d'Effiat's functions as Superintendent of Finance, and within the year Claude Bouthillier's son, Léon Chavigny, was appointed Secretary of State for foreign affairs, which he conducted in close collaboration with the King and the Cardinal.

Chavigny was a respected figure at Court. Richelieu encouraged his taste for high living, since it gave him a hold over Chavigny. When, as sometimes happened, the Cardinal was dissatisfied with his work, he would write and tell him that if he were to devote as much energy to his official duties as to the acquisition of personal wealth, it would be a distinct advantage. His lavish style of living involved him in what were often very large debts. Within the course of just a few years these amounted to 1,800,000 livres. But the spendthrift's debts were always paid. The Chavigny estate, which he had received from the King, was highly profitable. He had succeeded in making himself indispensable not only to Richelieu but to the King and Gaston d'Orléans as well. His critics said that he was rude and offensive to his subordinates, but to his superiors he always remained a sycophant. He was never more than a minor official who could be disavowed, transferred or dismissed. In his official capacity he was not authorized to act on his own initiative. And yet he was more than just a Secretary of State. He had direct access to the King and acted as his adviser in all departments. But his most important function was that of mediator between Orléans, the King and the Cardinal. He also presided over the so-called Council of Princes for Orléans. When Richelieu wished to win the King over for some project of his own, he would often use Chavigny, for Chavigny was well aware that without the Cardinal he himself would be nothing, and gave him his complete devotion. This we know from Chavigny himself, who said of the Cardinal: "He is the only master I recognize." Whenever Louis XIII was suspicious of his Prime Minister or out of humour with him, whenever his vacillating affections swung away from the Cardinal, Chavigny would enter the scene.

Richelieu frequently exploited his illness to his own advantage. Sometimes when he felt himself to be threatened by assassins, often when he needed peace and quiet, and especially when he needed to concentrate, he would plead illness. When he wished to avoid the monarch's personal presence, he was ill, and when he sensed that his master was in a bad mood, he was also ill. Then Chavigny had to come to the rescue and explain to Louis: "The Cardinal would sooner die a thousand deaths than incur Your Majesty's displeasure in the slightest degree." Often Chavigny would appeal to the monarch's better nature, and such appeals were usually successful, for the King was easily swayed and it was never very difficult to persuade him that if only harmony could be restored, if only the Cardinal could feel assured of the King's absolute trust, his illness would surely leave him.

Chavigny was Richelieu's observer and informer at Orléans's court. He surrounded the heir-presumptive with a whole network of spies and so kept him under constant surveillance. He remained a successful informer up to the time of the Cinq-Mars conspiracy, when, as we shall see, he failed not only to discover the plot in time but also to take effective action to stifle it once it was afoot.

But he stood by his master through thick and thin. "I am your grateful creature," he once wrote to Richelieu. And the term fitted.

When during the late thirties and early forties Mazarin gradually worked his way into the intimate sphere of the Cardinal's thinking and planning, where his acumen, subtlety and outstanding abilities as a negotiator made him indispensable to the Cardinal, it was not surprising that relations between Mazarin and Chavigny should have become strained. Chavigny was the one to suffer, but he did not complain. At that time Mazarin was working towards a distant goal, which lay beyond Richelieu's lifetime. The struggle between Chavigny and the Neapolitan was an unequal one, and by the time of Richelieu's death the Frenchman had already been worsted. He fell from favour at the outset of Anne of Austria's regency, and in 1652, at the age of only forty-four, he died.

Under the Ancien Régime in France the Secretaries of State originally came from the ranks of the notaries, who were charged with special duties for the King. This development can be traced back as far as the eleventh century. Ever since 1342 the King's notaries and secretaries had had to pass an examination. These men came into close contact with the King and were able to acquire influence. From 1547 onwards there were four Secretaries of Finance who, strangely enough, were engaged on virtually all aspects of state administration save those relating to state finance, for which an entirely new organization was created. They also had no authority in the realm of the law, which came under the Chancellor and the high courts. These Secretaries of State were principally concerned with the administration of the provinces and with foreign affairs. There were four treasurers (*trésoriers*), who dealt with normal expenditure, and a further four high officers of the treasury and two commissioners-general of revenue (*receveurs généraux des aides*), who dealt with special expenditures. Together these men formed the central authority and supervised the division of territory. France was divided into four large districts, each administered by an executive office headed by a treasurer, a treasury officer and a commissioner-general of revenue. These four districts were: the country north of the Seine and the Yonne, with its capital at Paris; Normandy, with its capital at Rouen; the region of Languedoïl with its capital at Tours; Languedoc with its capital at Montpellier. The individual districts were divided in their turn into *bailliages* for normal purposes and into so-called *élections* for special taxes. The Secretaries of State came to assume the duties of departmental ministers by a very gradual process. It was not until 1589, under Henry III, that war and foreign affairs were finally separated, which meant that from that time onwards two of the four Secretaries of State were each engaged on a single major sphere of activity while the other two continued to deal in a piecemeal fashion with all other aspects of state business—internal affairs, culture, trade, public works. This tendency towards specialization made considerable headway under Richelieu, but a large amount of state business was still dealt with as a combined operation or else handled directly by the Superintendent of Finance.

In the first half of the seventeenth century there was a new development: one of the financial intendants was placed over the others and made Superintendent. The precedent had been established as early as 1564, and the extremely successful Sully had been the exemplar of a Superintendent. The office he held was finally abolished by Louis XIV, after the downfall of Fouquet.

And so we find a Chancellor, a Superintendent of Finance and four Secretaries of State. Theoretically they were all equal in rank, their only superior being the King himself. But with the need to strengthen the authority of the Crown a "principal" or *"premier ministre"* was appointed, who then took over the general conduct of state business together with any duties which had not been allocated to a particular ministry. Only Richelieu and Mazarin could really be called prime ministers and, in theory at least, they too were merely instruments of the King's will. It was for this reason—and this has to be stressed again and again—that Richelieu was constantly obliged to impose his will on the King. This was also one of the reasons why Richelieu's opponents were prepared to go to almost any lengths, including threats of murder, in order to depose him. The great nobles had long been denied access to the state secretariats, a fact that only strengthened their resolve to oppose this new form of state administration. An attempt was made to win the upper class over to the concept of absolute monarchy by setting up advisory councils in which they could participate, but this attempt failed, owing to the aversion the great nobles had for administrative duties.

Under Louis XIII, of course, the provincial governors were still in charge and they were, almost without exception, members of the hereditary nobility. And then, besides the Secretaries of State, there were the *intendants*, the seventeenth-century counterparts of the *enquêteurs réformateurs* of the time of Louis IX, who had developed from the *missi dominici* of the Carolingian dynasty. Like their ninth-century predecessors, these *intendants* worked toward the unification of the State.

From the sixteenth century onwards, the men chosen as inspectors or commissioners with special or general authority to tour the provinces were usually so-called *maîtres des requêtes de l'hôtel*, ambitious young men who were completely dependent on the King; their tours of inspection were called *chevauchées* and they themselves *chevaucheurs*. In practice these emissaries came to be known by a variety of names, but the type itself, the type of the intendant, was constant. This development took place primarily under Richelieu, when the intendants became the executive arm of the central authority. It was for this reason that they were subsequently attacked by the Fronde in the reign of Louis XIV.

In Louis XIII's time the great majority of administrative questions relating to the provinces were settled on the spot. The Secretaries of State were mere agents. They informed the provincial governors, ambassadors and generals concerned of the King's wishes but were themselves able to bring only a very limited influence to bear. By modern standards the government departments of that day were extremely flexible. The only way of ascertaining the state of affairs is to take the activities of individuals under scrutiny.

Even titles meant very little. If certain advisers were

appointed Councillors or Ministers of State, this merely meant that they were allowed precedence on councils for internal affairs or at Court ceremonies. This was also the case in 1629 when Richelieu was appointed First Minister by letters patent. He received no specific and clearly defined political authority as a result of this appointment. All it involved was the question of precedence at Council meetings. Later, owing to the force of his personality and habit, and the death or the disgrace of the older members of the Council, he came to exercise absolute control over the *conseil* and was able to appoint new Councillors at will, men whom he could direct according to his lights and whose relationship to the monarch he could control. Between 1635 and 1642 there was, for the first time ever, a really efficient ministerial government, a wartime government. The different departments were made more independent of each other, especially the war department and the Treasury. It would be true to say, however, that nearly all the persons employed in these departments, who were of course *officiers du Roi*, executive officers of an absolute monarch, were Richelieu's confidants. Although the King referred to them as his ministers, they were not actually appointed as such and were not authorized to make political decisions on their own initiative. The monarch remained the sole source of political power. All decisions were made by the King himself or were at least attributed to him. And so the task of convincing the King, of persuading him to make political decisions, remained the cornerstone of French politics. This is why Richelieu's psychological relationship to the King was of such a serious, difficult and at times dangerous nature; it was in fact not dissimilar to the relationship of a modern Prime Minister to public opinion and his electorate. In his *Political Testament* the Cardinal stressed the fact that his fellow Councillors were constantly presenting different opinions and had every right to speak their mind to the King himself.

We have already met the Bouthilliers. Like them, Claude de

Bullion was a daily companion to both Louis XIII and Cardinal Richelieu. Under Henry IV he was already *maître des requêtes*; during the regency of Marie de' Medici, in 1612, he was appointed Administrator-General of Navarre, and the year before, in 1611, he had represented the Crown at the Assembly of Saumur. He was a member of the Queen-Mother's personal entourage and in 1615 he became her Chancellor. In 1619 he was given special duties, the most important being the financial administration of the provinces. Then in 1624, when Richelieu entered office, he was admitted to the sessions of the Royal Council. During the difficult years of Richelieu's rise to power, Bullion always took his part. Both in naval affairs in general and in the confrontations with the Duke of Guise to which they gave rise, he supported the Cardinal. He also lent him money, and on the Day of the Dupes he provided Richelieu with up-to-the-minute information on the development of the intrigue. He was a jovial figure, optimistic both by nature and by policy; he was tall and well built, which, as always in France, constituted a mark of distinction; he was also a man who took his pleasures seriously and who by and large was well liked. His nickname was an endearing one: "the little wine keg." As a brilliant conversationalist, he was particularly popular with the great nobles who revolved round the Court. But he failed to please Tallemant des Réaux, who, for want of a better, is so often invoked as an authority. Unlike the majority of contemporary reporters, Tallemant did not have a good word to spare for him. It is quite evident that he envied him his material success; he maintained that Bullion's property brought him in the best part of 700,000 livres a year.

Bullion, who eventually became Superintendent of Finance and Keeper of the Seals, had set out in life as a member of the staff of the Lesdiguières household. Soon he entered into a close, almost comradely relationship with Richelieu—in so far as the Cardinal ever permitted comradeship. For very good reasons Richelieu closed his eyes to tendencies towards self-enrichment. But from time to time he turned on this eternal optimist and once even raised his hand against him. Bullion, for his part, remained relaxed, trusting and open-hearted in his attitude towards the formidable First Minister. Tallemant, who was obliged to concede that Bullion was a better organizer than those who succeeded him, quotes him as saying: "If you will satisfy two appetites, that of His Eminence's household and that of the Artillery, I'll guarantee the rest." We shall be hearing more of Bullion in the chapter on state finance.

Pressure could be applied to the highest advisory and executive bodies of the administration in many ways. For example, even the highest officials had to obtain the King's permission before arranging marriages for their children. Bullion once asked Richelieu to use his influence with the King, for he had applied to him for permission for his son to marry and had received an evasive reply. But Richelieu was in no particular hurry to help him in this matter, and so he waited for six months before writing to Bullion, in January 1639, to tell him that there could be no question of a marriage for his son until certain financial conditions had been fulfilled. Among other things Bullion had to observe the terms of the decree limiting the annual income to which he was entitled by his office. By that stage in his career Bullion's friends estimated his income at 1,500,000 livres, although this may have been an exaggeration. Bullion agreed to all conditions, and his son married a Marquise de Toussy.

Letters in which Bullion and Richelieu discussed the use of secret funds are still extant. The relationship between these two men was indeed a strange one. They worked well together, and yet they were always falling out. Louis XIII had no grasp of financial affairs and Richelieu was always at pains to free himself from the cares and responsibilities imposed by such matters. As a result the Superintendents of Finance, under tight control, in many respects, were allowed far too much initiative in others, for they virtually dictated the government loan and taxation policy. Richelieu had no really effective control. The only visible signs of his auditorship were his sudden outbursts of rage and the accusations he levelled at his Superintendents of Finance. But when they were required to lend money to the Cardinal from secret funds, it was difficult to prevent them from doing the same things for themselves and their friends. And Bullion was a witness to the way in which Richelieu's fortunes had increased.

On various occasions Bullion and Claude Bouthillier had tried to draw up a more equitable system of taxation, for as things stood the Third Estate bore the entire burden. In 1640 they put forward proposals for a tax on the French clergy, but this called forth such a violent reaction that Richelieu immediately wrote to Bullion to say that if this measure were put into force, even his most devoted disciples could not expect to survive it.

Bullion, in collaboration with Chavigny, also dealt with foreign affairs. He had a voice in guiding Charnacé's mission in Holland, which we shall be considering later, and he maintained close contact with the English ambassadors. Louis XIII always thought very highly of him. He regarded him as the one man capable of exercising some control over Richelieu. But the King could scarcely have known the extent to which Bullion had enriched himself at the country's expense. When the apoplectic Bullion succumbed to a stroke in 1640, Louis XIII wrote to Richelieu saying that he deeply regretted his death and feared that it would be no easy matter to find so hardworking and reliable a servant again. At the same time, however, he commanded the Cardinal to impress on Bouthillier the need for more stringent financial measures, for otherwise there would be no money at all for the second half of the year.

Two things strike us when we consider these Secretaries of State. Their emergence illustrates the rise of the bourgeoisie from the ranks of the Parlement class. Further, most of them, passing their day in close contact with the King and the

7.   Cardinal Richelieu

8. Maximilian, Elector of Bavaria

Cardinal, owed their careers to Richelieu and were in some instances related to him.

This was the case with François Sublet de Noyers, who owed his start in life to the fact that his mother was a member of the Bochart family; Richelieu's maternal grandmother[1] was also a Bochart. Patronage and family influence remained all important. It was Feuquières who introduced Sublet to the Cardinal around 1628.

Sublet was later asked to supervise and manage the construction of fortification works in Picardy. His numerous letters to Richelieu were usually concerned with building problems, with questions of military defence and above all with fortification technique. According to the terms of his commission, Sublet was required to find his own workmen and specialists and to win the support of provincial governors and high military officers for these ambitious projects. But he also concerned himself with budgetary problems, with the theoretical aspects of fiscal policy and the supply of precious metals from Spain. He studied methods of debasing the coinage and tried to check the outflow of foreign exchange. He worked in close collaboration with the Secretaries of State and the high-ranking military commanders. At first he served Richelieu in an unofficial capacity. It was not until 1636, when he was appointed Secretary of State, that he came under his direct supervision.

Chavigny is said to have been jealous of the newcomer because of the favour he enjoyed not only with the Cardinal but also with the King, who always affectionately referred to him as "*mon petit bonhomme.*" When he was appointed Secretary of State, on February 17, 1636, he was forty-eight years old. In his official capacity he was chiefly concerned with military affairs. Physically a small man who had started his career as a clerk, Sublet was an indefatigable worker. He took over his multiple and responsible office from Abel Servien,

---

[1] Richelieu's mother, Suzanne de La Porte, was the daughter of François de La Porte and Claude Bochart.

the "*robin*" of the Dauphiné, whom Richelieu had been obliged to dismiss because of his quarrelling, primarily with Chavigny but also with Bullion.

Sublet inherited a large part of the internal opposition that had been the downfall of his predecessor, but he responded to all difficulties with his own tenacious devotion to duty. In the seven years of his tenure in office, he supervised the wording of 18,000 letters. He was constantly overworked. During the open warfare with Spain, when as an armaments specialist he was already hard pressed, he added to his general duties the functions of concierge of Fontainebleau in his capacity as Superintendent of Buildings, an office Richelieu had procured for him. His responsibilities were tremendous: he had to inspect troops, supervise their provisions, supply ammunition for the border territories of Picardy and Champagne, and in 1635, even before his official appointment, he was asked to find 6,000 pairs of boots for the army in Germany. He also had the supervision of incoming correspondence to the King from a large number of provinces. He was consulted in Church matters. He had to import tapestries from Flanders, send vagabonds to the galleys and build an academy and a college for the town of Richelieu. And time and again he was obliged to seek credit for his fortification works, for the wages of the King's intendants, for pensions and a host of other things.

When the King gave strategic instructions by letter, it was Sublet who prepared the draft. On such occasions he would often write to the officers himself, adding a word of encouragement, a comment on some special task or the latest Court gossip. And it was Sublet who kept the King and the Cardinal informed about the slightest changes in the disposition of the armies. He had to furnish lists of the numbers of men serving in the various regiments, calculate pay requirements from army lists, provide both ammunition and provisions and submit reports on desertions and mutinies. He constantly negotiated with financiers, exhorted his subordinates to greater efforts, and conscientiously checked that his orders were carried out. He supervised the collection of the *taillon*, the special levy raised to pay for the war, and he kept Richelieu informed at every step. Like the King himself, he had a phenomenal knowledge of detail. Unfortunately, his correspondence with Louis XIII has not been preserved.

When Sublet was at Court the King worked with him every day; if they were separated, he wrote to him through his personal secretary, Lucas. Richelieu thought highly of Sublet de Noyers's abilities, but he did not include him in the most intimate circle of his confidants, although he did entrust him with personal commissions. Sublet was asked to collaborate on the preparation of the *Political Testament*, and he also made many of the purchases for the Cardinal's library.

Very little is known about the way in which Sublet's career came to an end. He was dismissed two months after Richelieu's death, but no information has come to light concerning the circumstances.

There are a few other men who should be mentioned—for example, Louis Phélypeaux, Seigneur de La Vrillière, the son of a Secretary of State who, before his death in 1629, had tried unsuccessfully to ensure that his son would automatically succeed him in his office. But the son was also supported by Claude Bouthillier, and when Marillac, who represented the opposition party, nominated another candidate, Richelieu advised the King to reconsider Louis Phélypeaux's case, for if he were appointed now he would be indebted to both Claude Bouthillier and the Cardinal himself. And so Phélypeaux became a Secretary of State. He played a leading role in fighting the revolts in Languedoc in 1640, and had taken part in the suppression of the desperate uprising of the *"va-nu-pieds"* in Normandy the previous year. The provinces with which he was concerned from 1635 onwards were: Languedoc, Guyenne, Aunis, Burgundy, Bourbonnais, Nivernais, Normandy, Picardy, Touraine, Anjou, Maine, Perche and Auvergne.

Richelieu did not employ him on really important state business. It would seem that Phélypeaux too did not get on with Chavigny. The tone of his correspondence is businesslike and formal.

Henri-Auguste Loménie, Comte de Brienne, was also a Secretary of State. He inherited his father's office by *"droit de survivance"*, and until his father's death the two had worked together. Neither father nor son had any great influence on state affairs but their loyalty to the Crown appears to have been irreproachable.

These then were the high officials who worked with the King and the Cardinal.

But we must take care in assessing the influence of these executives. Modern standards are not applicable here. In the early days of absolute monarchy it was unthinkable that a Councillor should act on his own initiative. Georges Avenel is quite right when he says that the Secretaries of State at the beginning of the seventeenth century had nothing like the powers invested in a modern ministry. Far more influential than the Secretaries of State were the Superintendents of Finance; they really knew something about the workings of government, which could not always be said of those who nominally held power.

Father Joseph

But the circle of men who surrounded Richelieu in his professional life could never be counted complete without the man Richelieu found so congenial, François Joseph Leclerc du Tremblay, Father Joseph, whom Aldous Huxley has so admirably brought to life.

In every corner of Europe, in the Levant, in West Africa, in the North African Barbary States and in large areas of East Asia, there were in the first half of the seventeenth century certain indefatigable travellers of European origin who thought nothing of covering their twenty or thirty miles a day. With a discipline of iron, these men, seemingly guided by an invisible hand, prospected for trade on the grand scale and drafted commercial reports from which their compatriots at home learnt, for example, that this or that African potentate was selling gold dust, ivory, coconuts, groundnuts or even slaves on advantageous terms. But the drafting of such reports was not the real purpose of their tireless activity. The political intelligence service they conducted, under conditions of absolute secrecy, was far more important. And yet this too was not their ultimate goal. For these reporters were not laymen; they were Capuchin monks. Their principal task was to carry the Christian mission to distant parts of the world. They were there to serve the *Congregatio de Propaganda Fide*, the institution founded on January 14, 1622, by Pope Gregory XV. One of these monks, who had been a member of the mission ever since its inception, was Father Joseph, Richelieu's friend and adviser, the most passionately dedicated, astonishing and tireless of all the Capuchins (see Vol. I). In 1625, after being a member of this movement for only three years, Father Joseph was appointed prefect of foreign missions. In a sense he was already engaged in world politics in 1628, the time of the siege of La Rochelle, for it was then that he sent Father Pacificus of Provins to Africa and Asia to find out where Capuchin monks might be deployed to the best advantage. Father Pacificus was also a trained observer. He had already worked in Abyssinia and in the Near East and later pressed on as far as Persia, where he combined trade and missionary duties with considerable success. He was to prove one of the most effective political agents in Constantinople.

Richelieu thought so highly of Father Joseph's ability that for many years he considered him a possible successor. But after a life of dedicated and exhausting activity the lifelong friend died before his master, felled by a stroke. He was eight years older than the Cardinal. Others reaped the harvest that Richelieu and the Capuchin had sown and nurtured. The chief beneficiary was an Italian whom Father Joseph had once initiated into the great game of French politics: Giulio Mazarini.

It will repay us to take a brief look at the background from which Richelieu's *"Eminence Grise"* emerged.

Father Joseph, who was born on November 4, 1577, was the oldest son of Jean Leclerc du Tremblay, a nobleman risen from Parlement and Chancellor to the Duke of Alençon. His mother, Marie de La Fayette, was descended from provincial nobility. Her father, Claude, owned four baronies, one of which he made over to his grandson, François Joseph.

Before he took holy orders, Father Joseph had begun his career at Court. He was known there as the Baron de Mafflier. Both his maternal grandfather, Claude de La Fayette, and grandmother, Marie de Suze, were Calvinists. Like many other provincial nobles of their day, they had land but no capital. The La Fayettes had six daughters and no son. According to a practice quite common in their time, their daughter Marie was baptized and brought up in the Catholic faith, so that she might enter a convent later in life and thus make it unnecessary to provide her with a dowry. This kind of free interchange between the confessions had often brought relief to a hard-pressed family.

But Marie de La Fayette was removed from her convent and brought back into the world by a distant relative, the Duchess Anne d'Etampes. Like many other great ladies of her generation, Duchess Anne, who by then was seventy, had once been Francis I's mistress. She was a kindhearted woman and in later life fond of playing the matchmaker; it was in this capacity that she made Marie's fortune. She provided for the necessary dowry, and her charitable action was blessed with a fortunate outcome, for Marie de La Fayette's marriage to Jean Leclerc du Tremblay was a very happy one. The couple's first child was François Joseph. He was amazingly precocious. At the age of ten he delivered a funeral oration in Latin in honour of Ronsard before a large and illustrious gathering. Had he chosen to do so, he could have delivered his speech equally well in Greek. He learnt all his languages by ear, in the course of conversation. When he was only eight years old he went to a boarding school in Paris. The educational methods employed there prepared him for the Franciscan discipline. In the Collège de Boncourt corporal punishment was customary and undernourishment the general rule. One of François Joseph's fellow students later became Cardinal de Bérulle.

François Joseph was ten years old when his father died suddenly. It was a hard blow for the boy. He said later that this event had given him an enduring sense of the vanity and transience of life.

In 1585 his mother moved to a fortified house near Paris, for in Paris itself no man's life was safe. The house was called Le Tremblay. There the family enjoyed the protection afforded by the local farmers and their labourers. After his father's death François Joseph's mother took him out of school and kept him at home. There he received lessons from a private tutor, who insisted that above all his pupil must learn modern languages. And so the boy learnt Spanish and Italian at one and the same time and mastered them both. He studied philosophy, jurisprudence and higher mathematics, and could read Hebrew with ease at the age of fifteen. But he was also taught to ride and shoot. He read Plutarch and the biographies of hermits, and composed a treatise "On the Advantages of the Spiritual Life" before his twelfth year. One of the crucial experiences of his early years was his violent love for a young girl who was forced into marriage at the age of fourteen and then died in childbirth. The adolescent boy reacted to this event by developing a state of hypersensitivity productive of hallucinations. At times he felt himself surrounded by the souls of the damned, or he would suddenly be seized in the middle of a conversation by a sense of the actual presence of the dead girl. He would then turn deathly pale and fail to answer when spoken to. Some time later, after his mother had almost been killed by marauding soldiers, François Joseph decided to embrace the religious life.

The boy's self-absorption, verging on mysticism, was further influenced by a strange incident. One day he retrieved a famous book thrown away by a passing soldier, the *Barlaam and Josaphat*, a Latin version via the Greek and Arabic of the pre-Christian Sanskrit text of the *Lalita Vistara*. This age-old legend deeply impressed the boy and was transmuted in him into a heroic vision of Christianity.

The fact that Richelieu in his early years won this extraordinary man as his chief collaborator may well be considered one of the most crucial factors in his life. Father Joseph was the one person who, although one of Richelieu's dependents, surpassed him in insight into the fundamentals of politics. Richelieu's superiority lay in his capacity for concentration, for focusing all the powers of his intellect and will on a single issue; conversely, Father Joseph, with his ubiquity of vision, moved through the world of the present like a being beyond time, letting his energies flow freely and frequently dispersing them to no avail.

Before returning to Father Joseph, whose main sphere of influence was Central Europe, the basic condition of all French foreign policy has to be explored. For centuries, it had exerted a constant restraint on every French initiative abroad, and we must now attempt to outline the forces governing France's relationship to England.

CHAPTER VI

FRANCE AND ENGLAND

Richelieu has often been represented by right-wing historians as the man who disrupted the organic development of the French State and transformed it into an abstraction, thus making it impossible for any group, for any enterprising individual, to claim power on their own behalf.

Other critics, especially those in the nineteenth century who subscribed to the tradition of the French Revolution and its many consequences, have regarded him as a despot, and as the man who instituted the system of absolute monarchy which reached its peak under Louis XIV.

If we are to understand the Cardinal's achievements, it is essential to realize that in all he did he aimed at continuity and completion rather than outright innovation, and that all his policies were rooted in a centuries' old tradition. The emergence of the French nation and the French State was subject to the interaction of two main organizational principles: the feudal structure of medieval society and the authority of the King. From the very outset these two principles manifested themselves as both complementary and mutually antagonistic forces, which often threatened to erupt into open conflict.

If we now consider the emergence of the French nation in conjunction with the emergence of other great European peoples, we should acquire a clearer understanding of the origin of Richelieu's policies. Above all, if we consider the close and tragic relationship that continued for so many centuries between France and England, we will find that certain events stand out in greater relief than when the

Capetian kingdom is regarded in isolation. Consequently, before any attempt is made to establish the underlying causes of Richelieu's Spanish policy and to advance from that to an analysis of his actions in respect to Germany, Italy, the Netherlands, Lorraine and Sweden, it would seem necessary for us to give a brief sketch of the various phases of the relationship between France and England, for of all France's relationships with foreign nations, the one with England was the most intense and the most calamitous.

Throughout his life, Richelieu was deeply involved in historical research. He was constantly looking for precedents and demanded the investigation of treaties and agreements even of remote date which might yield prerogatives to the Crown. Numerous advisers, jurists and historians were at his disposal, and from their vast hoards of deeds and documents they provided the requisite arguments. These historical analogies were a tempting but dangerous field for speculation, but Richelieu appraised them with the cautious precision that typified his whole method. He used them primarily for purposes of rhetorical argument and as a means of reinforcing the proposals he submitted to the King.

He was constantly gathering information, and his enquiries were not restricted to his accredited representatives and special envoys; quite apart from these, he had a great and growing number of agents and private individuals both at Whitehall and in the City of London. The ceaseless flow of material he required for his files covered a wide range of subjects, from historical surveys of the most general kind and comprehensive political reports to details of daily life at the Court and descriptions of its various members.

In the early years of his ministry the European power that most concerned the Cardinal was the newly emerging power of England. The island kingdom constituted a major factor in his planning at that time. And here it must be said that he underestimated the strength of traditional resistance on both sides of the Channel. Although he had expected that the

French Crown would suffer reversals in carrying out its Huguenot policy, he always thought that time would heal these wounds; and the Buckingham episode seemed to him both foolish and pointless. One constant factor he seemed to discern later when he wrote of "the envy England has always borne us." But here he was belittling and distorting a crucial element: the patriotism of the island people.

Dominated by his political aims, his imagination overruled the tremendous historical and confessional differences dividing the two countries; he miscalculated, or rather his wishful thinking drove him too early to action.

Like his predecessor La Vieuville, Richelieu deliberately encouraged the marriage between Louis XIII's sister and Charles I. It is unlikely that he actually planned this marriage as a means of undermining England and temporarily excluding her from European politics, although in fact this was very largely what happened. The deep designs later attributed to him in this connection probably had no substance in fact. There can be little doubt that he regarded this marital bond as a means of drawing the two royal houses closer together. Later, in the thirties, he was of course preoccupied with the fact that the politics of dynastic marriages, which until 1600 had been governed entirely by the feudal laws of succession, were becoming an anachronism, owing to the progressive disappearance of the feudal class which he himself advocated. But this knowledge did not prevent him from using the terms of the marriage treaty as a pretence for French interference in internal English affairs for years. His endeavours contributed to the first really serious crisis ever to face the European monarchies—the deposition and execution of Charles I—and also helped to create a favourable climate for the emergence of Cromwell's dictatorship. Although the Cardinal certainly did not aim at such an outcome, he none the less benefited from it, for the way was now open for France to become the leading Continental power. Richelieu thus had a relatively free hand in Europe and was able to pursue his own policy, above all in

Germany, without having to reckon with really effective English intervention. There was of course always a possibility that the Stuarts might suddenly rally to the Spanish cause.

It is easier to assess both the causes and the development of Anglo-French relations in more recent times—including the War of the Spanish Succession, the wars on the American continent and the battles of Trafalgar and Waterloo—in terms of Richelieu's seventeenth-century political outlook, than in terms of our own. Historically speaking, his occupies a central position, but because of the great loss of national identity sustained by the European peoples of today, ours tends to disregard certain relevant criteria. If we are to grasp the reality of the situation Richelieu was faced with in his dealings with England, we shall have to bear in mind the whole sequence of battles and political tensions, the devastating wars and the silent hostility of uneasy peace, that had been going on for the best part of a thousand years. It is worth while, therefore, to consider a few of the more characteristic phases in the development of these two peoples, who differ so widely in national character, institutions and religious background.

In the early days of the Capetian dynasty, the territory that later constituted France was divided up into seven main areas. Five of these lay in the north: the Duchy of France, which was linked with the monarchy, the Duchy of Normandy, the Duchy of Burgundy, the County of Flanders and the Duchy of Champagne. In the south there was the Duchy of Aquitaine united with the County of Poitiers, and the County of Toulouse. These were the great feudal estates. Each was governed by a powerful feudal lord and each contained within its boundaries a number of smaller estates. Thus the Duchy of France embraced the Counties of Maine and Anjou, Paris and Orléans; the County of Flanders embraced other counties such as Hainaut and Brabant; the Duchy of Normandy embraced the County of Brittany; the Duchy of Burgundy embraced the Counties of Nevers, Charolais and Bourbonnais;

Map 1. France under the Capetians

the Duchy of Aquitaine embraced the Duchy of Gascony and the Counties of Marche, Angoumois, Périgord, Auvergne, etc.; the County of Toulouse embraced the Counties of Rouergue and Quercy and the Viscounties of Narbonne and Béziers, etc. But this was not the end of the subdivisions, for the lords of the lesser estates were also entitled to give land in fee.

The net result of all this was constant local anarchy. Ceaseless feuds were carried on between one province and another, one town and another, one castle and another. And the consequence was devastation, pillage and famine. During the eleventh century, order began very gradually to emerge, but it was only from 1110 that the King succeeded in binding important feudal territories in allegiance to the Crown. The methods used were the same the great feudal lords had used to obtain the allegiance of their vassals.

For centuries the relations between the French and the English were subsumed in the baleful term "hereditary enmity." But both the French and the English had lived under Roman rule and, despite invasions and clan warfare and the sway of feudalism, both these peoples had kept certain traits of Roman origin, which enabled them eventually to establish nationwide order. The island kingdom, of course, did not face the same historical task that fell to the French Crown.

From their modest foothold on the Isle-de-France the French kings battled against opposing authorities, winning new territories only to lose them again, but finally emerging as the rulers of a large territory, which then became the new French state. By contrast, England had already been moulded into a unified kingdom as a result of the Norman Conquest. But in France the movement towards national unity was a slow and arduous process. The French Kings had to endure severe set-backs in their struggle with the feudal lords—especially the English Plantagenets, the most powerful of all the French vassals—and to fight their eastern neighbours as well. France could never really feel secure. Unlike England, whose frontiers were guarded by the sea, she could not afford to disregard the outside world and withdraw within her borders in times of national exhaustion. Scotland, Ireland and Wales repeatedly forced the English to take the field, but even when they had the support of Continental allies, England was never in mortal danger.

A constant and formidable drain on British strength, however, were the claims made by successive English Kings to the crown of France.

Owing to the Norman element in the British national character, there subsisted a spiritual and emotional bond between the two peoples, which was never completely broken even in periods of extreme hostility. From 1066 until well into the fourteenth century England had two languages. Apart from Latin, French was the language used by the ruling class, in government, and in the universities. The language of the Conquerors gave ground only very gradually, but its eventual assimilation with Anglo-Saxon led to the emergence of English as a language of immense vitality and range.

The dramatic five-hundred-year period following the Norman Conquest is usually conceived of and subsumed as what has come to be known as the Hundred Years War. Yet that war was only a continuation of the long series of battles for sovereignty between the two nations, from the eleventh to the fourteenth century. The extremely complex grounds cited and fiercely upheld by both sides were based on old marriages, hereditary claims and hereditary rights.

Philip I of France (1060–1108) had begun the unsuccessful fight against William the Conqueror until the latter's death in 1087. During the reign of Philip's son and successor, Louis VI (1108–1137), largely owing to the impetus given by his friend and adviser Suger, the great Abbot of Saint-Denis and an early opponent of feudal despotism, an almost mystical sense of national unity began to make itself felt in France. It was particularly evident when the German Emperor Henry V, an ally of England's, threatened Reims. On that occasion a powerful French army gathered round the oriflamme, the sacred banner of St Denis, and saved the town.

Louis VI's son, Louis VII (1137–1180), surnamed the Crusader, married Eleanor, Duchess of Guyenne, the daughter of the late Duke of Aquitaine and the granddaughter of the first troubadour. As a result of this marriage Louis VII stood to inherit the rich lands of Guyenne, Poitou and Gascony. Eleanor accompanied her husband to Syria, and there she was censured for loose conduct, in particular for having entered into a relationship with her own uncle, Raymond of Antioch. These charges led to the dissolution of the marriage in 1152.

Shortly afterwards this mighty heiress married Duke Henry of Anjou-Plantagenet, later Henry II of England. Henry inherited Anjou, Maine and Touraine from his father and Normandy from his mother. By his marriage to Eleanor he acquired Guyenne, Poitou and Gascony. The entire domains of the houses of Normandy, Anjou and Aquitaine had become his. When he came to the throne he not only founded the dynasty of the Plantagenets, who reigned in England from 1154 to 1399, he also brought the Continental territories of his inheritance to the English Crown. His successors upheld England's claim to these territories until after the reign of Louis XIII.

Eleanor bore her English husband five sons and three daughters. But over the course of the years she was to prove his most dangerous adversary. She first encouraged and then led her growing sons in their revolt against their father, and he retaliated by making her his prisoner. But Henry did not give up his claim to Eleanor's inheritance. In pursuit of it he declared war on Louis VII of France, to whom he had once sworn an oath of allegiance.

In his seventeenth political maxim Richelieu stated:

"The English lay claim to Guyenne and La Rochelle both by descent from Queen Eleanor, the only daughter of the Duke of Aquitaine, who, having been repudiated by King

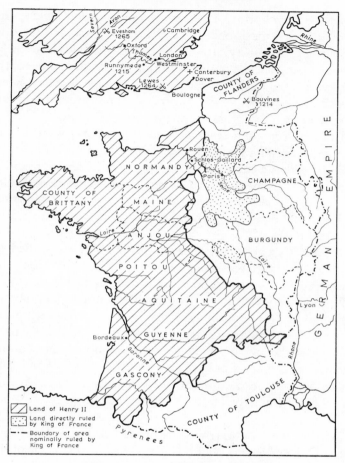

Map 2. France and England in the time of
Henry II of Anjou-Plantagenet

Louis the Young [Louis VII], subsequently married Henry
[II] of England, and also by the terms of the treaty of
Brétigny. Consequently, it would be dangerous to allow them
to gain possession of our harbours, lest they should renew
these claims."

Of the sons born to Eleanor of Aquitaine and Henry, the third, Richard the Lionheart, and the youngest, John, made their mark in history. John's reign was to have extremely grave consequences for the future of the English monarchy. He was his father's favourite son, and on one occasion King Henry expressed both his compassion and his affection for him by calling him "John Lackland." But his father's affection did not prevent him from becoming a driving force in his mother's conspiracy against the King. John, always a clever and sometimes a successful tactician, used his irresponsibility adroitly to his personal advantage; it remains remarkable, however, that although his character traits brought him to a bad end, the disastrous consequences of his selfishness led to crucial reforms.

Henry II's two eldest sons, William and Henry, died in 1156 and 1183 respectively. In 1189 Richard the Lionheart succeeded to the throne. Physically immensely vigorous and full of life, he joined the Crusades and did not remain long in England; his brother John exploited his absence by attempting to seize the throne. Although Eleanor took Richard's part, John none the less appeared to be succeeding in this venture. Richard meanwhile was in Sicily, then in the Holy Land, and finally he became the prisoner of Duke Leopold of Austria and then of Emperor Henry VI in Germany.

Richard the Lionheart was the brother-in-law of Henry the Lion, Duke of Saxony and Bavaria, the great opponent of the Hohenstaufens. At the end of the sixties Henry's marriage to his first wife, Clementia of Zähringen, was declared invalid at his instigation, whereupon he married the English princess Matilda, who greatly influenced him and prevailed upon her husband to endorse the policy pursued by the Hanseatic League in the interests of its Baltic and North Sea trade. This Hanseatic policy, together with his own *Drang nach Osten*, brought Henry the Lion into conflict with many of the princes of the Empire and even with the Emperor himself.

At first he had supported Emperor Barbarossa's Italian policy, and in 1172 had even accompanied him on a pilgrimage to Jerusalem. But he was accused of having conspired with the Byzantine Emperor Manuel I, and when Barbarossa's son Henry summoned Henry the Lion's help against the Lombards in 1176, he refused. As a consequence the Imperial army was defeated at Legnano. In 1180 Barbarossa and his princes proceeded against Henry the Lion, placing him under the ban of the Empire and confiscating his duchies. In the end he was obliged to flee the country and live in England.

In 1174 Matilda had borne him a son, who grew up at the English Court and subsequently became Emperor Otto IV. It was not until Barbarossa's son had succeeded him as Henry VI that Henry the Lion was able to return to the Empire. The English marriage contracted by this German prince had its repercussions by way of the Guelphs until quite late in the history of the Hanoverian house, although not so incisively as the marriage some centuries later between Frederick V of the County Palatine and the daughter of James I of England.

Richard the Lionheart and John Lackland

Before departing for the Holy Land, Richard the Lionheart appointed Chancellor William Longchamp, Bishop of Ely, as his deputy; thanks to the Queen-Mother and the loyal barons, it finally proved possible to buy Richard's release. On March 13, 1194, he returned to England, but on May 12th of the same year he was again fighting in Normandy against Philip Augustus of France, who was then gaining ground in his war with the English. Richard had succeeded in stemming the tide when, in 1199, he was mortally wounded by an arrow in the siege of Chalus, near Limoges. From that moment, all the advantages he had won were lost again.

Then John came to the throne, despite the fact that Arthur of Brittany, the young son of his late elder brother, Geoffrey, had a more rightful claim to the succession. Homage was actually paid to this fifteen-year-old boy in Anjou, Maine and Touraine, but it proved short-lived. In the year 1200 he fell into his uncle's hands and was murdered probably by John himself. Following this deed Philip Augustus of France brought an accusation of murder against John before a court of the Peers of France. He was found guilty and ordered to forfeit all his French estates.

However, before we go on to deal with the execution of this judgement and the ensuing events, it should first be mentioned that shortly after his succession John had fallen out with his nobles over the question of their military commitment to the Crown. He had also entered into a far graver dispute with the chapter of Canterbury over the choice of a new Archbishop. In the end it was Pope Innocent III who made the appointment; he nominated Stephen Langton, who was then resident in Rome. The monks of Canterbury approved the Pope's choice, whereupon King John ordered them expelled from their monastery. The Pope immediately authorized three bishops to place England under an interdict, and at the same time he permitted the English barons to take up arms against their King. The English bishops, loyal to the Curia, fled the kingdom. But the feudal nobles did not dare to fight, for John commanded a strong army of mercenaries and he had also taken the precaution of seizing as hostages a considerable number of children from the foremost families of the land. In order to cover the cost of his military preparations, John ordered large-scale confiscation of Church property.

Then, in 1209, Innocent III excommunicated him. John's initial reaction was to have a close watch kept on all harbours to prevent the papal bull from reaching England. But Philip Augustus of France was only too pleased to intervene as the Pope's executor. At this point in his affairs, the hard-pressed King of England decided—at a time when the whole of the Western world was imbued with the spirit of the Crusades—to seek an alliance with the Mohammedans. But when his emissaries approached the Emir el Hassis in Spain, they found him unaccommodating. After such "wickedness," Innocent III promptly decreed John's dethronement. He absolved all Englishmen from their allegiance to the Crown and called upon all Christian princes to drive out the godless tyrant. Langton was sent to France to Philip Augustus to inform him that he would be granted full remission of sins if he sent his armies to enforce the papal decree.

A great French army was immediately formed, and ships were concentrated for the transportation of the invasion force. But the English showed their abiding quality, as on many subsequent occasions, by a victory at sea, in which they sank a large part of Philip Augustus' improvised armada. Then King John appeared at Dover with 60,000 men. There the papal legate, Pandulf, sought out the King, whom he found undermined by his doubts about the loyalty of his people. Pandulf emphasized the invincible strength of the French army and the progress already made in the preparations for a new French fleet. He presented to him the inveterate hatred of his own barons and the wrath of the English exiles, who were working for his downfall in every country in Europe. He is even said to have quoted a prophecy made by an English hermit, Peter, according to which the King was to lose his crown before the Feast of the Ascension. The legate demanded that all the exiled priests, especially Langton, be allowed to return, and that full compensation be made for the losses sustained by both clerics and laity during the period of the interdict.

John spent the whole of May 14, 1213, closeted with the legate. On May 15th, he rose early and went to the Church of the Knights Templar in Dover, where he kneeled before the Pope's representative, held out both hands to him and, to the amazement of nearly all those present, declared himself the Pope's vassal. He then handed the legate a document, which stated that John, King of England and Ireland, in atonement for his sins against God and the Holy Church, of his own free will and with the agreement of the estates of his realm, delivered up the kingdom of England and Ireland to Pope Innocent III and his successors for ever, in order that he and his successors might hold it in fee from the Holy Church. He also undertook to pay a yearly tribute. No sooner had the legate concluded his triumphant mission than he recrossed the Channel, proceeded to the great army camp near Boulogne and informed Philip Augustus that, since England now belonged to the Curia, the King of France was no longer at liberty to throw even a rock at her. Philip Augustus reminded the legate of the vast sums he had spent at the Pope's behest in preparing for war, but the legate remained unmoved. At this Philip Augustus decided to disregard this new Papal command and to attack as soon as possible. But he fell out with the Count of Flanders, who went over to the English and helped them to win a second naval battle against the French, thus forcing Philip Augustus to abandon his plans for an invasion. It was then up to John to form a powerful alliance and invade France. Again he called his barons to arms, but they refused to board his ships until he had recalled all the exiles. John was forced to yield. Langton and the monks of Canterbury returned.

John still counted on the support of his nobles and put to sea. But the nobles declared that their period of service had expired and did not follow him.

John then placed his trust in his mercenaries and his allies, the Duke of Brabant, the Count of Holland, the Counts of Flanders and Boulogne and above all in the German Emperor, who was the one ally able to lend prestige to his venture.

At this point, Otto IV, the son of Henry the Lion and Princess Matilda of England, must claim our attention.

Guelphs and Ghibellines

At the death of Henry VI, Holy Roman Emperor and King of Germany, his three-year-old son Frederick by the Norman princess Constance, had already been elected. He was now passed over by a majority of the German princes, who elected in his stead another Hohenstaufen, Philip of Swabia. This, in turn, gave rise to a movement in favour of the Guelphs, and Otto the Guelph was put forward as an anti-king and crowned in Aachen. Philip and Otto, both bearers of the elective German crown, tried to obtain recognition from Innocent III. But the Pope vacillated. His principal interest in the matter was to safeguard the Curia's territorial possessions in Italy. In order to win the Pope over, Otto, with the backing of the Kings of England and Denmark, undertook to renounce all Imperial fiefs in Italy to which the Holy See laid claim.

Despite this offer it was Philip, the Hohenstaufen, who in 1204 finally gained the upper hand, but he was murdered on November 11, 1208, and Otto then received general recognition. In 1209 he journeyed to Italy, where he agreed to respect the Pope's choice of bishops and gave a solemn undertaking to defer to the Vatican in all religious questions. In this way he attained, for the moment, his objective and on October 4, 1209, was crowned Holy Roman Emperor in Rome. But from then on he began to break his promises. He took the provinces of Spoleto and Ancona, which were united with the Vatican territories; he attacked Apulia, which belonged to the King of Sicily, Frederick of Hohenstaufen, and began to prepare for the invasion of Sicily itself. At this point, on November 18, 1210, the Pope excommunicated him. He relieved the German princes from their oath of allegiance and advocated—however unwillingly, for he feared the union of Sicily and Germany— the nomination of Frederick as an anti-king. In 1212 Otto hurried back to Germany. In the following year he laid waste to the territory of the Landgrave of Thuringia and drove Ottokar of Bohemia from his realm. But despite, or perhaps because of, these acts of violence, his rival, Frederick of Hohenstaufen, was received with jubilation by his followers and soon gained the ascendancy.

In order to help his English uncle King John against Philip

Augustus and uphold John's right to his mother's inheritance of Aquitaine and Poitou, and particularly in order to regain the favour of England's new feudal lord, the Pope, Otto joined the great coalition against Philip Augustus.

On July 27, 1214, the armies met near Bouvines, north-east of Lille, where the King of France won one of the greatest and most fateful victories in the whole history of medieval warfare. But it was not only a victory for the French dynasty. It was also a victory for the Hohenstaufen, for Frederick was allied to Philip Augustus, and when John and the Emperor Otto and all their followers had been defeated, Frederick of Hohenstaufen was crowned Holy Roman Emperor in Aachen in 1215.

Once the decision he had sought as England's ally had gone against him, the domineering Otto withdrew to his own Duchy of Brunswick. He was now powerless, isolated and cordially disliked. The victory at Bouvines was the outcome of one of the rare historical instances of a Franco-German alliance.

In 1184 Philip Augustus had conquered the County of Vermandois in Flanders, and while Richard the Lionheart was a prisoner in Germany he had taken the Norman Vexin. In 1204 he had taken possession of Normandy, Anjou, Maine, Touraine and Poitou. But his principal objective remained the invasion of England. By this time his newly formed State was already far removed from the medieval concept of universalism. As in 1124, when Reims was threatened, so too after Bouvines there was a strong patriotic movement in France.

The End of John Lackland and the Great Reforms

After his defeat, John returned to England in his customary blind rage. Claiming that his nobles had abandoned him, he marched through the kingdom, burning and laying waste wherever he passed. But Langton, who had also returned home, opposed the King. He excommunicated all those who had participated in the King's vengeful acts and eventually John was obliged to summon the great barons to appear before him once again. Meanwhile, however, Langton had already convened an assembly in London, and when the King entered the hall he found the Archbishop at the head of the assembled barons with Henry I's Charter in his hand. It was not the first charter England had received following the Norman Conquest, nor was it to be the last.

Why all these details of remote history? Because they allow us to recognize the indissoluble links connecting many of the events of the distant past with the conditions and attitudes prevalent under Louis XIII, James I and Charles I and directly influencing Anglo-French relations at that time. Indeed, these remote events conditioned the general character of state policy long after those monarchs had disappeared from the scene.

King John's reign, which we have dealt with at some length, demonstrates, first, the consequences of the King's decision to cede to the Vatican rights of sovereignty over England; second, the reaction of the English people to this decision; and third, the great advances in constitutional law the estates were able to carry out because of the popular reaction.

The following incident shows how long the English continued to fear papal claims:

Between 1592 and 1617 the English ambassador Thomas Edmunds carried out a number of missions in France. James I forbade him to visit Richelieu in his home because the Cardinal refused, on grounds of rank, to offer the ambassador his hand and was quite determined that he should not precede him when entering or leaving the room.

Richelieu, commenting on this incident in his Memoirs, said that James I wished to prevent a situation from arising

"in which he would have been acknowledging papal superiority and, as he himself later said [to Châteauneuf, the French ambassador in London], sanctioning Bellarmine's doctrine, according to which Cardinals were higher in rank than the Kings themselves.

"He was made even more sensitive on this point by virtue of the fact that the Popes claimed that they had rights to England and insisted that England had been a papal dependency ever since John Lackland surrendered it to them in order to obtain their authority to drive out Louis the Dauphin, son of Philip Augustus, who had been called and chosen by the English estates and had taken possession of the kingdom."

This comment of Richelieu's is a valuable one, for it shows the extent to which England's subordination to Rome, agreed to by John in the thirteenth century, lived on in the minds of Kings and statesmen of the seventeenth century.

But what really matters for us is that we should establish the connection between John's errors and the truly epoch-making advances in constitutional law outlined below, from which England's special character and her special position among the nations of the world have derived.

In 1071 William the Conqueror had entered into a mutual contract with his nobles whereby he undertook for his part to redress all grievances brought before him. For the Anglo-Saxons he restored the laws of Edward the Confessor. When Henry I was proclaimed King, his oldest brother, Duke Robert of Normandy, claimed the throne by right of primogeniture. In order to obtain the support of both the Norman and the Saxon barons against his brother, Henry invited them to confirm by oath a new charter similar to the one guaranteed by his father. It was this document that Langton brought before the London assembly a hundred years later. Henry's successor, King Stephen, had given like guarantees and conceded certain rights to the Church. In 1154 Henry II in his turn renewed Stephen's charter, and had a copy placed in every church in the land. A few copies are still extant. But the charter that won lasting fame as the "Magna Carta" was the one to which John Lackland was forced to fix his seal.

Before the King actually signed this charter, however, much

was yet to happen. Once John became his vassal, the Pope was no longer interested in furthering the cause of the English barons. Their great leader, Fitz Peter, died in October 1213, but under the leadership of Langton the barons continued to press the King hard. Soon after Easter, 1215, John rejected the demands they made at Brackley and was supported in this action by the papal legate, who insisted that Langton should excommunicate the rebel leaders. This Langton refused to do. Opposition to the King then developed into civil war. The barons were repulsed at Northampton but welcomed by the citizens of Bedford and then London. With the towns behind them, their victory was assured and the remaining barons of England flocked to join them. On June 15, 1215, John granted Magna Carta at Runnymede.

As was only to be expected, however, no sooner had he given the pledge than he tried to retract it again. His mercenaries, whom he should have dismissed according to the terms of the Charter, encouraged him in this, adding fuel to the flame of his anger. John increased his levies. With this the treaty was broken and civil war broke out again. At that point the barons received a bitter blow, for the Pope himself suspended the Charter, which he declared had been obtained under duress and was consequently invalid. He instructed Langton to dissolve the confederation of barons, and on this occasion went so far as to threaten him personally with excommunication. Langton journeyed to Rome, where he was repudiated. Meanwhile John's forces were growing, and one castle after the other fell into his hands.

At this desperate juncture, when John was about to take a terrible revenge, the English barons sent a delegation to Philip Augustus. Driven to extreme measures, they offered the Crown of England to his son, Prince Louis of France. Philip Augustus accepted their offer. This was the incident Richelieu reported in his Memoirs.

The French heir-apparent succeeded in assembling a strong army, thanks principally to his wife, Blanche of Castile. He landed at Sandwich and marched on London, which he entered on June 2, 1216, to a friendly welcome from the populace. There he promised the rebels that he would reign according to the Charter and would restore their lands to them. But several of the English barons were already inclined to look upon this "appeal to the foreigner" as a slight to their honour and began to waver.

As long as Pope Innocent III was alive, John could count on his support, and Louis's war in England proved a slow business. As the royal fortresses continued to hold out against him, mistrust and indecision grew in the rebel camp. Several of the English barons were negotiating with the King. At that time John was north of the Wash, which he proposed to cross with his army. By the time he reached the ford, his soldiers were already safely across, but a long row of carts laden with his treasure and provisions were carried away on the rising tide. When he saw this mishap, the King fell into one of his violent rages and briefly lost consciousness. He was carried to the Cistercian monastery at Swineshead, where he is said to have drunk great quantities of beer before being taken on to Newark. There he just had time to confess, name his son Henry as his successor and dictate a letter to the newly elected Pope Honorius in which he commended his children to him. Then, on October 19, 1216, he died.

Henry III

On October 28, 1216, the papal legate crowned John's ten-year-old son Henry III of England. The child was required to ratify John's acknowledgement of papal sovereignty and it was as a vassal state that England was entrusted to the guidance of the Earl of Pembroke, who was appointed Lord Protector. Pembroke's first action in his new capacity was to reissue Magna Carta. The remaining English nobles then deserted the French prince. When John died, their resentment died with him: the newly crowned child was their legitimate

King. Prince Louis's situation deteriorated rapidly, and in the end he found himself besieged in London. He asked his father for help, but Philip Augustus did not want to fall out with the Pope. Louis's wife, Blanche of Castile, succeeded in sending fresh troops, but the transport was intercepted by the English. This spelt the end of the Capetian enterprise in England. On September 11, 1217, Louis signed a treaty with the Lord Protector that enabled him to return to France on tolerable conditions.

At this stage England's internal development was already totally different from the kind of development that had taken place on the Continent, especially in France.

Magna Carta

In no Christian land was the dispute between the Crown and the nobles so consistent or stubborn as in England.

When—chiefly in the nineteenth century—the concept of popular rights acquired the romantic connotation it now has, Magna Carta came to be regarded as a legendary symbol of the English Constitution. This was one of the factors leading to the emergence of the anachronistic conception of England as an age-old democracy. In point of fact, however, as we have already indicated, the sixty-three articles of the Charter were principally concerned with the ratification of long-existent rights and privileges together with subsequent amendments and additions introduced since the Conquest, none of which could be said to transcend the essential character of feudalism. What the Charter did was to state explicitly the limits of the King's power in the Anglo-Norman feudal monarchy. Another major point was the requirement that taxes were to be levied only by "general consent." However, it is quite evident from the full text of this provision that what was really meant was the "general consent" of the feudal barons. The document also contained provisions of great and lasting importance concerning the separation of ecclesiastical from secular law. The

Charter also guaranteed to "freemen"—but not the "unfree"—
a lawful trial before being punished for any offence. The
Charter ratified the privileges enjoyed by the town of London
and gave foreigners the right to trade in England. Thus the
Englishman's inalienable constitutional rights appear as both
the inheritance of the past and the foundation of the future.

In France, on the other hand, the early influence of Roman
law had produced a tendency towards systemization and
legalism, and statute law was developed at the expense of
common law. In thirteenth-century England the *corpus juris*
had been rejected as "dangerous."

And so in respect of their national institutions these two
countries developed along entirely different lines. The same
was true of their relations to the Curia. France established a
positive relationship as between equals. The Gallic tempera-
ment was quick to counter any apparent or real attempt on the
part of the Church to interfere in French affairs. By contrast,
England's relationship to Rome was far more extreme,
ranging from total submission to total separation.

To recapitulate: the two crucial events were England's
acceptance of papal sovereignty on the one hand and the
proclamation of Magna Carta on the other. Both were to
exercise a decisive influence on the development of the English
Constitution, the English Church and England's relationship
to the Continent. After King John's time the desire for emancipation from Curial tutelage gained momentum in England.

Innocent III and Philip Augustus

By his policies Innocent III lent an added impetus to the
powerful movements that, although not immediately apparent
at a political level, emerged later in a number of different
forms when popular feeling against the Roman Church
finally erupted. The Curia's attempt to assert authority over
all the Kings of the Christian world eventually led to dire
consequences. The Pope interfered in the internal affairs of all

Christian states, he treated their rulers as his subjects, he hurled interdicts and anathemas and finally exhausted the awe of those instruments of spiritual dominion. He sought to extend his suzerainty wherever possible and to make all Christian Kings his vassals. England was not an isolated case. The kingdoms of Sicily, Denmark and Sweden had also acknowledged the Pope's supremacy. Sancho of Portugal, like his predecessor, Alfonso I, paid the Pope tribute, as did King Peter of Aragón, who in 1204 had laid his crown on the high altar of St Peter's and was then crowned by Innocent III.

Philip Augustus offered resistance, whereupon the Pope laid France under an interdict. He received a proud answer for his pains. When he tried to interfere in France's English policy, the French King told him not to meddle in matters that concerned no one but himself and the King of England. And when Innocent III temporarily supported Otto of Brunswick, Philip Augustus wrote to him:

"I am surprised that you should continue to support a Prince whose family interests make him an enemy of your lands. Your Holiness must realize that by the ill-considered support which you are affording this man you will appear to be not only inflicting an injury on my nation but offering an insult to all Christian Kings. If you persevere in this policy I shall take the necessary counter-measures."

Much later the Pope was to write to Philip Augustus: "It is not without a sense of shame that I tell you of my troubles, for you had often warned me." From the tone of these exchanges between the French Court and the Curia, it is quite evident that the day when the Holy See was to become a pawn of French foreign policy was not far removed.

Philip Augustus' Successors

Following Philip Augustus' forceful reign and the early death of his son Louis VIII, who as Prince Louis had very nearly succeeded in establishing a personal union between France and England, the French feudal lords rebelled in 1226. On this occasion their revolt, which continued until 1232, was directed against Louis VIII's widow and her eleven-year-old son, Louis IX (1226–1270), later called St Louis.

The rebellious French nobles, taking a leaf from the English barons' book, entered into an alliance with England. They were not opposing the French Crown as such, but had risen against the Queen-Mother, a lady of Castilian origin, insisting that she must cede her powers as Regent and that her eldest son must make way for his uncle, the Count of Boulogne. At the same time, however, these feudal lords were also intent on exacting revenge for any personal offences to themselves and on gratifying their desire for wealth and power. As a result they threatened to destroy all that had been accomplished for the monarchy.

The leader of this revolt was the Breton Pierre Mauclerc, a Capetian of the junior line. He and his confederates placed all their hopes on King Henry III of England, who was to learn within his own borders what the great nobles of French extraction were capable of doing to a *"primus inter pares."* In fact, from the very beginning of his reign Henry was so hard pressed by his barons that he was unable to come to the aid of the French rebels in time, and so let one of the most favourable opportunities for a decisive victory in France slip through his fingers.

Almost all the great feudal nobles had taken up arms against the Queen-Mother and they were joined by many of the members of the younger branches of the royal house, who were also to rise against the Crown centuries later in the Frondes. At the same time a campaign of slander was launched against Blanche of Castile, which proved far more dangerous than the tumult raised by the warrior lords. In every corner of the land the troubadours—who were also the reporters of their day— impeached the Queen-Mother's honour. She was said to be an "extortioner" who was "bleeding" the French people, a "bloodsucker" who had transferred her profits to her native land beyond the Pyrenees, an "adultress who had poisoned her young husband" and who had been the mistress of her former adherent, Count Thibaut of Champagne, who at that juncture seemed to be veering towards Mauclerc again.

Both under Philip Augustus and during Louis VIII's brief reign, Blanche of Castile had distinguished herself by her energetic support of her husband in his actions against the English, and after his death she demonstrated quite astonishing powers of statesmanship. It was she who prepared her son for his destined place as one of the greatest of all French Kings.

Although a widow harassed on all sides, she overcame the combined power of the feudal nobility and discredited their slanders. In her struggle she was able to count on the support of the Curia, for Curial policy had shifted yet again and Rome needed a strong France as a bulwark against the Hohenstaufens. But it was the Hohenstaufen Emperor Frederick II, the friend of Philip Augustus, who proved Blanche of Castile's most faithful protector. He gave her his word that he would not allow any German prince to side with her enemies: the Emperor had not forgotten Bouvines. Subsequently St Louis requited Frederick's attitude towards his mother, but one of his brothers, the Count of Anjou, was to make short shrift of this family debt of gratitude.

Meanwhile the rebellious vassals awaited the English landing with extreme impatience. It was then that the Third Estate spontaneously rose to an impassioned defence of Louis IX and his mother—something quite new to French history. Blanche of Castile had had her son crowned and anointed in Reims with all possible speed, after which she removed him to the safety of Montlhéry and then to Paris.

Doubtless the rebels were restrained by awe, the strength of which is difficult to appreciate today, from declaring open war on the Lord's anointed. Instead, they invaded Champagne, the territory of Count Thibaut, whose support for their cause had not been unequivocal. Thanks to the backing of a broad section of the French people, Blanche succeeded in negotiating with one group of rebels while containing the other by military means. It was an extraordinary achievement. In the end Thibaut remained loyal to her and she freed his territory without recourse to arms.

Richelieu often spoke with admiration of the Castilian stateswoman. On the occasion of Louis XIII's coronation he wrote: "Marie de' Medici has acted like a second Blanche of Castile." At the time of the conspiracy of princes, he again said that Louis XIII's mother had drawn strength from the example set by Blanche of Castile, the mother of St Louis. Her memory was still green in the minds of Frenchmen in the seventeenth century. But then her achievements as Regent, wife and mother had been of an exceptionally high order.

The rebels continued to look to England for help. But the English barons denied their King the forces he required to intervene successfully on the Continent. When he did finally land in France and set up his headquarters in Nantes, his army was so weak that he did not dare to attack and soon he was given many good reasons for returning home in all haste. Deserted by England, the confederation of feudal rebels broke up. Mauclerc made one last attempt along lines the Regent herself was to pursue with such great skill: he tried to unite his own daughter with the Count of Champagne, against whom he had been fighting only a short time before. But the Queen-Mother quickly intervened and led the unreliable Thibaut, whom she herself had rescued, back to the path of duty and absolute allegiance. She had been successful on every score and the French monarchy drew tremendous strength from her victory.

By the terms of the treaty of Meaux, which Blanche concluded with the Count of Toulouse in 1229, the Count was required to raze the walls of his capital city and thirty other towns in his province of Languedoc, to allow the citadel of Toulouse to be occupied by royal troops for a period of ten years and to persecute the "heretics" within his borders—

the Albigenses—with fire and sword. This provision, carried out under the control of the Inquisition, was to bring great bloodshed and misery. The Count was also required to make his peace with the Church and do penance by fighting in Palestine for five years.

But the most important consequences of Blanche's regency arose from her policy of dynastic marriages.

She had borne her husband ten children, several of whom died in childhood. Of her sons, St Louis, her first-born, Robert, Jean, Alphonse, Philippe and Charles survived. The only surviving daughter entered a convent.

She married her eldest son, Louis, to Margaret, the daughter of Raymond Berenguer, the Count of Barcelona and Provence; her youngest son, Charles-Etienne, she married to Béatrice, Margaret's younger sister. Béatrice was Berenguer's favourite daughter and his heiress. As a result of this marriage Charles-Etienne acquired Provence in January 1246, and in May of the same year his brother, the King, ratified the provision in Louis VIII's will whereby Charles was to receive the Counties of Anjou and Maine.

As a matchmaker Blanche of Castile showed astonishing intelligence and foresight. Her achievements in this sphere were to make themselves felt far into the future and far beyond the borders of France.

The Counts of Arles, who had once ruled over the major part of Provence, had been able to make themselves independent of the French Crown because a large part of their territory on the eastern bank of the Rhône was an Imperial fief. But in 1112 the male line died out and Count Raymond Berenguer inherited their lands.

The Counts of Toulouse had been rivals of the Berenguers and the two families had fought one another over a considerable period. In 1125 a treaty was concluded giving the Berenguers the southern part of the territory including the towns of Aix, Arles, Marseille and Nice and the County of Forcalquier, which skirted the Durance, while the house of

Toulouse received Valence, Die, Orange and Venaissin. Avignon remained a condominium. Then, in 1166, the Berenguers united Provence with Aragón. In Richelieu's day this was still an important political factor in the struggle between France and Spain. But with the death of Raymond Berenguer V in 1245, the male line of the Berenguers came to an end, and through his marriage to Béatrice, St Louis's youngest brother acquired Provence.

Robert, who was born in 1216 and fell in Egypt in 1250, received the County of Artois under the terms of his father's will. He married Matilda, the daughter of Henry II of Brabant.

Blanche of Castile's seventh child, Alphonse, who inherited Poitou from his father, married Jeanne, the daughter of Raymond VII of Toulouse in 1241. When Raymond died, the Capetian prince inherited through his wife the greater part of Languedoc together with Venaissin, which lay on the eastern bank of the Rhône, and proceeded to administer these territories in an exemplary manner.

Louis IX (St Louis)

Like Louis XIV, Louis IX was faced with a violent revolt of the French nobles during the early years of his reign. The monarchic authority established between 1182 and 1226 by Philip Augustus and his son, Louis VIII, had been bitterly opposed by the feudal lords. Under Louis IX their opposition was finally subdued. By negotiating with the dispossessed nobles Louis won legal title to the possessions Philip Augustus had won by force of arms. Some of the nobles sold their rights to him, others agreed to recognize the King's brothers as their successors. In a treaty concluded in 1258, the King of Aragón gave up all his fiefs in Languedoc in return for an undertaking by France that she would renounce her rights of sovereignty over the Counties of Roussillon, Bésalu, Cerdagne and Barcelona. These exchanges, on which many legal claims were subsequently based, paved the way for the strict separation of

Spain from France that was to follow. But the King of Aragón still retained control of Montpellier.

In the following year, 1259, Henry III of England renounced all rights to Normandy, Anjou, Maine, Touraine, Brittany and Poitou. In return he received, as feudal tenures, Quercy, Agenais, Limousin and that part of Saintonge lying beyond the Charente.

The French Crown did not retain direct control over all these provinces. Some of them were given to Louis IX's younger brothers by way of royal grants.

At that time the French monarchy still had a feudal structure. Its administrative machine was rudimentary and the only way for the King to retain control of newly acquired Crown territories was to give them in fee to various members of his family, thus setting up new dynasties. Wherever they went these new dynasties introduced the language and customs of France. And if the Capetian princes subsequently enlarged their territories, then this was also of benefit to the French Crown.

At the end of Louis IX's reign the monarchy exercised direct control over the Duchy of France, Vermandois, Valois, Normandy, Touraine, Maine and Berry, over the County of Mâcon and the eastern part of Languedoc, and through the medium of eight separate dynasties, all related by blood to the royal family, it also exercised indirect control over Burgundy, Brittany, Boulonnais, Artois, Poitou, Auvergne, the County of Toulouse, Anjou, Provence, Nivernais and Bourbonnais.

Louis IX was a great legislator. He was the most just and devout of the Christian rulers of his day, his policies and victories strengthened the monarchy, and he brought order to the kingdom and succeeded in establishing a truly Christian *imperium*. Drawing on his mother's experience, he entered into a dual and equal alliance with the clergy and the bourgeoisie on the one hand and the feudal lords on the other, thus counteracting a force that had vitiated French society in the past, when the nobles, with their traditional expectancy of preferential treatment, had succeeded in isolating each of these groups from one another and all three from the Crown. Louis IX paved the way for a rapprochement between these different social groups by convening the Estates-General. Moreover, in direct contrast to King John of England, he limited the claims the Vatican was entitled to make on the French clergy, especially those relating to the imposition of taxes, by the proclamation of a Pragmatic Sanction and by appointing the King of France as the temporal lord and protector of the French priesthood. He allowed the French towns to appoint their own municipal authorities and to conduct their own domestic affairs. Only in respect of the administration of justice and of military service were they directly subservient to the Crown.

But Louis's most significant achievement was in imposing royal justice on the feudal nobility.

The law he introduced to deal with private warfare, which he called "*quarantaine le roy,*" bears the unmistakable imprint of his personality. Under its terms nobles who declared war on one another were required to wait for a period of forty days before taking up arms, in order that the weaker of the two contenders might appeal to the King if he wished, in which case the dispute would be settled by a royal court and not by force of arms. But Louis IX, not content with substituting the principle of justice for that most fundamental of medieval principles, the feud, went even further by introducing courts of appeal. He created the four great *bailliages*: Sens in the Duchy of France, Amiens in Vermandois, Mâcon in Burgundy and Saint-Pierre-le-Moûtier in the Auvergne. These courts of appeal were superior to the local courts of justice.

The judicial Parlement, which was perfected during the thirteenth century and became one of the principal institutions of the French monarchy during the entire course of the Ancien Régime, had its origins in these same courts of appeal; gradually it came to replace the feudal Parlement. After

Louis's return from his first Crusade in 1254, under his encouragement the Parlements began to convene regularly, in some case annually. Since the Parlement had in fact become the supreme royal court, it was attended by princes of the blood and by officers of the Crown such as the Chancellor and the Constable. When legislative and procedural matters became more complex, specialists in legal matters, the so-called *légistes*, were recruited from the universities. They had no actual voice in the proceedings and no deliberative function. They simply prepared the cases for the barons and prelates, who then passed judgement.

Louis IX's reign saw the emergence of an administrative body under the Crown. The senior officials were the *sénéchal*, the *bailli*, the *prévôt-général* and the *officiers du roi*, whose duties had already been partially defined under Philip Augustus and Louis VIII. Louis IX invested these representatives of the Crown with rights and privileges similar to those enjoyed by the Counts and Viscounts under the two preceding dynasties, especially under Charlemagne. The institution of this new privileged class eventually led to the downfall of the lesser feudal nobility. Louis's achievements in this sphere were developed extensively during the reign of Philip IV.

The age of Louis was still overshadowed by the tremendous struggle between the Guelphs and the Ghibellines, between the Curia and the Hohenstaufen Emperor Frederick II. Louis IX was King of France at a time when the ancient structure of Christianity was undergoing the most radical transformation.

Today this great French King is still visibly, indeed audibly, present. Few of the great figures of the late Middle Ages were described by their contemporaries with such penetration, few found such a chronicler as Joinville, such an observant critic as Fra Salimbene. St Louis has become a central and an enduring image in the mind of a great people, an image that time and again through the centuries has emitted a radiance beyond compare. He was an eleventh-century Christian living in the middle of the thirteenth century, a fearless and blameless knight, strict in his conduct, yet cheerful and spirited in his dealings with others. He possessed the highest qualities of kingship, shown particularly in the sphere of foreign policy. He fulfilled all his obligations within this sphere with untiring zeal and without once exceeding the bounds of the moral code of his day. Of the territories he had inherited from his ancestors, he retained only those to which he considered he had a just claim. What he held, however, he held with a grip of steel. In everything he did he enhanced to the greatest possible degree the prestige, the dignity and the effectiveness of the French monarchy.

He was the greatest landowner in his kingdom. The old Crown lands of Picardy, the Ile-de-France and Berry were augmented by the territories of Normandy, Anjou, Maine, Touraine and Saintonge, which had all been taken from the Plantagenets. Auvergne, the legacy of the Montfort family, and the territory previously held by the Seneschal of Beaucaire were also acquired by the Crown. The great feudal estates still existed, but by a series of treaties and dynastic marriages Louis's mother had already brought many of them—Flanders, Brittany, Champagne, Burgundy and Languedoc—to the point where they must eventually come to the King. The County of Toulouse had only a nominal existence. This tendency towards centralization was advanced still further by the activities of the Inquisition in the territories of Raymond VII and Raymond Berenguer; Louis IX, a devout son of the Church, was persuaded that these proceedings were necessary. The only feudal estates that were independent of French influence were Aquitaine and Gascony, the domains of the English Kings, and it was there that trouble was to break out anew.

In 1242 there was yet another war between England and France. Louis IX defeated the weak King Henry III of England and the Count of La Marche at Taillebourg and Saintes. It was only his own sudden illness and the outbreak of dysentery in his army that prevented the victor from marching on Bordeaux. The Count of La Marche submitted. These victories also bore fruit in the south. With the peace of Lorris, concluded in 1243, the feudal system began to disintegrate in Languedoc, completing the process initiated by the peace of Meaux.

By then only Aquitaine remained independent. Louis IX granted an armistice for this territory, although he could have driven the English from the Continent had he wished to do so.

Henry III of England was no longer in a position to maintain himself on French soil. But Louis regarded the remaining Continental possessions of the Plantagenets as legitimate. He did not avail himself of the opportunity of seizing Bordeaux and Gascony, and in the end he magnanimously allowed his opponent to retain Périgord, Limousin, Quercy and parts of Saintonge and Agenais. As far as the rest of the Plantagenets' Continental territories were concerned, however, he forced the English to renounce their rights of sovereignty over Brittany, La Marche, Angoumois and Auvergne. The famous treaty of Paris concluded in 1259 between Louis IX and Henry III was criticized by French patriots at the time and has been criticized ever since as far too generous. Louis himself, however, regarded this agreement as a lasting instrument of peace and he observed its provisions. In this way the great French King was able to call a temporary halt to the constant strife that had beset Anglo-French relations since 1066.

In the early days of their activities, the "officers of the Crown" had often infringed upon the rights of individuals living within the Crown territories. In 1247 Louis instituted an enquiry to examine all such cases of injustice, so that those concerned might be compensated. In doing so he created the office of the *enquêteurs*, the inspectors who toured the King's territory after the fashion of the *missi dominici* of Charlemagne's day.

Louis was called upon to act as arbitrator throughout the

length and breadth of Christendom. In this capacity he tried to effect a reconciliation between Frederick II and the Pope. Throughout his life he exercised a truly moral authority. Even Henry III of England declared that he was proud to be his vassal, for Louis was the foremost knight of Christendom. In 1270, when this great ruler died in Tunis during the last Crusade, every country of the Occident mourned his passing.

In the sphere of state unity, Louis IX transformed the unintegrated Crown dependencies into a genuine community; he encouraged the development of the towns; he furthered the cause of justice and as a Christian King he none the less preserved the dignity of the French Crown and the independence of the French Church vis-à-vis the Curia.

During Louis's reign, the dispute between Pope and Emperor gave the Capetian house extraordinary opportunities which might well have raised it to a position of pre-eminence in Europe, while England, weakened and withdrawn into herself, was concentrating all her powers on an internal development that was the precursor of a great but still distant future.

The Expansion of the Capetian Dynasty

We have already seen that in 1204 the Angevin lands in France were regained by Philip Augustus; in 1246 Blanche of Castile's youngest son, Charles-Etienne, was invested with the fief of Anjou. But his star was to rise much higher, for he became deeply involved in the central event of the age, the dispute between the Holy See and the Emperor. Frederick II, a syncretist sceptic who fostered an early and magnificent Renaissance, was the son of antagonistic parents, the cruel Emperor Henry VI of Hohenstaufen and Constance, heiress of the Norman kingdom of Sicily and many years her husband's senior.

The crisis in the affairs of the Hohenstaufens necessarily

drew the French King's attention to what was happening in Italy. Pope Clement IV, in an attempt to deprive the Hohenstaufen heirs of the kingdom of Sicily, invested Charles I of Anjou with this territory and then crowned him King of Sicily in Rome on January 6, 1266. Alexander IV had already tried to displace the Hohenstaufens with one of the sons of Henry III of England.

Charles of Anjou acted quickly. In 1266 he marched at the head of an army of French knights strongly reinforced by mercenaries against Manfred, the bold natural son of Frederick II. The battle of Benevento saw the bitter end of the greatest German dynasty in the Mediterranean world. Manfred was deserted by his barons and defeated on February 26, 1266. He himself sought and found death in the battle. A year later, when Frederick's grandson Conradin marched to Italy to win back the Hohenstaufen legacy, he too was defeated by the French, at Tagliacozzo on August 23, 1268, and taken prisoner. After a sham trial he was beheaded in Naples. From that point on the Capetian ruled over southern Italy with an iron hand. He was also the suzerain of most of the towns of Lombardy and Tuscany, and so exercised effective control over them as well. It was then that the Roman prelates realized that this new ruler offered a far greater threat to the Pope than ever the Hohenstaufens had done.

Pope Nicholas III tried to extricate himself from this difficult position by asking one of the Christian princes, a new man with a considerable reputation, Rudolph of Hapsburg, to act as arbitrator. But Charles of Anjou refused to countenance any attempt at negotiation.

Rome was left to rue the many occasions when St Louis had tried to bring about a reconciliation between Frederick II and the Vatican. Charles of Anjou, who reigned until 1285, was altogether different from his great brother. By main force he ensured the election of Pope Martin IV, the erstwhile Keeper of the Seals to the King of France and his own devoted servant. Pope Martin was the man who had conducted the negotiations leading to the decision to invite Charles of Anjou to take over the kingdom of Naples and Sicily. He remained at all times Charles's dependent and allowed him to do as he pleased. Although Nicholas III had still dared to offer resistance, none came from Martin IV. Charles was succeeded by his son, Charles II, who reigned from 1285 to 1309. In the year of his death the Papacy was removed to Avignon, an event of far-reaching consequence.

Charles II's principal aim was to revive the policy of conquest in the East, which lost increasingly the impetus of militant faith to become an instrument of power politics and greed. The proverbial luck of the Anjous, which had raised him to such high estate, was to carry his family much further; in 1307 Charles Robert of the Neapolitan line of the house of Anjou became King of Hungary, and his son, Louis I, subsequently extended the borders of his realm to include Moldavia, Wallachia, Bosnia, Serbia and western Bulgaria, then took Dalmatia from the Venetians, annexed various Russian territories, and finally, in 1370, became King of Poland. The powerful hold on the imagination exercised by the charismatic aura of the dynasties on the peoples in the warring Middle Ages explains the marvel aroused by such an extraordinary expansion of the domains of their own ruling house and its sidelines.

It is noteworthy that, by voluntarily advancing the Anjous in Naples and Sicily, the Curia paved the way for the Italian policy pursued by the Kings of France at a later date, and equally that the hostility of French dynastic policy towards the Holy Roman Empire, which led to the downfall of the Hohenstaufens, left the German peoples with a store of bitter memories. And most important of all, through Charles of Anjou, France embarked on a Curial policy that for a time reduced the Holy See to complete subservience to the French Crown, thus exerting a crucial influence on Anglo-French relations and on the development of the English Church. We must now consider that development.

The Development of the English Church and French Curial Policy

The fate of Thomas à Becket, Archbishop of Canterbury, the great champion of the papal hierarchy, is well known. Becket opposed the Constitutions of Clarendon, formulated in 1164, consisting of sixteen articles intended to resolve points of dispute between the King and the clergy; among other things, they made all appeals to Rome subject to the King's approval. Ten of these articles were condemned by Pope Alexander III. What was at stake, therefore, even at this early stage, was the sovereignty of the State vis-à-vis the Church. Becket paid with his life for his resistance to this development of secular power, and so became a martyr and national saint. Three hundred years later he was accused and condemned of treason and *lèse-majesté* by Henry VIII, who availed himself of the opportunity thus afforded to take possession of the rich treasures in Becket's shrine. Between his death and this infamous deed lies the period in which England moved from an originally particularly outspoken integration with the universal Church to her severance from Rome and the establishment of the Church of England.

The event that contributed more than any other to the grave outcome was King John's recognition of papal sovereignty over England and Ireland in the early thirteenth century. The papal treasury thereafter received a rich income from its great vassal, and Pope Innocent IV is known to have referred to the King of England as his "servant." In their English policy the Popes played off the barons against the Kings with remarkable skill. Under Henry III, who succeeded King John, English opposition to Roman influence became more pronounced.

During his struggles with the Hohenstaufens, Pope Alexander IV decided to further the cause of Henry III of England by supporting the election of his brother, Richard of Cornwall and Poitou, as King of the Romans. He also had held out the prospect of the throne of Sicily for Henry's son Edmund, Earl of Lancaster. Henry eagerly accepted and for his part undertook to pay high subsidies to the Curia in order to achieve these objectives. But the English nobles took violent exception to the proposed subsidies and the projects came to nothing. Instead the Provisions of Oxford were submitted to the King, which he was obliged to confirm by oath. These provisions deprived the King of important powers. For the first time a strong national movement hostile to all foreign influence arose in England.

The King's stepbrothers and his numerous foreign advisers, many of them relatives of his Provençal wife, were expelled and the papal legate was again denied entry into England. But Simon de Montfort, the friend of Bishop Grosseteste of Lincoln and the leader of the barons, who defeated and deposed his monarch in the battle of Lewes on May 14, 1264, was held in high esteem. Even at that time this feudal rebel had the lesser clergy and the common people on his side. When, following Lewes, he was excommunicated from the Church, his rebellion assumed a religious character, his followers took the cross as their emblem and claimed that they were fighting for a holy cause. This was not a first step towards secularization, nor was it the beginning of a democratic development, but it was a hint of things to come. Montfort was declared Protector of the Realm. In 1265 he summoned the nobles to discuss affairs of state, together with two knights from each shire and two burgesses from each borough. It was for this reason that he came to be regarded as the founder of the Commons. But he was not to be permitted to finish his work. Before the year was out Henry III's son Edward defeated the rebels at Evesham, where Simon de Montfort was killed. With this the rebellion came to an end. The King was reinstated and the papal legate, Cardinal Ottoboni, returned with all due ceremony. But the rebellion, although short-lived, had considerable repercussions.

With the death of Simon de Montfort the last of the great

Normans who had furthered the development of England vanished from the scene. His method of procedure had always been pragmatic and, as such, typically English.

The sharp distinction between the conquering Normans and their conquered subjects had become blurred with the passing of time. By a slow and gradual process—accelerating only in its final, dramatic phase—a new ruling class arose, whose members revealed a special talent for statesmanship.

Two crucial factors in the development of the English national character were the emergence between the thirteenth and the fifteenth centuries of an intellectual elite at the Universities of Oxford and Cambridge and the economic rise of the middle class, based primarily on the export of wool and cloth. One great achievement was the early emancipation of the peasants from villeinage. This was not brought about by revolution, but by the royal courts, partly as a result of the national pride in the peasant archers' victories over the French knights. The emancipation was opposed by the owners of the great estates, who had succeeded in drawing a large number of the gentry to their side, a fact that made it possible for regular bands to be formed and deployed in the disputes between the great nobles and the Crown and in the self-destructive feuds among the nobles themselves. The wealth of the great landowners had grown beyond all bounds. At the end of the Hundred Years War they were even rich enough to hire in great numbers the English troops who were then returning from France. In the course of time they had gone over more and more to sheep raising, for the sale of wool was the principal source of their income. A large part of England was enclosed as pasture land. The peasants lost their rights of commonage and their smallholdings. Their deprivation, later combined with a particular form of religious revival, eventually produced a mass emigration that led to the establishment of a "new England" and subsequently of an independent English-speaking great power across the Atlantic.

The unique quality of English history is also demonstrated

by the fact that the English legal system has always managed sooner or later to check injustices and the hardships they produce, and to bring them under the control of law. For one of the foundations of the English way of life has been the common law with its remarkable attendant of equity. In England the separation of ecclesiastical from secular law was first undertaken, with the consent of William the Conqueror, by the Italian jurist who became Archbishop of Canterbury, Lanfranc. The fact that this was done at such an early date meant that in England the common law was able to develop to the full, thanks to the influence brought to bear on it by the equity judgements pronounced both in Chancery and in the courts of law. Until the sixteenth century the Chancellors were high Church dignitaries. By the time William the Conqueror died in 1087, England already had the basic elements of a legal system that was to prove as strong and as pliant as steel and was thus able to adapt itself to changing times.

By the late thirteenth century England's relations to the Curia were already much more relaxed. Edward I, who reigned from 1272 to 1307, revealed himself as a disciple of Montfort, and during his reign England's unique creation, her Parliament, began to assume definite shape. In the summons to the session in 1295 we find the sentence *"Quod omnes tangit ab omnibus approbetur."* But the *"omnes"*—the *"all"*—simply meant those invited to take part in the discussions. At first the knights and the representatives of the towns had no voice in the actual decisions taken in Parliament. They were there to answer any questions that might be put to them. They had a duty to appear and were punished if they failed to do so. Later they were to voice their opinions without waiting to be asked and ultimately to summon the King to appear before them.

The English Parliament derives on the one hand from the great constitutional flair displayed by the Normans, who compelled the King to abide by the law, and on the other from the oath of allegiance taken by the King's vassals, which led in time to the formation of the Curia Regis, an administrative body in which the highest offices were the Exchequer and the Chancery. These were the cornerstones on which, whether in dispute or in collaboration with the Kings, later generations of the English estates were to build.

Only two years after the death of Edward I, England and the Holy See reached a crisis in their affairs, with consequences that proved to be far graver than anything in the past. This crisis was brought on by the removal of the papacy to Avignon in 1309.

St Louis had forceful heirs. His grandson Philip IV (Philip the Fair), who was the uncle of the first Valois King and a great patron of the legists and thus of Roman law, was in many respects a precursor of Richelieu. He fought the rebellious feudal lords with every means at his disposal. Above all, however, he continued to assert French secular rights in the face of papal demands; but where his grandfather had proceeded with wisdom and moderation, he was far more vehement. He was the herald of much later times, for he set up the sovereignty of the State as the ultimate criterion of political action, especially where fiscal policy was concerned. The methods he employed revealed absolutist tendencies. He set a Frenchman on the papal throne and then forced him to move to Avignon, thus depriving him of his independence.

During the Avignon exile of 1309–76, the English came to look upon the Pope as merely an instrument of French foreign policy, and this is a critical factor in what followed.

At Philip IV's bidding the French Cardinals, together with the Orsini, the ancient enemies of the Colonna, elected the Archbishop of Bordeaux, a Gascon by birth, to the papal chair. From that day until Gregory XI returned to Rome, every Pope was a Frenchman.

At last in 1378, in a turbulent scene, a Neapolitan was elected Pope. This was Bartolomeo Prignano, Archbishop of Bari, who became Pope Urban VI. He adopted a strong line with the Cardinals in an attempt to control them, but soon the pro-French party among them was pressing hard for his removal and using every available weapon in order to achieve it. Urban VI counterattacked vigorously: five of the Cardinals whom he considered his enemies were tortured and executed at his command. The French party responded by electing an antipope. The papal hierarchy was thoroughly shaken by these events, and the repercussions were greatest in England. Finally Urban VI embarked on a war against Queen Joanna of Naples, the daughter of Charles of Anjou. She had wholeheartedly espoused the French cause and was an adherent of Cardinal Robert of Geneva, the so-called "hangman of Cesena," who had been set up as antipope with the title of Clement VII. His election initiated the Great Schism, which lasted fifty-two years and produced no less than seven antipopes.

Urban VI died in mental darkness and was succeeded by another Neapolitan, Pietro Tomacelli, who became Boniface IX. Boniface was able and serious, and an excellent temporal prince, who watched over the administration of justice with great care, furthered the humanities and helped the poor. But he was not able to mitigate the evils of the schism.

The effects of French political intervention on the papacy and the strong English reaction against King John's submission to the Curia became apparent in English ecclesiastical affairs during the second half of the fourteenth century.

John Wycliffe

We must now consider the influence exercised by the English theologian John Wycliffe on the course of world affairs. In 1366 Wycliffe supported Edward III in his refusal to pay the Pope the feudal tribute to which England was still subject. He also advocated a tax on Church estates, and as a member of the royal commission to Bruges, to discuss ecclesiastical "provisions" with the papal nuncio, he proved a forceful and able negotiator. He was a contemporary of Occam, the *"doctor invincibilis"* who, like himself, defended the secular arm against papal authority; he made a clear distinction between theology and philosophy, between faith and reason, and he regarded general ideas as meaningless abstractions and practised a characteristically English form of pragmatism. One of his spiritual forbears was John Duns Scotus, who had great influence on the German mystics. Almost a hundred and fifty years before Luther's proclamation of the Wittenberg theses, Wycliffe had already expounded the essential content of the reformational protest. He disputed the primacy of the Bishop of Rome, condemned celibacy, denied both the doctrine of transubstantiation and the Pope's power of the keys and rejected the practice of auricular confession. For him the unadulterated teachings of the Holy Scriptures constituted the only valid authority, and he demanded the establishment of a national church independent of Rome.

He fully accepted the doctrine of divine grace. No martyr by nature, he was rather a cautious man with bold thoughts. He was closer to the early Puritans than to the Humanists of the Renaissance. Although he never exposed his life to danger, his teachings later caused countless thousands to risk theirs. Since his arguments were theological, they did not produce any immediate political effect within his lifetime. None the less, his opponents were able to convince the youthful King Richard II that Wycliffe had been one of the originators of the great Peasants' Revolt in 1381, which had threatened the whole social order of the day. The demands made by the peasants at that time were extreme, despite the fact that their wages had actually risen over the course of the preceding ten years and the cost of living had fallen; this meant that they were really revolting against the whole ruling order. They had seen their masters defeated in France and witnessed the surprise attacks made by the French fleet. Wycliffe's "poor priests" had told them of the scandalous wealth enjoyed by the great prelates. Langland's poem *Piers Plowman*, written in the vernacular, had been widely disseminated. The Statute of Laborers of 1351, favouring the great landlords, had embittered the agricultural class. We are told by Froissart that in 1381 Chaplain John Ball would sometimes preach to the congregation in the churchyard after Mass along the following lines: "People, things will not get better until all property is common property. It is intolerable that there should be lowly and common people on the one hand and noblemen on the other. We are all descended from the same parents, Adam and Eve. But while they go in silk and lace, we go in drill; while they have wine and herbs and wheaten bread, we have only rye and bran and straw, and drink water."

We shall be hearing more of peasant revolts.

There was undoubtedly a connection between Wycliffe's teachings and the Peasants' Revolt, which was eventually put down with considerable bloodshed. But the ruling classes of England were still so powerful, and the Church still felt itself to be so powerful, that neither of these groups considered it necessary to take severe measures against men like Wycliffe and Occam, who were in fact laying the foundations both for the peasant wars on the Continent and for the Reformation. Action was eventually taken against Wycliffe, though it was not severe. In London a council rejected his teachings, whereupon he retired to his parish of Lutterworth, where he continued work on his English version of the Bible. When Urban VI summoned him to appear in Rome to give account of himself, he did not comply, and on December 31, 1384, he died a natural death.

Just over thirty years later, on May 4, 1415, the Council of Constance condemned Wycliffe's "forty-five articles" and ordered his bones to be exhumed and burnt, which was duly done in 1428. It was this above all else that ensured the wide dissemination of his doctrine. Although his followers in England were gradually eliminated by the secular arm, his ideas prospered on the Continent, where John Huss, the peasant from Prachatice in Bohemia, became his disciple. It was in Bohemia that the seed sown by the English theologian was to find its most fertile soil, for Huss translated Wycliffe's theses into popular terms and thus established him as the great precursor of Luther. By his death at the stake, his influence was strengthened and perpetuated, like that of Jerome of Prague, a fellow martyr, who after studying in Oxford had first brought Wycliffe's writings to the Continent.

The followers of these two men were to revenge their condemnation at the hands of the Church a hundredfold, and the Hussite wars were to bring about far-reaching changes (see Chapter VII).

The new mode of thought, emerging when scholastic philosophy had reached its peak and was about to decline, cannot be isolated from the political, sociological and economic conditions of the time. In assessing these factors, however, we must take care not to overvalue any one of them at the expense of the others. Occam and Roger Bacon had heralded the birth of modern scholarship, and from them to Francis Bacon, who declared that "knowledge is power," it was only a short step. In point of fact, however, the whole of this new movement had been anticipated by Duns Scotus. In England nominalistic methods made short shrift of religious taboos; indeed, these essentially practical ideas were applied in direct opposition to Church tradition. By contrast, French thinkers, with their predominantly rational approach, engaged in an argument against the logics of ecclesiastical apologetics and carried on this discussion in successive generations.

The link between Wycliffe and Huss shows how closely knit the intellectual life of Europe was at that time. No territorial borders, however firm, were proof against the interchange of ideas in the medieval Christian world.

The judgements passed by the Council of Constance on the living and the dead created a crucial premise for the fearful crises of the sixteenth and seventeenth centuries and the fact that it was as the champion of Protestant Europe that England became a world power. The consequences of the first specifically reformational attitude adopted by England in her struggle with the pro-French Curia were of primary importance.

A further peculiarity of English history is to be found in the way in which the great feudal lords were exterminated during the Wars of the Roses and especially under Henry VIII, the first of the Tudors to follow the spirit of the times in striving for absolute power. What is significant in this connection is the fact that England—unlike France, who found herself in a similar situation at a much later date—was not left with a great gap in her social structure following the disappearance of her feudal nobles. Instead, a new aristocracy took their place. And so we find at the heart of England, by then a trading nation, this new class which had grown rich on Church property. It possessed many of the characteristics of the Roman optimates, or of the leading families of Venice in its heyday.

The Quarrel Between the Kings of England and France

Our survey has taken us forward into the fifteenth and sixteenth centuries. But we must now turn back to the thirteenth and fourteenth centuries, so that we may go to the root of the disputes between England and France.

The Plantagenet King Edward I was a Crusader who, added to his code of knightly honour and his physical prowess, had a highly developed sense of justice and closely observed the provisions of the law. His work was conceived in terms of the future and he relied for his support on the newly emerging classes. He always honoured agreements; he created state institutions that exist to this day—for example, the Courts of Chancery; he restricted ecclesiastical jurisdiction; he reorganized the system of feudal tenures, the administration and the maintenance of order. Parliament was able to extract substantial concessions from him, for while he was fighting Philip

IV of France for control of Gascony, Scotland sought French protection. Both because he wanted to and because he was obliged to—a frequent combination of circumstances in his case—Edward I laid the foundations on which the great and exemplary English institutions were to rise up.

Strong fathers, weak sons, strong grandsons. For twenty years Edward II was harassed by his nobles and suffered setbacks on all sides. But under Edward III further extensions were made to the Constitution, the intellectual life of the country underwent a great revival and trade flourished. The King secured the Flemish markets for the sale of English wool. Important literary works appeared in the English language. Although Edward II had lost his war with the Scots, in 1333 Edward III fought and won the decisive battle of Halidon Hill. Upon the death of Charles IV, his mother's brother, he again raised the never-abandoned English claim to the French throne. The endless business of claims, property, inheritance—and the peoples of Europe were delivered over to their fate. Under the Salic law, Edward III's claim was rejected. The Hundred Years War began.

The—for those days—tremendous sums of money Edward had to find in order to pay for his war undermined his relation with Parliament, and he was obliged to accede (though often on a temporary basis) to demands that presented the full range of constitutional rights of the English Parliament. Soon the right of petition was to be transformed as Parliament itself took the initiative in legislation, and in the Commons the members began to put motions in the form of laws.

The Good Parliament of 1376 was obliged to take action against abuses and intrigues at Court. By then the Commons —that is, the combined representatives of the counties and boroughs—had been separated from the Lords and had grown in importance. But despite the many tensions between the Crown and the Parliament, they were at one in their opposition to the Pope and to all interference from Rome.

By 1369 England's affairs on the Continent had already been

subjected to severe setbacks. Edward III's heir, the Black Prince, had returned from the battlefields of France a dying man, and from that moment on the fortunes of war turned against England.

From 1377 to 1461, under Richard II and later under the Lancastrian Kings, battles for supremacy raged between the Crown and the representatives of the people on the one hand and between the Crown and the feudal nobles on the other. The struggle to preserve the realm from disintegration at the hands of the extremely powerful feudal lords, which in France took place under Louis XIII and Louis XIV, came in the main much earlier in England. During the fierce struggle between the houses of Lancaster and York, English feudal power was definitely broken.

Under Richard II, the son of the Black Prince, an attempt was made to regain for the Crown some of the powers acquired by the Commons during the latter years of Edward's reign. Richard wanted to rule in his own right. In order to resolve the Anglo-French conflict, he entered into a dynastic marriage with Isabella of France, which preserved the peace both at home and abroad for a period of eight years. But those eight years were merely the calm before the storm. Under Gloucester's leadership the parliamentary opposition had gone to extreme lengths, accusing and condemning various high officials. During the unnatural calm of the years of peace the Crown had grown strong again, and now the time had come for the King to take his revenge. First Richard had the ring-leaders executed or banished and then he proceeded against Parliament itself. He set up a commission with full parliamentary powers as a first step towards getting rid of Parliament altogether. But then he became arbitrary, and the English have never taken kindly to arbitrary actions. He settled a dispute between the Dukes of Norfolk and Hereford by banishing them both, and upon the death of Hereford's father, Lancaster, he confiscated Lancaster's property. Hereford then returned to England, landing in the summer of 1399 while

Richard was engaged in an Irish campaign. The people of
England, who were greatly embittered, flocked to the Lancastrian. Richard fell into rebel hands and on September 29th
was forced to abdicate, whereupon Hereford was made King
as Henry IV. A rising in favour of Richard was suppressed,
and on February 14, 1400, Richard died in Pontefract Castle
under circumstances that have never been explained.

It should be noted that the first Lancastrian King of England
was elected by Parliament. Consequently, he immediately
reversed Richard's policy and restored to Parliament the
rights it had previously enjoyed. The position of the Lancastrian Kings and their followers was also undermined by the
need to obtain bigger and bigger credits to pay for the seemingly interminable Continental campaigns and for the battles
that were fought simultaneously against the Scots and the
Irish. At the time of the devastating conclusion of the Hundred
Years War, Henry VI, the last of the line, found himself
virtually in the position of a constitutional monarch. He was
at the mercy of the great nobles and his marriage to Margaret
of Anjou made him unpopular in the country at large. The
authority of the Commons reached its peak under Henry VI,
but it was still in the hands of the feudal lords and their
followers, the gentry, who enforced the election of their
partisans.

Our purpose in recapitulating so much of English history
has been to acquire an understanding of Richelieu's truly
remarkable attitude to England and thus of his whole English
policy. We have drawn attention to three main factors. The
first is the deep and virtually inborn awareness, common to
both Englishmen and Frenchmen, of the age-old enmity
between their two countries, which Richelieu was able to
suspend but not to eradicate; the second is the difference
between the development of French and English institutions;
the third concerns Church reform in England. This began
at a very early date and in a thoroughly nationalist spirit, and
in conjunction with the work of a French religious genius

(who left France and thus occupied no more than a marginal position in French affairs), it gave rise to Puritanism, the world-wide movement so alien to the French mind, which was to exert its influence far beyond Europe.

Some French Aspects of the Hundred Years War

The Hundred Years War, touched off by renewed dynastic claims on the part of England, dominated the late Middle Ages in France. Philip IV had three sons—Louis X, Philip V and Charles IV—none of whom produced an heir. When Philip IV's nephew, a member of the house of Valois, was crowned Philip VI of France, Edward III of England protested, claiming that as the son of Philip IV's daughter Isabella, he himself was next in line to the French throne.

In 1338 he landed on the Continent and joined forces with his allies from the Flemish towns and with Emperor Louis IV at Antwerp. In his pre-campaign diplomacy Edward had acted prudently, and the campaign itself began with an English naval victory at Sluys, which further demonstrated England's supremacy at sea. On August 26, 1346, Edward won the battle of Crécy and in the same year he defeated the Scots, who were allied with France, at Neville's Cross. A year later he gained possession of Calais.

At that time France was perilously weak. In Paris, Etienne Marcel had led a revolt for reforms in tax administration and freedom of association on the part of the estates, while in the north-east of the kingdom the "Jacquerie," the greatest peasant revolt in French history, had broken out. France none the less rejected the English peace terms, which were very harsh, and in 1359 the war flared up again. Soon the country was so destitute that peace had to be bought at any price, and on May 8, 1360, the peace of Brétigny was signed. On this occasion France ceded, besides Guyenne and Gascony, Poitou, Saintonge, La Rochelle, Agen, Périgord, Limoges, Quercy, Bigorre, Tarbes, Gaure, Angoulême, Rouergue,

Montreuil, Ponthieu, Calais and Guînes and also paid a high ransom for the release of John II, Philip's successor, who had been taken prisoner by the English.

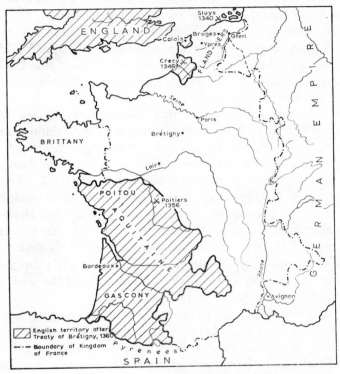

Map 3. France after the Treaty of Brétigny

The Valois Kings were still fully subject to feudal principles, and they created powerful vassals on all sides. This distinctly reactionary procedure is of particular interest to us, for it provided the background for the measures taken against the great nobles under Louis XIII and Louis XIV. France was undoubtedly in danger of being split up into a number of independent principalities, the fate of Germany. Time and again it seemed that large areas of the country would be lost to England, and later to Spain. Eventually, after the many battles conducted in accordance with the highest traditions of chivalry, and after the many French defeats in which the nobility were all but annihilated, it looked as if this long-drawn-out combat must end in an English victory.

The third of the Valois Kings, Charles V, died in 1380 and was succeeded by his eldest son, who became Charles VI. His second son, Louis of Orléans, inherited the Counties of Angoulême and Valois, which then remained in his family until the French Revolution.

It was under Charles VI that the threat to France was greatest. From 1392 onwards Charles, a muted, intuitive and decadent descendant of an ancient house, suffered inter-mittently from mental illness. He was married to Isabeau of Bavaria and lived with her in his lucid intervals. These became less and less frequent, and in his periods of madness he alternated between fits of frenzy and total apathy. His son Charles, later Charles VII, was born in 1403. He was the twelfth child of the marriage, and at the time of his birth two older brothers were still living. It was Charles VII's daughter Catherine, married to Henry V, who introduced the seeds of madness into the house of Lancaster.

Following Charles VI's breakdown, a bitter struggle for the regency took place between his brother Louis of Orléans, his uncle Philip the Bold of Burgundy, and Philip's son John the Fearless. On November 23, 1407, Orléans was murdered in Paris on the instructions of John of Burgundy. This outrage led to fierce strife between Orléans's followers (called "Armagnacs" after their commander) and the "Burgundians." This civil war was the ultimate cause of France's defeat at the hands of Henry V of England. Though a reconciliation was effected between the warring factions, it was not genuine and did not stop the Armagnacs from taking their revenge. In 1419, John of Burgundy met Charles of Valois, the heir-apparent, on the bridge over the Yonne in Montereau, osten-sibly to settle their differences, but John was cut down with an axe. This drove John's son and heir, Philip the Good of Burgundy, the founder of the Order of the Golden Fleece, into an alliance with the English. In the patched-up peace settlement concluded between France, England and Burgundy in 1420 at Troyes, Philip succeeded in having Charles excluded from the succession. And so yet again in France we find the princes of the blood conducting a struggle for internal power along purely feudal lines when the national enemy was firmly established on French soil.

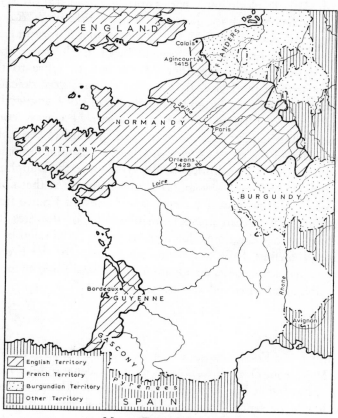

Map 4. France after 1427

The feud between the French and the Burgundian branches of the house of Valois was further inflamed by Queen Isabeau. After the murder of Orléans, the Armagnacs had her banished from the French Court, whereupon she went over to the Burgundians. The Queen appears to have been the principal author of the treaty of Troyes. When the question of her son's exclusion from the succession was under discussion, she herself declared that Charles was not her husband's son. The Dauphin was a very unstable person, and the doubt induced by this declaration preyed on his mind and for years seriously impaired his development. Charles normally resided at Bourges, a fact which earned for him the derisive title of *le Roi de Bourges*. He was defeated by the English and the Burgundians at Cravant in 1423 and at Verneuil in 1424. He was forced to cede first Champagne, then Maine, and to retire to the farther bank of the Loire. In 1426 the English were defeated at Montargis by Jean Dunois, later the Count of Longueville, the Bastard of Orléans, who was Charles's best army commander; but in 1427 they again pressed forward to the Loire and encircled the city of Orléans. Charles was quite prepared to give up this key position as well and escape to the Dauphiné, the only French territory still under his control. At that point it looked as if no power on earth could prevent France from becoming an English possession. The King of Bourges had all but lost his kingdom. But then from the mystic depths of patriotic feeling, from a spontaneous upsurge of the French national consciousness, an apparently irrational force emerged in a unique and marvellous figure.

Joan of Arc

When the French cause was at its lowest ebb, Joan of Arc, the Maid from Domrémy, appeared on the scene. In May 1429, under her leadership, Orléans was relieved and Reims retaken. In Joan's presence Charles VII was consecrated in Reims Cathedral and anointed with oil from the ampulla that, according to hallowed tradition, a dove had carried to Clovis, King of the Franks, on the occasion of his conversion. To the fifteenth-century mind, Charles was now incontestably the rightful King of France.

In the course of one of the great political trials of world history, Joan was condemned in Rouen, under disregard of the formal rules of procedure. The outcome was a foregone conclusion—under political pressure she had to be convicted of witchcraft and condemned to death at the stake. Her judges were all hostile to Charles VII. Their careers and their benefices were dependent on the English. The University of Paris, the great monasteries of Normandy and the canons of Rouen were all pro-English.

Joan of Arc had driven the English from Orléans, but not from France. She had seen the King crowned in Reims, but there was still a second King on French soil, the King of England. Much remained to be done and it was done by the people of France, who produced one of those supreme efforts they have so often shown themselves capable of. But all that was achieved in the twenty-two years following Joan's death was achieved by the spirit she had created and the power she had unleashed. Despite military reversals, despite the pro-English sympathies of certain towns and territories, once Charles VII had rid himself of La Trémoille, he went from strength to strength. France was reconquered.

There was another important reason for Charles VII's victory, quite different in nature from the Maid's mystical inspiration—the appearance of Jacques Cœur, one of the early capitalists, on the French scene.

Jacques Cœur was the son-in-law of a master minter of Bourges. He was an organizer of genius and was responsible for developing the Levantine trade. Charles VII appointed him his *grand argentier*—his Minister of Finance. By fifteenth-century standards Cœur, like the Fuggers, had amassed an enormous fortune. This had come partly from trade and partly from mining, for he had also exploited the mines of the Beaujolais and Lyon districts. The motto on his coat of arms, *A vaillans cuers riens impossible*, stamps him as a precursor of the great entrepreneurs of modern times. It was he who financed the King's wars, and when Charles proceeded to the reconquest of Normandy, Cœur said to him: "Sire, what is mine, is yours." Just as Charles V would never have been elected Emperor without the Fuggers, so France would never have risen from her near exhaustion to perform the vital task then facing her without this entirely new force of credit.

At a time when many Frenchmen were in want, Jacques Cœur's lavish style of living provoked hatred and envy, and false accusations were made against him. He was found guilty and saved himself by fleeing to Rome. His case was later reopened by Louis XI and his name was cleared.

The one certain fact to emerge from the Hundred Years War was that danger and death had drawn the people of France together into a nation, and they would now always keep a sense of their common identity.

The English, for all their pains, had been forced back to their island; but now the Atlantic beckoned them, and the sea routes of the world.

France after the Hundred Years War

What was the price France paid for victory? The chronicler Thomas Basin described the aftermath of war:

"From the Loire to the Seine, from the Seine to the Somme, the farmers are dead or deported, the fields lie fallow. . . . I have crossed the broad valleys of Champagne, of Brie, of Beauce, of Gâtinais, the district of Chartres, of Dreux, Maine, Perche, the Norman and French Vexin, Beauvaisis, Caux, I have journeyed from the Seine to Amiens and Abbeville, I have passed through Soissons, Valois and that whole area which extends as far as Laon and even Hainaut, and I have

9.   Bust of Gustavus Adolphus of Sweden

IOANNES TILLIV

10.   John, Count of Tilly

seen nothing but waste land, stripped of vegetation and devoid of people, fields turned to dog grass or to bush. . . . Only in the immediate vicinity of the towns, the fortified villages or the castles was there any sign of cultivation and then only to the extent to which the lookout on the tower was able to note and report the approach of marauding bands. Boundaries had been forgotten, the continuity of life disrupted; resettlement proceeded slowly."

Gaxotte tells us that the old order was entirely destroyed. The old French peasant stock had all but disappeared. Many who had sought refuge in the towns did not return to the country when peace came. In the cities the intermixture of nationalities increased. Apart from granting tax reliefs, there was little the monarchy could do to revive agriculture, but what it could and did do was to revive the crafts by encouraging the immigration of founders, glassblowers, coppersmiths, armourers, carpenters, miners, spinners and dyers. These artisans came from Catalonia, Italy, Germany, Switzerland and the province of Liège, and they settled in Paris, Rouen, Tours, Reims, Lyon, Montpellier, Nantes, Toulouse and Bordeaux. The most important of the foreign industries established by the King at that time was silk weaving.

The relationship between the various classes was also radically altered. In the Middle Ages the wealth of the Church lay in its land, but the majority of French parishes had lost half or even two-thirds of their land as a result of the war. We possess a report compiled by a certain Jean Mouchard who visited all the parishes in the diocese of Paris south of the Seine between 1458 and 1470. On August 11, 1466, he wrote: "In Jouy-en-Josas I found no priest and only four parishioners. The church has been destroyed." In 1412 the land belonging to the priory of St Catherine near Orsay produced 107 livres, 6 sols, 6 deniers, one goose and sixteen *muds*.[1] In 1461 it produced only a third of this revenue. In Bures there was only

---

[1] An old French measure of capacity, which varied from province to province. The word derives from the Latin *modius*.

one parishioner, in Fontenay the ruined church was over-grown with vegetation, and the Abbot of La Roche lived all alone in his monastery. In 1462, faced with starvation, he sold a Bible, a chalice and a missal and in 1468 two thousand slates from the monastery roofs. The convents of the diocese were deserted. Everywhere conditions were the same. Many young clerics had joined the marauding bands that plundered the countryside. Many priests had stayed on in Paris. The inhabitants of Savigny-sur-Orge said that they had seen their parish priest only once in four years. All this we learn from Gaxotte's vivid account.

The war that had brought about these conditions was contemporaneous with the schism in the papacy. Thus social disorder was accompanied by the loss of Christian unity. In 1437, three years after his reconciliation with Burgundy, Charles VII, on his own authority, bestowed on the French Church an organization based on conciliar theory. In the Pragmatic Sanction of Bourges, a true product of the Gallic mind, the General Council was invested with greater authority than the Pope and was empowered to depose him, and he was accorded no right whatsoever to take such counter-measures as the annulment of the council's decrees or the dissolution of its assemblies. Bishops were to be elected by their canons and abbots by their monks. So much freedom was bound to lead to abuses, for freedom is predicated on a strong sense of responsibility, and this was not forthcoming. Fierce conflicts of all kinds broke out. Of the new appointments to the twenty high ecclesiastical offices that fell vacant between 1444 and 1453, seven were secured by force. Countless actions were brought, civil war broke out in various places and newly elected dignitaries were constantly being deposed. In Vendôme a bishop was insulted and abused; his mitre was snatched from his head, his hair was torn out and he was thrown on to the street, where a howling mob surrounded him. In 1492 the Metropolitan of Paris, the Archbishop of Sens, had gone to Notre Dame to say Mass in the presence of Charles VIII.

When the Archbishop left the church he walked in procession behind the cross borne by his deacons and began to bless the crowd. At this point he was attacked by a group of canons who had refused to submit to his authority. They tore his surplice from his back and smashed the cross.

The King interfered in all ecclesiastical elections and used pressure to secure posts to men compliant to his will. A state of authoritarian anarchy was brought about. The Church was secularized, bishoprics became sinecures for great nobles, politicians, courtiers, who engaged in intrigue between the King and the Pope. They lived in Rome or Paris, in princely style, undertaking ambassadorial functions and amassing benefices to keep up their lavish style of living.[1]

If the Church was in a bad way, the condition of the nobility was scarcely any better. Their estates had been devastated, a large proportion of their sons had fallen in the war. Many families had died out entirely. The French nobleman had once been a free warrior, but by the end of the Hundred Years' War he was completely dependent on the King. The greatest of the noble houses—Anjou, Armagnac and Valençon —had either been wiped out in the course of the war or had been destroyed by royal justice, especially under Louis XI. Brittany was the only surviving feudal power and the house of Orléans kept in the background, waiting for better times.

If the thirteenth century, the century of St Louis, saw the emergence of royal justice, the fifteenth century witnessed the development of the Treasury and the army. No soldiers without money, no money without allegiance, no allegiance without soldiers. First the King conquered the English and then he conquered the French. And it was the people of France who gave him the money with which to conquer their bleeding land and hold it for himself.

From 1066 to 1453 there were only brief interludes of peace

---

[1] For example, the Cardinal d'Estouville, Chamberlain to Sixtus IV, had four bishoprics, four monasteries, four priories and many benefices in Italy. He also had several mistresses, all of whom bore him children.

in the warfare between France and England, and the struggle continued under Louis XIV and his successors. By that time of course it was no longer a question of provinces but of whole continents. Trafalgar and Waterloo are battle-cries in the memories of these two nations. In the seventeenth century, after six hundred years of almost continuous warfare, the mood was much the same. At that time the strength of patriotic feeling on both sides of the Channel was tremendous. When Richelieu adopted Francis I's plans for an English alliance and proceeded to apply them in an intensified form, thus reviving the conciliatory policy pursued by Henry IV, he found himself constantly in conflict with these patriotic forces. Here too he had to engage in an unpopular policy, for after the French religious wars the confessional differences between England and France, with the French Huguenots counting on the support of their English brothers in the faith, appeared to constitute a further impediment to an Anglo-French rapprochement. Meanwhile, however, Spain, backed by her great empire, had entered the scene and assumed the dominant role.

The Tudors

When for practical political reasons Richelieu decided to go against the inborn prejudices and instincts of his own people and adopt a friendly attitude towards England, he furnished the following typically simplified grounds for his action:

"The first reason is that England lies like a bulwark before France, which is why the Dukes of Burgundy attached great importance to their friendship with England, for it enabled them to keep a check on French power."

He went on to say:

"If the King of England enters into an alliance with France, Spain will no longer be able to restrict our freedom of movement or impede the realization of our claims."

Following her discovery of the New World and her immense territorial acquisitions overseas, Spain under Charles V became a new factor in European politics, completely altering the balance of power and for a time threatening the very existence of both France and England. In this new situation, Anglo-French relations, marred for centuries by constant warfare, necessarily underwent a fundamental change.

In order to understand what happened, we must take account of the Tudors, the great English dynasty that succeeded in concentrating all power in the Crown without falling into the pattern of absolutism that evolved on the Continent.

The founder of the Tudor dynasty was Henry VII, a temperate and thrifty monarch, who had come to the throne upon the death in battle of Richard III and had married the eldest daughter of Edward IV. He faced continuing opposition from Lambert Simnel and Perkin Warbeck, who posed as descendants of the house of York, and a revolt led by the Earl of Suffolk; but meanwhile hoping to strengthen his young dynasty by linking it with the rulers of the newly emerging Spain, Ferdinand the Catholic and Isabella, he tried to arrange a marriage between Prince Arthur, the heir-apparent to the English throne, and Princess Catherine of Aragón. In 1501, after lengthy negotiations, he succeeded in this aim, but in the next year Arthur, at the age of sixteen, died. The friendship with Spain brought rupture with France, but after a short campaign in France the treaty of Etaples was concluded on November 3, 1492, on terms favourable to England. In order to spare her new ally a war on two fronts, Spain had negotiated a truce between England and Scotland prior to the campaign. A further result of the Spanish mediation was the marriage of King James of Scotland to the eldest daughter of Henry VII, which further ensured Henry against Scottish attacks and thus enabled him to carry out financial and legislative reforms. He left a secure throne to his second son, who succeeded him on April 21, 1509.

Henry VIII now embarked on his astonishing career. When he was still a boy, he had met Erasmus of Rotterdam at Court, and Erasmus recorded his amazement at finding such extraordinary gifts in one so young.

Following the premature death of Prince Arthur, Catherine of Aragón was married to his brother Henry. Such a union was forbidden under canon law, so the original marriage between Arthur and Catherine had to be annulled in Rome before the second could take place. The annulment was granted on the ground that the marriage had not been consummated. This became an important factor in Henry's later divorce proceedings, in which he called the validity of his marriage to Catherine into question, asserting that the ground for the original annulment had proved false.

Henry VIII, a fine athlete with a humanist education, had inherited from his father a stable throne and a well-filled treasury. At first he left foreign policy in the hands of his favourite, Cardinal Wolsey, Archbishop of York. In the beginning, Wolsey pursued a course designed to maintain the balance of power in Europe, but later his actions were guided by his personal ambition to become Primate of England and Pope. What he had in mind for his sovereign was no less than the Emperor's crown and the role of arbitrator to the whole of Christendom. At the same time English claims to the French throne were raised yet again.

The struggle for European supremacy, which had never really ceased, now appeared as a contrapuntal accompaniment to the emergence of single nations as united and absolute monarchies. But if we compare Charles I of Spain, Francis I of France and Henry VIII of England, the three Kings who attempted to assert their supremacy over Europe in the sixteenth century, we find tremendous ideological differences.

In 1511 Wolsey persuaded Henry to join the Holy League formed to counteract the influence of French power on the Continent. Wolsey's chief interest in this affair was to safeguard the interests of the English wool traders in the Netherlands, which had become a sphere of Hapsburg influence as a result of Maximilian's marriage to the daughter of Charles the Bold of Burgundy. But this Continental venture merely served to undermine England's excellent financial position. Although Henry and the Emperor Maximilian were victorious at the battle of the Spurs near Guinegate, it was an expensive victory, for all that England gained from it was the fortress of Tournai.

Events in Italy

Francis I of France and Charles I of Spain, Maximilian's grandson and successor, were both eager to enter into an alliance with Henry VIII. Francis I had strenuously tried to become Emperor himself. His reign had got off to a glorious start with the battle of Marignano, which completely transformed the balance of power in Italy. Early one morning the Venetian ambassador to the Vatican had called on Leo X, rousing him from sleep to inform him of the victory of France and Venice over the Imperial army, and after that the Pope all but threw himself into the arms of Francis I. He met him in Bologna in December 1515, and there solved a diplomatic problem by obtaining assurances from the King of France that he would not attack the kingdom of Naples. He also succeeded in strengthening the position of the Medici in Tuscany, who were closely related to Francis I. Only ten years later, however, following his defeat at Pavia, the King of France became Charles V's prisoner, and after that supremacy in Italy reverted to Madrid and Vienna for a long time to come.

In the interval between Marignano and Pavia, Luther had posted his theses on the door of the castle church in Wittenberg; in Spain Charles I had ascended the throne, the insurgent *Comuneros* had been suppressed with great violence, and Charles had been elected Holy Roman Emperor as Charles V; the Diet of Worms had been convened; and Henry VIII had completely abandoned Francis I. Although they had met near

Calais in 1520, Francis had been unable to obtain even verbal undertakings, let alone the formal treaty he had hoped for.

A German, Pope Adrian VI, succeeded Leo X and remained loyal to the Emperor. After his death, however, Clement VII altered course. It seemed to him that the chief threat to the Vatican lands in his day came from Spain and the Empire. He reverted to the pro-French policy pursued by Leo X on the occasion of the Imperial election. Initially the more powerful princes had all been opposed to Charles of Hapsburg. From the summer of 1517 onwards, Francis I had worked on the German electoral princes. Margrave Joachim of Brandenburg was the first to sell him his vote. His brother, Albert, Archbishop of Mainz and Bishop of Halberstadt and Magdeburg, also bartered with the King of France through Ulrich von Hutten. Then, on January 15, 1519, Emperor Maximilian died before he could pay out the money he had promised to the Electors in return for their support of his grandson, Charles I of Spain. The latter's representative censured the College of Electors in the strongest possible terms and then started bidding on his own account. The Archbishop of Mainz sold his vote no less than five times. Louis, the Count Palatine, did not lag far behind him. Francis I's election prospects appeared so favourable that the Archduchess Margaret thought it advisable to put forward Ferdinand of Styria. The one elector who was utterly incorruptible was Frederick the Wise of Saxony, who let it be known that he for his part would refuse the Imperial crown if it was offered him; Leo X had considered him as a possible candidate at one point. But then the course of events was changed by a spontaneous and powerful movement initiated by the nobles of South Germany in conjunction with the Rhenish knights, who declared that they would enlist the help of all Germans who "did not wish to become French" and would go to any lengths to prevent the election of the Valois King. The Prince of the Church, Leo X, who was constantly embroiled in political and nepotist intrigue and was easily swayed, sensed that the scales were being tipped in favour of the Hapsburg; in 1521, only two years after Charles was elected, he entered into an anti-French alliance with him. But as Emperor Charles still retained the mistrust of the papacy instilled in him by Leo X's initial opposition to his election, and it was subsequently confirmed by Paul IV's anti-Hapsburg policy.

As for Wolsey, he had quite failed to appreciate the strength of German nationalist feeling, just as he had failed to appreciate the financial strength of the Fuggers in Augsburg. Henry VIII's representative at the Electoral Diet in Oberwesel, who had fondly expected to be the man behind the scenes, was ultimately left to report that French hopes had suddenly sunk very low and that the Hapsburg would win the election.

Wolsey's Foreign Policy

In the course of the Franco-Spanish struggle in Italy, Wolsey intervened on both sides and not always at the right time.

When Clement VII revived Leo X's anti-Hapsburg policy, Henry VIII petitioned for the dissolution of his marriage to Catherine of Aragón. Clement's predecessors had invested Henry with the title of "Defender of the Faith" following the publication of his polemical treatise in defence of the sacraments (*Assertio sacramentorum*), in which he attacked Luther.

At first it had seemed as if the Pope would accede to Wolsey's urgent requests and pronounce the annulment of Henry's marriage. But then he came under strong pressure that forced him to alter course and make temporary peace with the Emperor. As a result he reopened the case and Henry and his unhappy wife, an aunt of Charles V, were required to appear before an ecclesiastical court in Rome. Henry took out his rage, immoderate as ever, on Wolsey, and in the following year he was accused of high treason and placed under arrest. He was saved from the scaffold only by death, which overtook him on the long journey from York to the Tower of London. He was followed as Lord Chancellor by Thomas More, who had completed his deep-probing analysis of the State, *Utopia*, at virtually the same time that Machiavelli finished his *Il principe*. It was under More's chancellorship that Thomas Cromwell, an admirer of the great Florentine thinker, first came to the fore, and he soon succeeded More. Thomas Cranmer also rose to royal favour and was appointed Archbishop of Canterbury. Few of Henry's favourites escaped the executioner's axe—nor did Anne Boleyn, who, like Catherine, failed to give him a male heir. Of the five children of his marriage with Catherine, only Mary survived. Anne Boleyn's daughter was to become Elizabeth the Great.

The Reformation parliament was convened in 1529 in Westminster. In 1530 the whole of the English clergy were summoned before the royal court of justice, where the attorney general accused them collectively of having failed to protest in 1518 when Wolsey had added to his ecclesiastical and secular offices the office of papal legate; in Henry's opinion, Wolsey had thus committed an act of treason against the King. Heavy fines were imposed on the English Church, some of which Henry was prepared to remit on condition that the Church recognize him as its protector and, as far as the law of Christ would allow, its supreme head. The Pope was not to be cowed by such threats. He had the backing of the Emperor, and a full three years after this harsh confrontation between the English King and the English clergy he still forbade Henry to divorce Catherine and enter into another marriage.

By then the dissolution of the monasteries, which Wolsey had initiated, was well under way. The break with Rome, although not yet formally announced, was already an accomplished fact, and it was to this that England owed the special position she then acquired as the leader of the Protestant world. There were still fierce pockets of resistance to be overcome at home, but after Henry VIII it was quite impossible for England to revert to the old ways. The cause of this development is not to be found in the Pope's refusal to grant a royal divorce but in the specific character of the island people, who for centuries had been moving towards independence.

Edward VI and Mary Tudor

Only three of the children of Henry VIII's six marriages survived childhood: Mary, the daughter of the Spanish Infanta; Elizabeth, the daughter of Anne Boleyn; and Henry's only son, Edward, whose mother, Jane Seymour, had died at his birth. Henry's instructions regarding the succession were contradictory. His legitimate son, Edward, was to succeed him. But if Edward should die childless, the throne was to pass to Henry's two daughters, despite the fact that he had had them declared bastards upon the dissolution of his marriages to their mothers.

Edward VI reigned from 1547 to 1553, when he died at the age of fifteen. Mary Tudor, a Catholic who married King Philip II of Spain, succeeded him and was Queen of England from 1553 to 1558. It was during her reign that the only really serious attempt to establish the Counter-Reformation in England was undertaken, and it was unsuccessful: England had opted for reform. By the severity with which she proceeded against all who renounced the Roman Church, Mary Tudor had instilled in the hearts of the people a profound hatred of the Spaniards, who frequented the English Court as members of her husband's entourage.

In Edward's time the government of the country had been in the hands of Edward Seymour, the young King's maternal uncle, who had succeeded in having himself appointed Protector. As Protector he bore the title of Duke of Somerset. In 1547, the year of Henry VIII's death, he had gained a great victory over the Scots at Pinkie Cleugh. This, however, merely drove the Scots into a new alliance with the French, which enabled them to preserve their independence. Somerset fostered the reorganization of the Anglican Church. During his period of office the Book of Common Prayer was introduced and the groundwork was laid for revision of ecclesiastical law, which was completed under Elizabeth. Somerset also furthered the Protestant cause by granting asylum to refugees fleeing religious persecution on the Continent; the propagandistic effect produced by the appointment of foreign theologians to posts at Oxford and Cambridge is a point to be noted.

Elizabeth I

"The time is out of joint"—thus Hamlet in Shakespeare's drama. What time is not? Shakespeare's own time, caught up in a process of vast dislocations, forced a great people to bestir itself to great ends. The conflict of that era challenged the highest minds, but they also shattered the basic structure of established society and traditional institutions. All the peoples of Europe were tested to the very core of their being. Accustomed to violence and despotism and subject to both the powerful statesmanship and weak vacillation of successive rulers, the people of the island kingdom carried out institutional and ecclesiastical revolutions with the high seriousness demanded by a legal process based on age-old freedoms.

When Elizabeth succeeded Mary Tudor, Henry II of France accused her, since she had been conceived out of wedlock, of usurping the English throne, and he had Mary Stuart proclaimed Queen of England in her stead. Mary Stuart, then Queen of Scotland and the wife of Henry II's eldest son, later Francis II, was a niece of the anti-Huguenot Duke of Guise and the Cardinal of Lorraine on her mother's side and a grandniece of Henry VIII. At the time, Elizabeth was twenty-five years old, and if she had made the slightest slip she might well have been deposed. But Elizabeth knew how to wait. Her difficult childhood, in which she had been constantly exposed to personal danger, had taught her when to act.

Elizabeth's first adviser was William Cecil, later Lord Burghley, who fashioned her administration. Especially during his early years in office, literally every aspect of policy bore the stamp of his personality. Richelieu often spoke of him as his ideal of a statesman. He was a prodigious worker and never wasted a moment; objective to the point of dryness, a politician first and foremost, he was nonetheless a man of a decidedly Protestant cast. He was constant in his aims, from which he never deviated either in home or foreign affairs, and he destroyed all opposition with no compunction at all. But Elizabeth, unlike Louis XIII with Richelieu, did not become dependent on Cecil. Her moodiness and her propensity for forming sudden attachments to one or another of her courtiers were not the only qualities she had inherited from her father. She also had his stubbornness. She knew that her main asset was the hatred that had built up under Mary's rule.

Elizabeth remained the virgin Queen for reasons of state. She was well aware of the dangers inherent in the system of dynastic marriages. Developed in feudal times, in the era of absolute monarchy it was acquiring a force so disproportionate that time and again the fate of nations was influenced or even decided by this factor alone. No sooner had she ascended the throne than the English Parliament begged her to choose a husband. Her former brother-in-law, Philip II, offered—as he put it in a private letter to his representative in London, the Duke of Feria—"to sacrifice his conscience and do her the highest honour." However, Pope Paul IV, whose pro-French propensities Elizabeth was to exploit on many subsequent occasions, made it impossible for her even to consider Philip's conditions. And so she rejected the Duke of Feria's overtures, amusing herself in the process. It did not take Feria long to realize that this great dynastic transaction was a lost cause. Initially, however, Elizabeth continued to pay the Spanish ambassador every possible attention, especially during the period when her plenipotentiaries were negotiating a peace treaty with France. Although there was no actual warfare between England and France at that time, there was a need to deal with the after-effects of past battles.

While Spain and France had been fighting for control of Italy, there had been some hope for English territorial claims on the Continent. But on April 2, 1559, the peace of Cateau-Cambrésis between France and Spain brought the era of the Italian wars to an end. It had begun in 1495, when Charles VIII of France set out on that improvised campaign which reads today like an episode from a chivalric romance. If Charles VIII had given the same thought to French foreign policy as Henry IV, he would have realized that the Netherlands question, the German question and the problem of France's relations to Spain and England were more important than his romantic Italian campaign. The Italians opposed him with the cold realism of accomplished diplomats, which Louis XI could doubtless have matched but not the ill-advised Charles. The question of the Italian territories remained the prime consideration of French foreign policy under Henry II and Francis I until Spanish supremacy over Italy was established by the treaty of Cateau-Cambrésis, which radically changed the whole complexion of European politics. The problems posed by the Netherlands and by Germany, which were aggravated by religious division, then became the major concern of the day. At the same time, tension at sea between Spain and England grew slowly but inexorably in the new situation created by the Spanish discoveries overseas.

In the decisive year of 1559, Philip II married Elizabeth of Valois, the daughter of Henry II. Even before Cateau-Cambrésis the Spanish had been alert to the dangerous possibility of an Anglo-French alliance. Philip's third marriage should be regarded, therefore, as a traditional counter to the threat of an Anglo-French rapprochement. With the outbreak of the French religious wars in 1562, however, France's value as an ally was greatly reduced. But there was a further obstacle barring the way to closer ties between England and France:

the Dauphin, Mary Stuart's husband, was then signing himself "King of England, Scotland and Ireland."

The second year of Elizabeth's reign was a crucial one. In it the first Parliament convened in her name passed two ecclesiastical laws of fundamental importance: the Act of Uniformity and the Act of Supremacy. The Anglican service, introduced under Henry VIII, was thereafter the only form of divine service officially recognized by the State. When Elizabeth came to the throne, the English Catholics had made up more than fifty per cent of the population. When she died they numbered no more than five per cent.

In 1563 the Book of Common Prayer, first introduced under Elizabeth's stepbrother, Edward VI, was officially adopted for use in the Anglican Church. In this revised version of the Prayer Book, Elizabeth was no longer referred to as the supreme head on earth of the Church of England, the title claimed by her autocratic father, but as supreme governor, a formula more acceptable to the Curia. This compromise solution has remained in use up to the present day. Since England was able to avoid the religious wars that ravaged the Continent, the theological disputes of sixteenth-century Europe claimed fewer victims in England than in France or Germany. But in 1570 Elizabeth's Privy Council began to execute many priests and noblemen, including some of outstanding merit like Edmund Campion, and even commoners. However, all were condemned not on religious grounds but on grounds of high treason. The executioners were kept busy with fire and rope. These extremely harsh measures, having no precedent from the early period of Elizabeth's reign, were introduced following the Massacre of St Bartholomew and the proclamation of the papal bull in which Pius V excommunicated Elizabeth and declared her deposed. The Queen's Catholic subjects were thus released from their allegiance to her. In 1580 the Pope's Secretary of State is said to have told a Jesuit, in reply to a question regarding the moral justification of regicide, that "since it is through this woman that millions of souls have been alienated from their belief, there can be no doubt but that if some faithful servant of God were to dispatch her from this world, his action would not only be blameless but meritorious."

If the Church of England had had its way, then the English Puritans, who took their instructions from Geneva, would have been persecuted quite as severely as the followers of the ancient faith. It was the declared intention of the Puritans, or Calvinists, to destroy all hierarchies, and it was from their ranks that the anti-royalists emerged. They did not recognize the Anglican bishops, they inveighed against the profligacy of the upper classes and they wanted to see the State administered by a Protestant council of elders along the lines prescribed by Calvin. The people respected them, for the people always respect an attitude that is one hundred per cent consistent. And it was their obvious popularity in the country that saved them. When an anti-Puritan measure was presented to Parliament, it was thrown out.

Developments such as these caused growing concern to Philip II of Spain. With one eye on France he slowly renounced his previous amicable relationship with England, but he was loath to do so. In 1569, at a time when both Catholic arms in France and Spanish arms in the Netherlands were enjoying a spate of success, Mary Stuart's uncle, the Cardinal of Lorraine, suggested to Philip II the formation of a Franco-Spanish offensive alliance against Elizabeth. Despite France's internal weaknesses at that time, it is quite clear that the combined forces of the two great Catholic powers would have been more than a match for the English, who had not yet consolidated their strength. Yet even at that late date Philip II rejected the alliance. He did not trust the French. The Continental victories of Catholic arms in that year also gave rise to a rebellion in the northern counties of England, which, like the rebellions of 1536 and 1549, enjoyed an initial success. On this occasion the rebel leaders were Northumberland, Cumberland, Westmorland and Richard Morton. They were not actually trying to depose Elizabeth but they did want to ensure Mary Stuart's right of succession. Their rebellion was suppressed, and it was then that the Pope pronounced Elizabeth's excommunication. At the time England was swarming with refugees from every corner of Christendom, and on the Continent seminaries had been founded for the express purpose of training agents to carry the Catholic mission to England, an undertaking that might well cost them their lives. Savage, the man instructed to murder Elizabeth, was no hired assassin but a student of theology. Like Babington, Mary Stuart's correspondent, he had spent his formative years in the seminary of Douay.

What finally persuaded Philip II to forgo his traditional links with England was the tremendous impact of the victory of Protestant ideas in the Netherlands. Elizabeth tried to avoid a definitive break, but it was becoming increasingly clear that the dispute between the Spanish empire and the newly emerging power of England was prompted not so much by religious differences as by power factors, above all by economic factors, which were to exercise an enduring influence on both nations. We shall be discussing this question later in connection with both Spain and Holland.

Burghley acted on the principle that the Netherlands were England's Continental counterscarp, without which she could not survive, and he constantly impressed this axiom on Elizabeth. None the less, in 1575 Elizabeth offered to mediate in the Netherlands on behalf of Philip II, on the condition that Philip modify for the benefit of English merchants the strict religious laws currently in force in the Spanish dominions— a condition that seemed to her to present no difficulties. She also requested that Philip recall Don John of Austria from the Netherlands, because he was disturbing the peace. This second requirement conformed with Philip's own wishes, for at that time the victor of Lepanto was cherishing chivalrous plans for freeing Mary Stuart and was already making preparations for an invasion of Scotland.

Meanwhile the consolidation of the Church of England was progressing to the constant accompaniment of conspiracies and insurrections, but all within local limits. Whether these revolts were kindled by missionary Jesuits in the name of the Counter-Reformation or by foreign states, Mary Stuart, the Queen's rival and opponent, formed a natural centre for all such movements, and she was always directly or indirectly involved.

Queen Elizabeth the Great did not find it easy to sign death warrants, not even in the case of Mary Stuart. Her political task was as confused and complex at home as abroad. In her case, caution and the art of dissimulation had taken root early in life. Contrary to the general practice of her times, Elizabeth showed both statesmanship and moderation in punishing offenders. But her intended victims, her collaborators and even her favourites were all kept in a state of uncertainty. She never let them know how high their credit was. As a dissembler she excelled even Burghley, for she was able to employ tactics that were both illogical and contradictory. Richelieu was also a master of camouflage, but he always proceeded logically; he was the professional poacher, who knew exactly where his snares were laid.

The defeat of the Spanish Armada, one of those crucial events that leave a mark on the character of a whole nation, came in the middle of Elizabeth's reign. This was the starting point of England's development as a world power, which she accomplished despite the fact that her population then numbered only four and a half million.

Decentralizing and particularist tendencies in France were suppressed by the movement towards absolute monarchy. But n England the conflict between the State and the estates, which soon became a conflict between the State and the people, was conducted without giving rise to a period of absolutism.

During Elizabeth's reign two factors that had greatly contributed to the self-assurance of the island kingdom reached the peak of their development: the incomparable daring of

English seamen, exemplified by such men as Sir Francis Drake and Sir Walter Raleigh, and the intelligence service, which had been thoroughly revised since the days of Henry VIII. Walsingham transformed it into an instrument that enabled him to hear in London what men were thinking in Rome. It was in this almost invisible web that Mary Stuart was enmeshed.

The age of Elizabeth was the last in which England still formed an integral part of the old European order. Politically and economically it marked the beginning of a great venture; intellectually the Elizabethans, fearing the destruction of their heritage, made use of all the past had to offer. The poets celebrated the greatness of England's past, the scholars heaped upon it their noble mounds of learning. But above all the Elizabethans savoured their heritage, although this did not prevent them from denying it when the spirit of their own age demanded. The great Elizabethans found themselves confronted with the gorgon's head of Puritan iconoclasm, whose chilly aura subdued their revels and penetrated into the innermost recesses of their world.

James I

In the first volume of this work there are profiles of James I and his favourite (see p. 165 ff. and p. 180 ff.). We must now consider these two men from a different point of view.

Towards the end of her life Queen Elizabeth found it quite unbearable to discuss the succession with her advisers. There had been a time when Mary Stuart's son, James VI of Scotland, who later succeeded to the English throne as James I, had looked upon all of Elizabeth's influential ministers as his sworn enemies. In all of Elizabeth's actions he perceived signs of intrigue directed against his own claim to the succession. He saw pretenders and rivals on every side. Many of them were real enough.

James, who had written scholarly works on absolutism and

the divine right of kings, had made secret contacts with the English Catholics at an early date. He had also approached Clement VII, addressing him as "Holy Father." James later described an incident in which, he claimed, the Pope had exhorted him to return to the Catholic faith, whereupon he himself had suggested that the theological issues dividing the Church should again be submitted to a General Council and had undertaken to abide by the Council's decision. The Pope, James declared, was not interested.

Both during and after the Essex crisis James's agents had been very active in England. Their orders were to discover whether there was any possibility of Elizabeth's being deposed and whether the Catholic opposition was prepared to back James's claim. Certainly the King of Scotland had followers in England, among both the nobility and the gentry. He was constantly urging them to keep themselves in a state of readiness in case matters should ever come to a conflict of arms. James's wife was Danish, and at that time he was undoubtedly counting on the support of the Danish navy. His own Scottish nobles were ready to march at a moment's notice.

One of his Continental confidants and advisers was the Grand Duke Ferdinand of Tuscany, who acted as intermediary between Henry IV of France and the Pope during Elizabeth's lifetime. Ferdinand was Marie de' Medici's uncle and was closely connected to James VI of Scotland through his marriage to a member of the house of Lorraine.

It was only after the death of Essex, when it had become abundantly clear that Elizabeth's position was unassailable, that James cautiously but consistently approached those English ministers whom he had previously regarded as his chief adversaries. Lord Burghley's son, Sir Robert Cecil, was the first to respond to his advances, in order, as he later claimed, to ensure the Queen's safety and peace of mind. At the time, however, he did all he could to keep the Queen in ignorance of this new departure. At the same time, James VI instructed the Earl of Lennox to assure the Queen of his devotion and loyalty. Lennox was favourably received by Elizabeth, whereupon James authorized him to offer military help against the Irish. When the Catholic leader, James Lindsay, tried to obtain a declaration of religious tolerance for the Scots Catholics, James VI fobbed him off with empty phrases. At that time James negotiated tirelessly with men of every shade of opinion and held out hope to Protestants and Catholics alike.

On March 24, 1603, the day of Elizabeth's death, there was great anxiety in England. It was rumoured that a Spanish invasion was being mounted from Flanders. But once it became known that James VI of Scotland would succeed to the throne and so bring the two kingdoms together, the anxiety was soon dispelled. The Scots King lacked the means for a stately entry into his new domain, and contemporary observers reported that on his arrival on English soil he made a shabby appearance and that his Scots accent seemed alien. But he was given a triumphal reception. The Catholics lived in high hopes, and James did in fact promise to mitigate the penalties imposed on them, although he made it a condition that they renounce all missionary activity. But since they regarded missionary activity as their principal duty, this merely prompted them to conspire against the King, in the certain knowledge that they could count on help from abroad.

In 1605 the Gunpowder Plot was discovered. If it had succeeded, the Protestants would have lost all their leaders. The conspirators had calculated that in the ensuing confusion it would have been a simple matter for them to sway the populace in their favour. Instead, this ill-considered and cruel conspiracy resulted in the imposition of extremely harsh conditions on the English Catholics for a long time to come.

James's foreign policy was not immediately affected by these internal events. In June 1603, acting in concert with Robert Cecil, he had come to an arrangement with the French, which led to the signing of a trade agreement. In August 1604 he gave his signature to the understanding with Spain. This

reconciliation between England and Spain, effected immediately after Elizabeth's death, was an object of great concern
to Henry IV of France. He had long since come to regard
Burghley's fight against Catholicism as a political constant.
For Elizabeth, Spain had been the source of all danger, and the
same held true for her younger contemporary, Henry IV of
France. Elizabeth had never really freed herself from the fear
and tension she had known before the defeat of the Spanish
Armada. Mary Stuart, living or dead, gave her no peace, even
appearing to her in her dreams, and her memories of Mary
Tudor's reign continued to oppress her throughout the whole
of her life. Henry IV, for his part, had not forgotten the
Massacre of St Bartholomew or the French Holy League,
which had been directed from Spain. Despite the many
vicissitudes of Anglo-French relations, the two sovereigns had
always been at one in their opposition to Spain.

It is not surprising, therefore, that the first thing Henry IV
did upon the death of Elizabeth was to send his close friend
Rosny, the Duke of Sully, to James I. Sully's reception got
off to a bad start for, as we have already seen, the English
Admiralty, secure in the sense of its own immense superiority,
took the opportunity of insulting the French flag.

The instructions Henry IV gave to his alter ego on this
mission had been worked out with great care. Sully was to
obtain a contractual guaranty of English help for the rebels
in the Netherlands and was to impress on James and his
ministers that the Spanish Netherlands constituted a source of
mortal danger, not only to France but to England as well;
for Spain was at liberty to mount an invasion from the Netherlands against either country whenever she pleased. Sully was
also to express his sovereign's conviction that an Anglo-
French agreement would immediately bring the Scandinavian
countries into the alliance, and that England might rest
assured that, as a sea power, she would occupy the key position
in the international conflict that was bound to come. If
England should decide to stand aside, the consequences would

be ruinous, for if James I were to follow an isolationist policy, his kingdom would be subjected to an endless succession of Catholic conspiracies and revolts. On the other hand, an Anglo-French union would at last establish a balance of power in Europe.

The accounts Sully gave of his English mission, at that time and later, were graphic and direct and very far removed from the official style of later French diplomats. Both in his Memoirs and in his letters to Henry IV describing his audiences with James I, he shows himself to have been a highly imaginative but excellent reporter:

"The King of England speaks fluent French with a strong Scots accent. . . . The first thing he said to me was: 'I have been told that my cousin the King of France is mocking his friends and royal kinsmen; he calls me a Captain of the Fine Arts and the King of the Clerks.'" After parrying similar thrusts, Sully found it extremely difficult to get down to business, for the King kept on reverting to private matters. In the end James did say that he was not of a mind with those old impenitent Englishmen who still thought in terms of the Hundred Years' War. He also said that he had no interest in Brittany and warned the French ambassador not to pay any attention to the nonsense being talked in London society.

Sully made no more headway with the English ministers, who were distinctly cool. They listened to him but said nothing.

But there is also a report of a farewell audience, which allegedly was held in private. According to Sully, James I said to him: "The fact that my brother Henry has sent his best friend to me must not go unrewarded." James is also supposed to have asked what progress the Duke had made in his talks with the English ministers and, on learning that these had proved negative, to have said: "Tell me everything. I have time. Today's hunt has been put off." At this Sully claims to have told the King of all the issues he had been required to raise and to have been told in reply: "So the King of France wishes to see the Netherlands freed from Spanish rule. But supposing this project, which would also be in my interests, were realized? What then? How does the Most Christian King envisage the future development of the Continent? What does he think of the Spanish conquests in other parts of the world?"

At this Sully became very formal and asked the King to swear by the Holy Sacrament never to divulge to a living soul a word of what he was about to say. He then invited James to consider the rise of the house of Hapsburg over the past hundred years. It had already extended its rule over Spain, Germany, Italy and Flanders; it was about to crush Holland and it boasted kingdoms in America and in the East Indies that were bigger than Persia and Turkey put together.

Sully then developed his grand design. The Stuarts and the Bourbons, he said, should enter into an intimate and lasting alliance, which the Kings of the North would also join. Holland would be freed and the Protestant princes would all forsake the Hapsburgs: Bohemia, Hungary, Moravia and Silesia were waiting for a liberator. Savoy would be easily won. All that was needed was to take the kingdom of Naples from the Hapsburgs. Even the Pope was complaining that he was hemmed in by the Austro-Spanish dynasty.

The first and most important step was to annex the combined Spanish-Portuguese territory in the East Indies for England. The Indies were Spain's vulnerable point; the Spanish-Portuguese fleet could be defeated in the Indian Ocean. Too many wars had been conducted in Europe already. The old continent had seen enough of bloody victories, defeats and useless peace treaties. They must now think of the world markets that would be opening up to a new Europe. What an opportunity for the King of England to acquire undying fame!

At this point in his discourse Sully suddenly noticed that the King looked startled, almost as if he were listening to a madman. He immediately broke off and said, "These are just my own thoughts, secret thoughts, which are concerned with the distant future." He then reminded the King of his oath and, returning to his brief, said to James: "What we ought to be thinking of now is the conclusion of the treaty for the liberation of the Netherlands. We must help these industrious peoples who have so much in common with the English; but we must help them secretly, without declaring war. We must send money and recruit soldiers for Holland. But first we must prevent Spain from taking Ostende."

The authenticity of this report has been questioned by historians.

Where the original letters to Henry IV are missing, we have the copies Sully reproduced in his Memoirs. But perhaps this question of authenticity is not the thing that really matters. Whether Sully presented these far-reaching ideas to the King of England or not, they still remain very impressive designs, many of which were actually realized—his observations on the Indies, for example. What matters is that he thought of them and committed them to paper, which means that a statesman of the early Bourbon period had anticipated Richelieu's ideas and even gone beyond them.

Sully claimed to have told James I in 1603 that Spain and Portugal could be defeated in the Indian Ocean. The Spanish-Portuguese fleet was defeated in the Indian Ocean by the British in 1612. The East India Company acquired Madras in 1639, two years before Sully's death and three years before Richelieu's.

Colonial Questions

This same Duke of Sully once wrote: "Lands that are separated from the main body of France by foreign countries or the sea will always be more of a burden than a benefit." On another occasion he declared that the mental outlook and natural disposition of Frenchmen were not suited to the conquest of great territories far from home. Here he was alluding to a supposedly constant trait in the French national character, but it has always been counteracted by an opposite tendency, in which the power of the will is directed outwards, and Richelieu was one of the great exemplars of this. Sully regarded the construction of a French fleet as a defensive measure. Not so Richelieu: he saw the French navy as an assault force. It is interesting to note the reactions of Spain and England to the Cardinal's naval preparations. The Spanish, persuaded of their great superiority at sea, received the news with equanimity. The English behaved very differently. The King of England had long since regarded himself as the "sovereign of the seas," although until the time of Cromwell, when the Navigation Acts changed the situation completely, there was little objective evidence to support such a claim apart from the unique daring of individual English sea captains. But these astonishing individual achievements were the result of a general awareness on the part of the English of their maritime mission, which more than compensated for any technical deficiencies in the British fleet.

The colonies did not assume a dominant role in England's economic policy until the eighteenth century. The early pioneers of colonial expansion were not Englishmen. In 1496 Henry VII authorized the Venetian John Cabot and his sons to undertake voyages of discovery under the British flag and to take possession of uncharted lands; he then invested them with the tenure of newly discovered territories.

Cabot and his sons landed on the American mainland before Columbus did. But England failed to exploit their discovery. The only advantage it brought her was the knowledge that the fishing grounds off Newfoundland would provide a useful source of food for English mariners. Raleigh later maintained that England would pay dearly if Newfoundland were lost. For views such as this, which were not shared by the majority of his countrymen, Raleigh himself was to pay dearly. Most of the progressive and far-reaching plans formulated in England at that time came from the merchant class and not from the nobility, who had always looked to Europe as the natural goal of English expansionist policies. It was a London merchant, Robert Thorne, who advised Henry VIII to seek both a north-west and a north-east passage, and even suggested that a route to India might be discovered via the North Pole. During Mary Tudor's reign Anglo-Spanish rivalry at sea was halted.

As we have already seen, the initial impetus to English emigration came from the impoverishment of the peasants following the change-over from agriculture to sheep farming. This was subsequently reinforced by the effects of English internal policies at the time of Cromwell as well as the prospect of an easy life and an assured future in the colonies. These high hopes were based primarily on the impressions Sir Walter Raleigh had formed of the territory he called "Virginia" in honour of Queen Elizabeth, where, he said, the people lived as in the golden age.

Under both James I and Charles I the English navy was neglected. English prowess at sea, astonishing though it was, was employed only for surprise attacks on the Spanish and French coasts and privateering ventures directed against the Spanish silver fleet and French merchantmen. These sudden attacks provoked strong complaints and strengthened anti-British feeling in the countries concerned. Richelieu was obliged to act against French public opinion in this particular respect. He insisted repeatedly that France could not afford to waste time on such incidents but must concentrate on the primary objective of winning England as an ally against Spain. English piracy must be treated with contempt, as something that was scarcely worth noticing. Richelieu extended this diplomatic policy of indifference to include even English naval support for the Huguenots. He attributed such incidents as England's conquest of the Isle of Ré in 1627 and the treaty the English concluded in October of the same year with La Rochelle to that "extravagant and exalted halfwit, Buckingham." If any English ships should be captured by the

French in reprisal, he wrote, then this must on no account be permitted to cause a rift with England. Undue importance should not be attached to such incidents. At that time Richelieu authorized Châteauneuf, his ambassador to England, to submit a plan to Charles I for improving maritime relations between their two countries. His final instructions were: not to be over-sensitive where French honour was concerned.

The English were always trying to prevent French merchants from trading with Spain; they would board French ships on the high seas, and refused to recognize the French flag. Richelieu played all this down. Charles I, on the other hand, told the French ambassador quite openly that if his brother-in-law the King of France wished to live at peace with him, he must give up his plans for a French fleet. Richelieu wanted peace with England. But Anglo-French rivalry in the colonial sphere soon proved unavoidable. Despite Richelieu's wise attempt to establish an early form of entente cordiale, competition between England and France in Asia and America revived their ancient feud and led to serious disputes, which reached their peak under Napoleon I.

Here we see the extent to which Richelieu's foreign policy was influenced by his own rare ability to deal with all the problems confronting him at different levels. He was able to subordinate the short-term considerations which arouse public opinion to the more enduring and important requirements of French national policy. This kind of long-term policy, conducted by this extraordinary man in accordance with a hierarchical system of values, was one that politicians of later eras were seldom able to emulate.

In Richelieu's day it was the Dutch who magnanimously advocated the freedom of the seas. Their endeavours on this account have been recorded by Hugo Grotius. This astonishing example of international liberalism was a positive act undertaken by a nation powerful enough to be able to afford such magnanimity. For the Dutch could command respect for their shipping. The same could not be said of England. England felt sure of herself at sea, and justifiably so, for she had an impressive list of extraordinary achievements and lucky incidents to her credit. But England was not yet a dominant maritime power.

The English politician and orientalist John Selden composed a treatise entitled *Mare clausum* in response to Hugo Grotius' magnificent *Mare librum*. Selden was an opponent of absolute monarchy who had been imprisoned under Charles I, though he later spoke against the Puritan demands in the Long Parliament. In his treatise he claimed that England was entitled to the absolute sovereignty of the seas surrounding her shores. His ideas exercised a decisive influence on the Navigation Acts passed under Cromwell. The Dutch attitude to this maritime problem revealed a sense of power and security, but Selden's work leaves the reader with the impression that there was a discrepancy between England's conception of herself as a great maritime power and the actual state of her naval affairs. Nonetheless, it was owing to this auto-suggestion, to the power of England's will and England's self-confidence, that her colonial empire constantly expanded on two continents, while at the same time an English fleet was built up that soon relegated Holland to third place in the naval hierarchy and, after Holland's successful resistance to the Spanish, very nearly let that country fall a victim to Louis XIV, the man who received and squandered Richelieu's heritage.

Prelude to Richelieu's English Policy

Throughout the whole of his reign James I tried to mitigate the conflicts which marked his century and wherever possible to resolve them by peaceful means. He sought to avoid all aggressive measures and, as a true Stuart, declined to pursue an anti-Spanish policy. Under James the British fleet again lost much of its striking power. A supporter of the Church of England and an opponent of feudal rule, which he had come to know only too well in Scotland, he moved with the times in advancing the cause of royal power, but in this respect his contribution was primarily theoretical. The reaction to it was delayed until his son's reign.

Three years before the beginning of Richelieu's first period of office, an event took place that produced grave repercussions in the future of Europe. This was the marriage between James I's daughter, Elizabeth, and Frederick, the Count Palatine. This dynastic union was celebrated by splendid festivities, which included a performance of Shakespeare's *Tempest*. In the light of subsequent events, the choice of play could not have been more apt.

In 1616 and 1617 La Vieuville was pursuing a policy of wooing England that was based on Henry IV's political thinking but also showed traces of Richelieu's influence. This "new line" was highly unpopular with a large section of the Catholic majority in France. The corresponding policy in England was no more popular with the English, who, as we have already indicated, felt great sympathy with the French Huguenots.

On January 5, 1617, three months before Concini's death, Louis XIII instructed Cauchon du Tour, who had been sent on a special diplomatic mission to England, to counteract any impression that the French Crown was in danger of losing its authority. Louis had heard that the Duke of Bouillon, the sovereign prince in Sedan, had turned to James I for help, but he had every confidence in his royal brother and was convinced that he would respect the principle that a vassal could appeal for help only to his own sovereign.

The same subject prompted Schomberg's departure for Germany. A Fronde was afoot in France under the leadership of Henri de Bourbon, Prince of Condé, the Duke of Nevers, the Duke of Vendôme and the Duke of Bouillon. Their rebellion had international implications, and it was the subject of a royal declaration issued February 18, 1617, which Henri, Duc de Rohan, described as "an excellent and precise summary." Its author was Richelieu.

The Duke of Bouillon had appealed to every Protestant Court in Europe including the Court of King James. He had spread the rumour that Spain was supporting the claims raised by Charles de La Marck, Comte de Maulevrier, to the principality of Sedan and that the house of Austria was sending reinforcements to the Spanish general Spinola, who was threatening the principality. The Netherlands branch of the Hapsburgs were said to be the prime movers in this action. The rebels' object was to win the whole of Protestant Europe, the Calvinists in particular, as allies against the alleged Spanish intrigues. Even Concini, the Marquis of Ancre, was informed by Bouillon of these "dark plots." In actual fact the rebels' allegations were put out simply in order to justify and camouflage the massive recruiting campaign they themselves were conducting, and as a means of rallying the Protestant forces of Europe. For this was not just another in the series of chronic revolts by the French nobility. What threatened here was the as yet unbroken power of the Huguenots, still capable of unsettling the Bourbon monarchy whenever they pleased. And in this connection the many close personal relations between the French and the English Protestants were an important factor.

On January 26th du Tour received the following instructions in London:

"You are to explain [Bouillon's] behaviour to my brother the King of Great Britain. Details are contained in the memorandum which I am sending to you. In short, you are to assure the King that I have complete trust in him and am convinced that he would never support rebellious subjects in an action directed against their lord but would rather join forces with me in leading insurgents back to their true allegiance."

If we compare these instructions to the French embassy in London with the instructions Richelieu sent in the same year to Schomberg, the special envoy to the German Courts, and to de La Noue, the special envoy to Holland, it becomes quite evident that this proposed union between the provincial rulers and the Huguenots was felt to constitute a real threat to the emerging French State. This casts a revealing light on Richelieu's Huguenot policy.

Some indication of the tension with which the English reaction was awaited in 1617 is given by the fact that this affair had not been entrusted to the regular envoy, Desmarets. Instead it had been considered necessary to send as special representative to the Court of St James's Charles du Tour et Maupas, a man personally known to James I and of whom he had formed a high opinion during his period as French envoy to Scotland.

At the end of February, Baron du Tour was able to report to Louis XIII from Dover that there was no need to fear an intervention in favour of the rebels on the part of England, for although James I was fitting out a fleet it was quite evident that this was intended for India and would on no account be used against France.

Richelieu was not satisfied with the outcome of du Tour's mission and on April 6, 1617, he wrote to Desmarets, informing him that du Tour had failed to dispel the prejudices James I had formed concerning the internal situation in France. It is to be assumed that this criticism of du Tour won Richelieu the goodwill of Desmarets, for the latter had not been enthusiastic about his colleague's special mission.

In the same letter the Cardinal also referred to a strange piece of information Desmarets had sent him: Sir Walter Raleigh had recently been released from a long term of imprisonment in the Tower. Desmarets had met Raleigh, who had told him that he was to be sent on another difficult mission overseas, but that he was most discontented and dejected; he then assured Desmarets that he remained a "warm admirer of the French Crown." Unfortunately the circumstances of their meeting had made more detailed conversation impossible.

The implications were obvious. Richelieu instantly saw

11. Louis XIII, King of France

12. Pope Urban VIII

in Raleigh's allusion possibilities for his naval plans and wrote to Desmarets: "Please be so good as to inform me whether the negotiations with the person whom you have mentioned have produced any results. This would be of interest if you should consider that the person in question might be eligible for service under the King of France."

But nothing came of this initiative. On April 24, 1617, the Marquis d'Ancre was murdered and on the 25th Richelieu went into exile. Between then and 1624 we find no further evidence of Richelieu's influence on French policy vis-à-vis England, except perhaps in respect of the plans La Vieuville continued to cherish for a marriage between Henrietta of France and the English heir-apparent, who had just returned from his disappointing journey in search of a Spanish bride. Meanwhile, in 1618, Sir Walter Raleigh died under the executioner's axe.

During the period of Richelieu's enforced absence from the political scene, the peace between France and England continued undisturbed.

We have already seen that at the time when Charles's marriage to Henrietta of France was being negotiated, Richelieu was well aware that he could only break the Huguenots' naval power with the help of England and Holland, for at that early stage the French navy was virtually nonexistent. The fact that he was able to obtain such help from both countries, in exchange for what was no more than a loose undertaking to support the Dutch in their struggle for freedom, is one of the astonishing feats that testify to his skill as a negotiator.

On June 2, 1625, a new special envoy, La Ville-aux-Clercs, was sent to London, and on June 1st or 2nd of the same year Richelieu wrote to him as follows:

"Le Sieur de la Ville aux Clercs is to inform the King of Great Britain and the Duke [of Buckingham] that Rohan and Soubise and the citizens of La Rochelle still persist in their

insolent conduct . . . that the King will carry out the undertakings made to the said Rohan and Soubise in the treaty of
Montpellier and will give honourable commands to them both
in his army and navy in Italy . . . that he intends to take new
and massive action against [the Huguenots].

"In this way it will be possible to assess whether this [last]
proposal offends the susceptibilities of the King of Great
Britain and the Duke. . . .

"And in case the Sieur de la Ville aux Clercs should be
questioned as to whether the King [of France] desires war or
peace with Spain, . . . he should reply that His Majesty will
not act in either regard unless he deems it useful, necessary
and to the advantage . . . of his allies."

And in point of fact, as we have already seen, Montmorency's victory over the Huguenot fleet in 1625 was fought
largely in Dutch and English ships. This victory was particularly unpopular in England, where both the English town
dwellers who engaged in foreign trade and the English
Protestant nobility felt growing concern for their French
brothers in the faith. English preachers condemned government policy from the pulpits. Even on board the English ships
there was violent opposition to Admiralty orders, and Lord
Pembroke wrote to one rebellious captain to say that the
report he had received of a mutiny among the English sailors
was the best news he had heard for a long time.

James's decision to sacrifice his popularity at home for the
sake of his foreign policy was extremely daring, and its only
justification was the assumption that France would commit
herself wholeheartedly to the reconquest of the County
Palatine.

At the beginning of his reign Charles I continued his
father's unpopular pro-French policy. The representatives in
London of Christian IV of Denmark tried their utmost to
persuade the English to undertake a naval engagement in the
Weser estuary and to land English troops on the Continent

on a massive scale. They spoke of military developments that would be taking place in the very near future, although in point of fact the Danes were in no position to dictate the course of events. One of the prospects they held out was the immediate intervention of the Elector of Brandenburg and his brother-in-law, the Prince of Transylvania. They assumed an air of great confidence and maintained that the German Catholic League would be forced to surrender every one of the territories it had conquered. But Charles' favourite, Buckingham, regarded North Germany as no more than a minor theatre of operations. He quite failed to appreciate the crucial importance of Swedish arms and he was not prepared to pay £15,000, which Gustavus Adolphus was demanding from the English as the price of his intervention on the Continent. Meanwhile the Danish King was totally dependent on England. But he too received nothing, and the Danish cavalry, which had received no pay, was refusing to fight. Christian IV blamed the English for his defeat at Lutter. And in fact the Scandinavian countries received virtually no advantage from their political link with England. Although Buckingham had entered into an offensive and defensive alliance with the United Provinces, his plans—if they can be called plans—were now directed exclusively against Spain. He gave orders for a number of surprise attacks to be carried out on the Spanish coast. In one of these Cadiz—Spain's richest harbour—was conquered, sacked and laid waste. He tried to capture the Spanish silver fleet and so cut Spain's lines of communications with her American possessions. The attempt failed and in December 1625, after sustaining heavy losses, the English ships returned home without having accomplished their mission.

Richelieu benefited from this ill-conceived action, for Spain then adopted a more conciliatory attitude towards France. The pro-Spanish party of the *dévots*—the Queen-Mother and her large following together with Gaston d'Orléans as pretender—then gained the upper hand, for the Huguenot problem had meanwhile become so urgent that the King and the Cardinal were obliged to deal with it once and for all and, as has already been mentioned on repeated occasions, any large-scale military action against the Huguenots was fraught with grave dangers as long as Spain threatened the French borders. France could not rely on her alliance with the Protestant sea-powers in the operations she contemplated against the French Reformers. Consequently she had to alter course. The French religious dispute was reassessed for the benefit of Spain. The new, if temporary, motto of French diplomacy in Madrid was "Counter-Reformation"—France and Spain had a common duty to oppose the Protestants. The *dévots* were triumphant and Richelieu did nothing to discomfit them. For the moment their triumph fitted in with his plans.

Bérulle, their leader, developed a project for an attack on England by a combined Catholic force, and even this Richelieu did not at first oppose. Throughout this whole episode he was intent on doing one thing at a time: The Spanish must give ground in Italy; the threat of invasion must be removed; the Spanish must be restrained from intervening in the Huguenot action and perhaps even persuaded to furnish naval support for the blockade of La Rochelle; and then, after the defeat of the rebellious Huguenots, France would have a free hand at home and abroad and could revert to her traditional anti-Spanish policy.

We have already seen how precisely Richelieu achieved all these strictly defined aims (see Vol. I). During the siege of La Rochelle, despite their mistrust, the Spanish remained inactive and if anything even furthered the French cause. The pro-Spanish circles in France were appeased and whole-heartedly supported the Crown in this civil war. The Spanish themselves mobilized a fleet in support of Louis XIII's action, although it never saw service, because the Duke of Olivares, then responsible for Spanish foreign policy, remained justi-fiably wary of French intentions throughout the whole episode. It is of course true that in 1628, despite all Richelieu's efforts, Buckingham appeared before La Rochelle with an English fleet, which meant that England was again at war with France. But then Felton murdered Buckingham, and that virtually put an end to English participation in the siege.

In the further course of this history we shall come to see that Charles I of England was prompted by Richelieu's Continental policy to go against the popular mood in England and revert to a pro-Spanish policy. We have already spoken of the marriage between James I's daughter Elizabeth and Frederick, the Count Palatine. To appreciate the far-reaching importance of this marriage for the political life of Europe, we must now turn to events on the Continent and more specifically to events within the Holy Roman Empire.

CHAPTER VII

GERMANY

One of the important movements leading up to the outbreak of the Thirty Years War originated in Bohemia.

The Hussite or Wycliffite doctrine had been disseminated by itinerant preachers. It had caught on in the Upper Palatinate and penetrated as far as Poland, giving rise to the bloody clashes between established authority and the Taborites, the extremist Czech-nationalist wing of the Hussites, who, under the fanatical leadership of John Zizka, rejected all thought of compromise. It was not until 1434, when Zizka's successor, Prokop, was defeated at Lipan, that the Taborites were eliminated as a political force. But even then the embers continued to smoulder among the peasantry. This is clear from the career of Thomas Münzer, an agitator who fled from Zwickau to exert great influence in Prague a hundred years after the death of Huss. He intervened in the German Peasants' War and his appeals to the people, made with great revolutionary fervour, called for the overthrow of all the ecclesiastic and temporal institutions handed down from the Middle Ages, in the name of Christian justice.

The pamphlet in which Martin Luther attacked both the person and the doctrines of Thomas Münzer is well known. It is quite as harsh as his proclamation "Against the Murderous and Felonious Bands of Peasants," and it did much to consolidate the position of the German princes, who had emerged victorious from the Peasants' War.

Of the principal forms assumed by the reformational protest, it was the utterly uncompromising doctrine of Calvinism that most appealed to the descendants of the Hussites.

By contrast, the Lutheran doctrine remained an essentially German phenomenon. Martin Luther had given expression to his religious genius and spiritual passion in the powerful creative language of a great poet. In every sense of the word he was a child of his time, and as such he was faced with the task of creating a new language, one that could speak to the German peoples of his day and revivify for them the Christian message formalized in the language of the Roman Catholic Church. Lutheranism reached its apotheosis in the music of Johann Sebastian Bach and continued to exercise its influence as an essentially German spiritual force long after Bach's death, liberating intellectual potentialities of a quite specific character in the wider spheres of secularized intellectual endeavour, independent of all religious bonds.

Calvinism, on the other hand, generated an absolute and uncompromising dynamism, which in its effects unleashed fratricide in the German lands and a revolt in Bohemia which developed into a devastating war that continued unabated for thirty years.

Conversely, in the oppressive years preceding and presaging the outbreak of war, an anti-war pamphlet disseminated from Wittenberg clearly demonstrates the conciliatory attitude of Lutheranism in contrast to the uncompromising harshness of Calvinism. This pamphlet, which is not the only one of its kind, includes this passage:

"As long as the Papists and we Lutherans were united, there was none of this talk of factions and parties. No man drove his neighbour from his lawful property. We lived together in peace and prosperity. We intermarried. Fathers brought up their sons, mothers their daughters, in their own religion. In those days we Christians knew neither persecution nor bloodshed.

"But in Bohemia Calvin has shown that he intends to suppress both the Papists and the Lutherans. He has initiated a reformation that is really a deformation or, to be even more precise, an annihilation. He has torn down the images in the churches and despoiled or burnt the holy relics. But if such force is used at the outset, when Calvin has scarcely gained a foothold, what will it be like when he has the upper hand?

"Consequently, in the face of such danger the Pope and Luther must not rest from their labours but must join together to protect German freedom, to re-establish German loyalty and constancy and must take the field with their combined power to extirpate the Calvinist weed once and for all.

"It would be most salutary if in the towns of the Empire the two religions were tolerated, both Lutheran and Catholic, and if in the Kingdom of Bohemia the poor peasants were to be freed from their thraldom in such heathen bondage. The Emperor would be in a strong position if he were the first to set such an example."

In 1555, forty-three years before the Edict of Nantes, the Catholics and Lutherans tried to settle their differences at Augsburg. During the initial stages of the negotiations Ferdinand, brother of Emperor Charles V, acted on his behalf. A compromise treaty was drawn up, from which the Calvinists were excluded. When the treaty was signed, however, the Pope said that he was acquiescing only with "a sense of sorrow," and he permitted the Catholics "to halt the struggle only until such time as they were strong enough to be certain of victory."

Prior to the Religious Peace of Augsburg, all Church lands whose ecclesiastical rulers had gone over to Protestantism had been secularized and all such transfers of property before 1552 were acknowledged at Augsburg. But the harsh principle of "*cujus regio, ejus religio*," which was to force so many to emigrate, offered a constant threat to internal peace. At Augsburg the *reservatum ecclesiasticum*, stipulating that spiritual princes who broke away from Rome would lose both their ecclesiastical benefices and their temporal power, was included in the text of the settlement in an attempt to modify this principle. But the reservation was to give rise to serious discord at a later date. The Edict of Restitution of 1629, one of the crucial factors in prolonging the Thirty Years War, was a development of this provision. The compromise settlement of 1555 also legally sanctioned the division of the German territories into two different confessions with equal rights.

From 1555 Ferdinand (later Emperor Ferdinand I) tried to pursue a conciliatory policy, especially in his relations with Lutheran Saxony, in order to consolidate the progress made at Augsburg. His attitude was dictated by circumstances. He did not have a free hand in Germany, for he had to defend himself against the Turks and their allies, the Transylvanians, and also against the Hungarian Protestants. Although he was still King of Hungary, only a narrow strip of Hungarian territory actually belonged to him. Ferdinand's son and successor, Maximilian II, was also obliged to deal with internal tensions with the utmost caution, because of the threatening situation in the East. It was not until Ferdinand I's grandson, Rudolph II, had come to the throne that this temporizing policy was changed—at first only slightly. This Emperor, a man of great complexity, introduced the Counter-Reformation hesitantly. The pressure was gentle but insistent.

As Protestantism spread victoriously across virtually the whole of Germany from the Baltic to the Danube, resistance built up only gradually. This resistance stemmed at first from the decisions of the Council of Trent, and was later intensified and systematized by the new and superior methods developed by the Jesuits. Their order had been founded in 1534 and approved by Pope Paul III in 1540.

In the first quarter of the seventeenth century, Electoral Saxony was still one of the leading contenders on the Protestant side, but it was prepared to make sacrifices in the interests of Imperial unity. The Palatinate, on the other hand, which was governed by the Calvinist party excluded from the Augsburg treaty, was extremely belligerent. The antagonism between Lutherans and Calvinists gave rise to great tensions, accompanied by bitter theological controversy.

Bavaria and Austria

The unity of the Catholic camp was undermined by historical factors quite apart from the religious issue, factors which had been largely responsible for the confusions long besetting the historical development of the German peoples. One was the rivalry between the house of Austria and the house of Bavaria, more long-lasting by far than the Austro-Prussian rivalry of a later age and relieved by only brief intervals of reconciliation.

In the early Middle Ages, Bavaria had embraced all the territories between the Adriatic Sea in the south and the Eger valley in the north, between the Lech and the Regnitz in the west and the Leitha in the east. These had been augmented by the border territories of eastern Italy, which had been a gift of the Saxon Emperors, and also by Styria, Carinthia and Carniola, by Lower Austria and by territories north of the Danube and west of the Bohemian Forest, which had been wrested from the Slavs.

From the ninth to the fourteenth century, periods of decline alternated with periods of reconstruction, sovereignty constantly changed hands, territories constantly changed their borders. It was a time of conflict and flux. Dukes were deposed and quite suddenly reinstated. Again and again estates were divided up into separate inheritances. Policy vacillated endlessly between East and West. Counsels of despair were followed by great and glorious designs, which on occasion even envisaged the conquest of Swabia and Burgundy. Imperial power, which itself alternated between shadow and substance, was sometimes supported and sometimes opposed. Bavarian sovereignty was extended northwards along the course of the Rhine as far as the Netherlands, then southwards to the Tyrol, east to the lost territories of Carinthia and

Styria, and even to Bohemia. Wars with the Saxons and wars with the Franks were followed by reconciliations of short duration. Such was the vacillating fate of an inland territory without established borders, exposed to the pressure of shifting populations.

Already at the beginning of the tenth century the Duchy of Bavaria was only a remnant of its former greatness. In the twelfth century the relationship between the Bavarian rulers and the Viennese Babenbergs was quite as problematical as their later relationship to the Hapsburgs. The Duchy of Bavaria had passed to Leopold of Babenberg in 1138 and subsequently to his brother Henry, known as Jasomirgott. Then Frederick I of Hohenstaufen temporarily appointed the Guelph Henry the Lion as Duke of Bavaria, vesting the Duchy of Austria in the Babenbergs as a hereditary possession. In 1180, after Henry the Lion had quarrelled with the Emperor, he was deprived of all his fiefs, and Bavaria passed to Otto I of the house of Wittelsbach. But from 1180 until the introduction of the right of primogeniture under Albert IV (the Wise) in 1506, and even later, the Wittelsbachs were unable to consolidate their ducal authority for any length of time.

The discord between two brothers of the house of Wittelsbach, Louis II and Henry III, contributed greatly to the rise of the house of Hapsburg, which acquired the Duchy of Austria after the death of the last of the Babenbergs. From then on the Hapsburgs and the Wittelsbachs both aspired to the title of King of the Romans. Although there were many agreements concluded between the two houses, many intermarriages and many interests held in common, the tension did not relax.

This rivalry was long recognized by leading French politicians as one of the fundamental conditions of German affairs, one that enabled them to intervene in Central Europe and, at a later date, to break the axis established by Charles V between Madrid and Vienna. Since the time of Francis I of France, Austro-Bavarian rivalry had offered the French a ready-made political instrument, and Richelieu made full use of it. Time and again Bavaria was obliged to seek French aid, under the Bourbons and later under Napoleon.

In the sixteenth century the people of Bavaria, especially the upper classes, showed a marked preference for the Reformed Creed. The reaction against Protestantism came later in Austria than in Bavaria and was consequently more violent. In both duchies the authority of the ruling house, painstakingly built up over the ages, was threatened by the Protestant nobility. In Bavaria, Bohemia and the Austrian crown lands this class, whose leaders and most influential members were men with a humanist background and often were trained in law, sought to maintain the rights and liberties of the estates.

Many of the German princes thought to profit from both sides in the confessional dispute. In the majority of principalities the Reformation had actually increased their power, for in the initial stages the Reformers had depended on them for protection and support. Thus the princes were able to enrich themselves by seizing Church estates. At the same time they were granted concessions and privileges by the Pope in return for their continued allegiance to the ancient faith. The importance of religious belief as a motivating factor varied from one prince to another. In his declining years Duke Albert V of Bavaria, the grandfather of Maximilian I, came to regard it as the only legitimate criterion. At first he had remained indifferent to the religious confusions of his day. But as time went on he gradually adopted a conservative outlook, apparently prompted first by concern for the welfare of his Duchy. The notion at which he finally arrived—that his ducal function was an office entrusted to him by God— became indissolubly linked with his conception of the inviolate sanctity of the traditional Christian Church.

In the end he drove the Protestant nobles from his Court in Munich with the words: "With those who do not share my belief I will not share my food." After offering a purely nominal resistance, his officials, who previously had viewed the religious innovations with tolerance, backed his new policy.

In 1556 Albert V summoned the Jesuits to Bavaria. In this he was clearly influenced by his father-in-law, Emperor Ferdinand I. Peter Canisius, the first German Jesuit, gave the following description of the condition of the Catholic Church at the time of the Reformation:

"We are more usurious than the Jews, more debauched and besotted than the Turks, more avaricious and cruel than the heathens, more licentious and self-indulgent than the beasts of the field; we are not faithful in marriage, rather our hearts and our eyes are full of adultery, ready at all times for all manner of lewdness . . . scarcely once in a month does it occur to us to live abstemiously and scarcely once in a lifetime do we observe the forty-days fast. We do not pay the tithe; instead, we withhold from the Church what is lawfully hers."

Such blunt polemics, making their effect by means of exaggeration, were written by men primarily concerned with keeping their own doorsteps clean, who took for their subject matter the signs of decay that had long been visible in monasticism and had furnished, quite apart from their theological implications, many actual grounds for protest and thus for Protestantism. Meanwhile, however, a probing internal reform had taken place within the Catholic Church. By contrast, a certain analytical bias in Protestant theology, which tended to sap genuine belief and to represent theology as the plaything of learned doctors, as well as the controversies between Lutherans and Calvinists, had lost for Protestantism the compelling impetus of its early days. Now it was the Catholics' turn.

The implementation of the decisions of the Council of Trent—the militant aspect of the Catholic campaign—was entrusted primarily to the Jesuits. Their task, in which they were sustained by a form of dynamic mysticism closely akin to that which informed the activity of St Teresa of Avila, was the apostolic mission. For the trained Jesuit the most important sphere of activity was that of education. Complete, unquestioning allegiance and dedication was the essential prerequisite of their work. All Jesuit exercises were subject to the one absolute requirement of *"motus rationalis creaturae ad Deum."* It is this that gave them their penetrating force. Jesuit educational methods in the seventeenth century were advanced to such a degree that many Protestants attended Jesuit schools. To the Society of Jesus anything lukewarm, anything conciliatory was anathema. They attacked Melanchthon no less fiercely than Erasmus.

The Council of Trent met from 1545 to 1547, from 1551 to 1552 and from 1562 to 1563, interrupting their sessions only in times of war. In 1551 the first Jesuit college was founded in Vienna, followed by others in Prague, Innsbruck, Ingolstadt, Munich and Dillingen. The foundations on the Rhine were also established at about this time. The University of Ingolstadt had been founded in 1472 by Duke Louis the Rich of Landshut. Originally it had been a non-denominational establishment with teachers of widely differing outlook and persuasion. The Catholic apologist, Dr. Eck, taught at Ingolstadt, but so did Reuchlin, Aventinus, Konrad Celtes, Jakob Locher and Urban Rhegius. It was not long, however, before the university was controlled by the Jesuits. The Collegium Germanicum in Rome also came under their influence, and by 1600 the towns of Würzburg, Augsburg, Passau, Salzburg, Olmütz, Triest and Breslau all had Jesuit bishops.

Emperor Rudolph II himself was educated at a Jesuit school attached to the Spanish Court. He established contact with the youthful Duke Maximilian of Bavaria, the German patriot whose determination to defend the Catholic faith equalled his loyalty to the Empire.

Maximilian was an outstanding statesman, an economical administrator with great practical gifts, an untiring worker and able to face any situation with fortitude and equanimity. His career clearly illustrates the difficult choice facing his family, between self-preservation on the one hand and loyalty to the Empire on the other, between the Hapsburgs as representatives of their own house and the Hapsburgs as Holy Roman Emperors. He was one of the most powerful of the German princes, and yet the policy he pursued brought him to the very brink of disaster. Eminent historians of later times, who have judged him from a point of view alien to both Maximilian and his contemporaries, have reproached him for having pursued false goals and for having acted against Bavarian interests. His task, they have said, was not to propagate Catholicism but to join forces with Frederick, the Count Palatine, for then the house of Wittelsbach would have become great. He has been reproached for "having had his head full of quixotic notions" and for having succumbed to Jesuit influence. If he had allied himself with Frederick, the Count Palatine, he could have parried the Austrian rise to power and could have established Bavaria as a dominant force in the Empire.

Such calculations were, however, simply beyond him, since he was incapable of regarding his Catholic faith as a relative value. It was in fact the most important factor in his life. To join forces with the Calvinist branch of his house was for him out of the question.

Maximilian was a slightly older contemporary of Richelieu, whom he outlived. He ruled from 1595 to 1597 as co-regent with his father, William V, and following his father's abdication in 1597, to 1651 in his own right.

Emperor Rudolph, on the other hand, ruled for only thirty-six years, from 1576 to 1612. He became King of Hungary in 1572, and in 1575 King of Bohemia and King of the Romans. On October 12, 1576, he succeeded his father as Emperor. Withdrawn from action, he lived in the Hradschin, the royal palace in Prague. He had considerable powers of perception and understanding, but the net result of it all was a paralyzing sense of futility. He busied himself with his extremely valuable collections and spent much of his time with astrologers and alchemists, with whose help he tried to divine the future. He appreciated the oddities of Arcimboldo and mannerist painters such as Hans von Aachen, and was a generous patron to the Protestant astronomers, Tycho Brahe and Johannes Kepler. He was a sick man who suffered from the taint of insanity introduced into his family by his great-grandmother Joanna the Mad, and concerned himself with affairs of state only in an arbitrary and piecemeal fashion. Extremely susceptible where the dignity of his office was concerned, he was subject to what was virtually a persecution mania. As a result

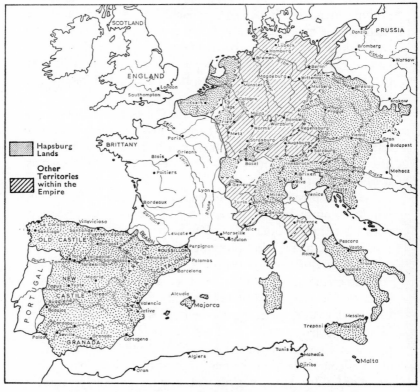

Map 5. The Hapsburg Empire, Middle of the Sixteenth Century

he grew more and more dependent on his sycophants. Although vacillating at first, he eventually allowed the Catholics to further the Counter-Reformation both in his hereditary domains and in the Empire.

The real driving force behind Counter-Reformation activity, however, was not the Emperor but Maximilian I of Bavaria. In 1607, following a hotly disputed decision of the Imperial Council, Maximilian occupied the town of Donauwörth, where the Protestant inhabitants had broken the law of the Empire by attacking a Catholic procession. His action provoked an almost instantaneous riposte: the Protestant estates banded together for purposes of self-defence, and on May 4, 1608, they founded the Evangelical Union of Ahausen under the leadership of Frederick IV of the County Palatine. In 1609 Strassburg and Ulm joined the Union, followed in 1610 by the Elector Sigismund of Brandenburg, the Landgrave Maurice of Hesse-Cassel, and various Imperial cities.

Inevitably, the Catholics responded in their turn: in 1609 the Catholic estates banded together to form the Catholic League. Maximilian of Bavaria became its leader and was joined by his uncle, the Archbishop of Cologne, and by the majority of the bishops who had remained loyal to Rome. And so, as in the days of the League of Schmalkalden and the League of Nuremberg, Germany was again divided into two hostile camps. The Religious Peace of Augsburg was a thing of the past, and the future was to bring great tribulations; for it was not only a German civil war that threatened but a great European conflagration with unforeseeable consequences, though the line-up of the contending parties had already taken shape during the Cleves-Jülich dispute. At that time a French army had been about to invade the Spanish Netherlands, and only the assassination of the French King Henry IV had then prevented the outbreak of a Continental war.

In the first two decades of the seventeenth century the rivalry between the Hapsburgs and the Bavarians tended at first to confuse the relations between the various Catholic principalities in Germany. The house of Hapsburg was obliged to take measures designed to reduce Bavaria's influence as leader of the Catholic group. There was a distinct danger that the Bavarian-oriented Catholic League might develop into a third force between Austria and Protestant Germany. Austria, keenly aware of the isolation this would bring, tried to retain the leadership by creating a special Austrian Directory under the Hapsburg Archdukes of Tyrol and Upper Austria, trying at the same time to persuade the Duke of Bavaria's Swabian allies to shift their allegiance.

Richelieu's Intervention in Germany

On November 29, 1616 Richelieu first took part in a session of the Royal Council. His appraisal of the European situation was cold and calculating, but his appreciation of the forces at work in the confused medley of opposing powers was amazingly accurate. In his view Catholic, Protestant, and class passions were all there to be exploited. The question of which should be exploited in any given instance was a purely tactical one, to be determined by considerations of time and place. Every human group, every human being was to be utilized or neutralized.

On December 29, 1616, the Cardinal had a hand in the important instructions concerning France's German policy that were sent to Comte Henri de Schomberg. This was in fact literally the case, for Richelieu's handwriting has been identified on the original manuscript. The principal issue at that time was the revolt of the French princes and great nobles under the leadership of the Duke of Nevers (see Vol. I) in the winter of 1616. Richelieu's primary task was to ensure that this revolt would not be supported by foreign rulers.

The diplomatic activities he conducted to this end in Germany, England and Holland took place almost simultaneously. Charles Cauchon, Baron du Tour et Maupas, was sent to James I and de La Noue was sent to Holland. The man chosen as the envoy to the German Courts was the great Schomberg, Minister of Finance and Marshal of France, the son of Gaspard de Schomberg, a native of Saxony, who as the Commander of German contingents recruited for service under the French Crown had established the important position occupied by his family in France.

His instructions specified that the principal object of his mission was to ensure that the name of the King of France was restored to its former glory within the German territories. The prestige France had lost as a result of the Wars of Religion, the revolt of the princes and the discord within the royal family had to be regained, a number of unfavourable prejudices had to be dispelled and the rumours of "internal weaknesses" in the French State to be denied.

The text continued:

"It must be pointed out that . . . we are neither so Roman nor so Spanish as to wish to espouse the interests either of Rome or of Spain to the detriment of ourselves and our traditional allies; . . . the confessional differences in France have not split the State: although divided in our beliefs, we remain united under the Crown. No Catholic in the King's service is so blind as to prefer a Spaniard to a French Huguenot in matters involving the State."

Later we read:

"It must be made clear to the German Protestant princes that we wish to prevent any further Spanish advance. This is to be effected by discreet offers of help, to enable them to counter the Spanish King's plans to obtain the Hungarian, Bohemian and Imperial Crowns for one of his children."

Schomberg was also furnished with all the information he would need to answer the criticism—often heard in the German principalities—that since the death of Henry IV France had been squandering public money. Richelieu's advice in this particular respect casts a revealing light on his diplomatic method, for he proposed that, far from attempting to refute these rumours, Schomberg should substantiate and even reinforce them by furnishing precise details of the immense material demands made by the French princes and the leading members of the nobility. Richelieu calculated that these statements of Schomberg's "would then be enlarged by the European *fama* and that this in turn would influence Louis's attitude." Richelieu often operated in this way, using foreign policy as a means of influencing French internal affairs.

The Cardinal further declared that ever since the reign of Francis I, and especially under Henry the Great, Paris had always worked for the "German liberties."

Above all Richelieu advised Schomberg to elaborate on the subject of France's behaviour in the Cleves-Jülich affair and draw attention to "France's disinterested attitude in Italy."

He then wrote:

"Any impression that Louis XIII's Spanish marriage was regarded as an act of political consequence must be dispelled."

And further:

"The Protestant princes of Germany must be convinced of our good intentions. . . . It must be explained to them that our only ambition is to ensure that the crown of King and Emperor is given to the man most worthy to wear it on behalf of Christendom."

Lest it should be suspected that these words were merely a cover for anti-Hapsburg sentiment, Richelieu went on to say:

"Both the Archduke Maximilian and the Archduke Ferdinand would be eligible. Ferdinand would be preferable in as far as he has children . . . for, since Maximilian is childless, the Spanish could again lay claim to the Imperial crown after his death, which they could not do in Ferdinand's case on account of his descendants."

And so at that time, although he was still bound to Marie de' Medici, Richelieu was prepared to give his preference to the Austrian branch of the house of Hapsburg in order to inhibit any possible claim by the Spanish line. But he was not prepared to go so far as to hold out any definite prospects to the Duke of Bavaria. The Cardinal stressed the fact that other nations were virtually panic-stricken at the thought of a union between Austria and Spain, lest this should lead to the disintegration of France. But he quickly added: "Nobody will believe that a man would set fire to his own house in order to please his neighbours."

He considered it important that Schomberg should counter the accusation, often expressed by the princes of the Empire, that the King of France was inclined to desert his allies. The opposite was in fact the case, but it would be necessary to find particular arguments for each particular prince. For each had to be satisfied and be given some expectations. Consequently, when speaking with a Bavarian it was desirable to speak as a Catholic. When speaking with a Brandenburger, on the other hand, or with a representative of the County Palatine, the possibility of friendly coexistence among the various confessions should be stressed.

What sort of a man was Schomberg, in whom Richelieu placed so much confidence? Later the Cardinal was to characterize him as follows:

"He was a nobleman whose profession was loyalty, a virtue characteristic of his nation. He was not clever, but his judgement was sound and he became Minister of Finance. In this office he did not enrich himself by so much as a *teston* and displayed absolute integrity at all times, although those working under him exploited his kindheartedness. He was a magnanimous man and completely honourable. By the grace of God he appeared and executed three tasks of crucial importance to the State, tasks occasioned by the most important actions of the century. His deeds were: the victory over the

English on the Isle of Ré, the relief of Casale and the battle of Castelnaudary, where the Duke of Montmorency was taken prisoner."

Maximilian I and the Bohemian Revolt

The inexorable progress of the Protestant movement in the Austrian dominions and in Bohemia was one of the principal reasons why Maximilian I of Bavaria decided to assume the leadership of the Catholic opposition. Although the development of the various confessions within these territories does not strictly belong to this enquiry, we must none the less establish the general pattern, for we shall understand Richelieu's foreign policy only if we have some knowledge of the events leading up to the Thirty Years War.

Just as in Bavaria under Albert V, so too in Austria and Bohemia a large part of the nobility had gone over to the new faith. This process is most clearly illustrated by the activities of Baron Georg Erasmus Tschernembl, a man of great intellectual power and the prototype of the "independents" who resisted the pressures of the Counter-Reformation and opposed absolutist tendencies.

Tschernembl, a native of Carniola, was a Calvinist. He was one of those feudal autonomists who maintained extremely active relations with leading Protestants, not only in the Hapsburg dominions and in Bohemia, but throughout the whole of Europe, and exercised a considerable influence on events in Bohemia.

It was in 1606 that Tschernembl, a man of great rhetorical gifts, came to the fore. At this time Stephen Bocskay's insurrection in Transylvania had produced a general crisis and the dispute in the house of Hapsburg, which was to end in the ascendancy of Archduke Matthias, was just beginning.

After the Transylvanian and Turkish hostilities had been brought to an end by the peace of Vienna (June 23, 1606) and the armistice of Zsitvatörök, Rudolph II's administration was obliged to grant the Protestant estates in Hungary their religious freedom. This greatly increased the self-assurance of the Protestants living in the territories subject to this agreement. For weeks Tschernembl, acting for the Upper Austrian estates, negotiated concerning the guaranties granted at the peace of Vienna and the safeguarding of the Hungarian estates. It was at that point that the Moravian autonomists under Zerotin seceded. In 1608 Tschernembl was to sign the alliance with the Hungarians. His relations with Christian of Anhalt, a prince who was intent on precipitating the downfall of the Austrian house, were very close.

When it became apparent that the religious aspirations of the Protestants were tending to coincide with the separatist aspirations of the estates, severe restrictions were imposed. This was done not by the Emperor himself—Rudolph remained quite inactive in the affair—but by an almost spontaneous reaction of the administrative bodies to what seemed a potentially revolutionary situation. The Hungarians, Moravians and Austrians rose against these restrictions.

In this situation, the Emperor's oldest brother, Archduke Matthias, had himself proclaimed head of the house of Hapsburg by the other Archdukes, on the grounds of Rudolph's pathological apathy. He won the support of the rebellious territories by granting concessions and accepted their homage, although only the Catholic subjects gave him their unreserved allegiance. Matthias then forced his brother to cede these territories to him. The only lands left to Rudolph were Bohemia and Silesia.

Tschernembl had once advised the Archduke to enter into an alliance with Henry IV of France against the Spanish and against Emperor Rudolph. Later, at the assembly of the Protestant estates in Horn, where he acted as the representative of Upper Austria, he told Matthias further that, since religious intolerance had cost Rudolph his lands, it could easily cost him his life.

Among other things, Tschernembl stated: "We are seeking

unions and agreements with the whole world. We have envoys everywhere. . . . If war comes, the prelates and the priests will be our first victims, and before we are done the whole ecclesiastical estate of the Roman Church will be wiped out."

Although Tschernembl took this tone with Matthias, when it came to political action he always urged moderation.

Despite the concessions Archduke Matthias had granted to his dissident subjects on March 16, 1609, in the Resolution of Capitulation, the crisis continued.

Tschernembl was an ardent member of the Bohemian resistance and he was also the author of a chronicle of the Bohemian revolt, which is a valuable source of information. He constantly fought for religious freedom for the Protestants and for their right to enter high office.

The one opponent for whom Tschernembl felt a violent antipathy was the Viennese Bishop Melchior Khlesl, a convert to Catholicism. In Bohemia it was said that Khlesl, the son of a baker, was brought up not "in the bakehouse but in the age-old school of Machiavelli." He was Archduke Matthias' principal adviser. What enraged Tschernembl and most of the other resistance leaders was Khlesl's conciliatory attitude. They accused him of deviousness and reprehensible luke-warmness. In point of fact, however, Khlesl later displayed a highly responsible attitude and great caution, which was to bring him into opposition to Archduke Ferdinand, who, brought up in Spain, was far from lukewarm. Khlesl spoke out against his succession far more openly than many of the members of the Protestant opposition and later, when Ferdinand determined to take stern measures against the rebels, it was Khlesl who advocated clemency.

On July 20, 1618, Bishop Khlesl was arrested and interned in the castle of Ambras. He was not allowed to go to Rome until 1622. At one point Ferdinand had angrily pronounced him a detestable little upstart and intriguer who ought to be done away with. Khlesl's admonitions had no effect on the

Emperor, and the rebels, whom he had tried to help, automatically rejected all proposals coming from him. The mediator's task is always a thankless one. Much later Khlesl was vindicated; in 1623 Ferdinand II acknowledged his innocence, although it was not until 1627 that the Bishop returned to Vienna; he died in 1630.

In 1618 the Austrian Hapsburgs were not powerful enough to indulge in rash actions; Maximilian I of Bavaria was in a better position.

Tschernembl and his associates were federalists and ardent disciples of self-government by the estates. Tschernembl's teacher, an advocate of the doctrine holding that the estates were fully justified in opposing the authority of the Crown, was François Hotman, a Huguenot born in Paris, who subsequently became an important jurist. Hotman had been a professor of canonical and lay law and Classical literature in Lyon and later in Lausanne, Strassburg, Valence and Bourges; he also lectured on Roman law in Geneva and Basle. Tschernembl made his acquaintance in Geneva and took over from him his ideas on an elective monarchy and representative government, which he proceeded to disseminate with great skill during the whole period of the dispute between the Hapsburg brothers. He was in advance of his age and also had a real grasp of practical affairs. He never underestimated his opponents, least of all Ferdinand II.

On July 14, 1609, Emperor Rudolph, who had already lost so many jewels from his Crown, granted the Letter of Majesty or Royal Charter to the Bohemians, who were still loyal to him. This document, to which distinguished men like Tschernembl contributed, was undoubtedly an important political achievement. It guaranteed religious freedom and also the right to build both churches and schools on Crown land. This right, vested in the three estates and not in the Protestants as such, did not apply to lands belonging to the nobles and the Church, although this limitation was soon high-handedly disregarded by the Bohemians. Emperor Rudolph, always playing for time, was fearful of his brother's extremist policy. As it happens, Matthias was also obliged to accommodate the Austrian estates in much the same way as was done in the Letter of Majesty. Of all the factors that exerted their paralysing influence on Rudolph's clouded mind, his presentiments of the future were doubtless the most crucial.

Ten years after the proclamation of the Letter of Majesty, on July 31, 1619, immediately before the outbreak of war, the leaders of the Bohemian resistance discussed and approved the provisions of the Bohemian Confederation, which they then drafted in the form of a state document.

In his excellent study, *The Revolt in Bohemia*, Hans Sturmberger quotes a diary entry of June 23, 1619, made by Hans Ludwig Kuefstein, a citizen of Lower Austria:

"In the night at twelve o'clock there was a great storm with thunder, rain and a fearful wind, as if it would destroy the whole town. And the eagle on the *Landhaus* was torn down and in the window of the hall the coat of arms of Styria and Carniola was smashed. God forbid it should prove an omen."

Sturmberger rightly interprets this statement as an expression of fear and uncertainty as to the wisdom of the chosen path. But by then there was no turning back, for the past had been cut off.

In Braunau in the diocese of Prague, the inhabitants had built a Protestant church. In 1618 the Archbishop of Prague prevailed upon the Royal Council to order the closing of the church. This action provoked a riot in the town, as a result of which eight Protestant citizens were arrested and imprisoned in Prague. The year before, when the Archbishop had ordered the destruction of a newly erected Protestant church in Klostergrab, there had been no resistance to his authority, but Protestant reaction to the Braunau incident was extremely violent, not only in Bohemia itself, but far beyond her borders in Moravia, Austria, Hungary, in the Protestant parts of the Empire, in fact throughout the whole of Europe.

The leaders of the Bohemian resistance took the Braunau incident as a signal for the beginning of hostilities. They had called an assembly of the estates in Prague, and Count Heinrich Matthias Thurn, Wenceslaus of Ruppa and several other extremists recklessly decided to make short shrift of their most hated opponents, the Emperor's councillors, Martinitz and Slavata, thus breaking all bonds with Vienna. On May 23, 1618, some hundred nobles rode into the capital; they entered the Hradschin, the royal castle that had been built by Charles IV and enlarged by the Jagellons, where the six councillors who administered the kingdom during the sovereign's absence were in session. A furious discussion took place and when tempers had reached a sufficient pitch Martinitz and Slavata were thrown out of the window, which was seventy feet from the ground. Despite his pleas for mercy their secretary, Fabricius, was sent after them. They all escaped with their lives, a fact interpreted by the Catholics as a miracle and by the Protestants as a lucky chance, for beneath the window lay a pile of rubbish consisting for the most part of old documents. "Defenestration" was a very ancient and seemingly inveterate Bohemian custom. The Hussite wars had also begun in this way.

By this act of self-help the Bohemian rebels committed an irreparable affront. Meanwhile, the Bohemian population, displaying very little revolutionary fervour at this stage, complained that the struggle for freedom and progress had been besmirched by attempted murder.

Although the conflict between the Hapsburg brothers had certainly weakened the archducal house, the leaders of the Bohemian revolt would not have taken such violent action but for the fact that Transylvania also chose to attack the

Emperor at that moment. Stephen Bocskay had died in 1606, the year in which the peace of Vienna was concluded. He was succeeded as Prince of Transylvania by Bathory Gabor, a son of King Stephen of Poland. Bathory was a harsh ruler and during his reign, which lasted from 1608 to 1613, civil war broke out. On October 11, 1613, he was murdered in Grosswardein, and Bethlen Gabor emerged as the new prince. Richelieu wrote in his Memoirs: "Only Bethlen Gabor, the Prince of Transylvania, stood his ground at that time and opposed the Emperor."

Initially, however, Bethlen contrived to establish a tolerable relationship with Austria, while at the same time prevailing upon the Turks to withdraw from his territory. But no sooner had the Bohemian revolt broken out than he openly went over to the enemies of the Hapsburgs and, again with Turkish support, invaded Hungary, where he conquered large territories and finished by taking Pressburg. After this the Hungarian estates offered him the crown, which he accepted. He then went on to threaten Vienna. In 1613 Emperor Matthias had asked the Imperial Diet for funds to arm against the Transylvanians. In 1614 he asked the General Convention of the Austrian dominions at Linz. He asked in vain.

The Ottoman Empire

A digression is now necessary in order to throw light on the kind of influence exerted by the Ottoman Empire on the events with which we are dealing.

The Turkish State had not been constituted by a single tribe, a single conquering nation, but by a number of tribes sharing the same religion and associated for warlike purposes, but constantly rebelling against their central authority. Both in structure and in the tensions marking their relations to one another, they resembled the feudal communities of the medieval Christian world, and like them their lives were governed by particular ideals, above all the concept of knightly honour. In the Middle Ages, East and West were much closer to each other than at the beginning of modern times. Both still had links with late antiquity, which, however, they assimilated in different ways, and there can be no doubt but that initially the Orient gave more than it received in the interchange of spiritual and material goods.

Thanks above all to masterful diplomacy, the Byzantine Empire had been able to withstand the repeated assaults of Asiatic peoples for a period of 1123 years. It fell to the Crusading armies of the Western world to conquer and sack Constantinople, and large areas of the surrounding country as well; thus they weakened the only surviving part of the ancient Roman Empire to such an extent that when the Turks attacked some two hundred years later, just as the Empire was beginning to rise again, it could no longer defend itself effectively. But when the victorious Turkish Sultan entered Constantinople, he was accompanied by art experts; unlike the Crusaders, he had the magnanimity to save and protect the Byzantine art treasures. He also preserved the whole administrative machinery of the vanquished Empire and adopted what was for the most part a tolerant attitude towards its customs.

On May 29, 1453, Mohammed II rode his horse into the church of Santa Sophia. He later transformed it into a mosque, but he granted freedom of worship to both Christians and Jews. He ordered his State in accordance with Mohammedan tradition and safeguarded its literary and scientific heritage; he was also receptive to the creative forces of antiquity and the Italian Renaissance. Cyriacus of Ancona, who has been called the ancestor of archaeology, came to Constantinople with Sultan Mohammed, and very soon the conqueror attracted Greek and Italian scholars and artists to his Court. The famous portrait of the Sultan by Gentile Bellini, whom the Signoria of Venice had sent to Constantinople in 1479 at the Sultan's request, is well known to us. The Sultan received many marks of respect from the city-states of Italy and even the smaller domains, such as Rimini of the Malatesta, which were eager to obtain advantageous trading agreements. Mohammed was a Renaissance prince, and that he was recognized as such by his contemporaries is quite evident from the medallion that Lorenzo de' Medici had struck as a token of his gratitude for the extradition of one of the Pazzi conspirators. The front of the medallion bears a likeness of Mohammed, and on the reverse side he is represented as a conquering hero in a triumphal chariot, being led by the "*bonus eventus,*" the god of success, to new victories. If Mohammed's reign had been longer, relations between the Eastern and Western worlds might have developed along quite different lines. During his lifetime Turkey played an important and productive role as a mediator between East and West.

All fifteenth-century accounts agree that, with the exception of a few isolated humanists, nobody in the Christian world was deeply affected by the collapse of the Byzantine Empire.

During Mohammed's lifetime it seemed to Western observers as if all that had happened on the Bosporus was that the Palaeologi had fled eastwards and had been replaced by a new dynasty. But when the great Sultan died—on May 3, 1481—a reaction to his views and his policy set in. Clearly Mohammed had gone too far for Islamic feelings.

His son, Bayazid II, was under the spell of Islamic mysticism and Dervish austerity. During his reign the Dervishes came into their own again. They brought their influence to bear on the people and strengthened the Oriental characteristics in the Ottoman nation. Bayazid regarded his father's fondness for the civilization of the Italian Renaissance as apostasy. The gallery of paintings Mohammed had acquired was sold off. The only members of the Christian world with whom the new ruler wished to associate were the engineers.

We possess a letter to Bayazid containing plans for a windmill, a ship's pump, and a large drawbridge to span the Bosporus. It was written by Leonardo da Vinci. Michelangelo, whom Bayazid had tried to engage as a bridge-builder in

1506, was warned of the Sultan's hostility to art. There was, however, one great man in the Western world who had an irresistible attraction for Bayazid, and that was the preacher Savonarola, who once declared that the Muslims sinned only from ignorance and, this apart, were far more pious than his Italian compatriots. Savonarola's sermons were published in Florence in 1496 and Bayazid had them all translated into Turkish.

Then Bayazid's son Selim, a martial ruler whose tremendous military conquests, most of them in the East, made Turkey the greatest state in all Islam, initiated an era of impassioned holy wars.

Selim's son was Suleiman the Magnificent, who in the interests of his imperial ambition fanned the power of faith to the point of fanaticism. During his reign the Western world was first exposed to the full impact of the Turkish wars. The Turkish peril, the Turkish threat, became a perennial nightmare for the inhabitants of every Christian land from the far south-east of the Continent to the centre of Europe, and for centuries the coastal dwellers along the Mediterranean were exposed to the terror of Turkish attack. But there was also an advantage in this Turkish threat; for like any force of nature, like any evil that feeds on rumours and the imagination, it had a unifying effect and elicited a co-operative response. In the face of the Eastern menace the European territories joined together to form an alliance of states centred on the lands of the Viennese Hapsburgs. Until late in the eighteenth century the Turkish wars continued to provide a training ground for the soldiers of Europe. Whatever the political ties of their respective governments, the English, Scots, Irish, Spanish, as well as the French, the Hungarians, Germans and Poles all fought against the Turks and received a firm grounding in the art of war. The hereditary nobles of Europe and those aspiring to their rank acquired knowledge and experience of warfare on the battlefields of south-east Europe—the hardest of all schools. Both sides went to war sometimes for conquest, sometimes for defence. Frequently the hard-pressed Turks were also obliged to fight a war on two fronts, for Asia was a second theatre of Turkish operations. From every pulpit in Christendom sermons were preached against the heathen Turk, and God was called upon to help destroy "the bastions of the false prophet Mohammed." Meanwhile the Turks invoked the help of the same God.

Following the battle of Marignano and his reconciliation with Pope Leo X, Francis I of France had planned a great Crusade in which all the rulers of the Christian world were to have taken part, including Mary Stuart's father, James V of Scotland (who had married into the house of Guise and supported French policy), Charles I of Spain, Emanuel of Portugal, Sigismund of Poland, Louis of Hungary, Christian of Denmark, the rulers of the city-republics of Venice and Genoa, the Medici of Florence and the Knights of Rhodes—a mighty company.

Ever since the Middle Ages the "Most Christian King" of France had been regarded as the natural leader of all Crusades. As late as 1510 the representatives of Louis XII of France had preached the gospel of the Holy War at the Imperial Diet in Augsburg, and during his attempts to win the Imperial election Francis I said, "If I am elected, then within three years I shall either be in Constantinople or I shall be dead." But, on February 24, 1525, ten years after his victory at Marignano, Francis I was defeated by Emperor Charles V at Pavia and taken prisoner. An unknown messenger was sent to the Turkish Sultan with a letter and a ruby ring from the King of France. He was murdered in Bosnia together with his companions, but the letter reached its destination. A second emissary, Giovanni Frangipani, subsequently handed the Sultan a second letter from the captive King. The Sultan's reply to this second letter has been preserved. In it we read:

"You, who are a Frenchman, the King of France, have sent your faithful messenger, Frangipani, to our door, the refuge

13. Albert, Count Wallenstein

14. Axel Oxenstierna, 1583–1654

of rulers. You have informed us that the enemy has occupied your country and that you yourself are at present in captivity. You have asked for help in order that you may be freed. All that you have said has been discussed at the foot of our throne, which is the refuge of the world, and our imperial wisdom has grasped all that is involved. . . . It is nothing new for Princes to be defeated and taken prisoner: have courage and do not allow yourself to be depressed. Our glorious ancestors, may God illumine their graves, waged war ceaselessly to repulse the enemy and conquer new lands. We ourselves have followed in their footsteps. . . . Day and night our horse is saddled and our sword girded."

French historians are of the opinion that the decision to take this ultimate step and call the arch-enemy into Europe was conceived by the Queen-Mother, Louise of Savoy, who was then acting as regent.

In every country of Christendom, even in France itself, people were soon speaking of "the blasphemous union of the lily and the crescent." The resistance within France to the foreign policy of Francis I was similar to that provoked by Richelieu's Protestant alliances.

On April 23, 1526, one year after Francis I had appealed to him for help, the Sultan led an army of one hundred thousand men with three hundred cannon into Hungary. On August 28th and 29th the Turkish army overwhelmed the Hungarians. The sixteen-year-old King of Hungary, Louis II, escaped from the battle with two companions but was drowned during his flight to safety.[1] Louis was childless, and the succession passed to his brother-in-law, later Emperor Ferdinand I. The Turks took Buda, where the Sultan occupied the royal castle and forbade all plundering. But on the Hungarian plains the troops indulged in the most fearful excesses. Far more people died as a result of their licence than in the actual battle,

---

[1] It was suspected that the Hapsburgs had had him murdered. This suspicion has never been confirmed or entirely refuted.

despite the fact that four thousand captives were slaughtered at Mohács.

Now that Hungary had been defeated—indeed, all but annihilated—the Austrian hereditary lands and Germany itself were exposed to the wave of Ottoman aggression. Emperor Charles V openly attributed the responsibility for the catastrophe to the King of France. For his part Francis I wrote to the German princes to say: "The Emperor has rejected the honourable peace conditions I offered him; neither the fearful calamities in Hungary, nor the death of King Louis, nor the misfortune of his own sister, the unhappy widow, are able to touch his heart. . . . If all forces had been united, which could have been done if the Emperor had wished, the infidels could have been repulsed." But by this time Francis himself was afraid lest Bohemia and Poland, which he already regarded as important to French foreign policy, should lose their independence to the Sultan. He sent a skilful politician, a Spanish renegade named Antonio Rincón, as his agent to Prague and Warsaw, and through him he also established contact with John Zapolya, the puppet King whom Suleiman had imposed on the Hungarians. But Hungary was divided. One part of the country backed Ferdinand I of Austria, who also laid claim to the crown. Zapolya maintained that he had been elected by the magnates of Transylvania and eastern Hungary. But the Imperial Diet in Pressburg branded him a usurper and an instrument of the Turks, and in December 1526 proclaimed Ferdinand the only legitimate King of Hungary.

As a result of the Porte's Persian war and the peace that Charles V and Ferdinand subsequently concluded with the Sultan—which was really more of a tactical armistice than a genuine agreement designed to regulate their mutual relations —the fighting shifted from Hungary to the Mediterranean. Kheir-ed-Din, known as Barbarossa, was appointed Captain-Pasha, commander of the Turkish fleet. Following this change of front the Sultan's relations with the King of France became even closer. A Turkish ambassador arrived in

Marseille and was received by the King. Meanwhile Barbarossa conquered Tunis in 1534, defeating the last of the Hafsid rulers, who had vainly tried to defend it. Then the famous corsair sent an envoy to France on his own account. By then both Algiers and Tunis were in Turkish hands and Malta, which belonged to Charles V's sphere of influence, was effectively neutralized. The fall of Rhodes had given the Turks control of the eastern half of the Mediterranean, and their North African conquests enabled them to threaten the western half. They were without question the leading Mediterranean sea power, replacing Venice, now on the decline, and playing the Mediterranean role that England was to assume at a much later date. At that time Charles V made the bold decision to lead an expedition against Tunis, and he reconquered it.

During this period of their alliance Suleiman was much more consistent than Francis I, who, as if plagued by a guilty conscience, went in constant fear lest his connection with Turkey should cost him a loss of prestige in the eyes of the Christian world. Consequently, whenever he succeeded in calling a temporary halt to his dispute with the Hapsburgs, he tried, if not to mediate, at least to give the impression of mediating between the Emperor and Suleiman. For his part the Sultan regarded his alliance with the "Bey of France," as he scornfully called Francis I, as one of the fixed points in his struggle with Charles V. The Sultan's military efforts were prodigious, and both the organization and the discipline of his army were admired by many of his contemporaries, especially the Spanish.

As a result of Francis I's alliance with the Turks, the French harbours in the Mediterranean entered into a period of great prosperity. A *hatti-sherif* of 1528 ratified very valuable French privileges in Egypt, and the treaties of 1535 gave to French ships the freedom of all seas subject to Turkish control; their captains were at liberty to drop and weigh anchor in all Turkish ports, while French merchants were allowed to buy and sell in all the territories of the Turkish Empire and to engage in unlimited trade on condition that they pay a five per cent commission to the Turkish authorities. French citizens domiciled in the Turkish Empire came under the jurisdiction of the various French consulates. They also enjoyed complete freedom of worship and were given the custody of Christian sanctuaries. They were able to arrange for their property to be transferred to their heirs in France without difficulty. Ever since the time of Francis I, France has received preferential treatment within the Turkish Empire. Other nations, such as the English, Spanish, Sicilians and Genoese, were required to sail under the French flag when they entered Turkish waters, which must have given great satisfaction to the French, who had always been the underdogs at sea. The King of France was the only European monarch whom the Sultan treated as an equal. He was no longer referred to as the "Bey" but as the "Padishah"—the Emperor. In Richelieu's time Louis XIII was still accorded the title of Emperor by the Turkish Court and he always signed himself as such in his correspondence with the Sultan. By contrast, the Holy Roman Emperor was addressed as King of Hungary by the Turkish Sultan. The Turks still used these titles for Louis XV and Maria Teresa in the eighteenth century. Thanks to her special position, France was able to influence the customs of the Near East peoples from Syria to Egypt and the countries of North Africa. This process of social infiltration continued right up to the end of the Second World War; in the eighteenth century, when Turkish power was already waning, it produced the strange and extremely sophisticated culture of Constantinople.

Whenever France found herself in a difficult political situation in Europe, she had recourse to the Turkish alliance. In this Richelieu was no exception.

After 1526 the major part of Hungary was a Turkish dependency, and in 1541 the territory became a province of the Ottoman Empire. The battle of Mohács was one of those watersheds in history whose repercussions continue to make themselves felt long after the event. In the religious sphere the Sultan sided with the Protestants and so protected them from the impact of the Counter-Reformation. Religious intolerance was confined to the narrow strip of land subject to the Hapsburgs. In the Turkish province the Hungarians were even free to convert from the Lutheran to the Calvinist faith, if they wished.

With the conquest of Hungary the Turks had passed beyond the cultural borders of the old Byzantine Empire. The Hungarians in their turn began to develop characteristics that were essentially Turkish. The one native element to oppose the foreign influence was the specifically Hungarian form of humanism, which had always asserted itself in the face of adversity. In Hungary, as elsewhere, humanism was the province of a diminishing minority, but they remained true to the tradition initiated by the great Matthias Corvinus.

While the Austrian branch of the house of Hapsburg was engaged in simultaneous battles to the east, west and north, it received a measure of relief from the fact that since the end of the sixteenth century Turkey had been engaged in a serious conflict with Abbas I, the seventh Persian ruler of the house of Safavid. Abbas reconquered the West Persian territories that had been annexed by Turkey. After occupying Azerbaijan, parts of Armenia and Georgia and also Shirvan in 1601, he repulsed the Turkish attacks on Erivan and Tabriz, which were repeated almost annually up to 1613, and for a while his forces penetrated Turkish Asia in depth. From 1614 to 1617, when Richelieu first entered the government, the Turks launched various offensives, all unsuccessful, against their powerful neighbour. At the time of Abbas' death (January 27, 1628), his Empire extended from the Tigris to the Indus.

The victories of Maximilian and Ferdinand in Germany, especially in the initial stages of the Thirty Years War, would not have been possible but for the fact that the Turks were getting the worst of it in their campaign against the Persians from 1622 onwards; in 1623 Baghdad itself fell into Persian hands. At this time, too, internal difficulties began to emerge in the multi-racial Ottoman Empire. It is probable, therefore, that if the Thirty Years War had not broken out in Germany, the Sultan would have found it impossible to recoup his losses and gather strength again. The weakness of the Turkish rulers in the early seventeenth century is clearly illustrated by the fact that in 1622 the Janissaries[1] mutinied during a campaign against Poland. The advisers of Osman II, who was then only fourteen years old, decided to raise new troops in order to put down the rebellious Janissary corps and then to move the Imperial residence from Constantinople to Cairo. Had this succeeded, the realm founded by Mohammed II on the Bosporus would have been transformed into an Islamic Afro-Asian great power. But the Sultan's troops were defeated by the Janissaries and Osman himself was murdered.

Then again, if the European conflict had not been extended to world-war proportions, the most eminent of the Imperial commanders, Wallenstein, might have realized a lifelong ambition by undertaking a Crusade—an expansionist offensive to secure the eastern frontiers. But given the state of affairs in Europe, it was quite certain that the war which had broken out in Bohemia would prove interminable and that Turkey would receive regular subsidies and fresh impetus from the anti-Hapsburg powers.

One important reason that the Turks were able to threaten south-east Europe from the sixteenth century on was provided by the Hungarian Protestants, who had been turning for help to both the Turks and the Princes of Transylvania ever since

---

[1] Janissaries (Turk. *yenitsheri*—*yeni* new, plus *tsheri* soldiery), from 1329 recruited from prisoners of war who had joined the Turkish forces; from 1360 to about 1675 their numbers were swelled by children, mostly of Balkan origin. In the fifteenth century these infantry soldiers, who were all picked troops, numbered some forty thousand and in the seventeenth century a hundred thousand men. In times of peace they served as a police force both in the capital and on the plains. The commander of the Janissaries was the Aga. In time these praetorians became a source of danger to the Sultan. In 1826 they were finally eliminated by Mahmud II.

the onset of the Counter-Reformation. We shall be dealing later with the part played by Transylvania in the Austro-Turkish dispute, as a specific element of the French anti-Hapsburg policy.

Bohemia and the House of Hapsburg

Bohemia's relationship to the house of Hapsburg was always unsettled and full of contrasting and even contradictory factors, alternating between attraction and repulsion.

When Rudolph I, the founder of the Hapsburg dynasty, moved from the Alemannic into the Danubian territories, the sphere of influence thus created clashed with the Central European interests of the Přemyslides. Hapsburg expansion aims had originally tended towards Burgundy in the west, but the conquest of Aargau, the centre of Hapsburg power up to 1415, by Berne and Lucerne put an end to all such hopes. In the south-east the ultimate objective of Austrian policy was the acquisition of Bohemia and Hungary. The defeat of Ottokar II in the battle of the Marchfeld in 1278 initiated a new development, which was to give rise to countless crises right down to the twentieth century. Shortly after this decisive battle the concept of dynastic succession, which was to remain inviolable and to determine the fate of whole peoples for centuries to come, was introduced, giving rise to the Hapsburgs' policy of dynastic marriages, which was to have such enormous repercussions. A blood relationship was established between the two ruling houses of the Přemyslides and the Hapsburgs by the marriage contracted between the children of Ottokar and Rudolph.

In 1306, when the Přemyslides died out, Albert I came close to achieving Austria's objective in south-east Europe, but by the end of Rudolph III's reign in Bohemia it had already become apparent that Bohemia would resist any attempt on the part of her southern neighbour to exercise a lasting influence on her affairs. Upon the death of Rudolph III the

Duke of Luxemburg was elected King of Bohemia. Austrian and South German expansion was checked. But that was not the end of the Hapsburgs' struggle. Marriages were contracted with the Luxemburgs, hereditary unions were established, and in 1437, when the house of Luxemburg died out, Albert V of Austria appeared in Prague, albeit briefly, as the sovereign ruler of Bohemia. The sense of security instilled in the Bohemians by the fact that the Hapsburgs always introduced order into the Danubian territories vied with their inherent dislike of German dominance. "The Bohemians did not want the Hapsburgs and yet they were always electing them." This ambivalence was of course partly determined by external factors, by the constant shifts in the balance of power.

The Albertinian line of the house of Hapsburg died out with Ladislaus, King of Bohemia and Hungary, the son of Albert V of Austria, and in 1471 Ladislaus II, a Jagellon, ascended the throne in Prague. Then once again the Hapsburgs acquired the sovereignty of Bohemia by means of a dynastic marriage, for Ferdinand of Austria, who had married the daughter of Ladislaus II, succeeded to the throne. And in 1572, when the male line of the Jagellons came to an end, the house of Hapsburg, related by marriage to both the Přemyslides and the Jagellons, was left in sole possession of all hereditary rights.

The Bohemian resistance, which received great impetus from the intensive thought then being given to constitutional questions, opposed the principle of hereditary rule with consistency and determination. The fact that they did so is of great importance and would seem to form part of the historical mission of the Czech people.

In the second decade of the seventeenth century, when steps were taken in Vienna to procure the Bohemian crown and electorship for Archduke Ferdinand, the project met with many difficulties.

One factor above all posed a considerable problem for Ferdinand's succession, and it also greatly perturbed and even terrified the French. After Archduke Matthias' brothers had agreed to forgo their claim in favour of Ferdinand, Philip III of Spain suddenly announced in Vienna that he too intended to claim the Austrian throne. Philip was the son of a daughter of Maximilian II, and Ferdinand was only a nephew. The situation resulting from this initiative by the head of the Spanish line was resolved by a series of delicate, tenacious and highly secret negotiations which Ferdinand conducted with Spain's representative in Vienna. They also established the amount of compensation to be paid to Philip in return for the renunciation of his claim.

The secret agreement concluded between Ferdinand and the Spanish ambassador on March 20, 1617, was entitled *"Pactum de successione Regnorum Hungariae et Bohemiae."* But it is always referred to, and correctly, as the "Oñate Secret Agreement," for Oñate, the Spanish representative, was an important politician and wielded great influence in Vienna. He had arrived in Prague in February 1617 and he later played a crucial part in the negotiations from which Ferdinand emerged first as King of Bohemia and subsequently as Holy Roman Emperor. The price paid to Philip III for his withdrawal was extremely high. It also contravened the laws of the Empire, for in order to obtain the Bohemian crown and electorship Ferdinand undertook to cede to Spain the Austrian possessions in Alsace together with the fief of Hagenau and the County of Ortenau, and, upon his accession to the office of Emperor, the Italian principalities of Finale and Piombino. This would not only tighten the Spanish grip on France but also on the Holy Roman Empire, for Spain would acquire a direct strategic link between Spanish Franche-Comté and the Netherlands. In the east she would advance to the French frontier and control the Rhine.

Although at first the contents of the agreement were kept secret from Emperor Rudolph and the other Archdukes, for the time being it put an end to the dispute that had divided the house of Hapsburg. Once the Spanish had given their

K*   297

approval, steps were soon taken to ensure Ferdinand's "acceptance" as King of Bohemia.

At this point, however, the Hapsburgs' German opponents entered the scene: the Calvinist princes. Christian of Anhalt-Bernburg, who was the guiding spirit behind the inconsistent policy pursued by the Count Palatine, urged that the Bohemians be permitted to raise troops in all the territories of the Protestant Union. At the same time he tried to further an agreement between the Count Palatine and the Duke of Bavaria. One of his plans had its origin in the influence brought to bear by the French diplomats, whose private remarks tended in certain respects to depart from the instructions Richelieu had sent to Schomberg. Christian of Anhalt was the first to suggest that Maximilian of Bavaria should be offered the Imperial crown. We know that the Duke rejected this offer and that he also refused the Bohemians when they turned to him for help in defence of their liberties. He went against the opinion of his provincial council and his leading advisers and, without regard for Bavarian political interests, stood by his decision to remain loyal to the German Hapsburgs in their life-and-death struggle. He did this, moreover, despite grave doubts, which he formulated at the beginning of the thirties: "The Empire, no longer one, no longer Roman, no longer holy, is moving towards dissolution."

At that time Christian of Anhalt was still clearly intent on undermining the house of Austria. He was a member of the group centred on Holland and his politics were in the tradition of Henry IV of France. He maintained contact with every rebel group in the hereditary Hapsburg domains. Since 1600 he had been in close touch with the Protestants of Upper Austria. The centre for his activities as an agitator was Wittingau in Bohemia, which belonged to the Rosenberg family.

His Calvinist connections were legion. Not only was he in touch with the Dutch Protestants and the French Huguenots, but also with the Scots and English Puritans. His contacts with the great centre of Calvinist propaganda, the town of Geneva, which had become a refuge for the whole world, were extremely close, as was his relationship with Frederick V, the young Elector of the County Palatine, whose political actions he inspired. Later, it is true, Frederick came to doubt the reliability of his volatile and reckless adviser.

Heinrich Matthias von Thurn

Thurn's parents had been Protestants before him. He himself had won his spurs in the Turkish wars, and Emperor Rudolph had honoured him by appointing him Burgrave of the Bohemian fortress of Karlstein. He played a leading part in the drafting of the Letter of Majesty, and in recognition of his services he was nominated as one of the thirty "defenders of the faith" by the Protestant estates. He had been loyal to Emperor Rudolph but turned against Matthias, who greatly angered him by depriving him of his office of Burgrave and then by departing from Rudolph's policy of non-interference in the growing religious struggle. Matthias had sided with the Catholics and used every means against the Protestants, such as tearing down recently erected Protestant churches and forbidding the Protestants to build new ones. Thurn was certainly a brave men, but—like the Calvinist Wittelsbach, Frederick of the County Palatine, and the latter's general, Christian of Anhalt, who commanded the Protestant Union army, and unlike the Elector of Saxony—he had no sense of proportion or of reality, and was quite unfit to act as Commander-in-Chief at a moment of decision. He remained alienated from reality until his dying day.

Thurn regarded both Matthias and Ferdinand as usurpers. As far as he was concerned Rudolph had been the last legitimate Emperor. At first he engaged in small-scale operations against Ferdinand, marching into Moravia and pushing forward as far as Vienna, where only the timely appearance of Count Dampierre's cavalry saved the Emperor; but these were mere skirmishes compared with the battles to come. In view of the spiritual import and the historical significance of the Bohemian revolt, the intellectual gifts Thurn was able to place at its disposal appear disproportionately slight.

Both Thurn and Anhalt, like the Elector Palatine, whom they thrust into the limelight, were men of small stature. And yet in both Bohemia and Austria there were many excellent men in the ranks of the Reformers. The leaders of the revolt and those Bohemian nobles who took a major part in the execution of their brainless policy had little in common with the men of quality who distinguished themselves as the authors of the charter of the Bohemian Confederation, that impartial and politically mature essay in constitutional law. One of the principal authors was of course Tschernembl. The Bohemian Confederation was conceived as a means of opposing absolutism. Matthias had already sensed this new trend and had consequently adopted a negative attitude to an Austro-Bohemian federation that had been mooted in 1611.

According to the Bohemian "rebels," the princes should be replaced by the estates. The idea was not new, for it had already been advanced by both the French Huguenots and the French feudal nobles, but never before had it been formulated with the precision and clarity of the Bohemian Confederation. This document contained many intelligent and practical suggestions and went into the question of economic and customs unions. The obligations that would devolve on all citizens alike in times of national danger were also listed.

In 1615 the question of federation had been dealt with at a more theoretical level. But now the Bohemians were intent on putting theory into practice, for the estates and their privileges were in danger. The Bohemian Diet met on July 23, 1619. At first the delegates had wanted to include Upper and Lower Austria in their projected federation, which would then have extended as far as the Styrian border and would have constituted a Pan-Bohemian state. But Tschernembl persuaded them to reduce their ambitious plans to practical proportions, and it was largely owing to his influence that the Diet finally decided in favour of a strictly Bohemian federation. Even at that stage Tschernembl was still trying to avoid a definitive break with Emperor Ferdinand. On July 31st the Bohemians confirmed their Confederation by oath and on August 16th the special treaties with the territories beyond the Enns and with Lower Austria were ratified. Tschernembl's principal criterion was a religious one; he was determined to defend Protestantism.

It was only for a brief moment that the Bohemian Confederation had any real chance of being put into effect. But as a document it contained the quintessence of ideas, long present in doctrinal form, that had been disseminated throughout the whole of Europe in the effort to safeguard the ancient privileges handed down from the Middle Ages and to procure the new, fundamentally republican privileges then being demanded. What those advocating a constitutional monarchy were trying to establish by their struggle against the power of the princes was a constitution similar to that already in force in the United Provinces and in Switzerland. These men, fired by the spirit of Calvinism and still bound to the concept of the estates, were the precursors of a movement that was suppressed in Huguenot France and distorted into Cromwell's dictatorship in England, and attained its objective only much later.

The Bohemian revolt, prepared for by an elite of considerable intellectual standing and ruined by reckless gamblers, did not by any means receive the general support of the people of Bohemia. On the one hand there was the Catholic opposition and on the other the Lutherans, who were quite openly opposed to both the Calvinist element in the movement and the extremists such as Thurn and his followers.

The Imperial Election of Ferdinand II

The Transylvanian threat and the growth of Bohemian opposition served a necessary purpose in that they put a stop to the anti-Bavarian and anti-League intrigues of Viennese politics. The next step was to persuade Maximilian to agree to Ferdinand's election to the Imperial throne. In the same year that the charter of the Bohemian Confederation was drafted, Ferdinand stopped in Munich on his way to the Imperial coronation. He had written to Maximilian beforehand to assure him of his friendship and brotherly affection, and in the course of their conversation he held out the hope that Bavaria might acquire both the territories and the electorship of the County Palatine, which shows that Ferdinand's Bohemian plans had already matured at that time. Under the terms of the agreement concluded in Munich, Maximilian of Bavaria promised to support Ferdinand against the Elector Palatine and against the rebels in the hereditary domains.

In Frankfort, the time had come to take the poll before either the Elector Palatine or Christian of Anhalt was aware that Maximilian had completely rejected all thought of his own election, that their attempt to split the Catholic front by nominating him as a candidate had already been frustrated. When they discovered this, the Calvinists seriously considered the use of force to prevent the election from taking place, but in the event they lacked the necessary resolution. They did try to have the election postponed, in order to gain time, but here too they failed, because the Catholic Electors, headed by the Imperial Chancellor, the Archbishop of Mainz, insisted on adhering to the timetable laid down in the Golden Bull. On this occasion the Catholics had very definitely closed their ranks, whereas the Protestant group at the Electoral College was greatly weakened by the dissension between the Calvinists and the Lutherans. Meanwhile, the Protestant Union troops were encamped on all sides of the Imperial city, for the people of Frankfort had no liking at all for the Catholic princes. The Archbishop of Cologne feared a Massacre of St Bartholomew in reverse, for even Ferdinand himself was given a hostile reception. And yet Ferdinand had a great personal success in Frankfort, where his calm dignity and self-assurance, his consciousness of his family's perennial association with the Imperial crown, affected both himself and his fellow Electors. He had come to Frankfort as the King of Bohemia in order to vote on his own behalf. His right to the Bohemian vote was disputed and a delegation from the Bohemian estates was waiting in Hanau, asking to be heard. Ferdinand protested and the Bohemian delegation was not admitted; by this action the Electoral College recognized Ferdinand of Hapsburg as the rightful King of Bohemia.

The remarkable thing about the poll, taken on August 28, 1619, in the electoral chapel of St Bartholomew's Cathedral, was the fact that apart from the Bohemian vote, which he himself had cast in accordance with the regulations laid down in the Golden Bull, Ferdinand of Austria received the votes of Trier, Cologne, Mainz, Saxony and Brandenburg. At this the Elector Palatine (urged on, it is said, by his father-in-law) suddenly switched his vote to the majority group. Owing partly to his vacillatory weakness, this Imperial election was the first great defeat for the German Protestants. The Catholic League had shown that it was able to assert itself in the face of the mutually antagonistic forces of the Calvinist and Lutheran opposition and to obtain the support of Saxony, the principal Lutheran power, in the process.

At the end of November 1619, George Rákóczy, Bethlen Gabor's army commander, had been defeated at Ztropko by a force of ten thousand Cossacks sent by the King of Poland to help the house of Austria. As a result Bethlen Gabor was forced to withdraw into Hungary, leaving Count Thurn, who had mobilized the Bohemian army at Bruck on the Leitha, to retreat with all possible speed towards Moravia.

On August 27, 1619, the day before Ferdinand's election in Frankfort, the Bohemian estates had elected Frederick V of the County Palatine as their King. At the same time they proclaimed Ferdinand's dethronement. Ferdinand was crowned Emperor on September 19th; Frederick V's coronation in Prague did not take place until November 4th.

Angoulême's Mission and the Treaty of Ulm

Frederick, the Count Palatine, a Wittelsbach and the third son of Frederick IV, was born on August 26, 1596; he received a strict Calvinist upbringing and succeeded his father in the electorship. In 1613, as we have already seen, he married Elizabeth of England and through this marriage established a dynastic link with the leading Protestant power. His headstrong policies, which he began to pursue as early as 1614, received no support from England worth mentioning, save perhaps in a passive sense. But even the passive support of England was of consequence. He owed his election as King of Bohemia to his position as head of the Protestant Union. Both his father-in-law and his mother advised him not to accept the Bohemian offer. It has been said that it was his wife's ambition, among other things, that prompted Frederick to throw James's cautions to the wind. But here too it was Anhalt who was the real driving force.

On January 14, 1620, the estates below the Enns acceded to the urgent entreaties of their compatriots beyond the Enns and agreed to treat the Imperialists as enemies and to extend their alliance with Bohemia to include Hungary. At the same time they turned for help to Louis XIII.

There was a particular reason for this last step: shortly before, in the autumn of 1619, Ferdinand II had sent Baron Fürstenberg to Paris to urge the King of France to help stamp out the "Bohemian heresy."

In France a new revolt on the part of the princes and the great nobles was then imminent. Only four years had elapsed since Louis XIII had married the Spanish Infanta, Anne of Austria. France and Spain were at peace. Louis XIII was involved in serious disputes with his own Huguenot subjects. A story has been handed down to the effect that a Christmas sermon preached by Father Arnoux had moved Louis XIII to speak to Fürstenberg, but only in very general and noncommittal terms, of the possibility of a French force being sent against the Bohemian rebels. But the Foreign Secretary Puisieux was well aware that France was quite unable to make military commitments of any kind, and he was equally convinced that she could not afford to throw away the chance of an alliance with the German Protestants. France also had to consider the interests of James I, and avoid giving offence to Frederick V, the Count Palatine. The upshot was that no French soldiers crossed the border. Instead of military aid, Louis XIII sent a special envoy with a large retinue. This envoy was a prince of the blood, Charles, Duc d'Angoulême, a legitimized son of the house of Valois. His instructions were to try to mediate between the Protestant Union and the Catholic League. The best informed member of his staff was the Count of Béthune.

When Angoulême arrived in Germany, the Protestant and Catholic armies stood facing one another at Ulm. But there was discord in the Union ranks. A large number of the Protestant princes would have much preferred to avoid the bloody conflict, but the Margrave of Ansbach, whose plans were as frivolous as they were far-reaching, was a man given to bold decisions and he declared that he for one would not let down the elected King of Bohemia, Frederick of the County Palatine.

Meanwhile Angoulême went about his mission of reconciliation. Perhaps the treaty of Ulm would have been concluded without his intervention. But at all events the treaty was signed on July 3, 1620, embodying the terms of an agreement between the Protestant Union and the Catholic League. The signatories to the document were the levelheaded Maximilian of Bavaria and the Margrave of Ansbach, the commander of the Protestant Union army. Ansbach gave his signature reluctantly, but he gave it, for the discord in his own ranks left him no choice. The French mediator did not sign the document. The Catholic League and the Protestant Union undertook to refrain from all further hostilities, to withdraw their troops and even to disarm.

Article three of the treaty of Ulm specifically excluded
Bohemia from the provisions of the treaty. This was crucial,
for it meant that the Protestants were still at liberty to support
Frederick V of the County Palatine. The chief concern of the
Protestants, however, was to protect the County Palatine
from Spanish intervention and in this they received no help,
for the Spanish had not entered into a formal agreement with
the Catholic League and so were not subject to the treaty of
Ulm. The League of course was free to give Ferdinand armed
support in Bohemia. And so the net result of these provisions
was to make it impossible for the German princes to muster a
united defence against the Spanish advance, which meant that
the County Palatine would be at the mercy of the Spanish
general Spinola.

Angoulême had expected quite a different outcome. He had
been convinced that Emperor Ferdinand would extend
clemency to his Bohemian subjects and he had also thought
that Frederick V of the County Palatine would have the sense
to refuse the Bohemian crown. When Angoulême arrived in
Vienna with these optimistic notions, he found that, despite
the high honours and baroque pageantry of the official reception, his actual welcome was distinctly cool and his ideas were
unwanted. Exhortations to clemency and compromise were
no longer in demand. Bishop Khlesl's imprisonment had made
that perfectly plain.

Ferdinand's Intervention in Bohemia

Thanks to the treaty of Ulm, the Emperor's military
prospects in Bohemia had suddenly become very favourable.
Ferdinand was able to count on the support of the Spanish,
the Catholic League and also John George, the Elector of
Saxony, who went over to his side in 1620 because of his
aversion to the Calvinist Palatinate. The influence of the
Spanish ambassador, Oñate, remained the crucial factor at
the Imperial Court; so Angoulême was told that the King of

France had promised Fürstenberg that he would send auxiliaries and that mediation had never once been mentioned in their talks. Zdenko von Lobkowitz, Ferdinand's adviser, told the French prince quite bluntly that the Emperor considered further negotiations quite superfluous; a settlement was out of the question and the rebellious Bohemians must be forced back to the path of duty by the power of the sword; they must yield or perish. It has been suggested recently by certain historians that Puisieux was consciously trying to involve the house of Austria in a serious conflict. This interpretation seems improbable and is contradicted by the following passage in a letter from Richelieu to Father Joseph dated March 1626: "The armistice that the Duke of Angoulême negotiated in Ulm was the ruin of all of France's allies; for while they disarmed in good faith, their opponents remained under arms, and this spelt disaster for our German friends."

Such are the dangers of disarmament conferences.

Relations between the Spanish and Austrian branches of the house of Hapsburg were now closer than they had been since the days of Charles V. This gave rise to a strategic situation on the Continent of Europe that was felt to be a serious threat, not only among the large number of politically minded people in France, but also in England and in Italy, where even the Pope, as a territorial prince, regarded the King of Spain's zeal for the Counter-Reformation as a cover for extending Spanish political power. As a result of this new collaboration between Madrid and Vienna, the United Provinces were forced into a life-and-death struggle. Only the princes of North Germany were unable to adopt a unified and unequivocal policy.

Meanwhile, Frederick V of the County Palatine had taken up residence in the royal castle in Prague, which became the scene of countless comings and goings between the various representatives of the anti-Hapsburg bloc. At that time, shortly before the storm broke, a Bohemian Lutheran nobleman wrote as follows:

"We issue apologies and written defences, but others do not believe that our actions are justified thereby, neither do we pass the test of our own conscience. The Turks, the King of France, the Elector of Saxony, the father-in-law of our King, they all disapprove of our actions, even though one or the other might favour the revolution. When respected men came to us in the name of our King we gave them no hearing but, contrary to our oath, we threw them out of the window; we gave them no time to pray, let alone to defend themselves. We would not even listen to Emperor Matthias, to King Ferdinand, when they offered us peace, forgiveness, our rights and privileges and an arbitrated settlement. We have called upon our neighbours both within and without the Empire, we have invoked the Hungarians, the English, the Dutch, the Turks and the Devil himself. We have besieged Vienna and, in as far as it lay in our power, exposed the entire Holy Roman Empire to the Turks and the Tartars.

"Bethlen Gabor says that he is seeking power and not justice. Anhalt says that he is seeking gold; likewise the other colonels and captains. At least they are honest. But conscience must also be appeased, and so religion is dragged in. In truth, belief was ten times freer under the Hapsburgs than under the Calvinists. That is why the Elector of Saxony and the other Lutherans wisely took the Emperor's part. And what has our King done? He has destroyed images, drunk the health of the United Provinces in Bohemian beer and danced with Bohemian ladies.

"Whether we win or lose, our lot will be a harsh one. If we win, then all those who have helped Frederick will line up before us, greedy for land and gold at our expense. If we lose, we shall be subjected to the wrath of the Emperor, whom we have sorely offended. What else should we expect? We have taken from Caesar that which is Caesar's, and that which is God's we have offered up to the Turks."

The Offensive in Bohemia

When Maximilian I of Bavaria took over the supreme command of the League army, he was able to call on the services of an eminent military adviser who became one of the leading army commanders of the age, a man whose name will occur frequently in the further course of this history. This was Count Tilly, a native of Brabant. The army recruited by the Catholic League and led by Tilly was composed of Walloon, Flemish, Italian and Spanish soldiers. The Emperor himself was able to field only a small number of troops under the command of the ever-hesitant Bucquoy. The army serving the King of Bohemia was a mixed force made up of Germans of varying origins, Hungarians and English, but very few Czechs. In point of fact there were three Bohemian armies, each operating independently, led by Christian of Anhalt, Thurn and Count Mansfeld. But the one outstanding commander in the field at that time was Tilly. Maximilian was always able to rely on his prudence, his discretion and his steadfastness. He also employed Tilly on diplomatic missions to the Protestant Union and to Archbishop Wolf Dietrich of Salzburg, an opponent of the Jesuits against whom Maximilian had sent a punitive expedition in 1611.

Throughout the Bohemian offensive the troops of the Catholic League were accompanied by militant monks, including the famous pulpit orator, Father Dominic of Jesus Maria, who had been sent by the Pope. The presence of these clerics gave to the undertaking the character of a Crusade. Tilly commanded some twenty-five thousand men and the King of Bohemia twenty thousand. At the beginning of the campaign the Bohemian troops were not concentrated. Anhalt's force was occupying Pilsen, but Tilly marched straight for Prague by a more northerly route, whereupon Anhalt left Pilsen and tried to link up with Thurn and Mansfeld. In this he succeeded and in the night of November 7th to 8th the three commanders occupied the heights grouped around the White

Hill, skirting the western bank of the Moldau to the west of Prague.

The battle of the White Hill, which decided the fate of a whole era and has continued to influence the course of history ever since, scarcely deserves to be called a battle. Tilly himself later described the engagement, which had been joined at his command and against Bucquoy's wishes, as a "mere skirmish." But during this skirmish Christian of Anhalt was taken prisoner and the troops of the "Winter King," as Frederick was derisively called from then on, were put to headlong flight. Prague was occupied and Frederick and his Queen only just succeeded in escaping capture. In the Imperial army the regiments recruited by a certain Wallenstein (or Waldstein) greatly distinguished themselves. Wallenstein himself took no part in the action, for he had been placed in command of a detachment and ordered to occupy the city of Laun.

After the Fall of Prague

In 1620—prior to the battle of the White Hill—there had been three specific theatres of war: the Rhenish Palatinate on the western bank of the Rhine, which, with the exception of a few strongholds, was conquered by the great Spanish army commander Spinola between August and November; Upper Austria, where the League army was pressing forward from Bavaria; and northern Bohemia, where the Duke of Saxony had begun the occupation of Lusatia. Maximilian of Bavaria and John George took possession of guaranties, for the Emperor had undertaken to reimburse them for the full cost of the war and had authorized them to administer any territories they occupied until they received their compensation.

Tilly had risen from the ranks and had received his military training under Alessandro Farnese, the Duke of Parma. He had already fought with great distinction under the command of the Duke of Guise at the battle of Auneau, where the Huguenot army led by Fabian von Dohna was defeated. Later we find Tilly taking a prominent part in the Turkish wars. In 1605 Emperor Rudolph appointed him Field Marshal. His fame as a military organizer extended from Madrid to Warsaw. When his loyalty to Emperor Rudolph brought him into sharp conflict with Archduke Matthias, he resigned his command. He promised, however, that he would always remain loyal to the house of Austria. When Duke Maximilian of Bavaria, one of whose lifelong ambitions had been the creation of a strong Bavarian army, invited him to lead the Bavarian contingent in the army of the Catholic League, he accepted. In 1620, at the age of sixty-one, Tilly was appointed lieutenant general.

Bohemia after the Catastrophe

Meanwhile Richelieu was studying the international situation from exile. All extant comments of the Cardinal on the political situation exhibit his unwavering conception of a European order in which France was to play a dominant role.

Wallenstein was an altogether different personality. Making his way under the Hapsburgs, he rose to dazzling fame and exercised tremendous influence in both military and political spheres. Whereas Richelieu proceeded with clearheaded detachment and even made allowances for his own short-comings, the Bohemian vacillated between an exaggerated sense of his abilities and self-doubts so overwhelming that they deprived him of the power of action. Torn between these abnormally powerful inpulses, he not only constantly betrayed both himself and the principles and institutions he had elected to serve but also cancelled out his considerable perspicacity in practical affairs. His trust was blind, his mistrust malicious, and he superstitiously projected onto the stars the conse-quences of his actions, interpreting his own strength and his own weakness as divine dispensations. Wallenstein dealt with problems not by the Cardinal's method of deductive reasoning, but with his intuitive powers, focusing them suddenly, and often quite accurately, on the changing situations he was faced with; although he was often wrong in his political decisions, as an army commander he was usually successful. Strangely enough, in the final analysis his objective was the same as the one sought by the Cardinal and by another great figure of the age, the Duke of Olivares: the establishment of a nation-state governed by a central authority.

Wallenstein was the son of Protestant parents, who sent him to a school run by the Brothers of the Common Life, but the boy, who was known as "the Madcap," found the quiet pietistic life of the community repugnant. He was quite untamable and kicked over the traces to such an extent that his masters were unable to cope with him. Orphaned early, he was brought by a maternal uncle to the Jesuits in Olmütz, where one of the fathers, Veit Pachta, acquired a lasting influence over the boy. In later life Wallenstein himself said that this priest's influence had been crucial and that he owed everything to him. After leaving the Jesuits he attended the Lutheran University of Altdorf, where it was only the exalted position of his relatives in Bohemia that prevented his expulsion. Later we find him at the University of Padua, where he studied mathematics, astrology and military strategy. He was attracted by the profession of arms. Under Giorgio Basta he took part in a campaign against the Turks and the Hungarian Protestants. By then he was already attending Mass. Through the good offices of the Archbishop of Prague he married Lucretia Nikossie von Landeck, a rich heiress many years his senior. Her estates lay in Moravia and since she was the last of her line Wallenstein inherited the whole of her property upon her death, thus becoming a great landlord with estates in both Moravia and Bohemia. He appeared at Court during Emperor Matthias' reign, but it was Archduke Ferdinand of Styria, who by then had already been crowned King of Bohemia and Hungary, who drew him into his circle.

From his very first appearance it was evident that Wallenstein was a highly talented man, especially in the economic sphere. He was an entrepreneur on the grand scale. But the principal industry of his century—like the principal industry of Prussia, according to Napoleon—was war.

In 1617, when the Venetians besieged Gradiška and Dampierre's army was marching to its relief, Wallenstein quickly raised an army of his own and intervened. His name was mentioned in the secret records of the Venetian Council of Ten; he had made an immediate impression on the most highly trained of all observers.

The Consequences of the Austrian Victory

Soon after the battle of the White Hill, where Bohemia's hopes and aims and achievements had found a bitter end, it became apparent that the Imperial victory was far more complete than had at first been thought. Not only had Ferdinand become the undisputed master of Bohemia, but Frederick of the County Palatine, the only Calvinist Elector, had been excluded from the Electoral College. This meant that henceforth the Protestants would have only two votes to the Catholics' five.

The Emperor had quickly taken control of the Upper Palatinate, which was promised to Maximilian of Bavaria, and the County Palatine, which was occupied by Tilly and the Spanish general, Hernández de Córdoba. Frederick's followers were crushed as far afield as Westphalia and Lower Saxony.

Frederick, who refused to ask the Emperor's pardon, was accused of breaking the Imperial peace and placed under the ban of the Empire on January 29, 1621. Later that same year Ferdinand took further measures against the Calvinist prince, with the approval of Lutheran Saxony. On June 21st twenty-seven leaders of the Bohemian revolt were executed in front of the Town Hall in the old part of Prague.

His victory had brought Ferdinand a sudden increase of power, and under the influence of Spain he became the champion of the Counter-Reformation in Central Europe. This completely transformed the European situation.

Faced with this new balance of power, Richelieu, who had not yet entered into his second period of office, argued that the first thing to be done was to separate the Emperor from the Elector of Saxony, his only Protestant ally of any consequence. France's second aim, he declared, must be the neutralization of Bavaria. Protestant resistance in central and North Germany was not yet broken and the victorious Emperor could not afford to press his demands too heavily. In actual fact Ferdinand owed his success primarily to Maximilian of Bavaria, on whom—acting on his own authority and without the approval of the Imperial Diet—he conferred the electorship forfeited by Frederick of the County Palatine. The actual transfer was effected in 1623 at the Electoral Diet in Regensburg. As was inevitable, the Elector of Brandenburg refused to recognize the investiture, and this time John George of Saxony also protested.

Getting the Emperor's allies to pull together was no easy matter. Tension between the Bavarian garrisons in the County Palatine, Heidelberg and Mannheim, and the Spanish occupation troops on both sides of the Rhine was often extreme.

But the chief danger still lay in the future, for the Imperial and League armies had yet to assert their power in the north and to threaten the Baltic. When they did so, the Protestants began to fear that Ferdinand might try to turn the clock back to pre-Reformation conditions.

Meanwhile, in the turmoil that reigned in Bohemia after the disastrous events of 1620, positions of great economic power were established. Many families, even of humble origin, attained to might and prominence, which in a number of cases were retained by their descendants right down to the twentieth century.

After their defeat the rebels forfeited all their possessions to the Emperor. The confiscation council was instructed to establish to what extent individuals had "occupied a military, administrative, Court, civic or advisory office during the past rebellion, which commissions they had undertaken either at home or abroad, whether they had confirmed by oath and given their signature to the Confederation, whether they had attended [rebel] meetings and approved resolutions, whether they had incited others to like rebellion, whether they had passed scornful and derogatory remarks on the Emperor and his worshipful house or whether they were in any other way concerned in the rebellion."

It was in this postwar period of distress and greed that Wallenstein acquired the further wealth that was the necessary condition of his amazing rise to power. With his resources he was of course able to operate on a large scale in a profiteers' market. Many of the old Bohemian nobility had been extirpated, many had been made destitute, and nearly all had been driven from their homes. The Emperor had to be compensated in full for the cost of his war. Those who had helped him were richly rewarded, for Ferdinand's magnanimity knew no bounds. Even when estates were bought and paid for in hard cash, it was still possible to make tremendous bargains, thanks to the debasement of the coinage. On January 18, 1622, the so-called Mint Board was founded. This consisted of the Imperial Exchequer together with the following: Hans de Witte, a Dutch Calvinist and financier, who had lived in Prague since Emperor Rudolph's day and who acted as financial adviser to both Ferdinand and Wallenstein; Karl von Liechtenstein, who was appointed Governor of Bohemia on January 17, 1622; Wallenstein; Paul Michna, the Count of Weitzenhofen, who was the Emperor's Military Commissioner; and finally the banker, Bassevi. It is assumed that Wallenstein's later associates, Hans Ulrich von Eggenburg and Karl von Harrach, were also members of this commission. It had sole rights to mint coins in Bohemia, Moravia and Austria and was authorized to strike seventy guldens in small coin from one mark's worth of refined silver, as opposed to the forty-six guldens permitted previously. The Imperial

Exchequer received a payment of six million guldens from the Mint Board in return for this privilege.

But in order to find money to pay for the war the coinage was debased to a far greater extent than authorized in the regulations. Wallenstein, for example, struck as many as 123 guldens from one silver mark instead of the official seventy.

The first regiments Wallenstein raised for the Emperor cost him 63,185 guldens. After the conquest of Prague he bought and sold grain and wine and invested the profits in further regiments of mercenaries. Always mindful of the need for ready cash, Wallenstein exploited confiscations and the panic selling of the Protestants, and thus acquired over sixty estates, so that after only a few years, although the purchasing power of money was constantly sinking, his land holdings made him the richest man in Bohemia.

One of the ways in which this bold speculator augmented his income was by reselling at maximum prices estates that he had bought cheap. A further source of income was provided by booty, and false records, on which depleted regiments were listed as being up to strength.

In the course of time the serious irregularities in the activities of the Mint Board came to light. Wallenstein was accused by the Imperial Exchequer of having enriched himself by illegal means and was obliged to forgo the 200,000 guldens he was claiming for troop levies. This apart, however, all other claims lodged by Wallenstein were honoured in return for his pledge to raise a new army at his own expense.

Wallenstein acquired his sixty estates in northern Bohemia between the autumn of 1621 and the end of 1623. He bought the estate of Friedland and Reichenberg for 150,000 guldens and by the conditions of its tenure was entitled to style himself "von Waldstein und Friedland," to adopt the title of a Palsgrave and to set up a fidei-commissum. By then he was in a position to offer the Emperor a loan of three and a half million guldens, which sum was duly credited to his account. In 1624 Wallenstein's estates were raised to the status of a principality and he himself acquired the rank of a prince. Hans de Witte was involved in all of Wallenstein's transactions, including the enormous loans to the Emperor. In December 1621 Wallenstein had been appointed commander of the City of Prague and a month later, in January 1622, he was invested with the title and functions of a "Gubernator of the Kingdom of Bohemia." Then in 1625, when he was already engaged on his German campaign, the "Prince of Friedland and head of the house of Wallenstein" was raised to the rank of Commander-in-Chief of all the Emperor's troops stationed or likely to be stationed within the Holy Roman Empire and in the Netherlands. When Wallenstein raised his army he was made a Duke and appointed "General of the auxiliaries sent to serve in the Empire," which meant that the troops in Upper Alsace and in Italy were also under his command. But Wallenstein was to rise even higher.

At that time his annual income was assessed at six million guldens. This was derived partly from the capital assets he had deposited in the banks of Venice and Amsterdam, partly from his Bohemian and Moravian estates. Later he received a further income from the principality of Sagan in Silesia.

One of the few people close to Wallenstein was the Italian astrologer Seni (Giovanni Battista Zenno). With him he would spend whole nights in animated discussion. But Seni is supposed to have betrayed Wallenstein by furnishing Piccolomini[1] with regular reports. It is probable that he was being bribed by Gallas[2] and was well paid for his duplicity. Since he was also employed by Wallenstein himself on intelligence work, he seems to have been a double agent.

In 1623, when Baron Karl Harrach gave his daughter Isabella Katharina in marriage to the widowed Wallenstein, he firmly established the General's standing in the social hierarchy. In the same year the Emperor honoured Wallen-

---

[1] Octavio Piccolomini, see p. 429 ff.
[2] Count Matthias Gallas, soldier in Wallenstein's army; later conspired against him and succeeded him as Commander of the Imperial Army.

stein by addressing him as "dear Uncle." Harrach, who was a member of Ferdinand's most intimate circle, became his son-in-law's leading advocate at Court. When he died, in May 1628, Wallenstein lost his most effective support.

Despite their activity on the Asiatic front, the indirect threat offered by the Turks and the direct attacks mounted by the Hungarian and Transylvanian Protestants continued throughout the course of events in Bohemia. It was only the defeat of the Bohemians that forced Bethlen Gabor to sign the peace of Nikolsburg, on December 31, 1621. Although he was obliged to relinquish his claim to the Hungarian crown, he received, in addition to Kassa, Tokay and Munkács, seven counties in northern Hungary, together with the Duchies of Oppeln and Ratibor in Silesia, from which it is quite clear that Bethlen Gabor's power and influence were held in high esteem. For a short while the peace of Nikolsburg guaranteed Austria's south-eastern flank, until then under constant threat. But it was not long before the Hapsburgs' many opponents, especially the French diplomats, did their utmost to prevail upon not only the Prince of Transylvania (whom Richelieu greatly admired) but also the Turks to re-enter the European theatre of war.

In point of fact, in the autumn of 1622 Bethlen Gabor attacked again, but the victories of the Imperial and League armies within the Empire forced him to accept the treaty of Vienna, which was signed on May 8, 1624. By its terms he lost his Silesian possessions but gained the territory of Ecsed. Then in 1626, when he married his second wife, Catherine of Brandenburg, he was again brought into the centre of the great Protestant coalition.

In January 1625 Richelieu had sent his agents to Bethlen Gabor. In the summer of the same year Frederick V's emissary, Paul Strassburger, visited the Prince of Transylvania, who shortly afterwards entered into negotiations with the English, French and Venetian envoys in Constantinople. In the autumn Bethlen's representative, Dr. Quaedt, was active in North

Germany. In October Bethlen himself entered into direct contact with Christian IV of Denmark, having first obtained permission from the Turkish Sultan to form alliances with Christian powers; this had been expressly forbidden by the terms of the recently renewed Turko-Transylvanian alliance of Zsitvatörök. However, no firm agreement was established between Christian and Bethlen. The only concrete result of all this diplomatic activity was the conclusion of an offensive-and-defensive alliance in December 1625 between Bethlen and George William of Brandenburg.

Wallenstein's and Tilly's new victories in Germany again frustrated Bethlen's plans and persuaded him to negotiate the peace of Löcse with the Emperor in December 1626. His greatest hour would have come some four years later, when his brother-in-law, Gustavus Adolphus of Sweden, who had also married into the house of Brandenburg, appeared on the scene. But Bethlen Gabor, the bravest of the princes opposing the house of Hapsburg and the Counter-Reformation in his day, died in 1629 after a brief illness. His death brought a measure of relief to the Emperor in the thirties when, as a result of his Mantuan venture, he found himself faced with a potentially perilous war on two fronts. But here we are anticipating events by nearly a decade.

In 1621, when the twelve-year truce of 1609 between Philip III of Spain and the United Provinces had expired, war again broke out between Holland and Spain. As a result the question of Spanish troop movements from the valley of the Po to Luxemburg again became acute and Spinola was ordered to occupy the Rhenish Palatinate in order to safeguard the route. At this, the German Protestant princes appealed urgently to Louis XIII, literally begging him to send help. But help was not forthcoming, for Louis still lacked the means to intervene in Germany. Once this became apparent, the free Imperial city of Strassburg started to negotiate with Spinola and offered to withdraw from the Protestant Union. Strassburg was soon followed by the Landgrave of Hesse-Cassel and shortly afterwards by the Margrave of Ansbach and the Duke of Württemberg. When the few remaining members of the Union met in Heilbronn, it was clear that the German Protestant alliance, which had expired in 1621, could not be renewed. The only Protestants still under arms were petty princes and mercenary commanders. One such was the Margrave of Baden, who had lost his land and wished to reconquer it. A second was Count Mansfeld and another was the "mad bishop," Christian of Brunswick-Wolfenbüttel, who held the bishopric of Halberstadt. Leaders like these, who were always open to offers from abroad, were typical of the initial period of the Thirty Years War. Let us therefore briefly consider Mansfeld and Christian.

Mansfeld and Christian of Brunswick

The mercenary leader Count Peter Ernst Mansfeld observed the principle that war feeds on war as faithfully and as ruthlessly as any man. His family was one of the oldest in Germany, his forbears having had considerable power as Counts as early as the twelfth century. The family home, the ancient castle of Mansfeld, was situated in the county of the same name. Peter Ernst was a natural son of the Governor of Luxemburg and Brussels. He was born in 1580 and brought up in the Catholic faith. As one of the great mercenary leaders, he too possessed all the qualities of the entrepreneur. He was legitimized under Rudolph II in recognition of his outstanding military achievements in the Netherlands and Hungary. A violent man, Mansfeld was quick to revenge both real and imagined affronts. He was in constant need of money and was prepared to go to extreme lengths to get it. When the Imperialists broke their promise and did not install him in his father's estates in the Netherlands, he went over to the discontented Bohemians, joining Thurn's army at the head of four thousand men. He also served the Duke of Savoy. Wherever he passed with his army he brought fearful destruction. In 1619 he had been

15.　Henry, Duke of Rohan

outlawed by Emperor Matthias, but this he completely ignored. His only response was to march through the land at the head of his undisciplined horde, plundering every township he chanced upon. Together with Christian of Brunswick, he sold his services to the Dutch, whereupon, after ravaging East Friesland, he dismissed his army and travelled as a private gentleman to Paris and London in order to obtain financial support from both governments for raising a new army. In 1626 he reappeared in Germany at the head of his new force, but in Wallenstein he met his master, and was crushingly defeated at the Bridge of Dessau. Wallenstein, however, refrained from pressing home his advantage, doubtless because he was able to foresee Mansfeld's fate. In accordance with the Danish plan of campaign, Mansfeld pressed on through Silesia and into Hungary where he joined up with Bethlen

Fig. 1. H. U. Franckh: Mercenaries in the Village

Gabor's Transylvanian army, then fighting the Emperor with Turkish support. But Bethlen had already exhausted his resources and was forced to make peace. He advised Mansfeld to disband his own army without delay, but Mansfeld did not heed him. Instead he tried to rally his battered divisions by raising money from Venice and England, hoping both to meet what he owed in back pay and to recruit new troops. But on his way to Venice, at the end of November 1626, Mansfeld died in a small Bosnian village near Sarajevo.

We possess an apologia written by Mansfeld towards the end of his life. Even his own generation, who had witnessed the most fearful excesses in the territories of the Empire, regarded him with particular loathing. In this document we read:

Fig. 2. H. U. Franckh: Unsuccessful Ambush

"If soldiers are to live, they need money. If they are not given money, then they will take it wherever they find it, and will not restrict their demands to what is owed them. For they do not count their money, neither do they weigh it. And once they are let loose, their unbridled excesses will range far and wide. . . . They will take everything, they will plunder everything, they will strike, and strike down, all that stand in their path.

"In short, there is no disorder and no discord that they will not sow. For with their different nationalities, customs and societies, they are consummate masters in every form of villainy. The German, the Dutchman, the Frenchman, the Italian, the Hungarian, each makes his own contribution, so that no form of trickery or low cunning is unknown to them, and there is none they will not employ in their rapacious felonies. They respect no person, whatever his rank or office. No place is sacred in their eyes.

"All this we know and gladly concede: and have been obliged to witness many excesses of this kind with great and bitter grief. That is the great misfortune that makes dissension and war so horrible and so atrocious. The only remedy is good discipline. But discipline cannot be maintained where money and provisions are lacking. I know of nobody capable of proceeding in any other way."

As death drew near, Mansfeld confessed to a priest of the faith in which he had been born and bred, and then, having been helped into his armour and equipment, he stood supported by two officers and awaited death on his feet.

Mansfeld's brother-in-arms, Christian of Brunswick-Wolfenbüttel, wrote in quite a different vein. Here is a letter from him to the councillors of Paderborn:
"With the blessing of God, Christian.

"We send our gracious greeting, dear, distinguished, most noble, most honourable and most learned [Councillors]. Your communication has been duly delivered to us and from it we

323

have learnt your opinion; since we understand that you are not of a mind to resolve to send some person to us who might have agreed terms with us, and since therefore we do indeed sense your obduracy and evil intentions towards us, we would wish to have you warned severally and forcibly that unless you inform us forthwith and *in momento* of a change of attitude, in order that we may have peace, we shall without further notice burn down the whole monastery and shall give orders for all the farmers and their kinsfolk to be cut down and shot, so that their children's children shall rue the day; consequently, if you wish to avoid this ravage, you must send some person back with our trumpeter to reach an agreement with us, else all will proceed according to plan, in the light of which you must now make your decision.

"Signed at Horn, December 23, 1621.

CHRISTIAN"

Richelieu's Bavarian Policy

These then were the men who led the remnants of the Protestant Union armies and the Danish forces against generals of the calibre of Tilly and Wallenstein. Although Tilly and the League army had been extremely successful, Wallenstein's army, his towering personality and also his ruthlessness had enabled Vienna to regain the leadership and adopt an attitude towards Bavaria that Maximilian himself described as "the gratitude of the house of Austria." Maximilian was still strong, however. When Austria's position was undermined by the War of the Mantuan Succession, and serious conflict threatened in the north following the abandonment of the siege of Stralsund, Maximilian's prestige rose again. Like most of his contemporaries, he was convinced that Spain was out to subject the whole of Europe to Hapsburg rule. For a long time he regarded Wallenstein as an ardent advocate of a universal Hapsburg empire. Nor had he forgotten that the Spanish

Court had opposed his claim to the electorship and lands of the Count Palatine. Oñate had once said that he did not want Spain to have to share her dominant influence in Germany with a second-rate power. Maximilian also remembered that King Henry IV of France had been prepared to intervene in the dispute over the Cleves-Jülich succession and that the treaty of Ulm between the Protestant Union and the Catholic League, which had guaranteed him against attack during the Bohemian campaign, had resulted from French mediation. These memories played their part in persuading Maximilian after the mid-twenties to oppose Wallenstein's project for the formation of a Pan-German state. Maximilian's attitude, which was identical with Richelieu's, was largely responsible for ensuring the continuance of the old Imperial order whereby Germany remained divided. Because he agreed with Richelieu

Fig. 3. H. U. Franckh: Unexpected Attack

325

on the subject of German unity, Maximilian was tempted to regard an alliance with the French in a favourable light. At the same time, however, he constantly strove to separate France from her Protestant allies, in order to gain this great Catholic power as an ally for the League in Germany and thus reduce the Hapsburg influence. This Bavarian project had the support of the Curia.

In 1629 a memorandum was drafted by a group of Bavarian councillors in which the question of the French alliance was discussed to the following effect:

We have received news—and that is the whole basis of this French alliance—that not only England, Holland and the other partisans of the Count Palatine are using every means at their disposal to ensure his reinstatement, but that Spain has also promised the King of England that she will shortly

Fig. 4. H. U. Franckh: Armoured Trooper

restore the Upper and Lower Palatinate to him, although she is opposed to the restitution of the electorship during the lifetime of the present Count. Since we know which *media cognendi caesarem* the Spanish have, and also know that up to now they have held the leading Ministers at the Imperial Court in their golden chains, Bavaria can surely not be blamed if she considers her own interests. Although the Emperor's own attitude to the Electoral Bavaria is positive, his Minister of War and his other Ministers have shown clearly enough by their actions and comments (as, for example, that there are two Emperors in the Empire, and that the excessive authority enjoyed by the Electors must be reduced) that they are not well disposed towards the Elector of Bavaria or other Electors allied with him. By his levies which grow daily more immoderate, Friedland is trying to deprive the Electors and the estates of their liberties and to turn them into slaves. Above all, however, he is trying to subjugate Bavaria, and in order to do so he is working for the dissolution of the League army.

Maximilian I added his own glosses to this important document. For example:

"And although in general there can be no doubt but that this would cause His Imp. Maj. great displeasure, yet experience has shown that he [Friedland] does not altogether attune himself to the Emperor's orders or obey them, but rather acts in a way that is diametrically opposed to them and deals all the more harshly with those who complain to his Imp. Maj."

The authors of the memorandum went on to say:

France has stated that she is prepared to help Bavaria and to maintain its territorial acquisitions. Since France has been volunteering this help over a number of years and since she is also interested in establishing a balance of power vis-à-vis the house of Hapsburg on her own account, her offer must be regarded as genuine. France has great authority with England, Holland, the outlawed Count Palatine and especially the

Turks. Through French mediation Bavaria would also gain recognition of the electorship from the Elector of Saxony and the Elector of Brandenburg. If Bavaria were to reject the alliance she would offend the Pope, its original architect, and would also provoke France's enmity and drive her into an alliance with the enemy. And if France were to join with England and Holland in an attempt to reinstate the Count Palatine, then, given the attitude of Spain, his restitution would be certain.

Bavaria's position between 1624 and 1630 could scarcely have been put more precisely or more cogently.

Richelieu's Diplomatic Agents in Germany

Richelieu did not abruptly revive Henry IV's hostile Spanish policy. La Vieuville had already taken the first steps in this direction. But after 1624 Richelieu stepped up French diplomatic activity on all sides, especially in Germany, in an attempt to establish a combined anti-Hapsburg front. As soon as he had entered office the Cardinal increased the number of French representatives in the Courts and principal cities of both Protestant and Catholic Electors. The instructions issued to the various agents were largely identical: They were to continue France's traditional policy of backing the Protestant estates in their opposition to Imperial policy and were also to pursue France's principal aim of separating the Catholic League from the Emperor and neutralizing it.

Thanks to the information modern historians have culled from the documents of the period, many of the French agents employed in Germany at that time are better known to us today than they were to their contemporaries. We are told that in April 1624 a Monsieur de Vaubecourt and his son appeared at the Courts of the Rhenish Electors, where they introduced themselves as mediators. In a letter to Maximilian I of Bavaria Johann Schweikart of Mainz correctly assessed the position of the German princes when he said that if they accepted France's offer of mediation they would make the Emperor suspicious, and if they rejected it they would drive the French into the arms of their enemies.

Maximilian's appraisal of the situation was more subtle. He wrote: "In this [Vaubecourt's] proposal many different issues are merged; ultimately it is directed towards the restoration of peace in Germany, initially towards the restoration of the pre-eminence of the Electors and of the German Liberties and against those who threaten them, especially Spain."

It was a long time before anybody in Germany fully realized that after 1624 every French initiative was part of the "cold war" that France was waging against Spain and the house of Hapsburg.

In certain cases the foreign representatives appointed by France were not the kind of men we would expect. Their political colouring or their confessional leanings make them a strange choice.

The "zealots" or *dévots* (who were said by the *politiques*—the *bons français*—to be *espagnolisés*)—pursued a strictly defined policy. They wanted to see the Counter-Reformation victorious, they wanted Spain and Austria as France's allies, and they saw as their goal a Catholic world in which "His Catholic Majesty" and the "Most Christian King" would act in unison and the Protestants would be wiped out. It is, however, not easy to assess the exact nature of the opinions held by many belonging to this faction. Among the *politiques*, on the other hand, there were many who, while advocating tolerance for the French Huguenots, were ultimately aiming at the establishment of a French national church, which, like the Anglican Church, would be based on Catholic doctrine and would continue the Gallican tradition of opposition to papal supremacy. A powerful monarchy was of course essential to any such objective and consequently the *politiques* were royalists. But among the emissaries working for Richelieu and Father Joseph in Germany we find a number of men with a far more individual and sophisticated approach, such

L*

as François Langlois, Monsieur de Fancan. This remarkable man was born in Amiens into a family of jurists. His grandfather had been killed by the Spanish and his father, who did not long survive him, was said to have died of grief. Fancan, who had nine brothers and sisters, entered the Church and became the parish priest of St Germain l'Auxerrois in Paris. Later he was made a canon and then choirmaster, a post he relinquished in 1625. He was a born satirist and a highly gifted pamphleteer, and his historical and literary knowledge was of an exceptional order. After attacking Concini in a series of biting pamphlets, he took Luynes as his target, reproaching him for his ruthless behaviour towards the Queen-Mother. It was his advocacy of Marie de' Medici that brought him in contact with Richelieu. There are indications of an extremely close collaboration between the two men. Fancan also attacked Brûlart and La Vieuville and, like the Jesuits at that time, he wished to see Richelieu take control of French policy.

On December 22, 1624, Fancan was sent to Munich. His mission may be summarized as follows: He was to visit the Duke of Bavaria on the French King's behalf, but pretending to be on a private journey. He was to leave Paris in secrecy, so that neither the Secretaries of State nor his own friends and confidants could guess at the purpose of his journey. The only person to whom he was allowed to write was Schomberg, who had long been acknowledged an expert on Germany. His instructions contained nothing that was essentially new; he was to inform the Duke of Bavaria that the King's greatest desire was to bring about a lasting peace, and that to this end he wished to settled the affairs of the Count Palatine in the interests of both England and Bavaria. Fancan had two main objectives. He was to ensure that the Catholic League (i.e., Bavaria) did not support the Spanish in any way in Germany, and was to obtain Bavarian approval for the reinstatement of the Count Palatine in his ancient rights and privileges on condition that he embrace the Catholic faith. These requirements were to be formulated in the light of recommendations made by Father Hyacinth, a protégé of Father Joseph's and a product of the Vatican school who, as preacher to the Bavarian army, had been in constant contact with Maximilian since 1620; from 1621 on he had led an itinerant life, representing the interests of various States but especially the Vatican, and travelling between Rome, the Italian principalities, France, the Netherlands, Spain and various parts of the Empire, including Bavaria. Fancan was authorized to use threats if necessary. If Maximilian did not agree to his proposals Fancan was to hint that for reasons of state and against his own inclinations the King of France might find himself obliged to join forces with the English and reconquer the County Palatine. Then would come the bait. Fancan was to say that, as the Duke of Bavaria already knew, it was Louis XIII's intention to raise both the Duke and the house of Wittelsbach to the highest honours of the Empire (the allusion was of course to the Imperial crown). If the Duke decided to comply with France's wishes, then he should send an official envoy to Louis XIII and ask him to negotiate on his behalf.

On his way to Germany, Fancan passed through Liège, where he met Maximilian's brother, Ferdinand of Cologne, and his Court. Fancan had no credentials to present. He insisted on his status as a private citizen, well informed politically and expressing his personal views. But for a private citizen his demands were exacting, including the elimination of Spanish influence within the Empire, the complete segregation of Imperial and Spanish interests, and close secret relations between France and Bavaria. All this would enable Louis XIII to restrain his Protestant friends—England, Holland and the Scandinavian states—from open aggression. He also demanded that Tilly was to refrain from all further actions against England's supporters in Germany.

Maximilian failed to perceive the new political implications of the French agent's statements. He had distrusted Fancan from the very outset and even refused to receive him on the grounds that he was not an accredited representative. He found the whole affair highly suspect and rejected the French proposals, although he had previously agreed to proposals put forward by Father Hyacinth. It seemed to him that Fancan was reopening a considerable number of problems that had already been solved. It is clear from Maximilian's correspondence with his brother that he had been angered by the reports he had received from Liège and Cologne. In replying to them he stated that Bavaria and France had had a close relationship for the past three years and that Louis XIII was well aware that, although Bavaria expected nothing from Spanish mediation, she expected a great deal from French mediation.

Maximilian regarded Fancan's mission as a trick of La Vieuville's but in fact Fancan had received his instructions from Richelieu alone. The Bavarian Elector had expected that Richelieu would follow a policy far more favourable to his interests, and upon La Vieuville's removal from office he remarked that "because of his complete lack of understanding [La Vieuville] was totally unqualified and had thrown everything into confusion."

We have already seen that, when Fancan reached Munich, Maximilian took advantage of the Frenchman's lack of credentials in order to avoid negotiating with him. Although Father Hyacinth had spoken favourably of this "private" envoy-extraordinary, he failed to make any real impact. The truth of the matter was that the international situation at the time was all too uncertain and subject to constant change. Up to 1623 it had seemed that the English heir-apparent might well marry a Spanish Princess, which would have changed the whole international situation. Then in 1625, when Charles of England married Henrietta of France, this seemed to herald a profound change in the relations between France and Spain and between England and Spain. And of course, James I of England had firmly rejected proposals made by Hyacinth. Jocher, Maximilian's representative in Mainz, had informed Fancan to this effect. Lastly—and this was crucial—Maximilian did not want to prejudice his relations with the Imperial Court in Vienna.

The same Fancan was arrested in Paris some three years later following the death on June 4, 1627, of Gaston d'Orléans's first wife. In the *Mercure François* it was said that he was suspected of having maintained treasonable relations with foreign powers.

In Richelieu's Memoirs there is a lengthy passage about him, in which the Cardinal indulged in a rhetorical outburst of temper. There we read:

"On the day this Princess died, the King had a certain Fancan arrested in order that he should atone in some part for the crimes he had committed.

"This man had always declared himself, far more openly than prudence allows, to be an enemy of our present era; nothing could satisfy him save the fantastic hopes for a Republic which he nourished in his depraved imagination.

"His protest was not only against the present but against eternity as well; all the indications were that he knew no God save the god of his own madness.

"All his ends were bad, and the means he used to attain them were odious and evil; no notion for transforming our political condition was so wrongheaded or so cruel but that it would come to his mind at least once in the course of each day.

"It was his customary practice to compose pamphlets in which he sought to discredit the government, pour scorn on our monarch, malign his advisers, incite to revolt, find pretexts for disturbing the peace of the realm and destroying the monarchy in the name of patriotism.

"The Huguenots found such great favour in his eyes that, although he was a priest, all who had the reputation of being good Catholics were anathema to him.

"He had always maintained relations with Protestants abroad, to whom he rendered faithful service as a spy, and was all the more to be feared on this account since his clerical office tended to raise him above suspicion. In serving them he made use of his access to the houses of various Ministers, and under the pretext of giving good advice he raised false alarms in order to incite them to actions hostile to the State.

"He was a disciple of the devil, and truth never passed his lips; the sole purpose of all his duplicity was to sow discord among those whose unity was essential to the peace of the realm.

"His malice was so great that even in the royal household he employed all manner of stratagems in an attempt to estrange those whom nature and the Holy Sacrament had joined together.

"The King was resolved to impose on this malevolent man a punishment severe enough to match his crimes. But Richelieu . . . humbly begged His Majesty to content himself with the confinement of his person."

This case exemplifies the unreliability of certain of Richelieu's foreign agents and observers, who repeatedly contravened his policies, either by veering towards the Huguenots or by maintaining contacts with the party of the heir-apparent—sometimes both. We shall be meeting further instances of such opposition. Fancan, whom the Cardinal saved from execution, later became one of his principal and most dangerous polemical adversaries.

In the interval between Fancan's important mission to Munich and his imprisonment in Paris, various new developments were initiated. In 1625, the year when Louis XIII made temporary peace with the Huguenots, various attempts were made to bring about a general peace in Europe. Richelieu adopted a sceptical, even negative, attitude towards these endeavours. At the time he was still collaborating very closely with Schomberg. In a memorandum of that year we read: ". . . Archduke Leopold, acting in concert with Emperor Ferdinand, the Spanish ambassador, Osoña, and Prince Kimberg, has proposed to the King of France through the mediation of Monsieur de Marcheville that an alliance be concluded between Spain, the Emperor and the two Kings."

In an "Instruction for High Officials of the Ministry of Foreign Affairs," which was drafted in mid-May 1626, we read: "Monsieur de Marcheville will leave the Court after first announcing that he intends to visit his castle. He will then proceed secretly to Bavaria."

Then came an account of the many steps taken by the King of France to preserve the German Liberties, followed by a categorical assurance that Louis's highest ambition was to save his German friends from Austrian oppression. And further: "Marcheville is to confer with Father Hyacinth and Father Alexander, Father Joseph's correspondents. . . . The principal object of the mission is to win over the Duke of Bavaria, whom the King has not yet recognized in the office of Elector. An attempt must be made to mediate between the Duke and the Count Palatine."

These instructions, appended to the undated memorandum issued by the Foreign Ministry, were dated September 18th. But on December 6th fresh instructions were sent to Marcheville; they were signed by the King himself and countersigned by Phélypeaux. Marcheville was again sent to Maximilian of Bavaria, after which he was ordered to Denmark, where his ostensible object was to ensure that the Danes disarmed. In point of fact, however, this was no more than a tactical move designed to win over Maximilian and to ensure his approval of France's Protestant alliances. For we then read: "If the Duke of Bavaria fails to take measures in concert with the other Electors and through the mediation of Monsieur de Marcheville to settle the conflict with Denmark, then the King of France will proceed no further in this affair and will do nothing in respect of Danish disarmament. On his way to Copenhagen, Marcheville is to visit the newly appointed Elector of Mainz."

The more Richelieu was beset by problems at home the more attentively he pursued the details of foreign policy.

Between 1626 and 1630 he sent Marcheville as a mediator to Germany on repeated occasions. Then, on March 10, 1631, he appointed him French ambassador in Constantinople. His instructions on that occasion were very brief. They read: "Renewal of the capitulations."

Like Father Valeriano Magni and Father Alexandre of Alais, Father Hyacinth, who also served the Pope, travelled ceaselessly between Munich and Paris. The Curia did not hinder these monks in the execution of their missions any more than it hindered Father Joseph. Urban VIII had felt threatened by France over the Valtelline affair and had not been slow to express his indignation at Richelieu's intervention. But no sooner had the Imperial troops crossed the Alps than he took sides against Spain, although he was careful to avoid an open break with the house of Austria. He always treated the Spanish ambassador with the greatest consideration, and always assured the French ambassador that he had just spoken in the sharpest possible terms to his Spanish colleague. In actual fact, however, he made things as difficult as he possibly could for the Hapsburgs and openly refused to condemn Richelieu's Protestant alliances. Time and again Emperor Ferdinand had to contend with both the Pope's obdurate francophilia and the envy of the Catholic Electors.

England's Attitude

On January 11, 1626, Richelieu received emissaries from Buckingham, who had come to conclude an alliance. They were Lord Holland and Lord Carleton. Richelieu was apprehensive, for he was well aware how easy it would be for the English to strengthen Huguenot resistance. On the other hand he also knew that the English were in a position to persuade the Huguenots to yield. And at that time it lay in England's interests to work for a détente in French internal affairs, for then she might gain France as an ally against Spain.

On February 5th the delegates of the ostensibly reformed

religion, Holland and Carleton, arrived in the Louvre and were informed that Louis XIII was making peace with his Huguenot subjects, who had accepted the King's conditions. They undertook to stop fitting out warships, to allow the Catholics freedom of worship, to restore all Church property and to withdraw their demand that Fort Louis be razed. This peace initiative at home was in line with the peace settlement with Spain, which was concluded by Fargis in Monçon the following month. The negotiations leading up to these settlements had been conducted in a masterly fashion, and Richelieu was paying tribute to his own skill when he said that the Huguenots had agreed to sign because they feared that France would make peace with Spain, and the Spanish had signed because they feared that France would make peace with the Huguenots. But the Pope was displeased, and so too was Venice. The French Ultramontanes grew heated: a Cardinal had outwitted the Pope. Gaston d'Orléans, acting under the influence of Ornano, his steward, immediately placed himself at the head of the cabal, while Henry IV's natural sons, César, Duc de Vendôme and his brother Alexandre, the Grand Prior of France, together with the Duchess of Chevreuse and a majority of the great nobles, demanded that Richelieu be removed from office. This is the crisis that led to the execution of the Count of Chalais (see Vol. I).

While things stood thus in France, Marcheville departed on his German mission.

Denmark

Christian IV, King of Denmark and Norway and Duke of Schleswig-Holstein was born on April 12, 1577, at Frederiksborg Castle on the island of Zealand and was elected King by the Council of State on April 4, 1588, upon the death of his father, Frederick II. In 1596 Christian attained his majority and he then reigned until his death, on August 28, 1648. In 1597 he married Anne Catherine of Brandenburg.

As King he worked tirelessly in the service of the State, supervised the administration of justice and was not afraid to proceed against persons of high rank. He displayed great energy in the naval sphere and built an excellent fleet. In 1616 he founded the Indies Trading Company. It was thanks to his initiative that a number of new cities were built, including Christiania (Oslo).

His first war with Sweden (1611–13) was successful and ended with the peace of Knäred, the provisions of which were favourable to Denmark. This apart, however, his foreign policy showed little profit, and neither his intervention in the Thirty Years War nor the second war with Sweden brought him glory. And yet of all the Kings of the Oldenburg dynasty he has remained the most popular.

In 1634 he made an exemplary attempt to abolish serfdom; but this came to nothing, owing to the concerted opposition of virtually the entire Danish nobility.

In his capacity as Duke of Holstein, the King of Denmark was a prince of the Empire and had both a seat and a vote at the Imperial Diet. Until Denmark bestirred herself, the German Protestant party had been without an effective leader.

Frederick V of the County Palatine, who had fled to the Court of Brandenburg after the fall of Prague, had ceaselessly urged his father-in-law, James I of England, to intervene in Germany, and after James's death he continued to press his case with Charles I. In 1622 Frederick had made an abortive attempt to advance into the County Palatine, but the German Protestants had made no move; it was as if they were paralysed. Not even Bethlen Gabor's latest attack was able to incite the Protestant Union troops in the Rhenish Palatinate to mount an offensive. By then the Protestant Union was virtually at its last gasp. Spinola, the great Spanish general, was allowed to occupy the Rhenish Palatinate without a shot being fired. But for the money that foreign governments continued to pump into Germany, hostilities would have ended then and there.

French Policy towards England

Despite the vicissitudes of the international situation, French diplomacy remained extremely active. On April 27, 1625, instructions for the Count of Tresmes had been drafted. Following the death of James I, Tresmes had been chosen to bear Louis XIII's condolences to the English Court. He was told to avoid the subject of the proposed marriage between Charles I and Henrietta of France on this occasion and to concentrate on the necessity for reconquering the County Palatine. He was to inform the English that the French subsidies for Mansfeld had been guaranteed for the next seven months and that preparations were under way for further military action throughout the whole of Germany and in "still colder climes." If Mansfeld were to be employed in Holland against the Spanish, then this should only be done within the context of the Palatinate question. France was seeking no further territorial acquisitions. She had only one objective: to defend herself against the aggressive power of Spain. France, unlike Spain, would never exploit religion as a means of gaining Catholic princes as allies. The only request the King of France wished to make in the religious sphere was that the English Catholics should be treated justly.

On November 18th of the same year Richelieu sent Jean Varigniez, Monsieur de Blainville, a Councillor of State and Court official and a personal friend of the late Marquis d'Ancre, on a special mission to London. Blainville was expressly authorized to discuss German affairs in detail with both the English Ministers and the Dutch representative in London. He was to obtain assurances from England and the Netherlands that they would afford neither direct nor indirect support to the Protestants of La Rochelle.

He was then to advise the English Ministers that "out of deference to the King of England, the King of France will inform the Kings of Denmark and Sweden and also certain

Imperial and Hanseatic towns of the concern he feels over the pitiable conditions in the German territories."

Blainville was also to avail himself of every opportunity to emphasize how greatly alarmed France was by Spanish and Austrian ambitions. He was to prevail upon England and the United Provinces to provide Mansfeld with a sum equal to that provided by France. And then, like all French agents abroad, he was instructed to speak of strong concentrations of French troops on the borders of the Spanish Netherlands and to give assurances that Louis XIII would never negotiate with Spain unilaterally. In the intelligence sphere the French representative was required to obtain detailed information as to the fighting capacity of the English fleet and the plans for deploying it. Finally, he was told to get moves afoot in London to persuade the Prince of Orange to attack in the spring.

A clear-cut programme—but Charles I did not take kindly to Blainville's proposals. What disturbed English opinion was the fact that, while France was urging support for the German Protestants, she was at the same time trying to protect the interests of a religious minority in England. At that time Buckingham was still at hand to aggravate his sovereign's irritation. Clearly the prospects for a co-ordinated alliance between England, France and Holland were not promising.

Charnacé's and Marcheville's Mission

Within the context of Richelieu's Dutch, Danish, Polish and Swedish policies, there was one man who consistently played a leading part and who merits closer consideration. Among the great host of agents, many of them dubious figures, whom Richelieu and Father Joseph employed on all sides, there were some capable and eminent men. Hercule de Charnacé, one of France's most important foreign representatives from 1629 onwards, proved himself an excellent negotiator, a good judge of men and a keen observer. He was intelligent, energetic and quick to act on his decisions, a man of strong character, courageous and persevering, unbending in his purpose to the point of inflexibility, and nearly always successful, even in the most difficult situations. But in his personal life he was dogged by misfortune, subject to depression, and apt to attract envy and intrigue. His achievements were constantly jeopardized by counter-moves and devious manœuvres of his opponents. He exhausted both his fortune and his health in the service of the State, in his allegiance to his employers. In the end he sought and found death in battle. He had married Jeanne de Maillé-Brézé, of the family of Richelieu's brother-in-law, but his young wife died after only two years of married life. This personal tragedy left Charnacé in a state of despair and exhaustion, that deprived him of all power of action. We are told that Father Joseph concerned himself personally with Charnacé and that it was thanks to his great patience that he was finally induced to undertake a long journey in 1622. This suggestion, like all suggestions stemming from the Capuchin, also served a political end. Father Joseph had recognized the sick man's acumen, and so he sent him to Egypt, to Arabia, to the Holy Land, to Syria and Greece. Charnacé returned home by way of Russia, Poland and finally Germany, where he stayed for some time. Just as Father Joseph had expected, he brought back invaluable information. He had visited Gustavus Adolphus, the young King of Sweden, and the latter's cousin and enemy, Sigismund of Poland. Later, when he was serving as an army officer before La Rochelle, Charnacé had detailed political talks with Richelieu, in which he insisted that France must try to arrange an agreement between Sweden and Poland on the one hand and Sweden and Denmark on the other. His arguments served to strengthen Richelieu's own conviction. The much-travelled officer made a very powerful impression on Richelieu at La Rochelle, and from then onwards Louis XIII's principal adviser on foreign affairs did not lose sight of him. Charnacé distinguished himself in the battles with the English, especially on the Isle of Ré, and Richelieu gave instructions for his feats to be proclaimed from every pulpit in Anjou. In January 1629 the Cardinal entrusted Charnacé with an important diplomatic mission in which he was required to mediate between the Catholic League, Bavaria and Denmark on the one hand and Sweden and Poland on the other. French aims were unchanged: the consolidation of Protestant resistance within the Empire and the neutralization of the Catholic League.

The extension of Imperial power to the Baltic greatly alarmed the Cardinal. His fears on this account were prompted by one of those visions of the future which often continued to plague him even in his sleep; it seemed to him that this Baltic expansion threatened to increase the power of the Hapsburgs to an almost incalculable degree.

The aims of Richelieu's policy on the continent of Europe, and more especially within the sphere of German affairs, had scarcely changed since 1616, when the Cardinal had sent Schomberg his instructions. Meanwhile, however, France's freedom of action had been inhibited by the outbreak of further hostilities between the King and the Huguenots, which culminated in the siege of La Rochelle.

As we have already seen, however, both in 1626 and 1627 Marcheville had failed in his attempt to drive a wedge between Maximilian and the Emperor by offering to mediate between the Catholic League and Denmark.

Meanwhile, the victorious progress of the Imperial and League armies through Germany had reinforced Richelieu's oppressive vision of a great *imperium* stretching from the Adriatic to the Baltic; and it was only after the fall of La Rochelle (1628–9) that France was at last free to act again. It then seemed that the best way of countering the new development was by pursuing the ideas put forward by Charnacé during the siege and to draw the Scandinavian countries into the German scene without delay. Charnacé was chosen to persuade the Danes and the Swedes to compose their differences, and then to conciliate the Swedes and the Poles.

The possibility of such a move had not escaped Wallenstein. In March 1627 he had written to the Emperor urging him not to abandon the King of Poland, for the Swedes could prove an even more dangerous enemy than the Turks. In the same year he wrote to Arnim[1] in the same sense.

First, however, there was the Danish intervention. It was not as the King of Denmark and Duke of Holstein that Christian IV took up arms; had he done so he would have met with resistance from his estates. Instead he acted as a member of the European Union, and it was as such that he opposed the Austrian and Spanish Hapsburgs. His decision to attack was taken in the illusory hope that he would be joined by powerful allies from both east and west. But developments in Europe ruled out all possibility of effective support for the Danes. War broke out between England and France over La Rochelle and Turkey removed her forces from her western front in order to deploy them against Persia, thus giving Austria a respite in the south.

As early as 1623, when Tilly advanced into Westphalia, Denmark had felt threatened. The dubious Anglo-French defensive alliance with Holland was concluded in 1624 and Denmark became the military arm of the coalition. As far as Holland and England were concerned, their original intention, adopted before the resurgence of the Huguenot war brought a worsening of their relations to France, was to concentrate on war at sea. In view of her internal situation, France herself was obliged to avoid open warfare in any form. And so Richelieu concentrated his diplomatic activity on Denmark and did all in his power to strengthen Christian in his military resolve. The disarmament proposal put forward by Marcheville in Munich in 1626, which, he claimed, France would submit with a recommendation to the Danish King, appears to have been

[1] Field-marshall Hans Georg von Arnim, Commander-in-Chief of Saxony, an acquaintance of Wallenstein who frequently crossed his path.

a bluff designed to allay Maximilian's fears concerning the events taking place in North Germany and to persuade him to desert the Emperor.

In November 1624 the accredited French envoy in Denmark, Courmenin Deshayes, had promised Christian IV an annual subsidy of 600,000 livres and, as was only to be expected, had held out the prospect of a French attack on the Rhine to draw off part of the Imperial forces. Apart from these high subsidies for Denmark, France was also financing Mansfeld, although initially England had also contributed to this latter expenditure.

From the very outset Christian IV placed far too much trust in his allies and also in the military skill of such generals as Mansfeld and Christian of Brunswick.

And then, when Christian reached Hameln, he met with an extremely dangerous accident. He fell from his horse and his injuries were so severe that they kept him away from his army for months. This setback discouraged the Danish King and blunted his fervour. It also cost him time, and in that time the Imperialists greatly increased their forces.

Mansfeld was defeated, and after Wallenstein had finished his action in Hungary he met the Danes at Dessau on April 25, 1626, and won the victory. But it was Tilly who finally defeated the Danish forces, at the battle of Lutter on August 27th of the same year. These victories put the whole of North Germany at the mercy of the Imperial and League armies. Soon Christian was deserted by his principal allies. (The reasons why England and Holland failed to send help were clearly stated by Richelieu, as we shall see later.) Thanks to the great energy displayed by Wallenstein and Tilly, the King of Denmark was forced to lay down his arms.

It was not in defence of the faith that Christian had gone to war in June 1625. He had set out, trusting in his great allies, to secure his own country from the Imperialist threat and also no doubt in the hope of extending his dynastic territories. He had assumed the leadership of the German

Protestants, especially those of Lower Saxony, only to be deserted by his German confederates and eliminated as a military power. Only the Dukes of Mecklenburg had remained loyal to him, for which they paid a heavy price. Christian began suing for peace early in 1628. He asked for an amnesty, guaranties for the Protestants of Lower Saxony and the evacuation of territories occupied by the Imperial generals. Vienna, for its part, demanded the cession of Holstein, Jutland and Schleswig and closing of the Sound to foreign shipping. A compromise peace was finally reached, owing to Wallenstein's intervention.

The Danish war lasted from 1625 to 1629. The main efforts to bring it about date from the years 1623 and 1624. By the time the peace negotiations were under way, Ferdinand II had acquired a position of power unequalled by any Emperor since the days of the Hohenstaufen, and which he himself was never to achieve again. He owed this position to Maximilian I of Bavaria, to Maximilian's general Tilly, and above all to Wallenstein—which has to be kept in mind when we judge the man in his later years.

By now the Emperor was able to intervene in the Spanish war in the Netherlands. But the United Provinces responded to this new threat by gaining new victories. They took Wesel and exercised considerable influence throughout north-west Germany from the Dutch border to Westphalia. It had proved impossible to mount a really concerted attack on Holland, because against Wallenstein's wishes, large sections of his army had been moved to the Italian theatre of war to help in the Mantuan crisis, and it had also been necessary to mass troops on Germany's western border against the French. In the course of this latter operation Imperial troops had temporarily advanced into the bishropic of Metz. This policy, in which the members of the Catholic League had no say whatsoever, only increased the discontent among the Emperor's German Catholic allies. Wallenstein's victories had already been over-exploited, and when the Edict of Restitution was proclaimed—also against Wallenstein's wishes—the situation became strained to breaking point.

In Vienna, where, despite the short term Franco-Spanish secret treaty concluded during the siege of La Rochelle, the Spanish and the Austrians had been discussing anti-French measures since 1628, it was decided to impose harsh treaty conditions on Denmark. But, as we have seen, these were subsequently ameliorated when Wallenstein interposed his own far sounder view. Christian was allowed to retain his lands, but his allies were sacrificed. The Electors had been completely excluded from the negotiations, the objective of which was very clearly stated:

"Since in a number of years all sorts of confusions and misunderstandings have occurred, which have eventually led to great and serious wars and hostilities, and in order that these may be halted and further discord and the devastation of so many noble lands, principalities and provinces avoided [the parties have agreed to institute] a pacification move to re-establish and consolidate a noble and worthy peace and to inculcate enduring trust within Germany."

But the contents of the treaty of Lübeck were as follows:

Art. 1. Peace and friendship on sea and land; all are to be forgiven (no further recriminations, all to be forgotten, ended, assuaged, effaced, dead); everlasting unity.

Art. 2. No war damages. Christian IV retains Wendkusel, Jutland, Schleswig, Holstein, Stormarn, Dithmarschen together with all rights and regalia (without reparations).

Art. 3. Mutual exchange of prisoners.

Art. 4. The following are included in the peace: Spain, Poland, the Infanta in Brussels, the whole house of Austria, Electoral Bavaria, the Electors and estates of the Holy Roman Empire, Denmark, Norway, France, Great Britain, Sweden, the States-General of the United Provinces.

Art. 5. Ratification of the treaty (Christian IV 1629 June 13 (03) Copenhagen). No reprisals against the inhabitants of

Fehmarn, Nordstrand, Worde and Sulde. The Imperial soldiers are to withdraw in good order. Christian further undertakes to desist from all future actions against the Empire in the course of this war. Published 1629 June 07.

On July 19, 1629, after the treaty had been signed, Richelieu said in a letter to the Danish envoy in France, Johann Zobel, that the war King Christian IV had lost against Spain and the Emperor had been fought in the interests of England and for the restitution of the Count Palatine. France had been so involved with the siege of La Rochelle, the relief of Casale and the punitive expedition in Languedoc that she had been unable to send help. England had done still less, because the authority of the King of England had been undermined by Parliament. The Cardinal then passed judgement on the peace conditions with the following biting comment, which was effectively designed for the Danes themselves:

"These articles were the commands of a prince to his subject, of a master to his lackey."

In the period immediately preceding the conclusion of the treaty, Hercule de Charnacé, France's diplomatic representative, had been extremely active. He had left the French Court in Troyes in January 1629, and during the course of the actual peace negotiations he was still doing his utmost to prevent Christian from signing the treaty. His principal argument was that France was still confident of neutralizing the Catholic League.

After the peace treaty had been signed, Charnacé continued to press Christian to join the anti-Imperialist camp. Above all he tried to bring about a reconciliation and, if possible, an alliance between Denmark and Sweden. But despite all the advantages that Charnacé pledged to secure for Denmark if she joined forces with Sweden, Christian continued to observe the provisions of the treaty of Lübeck.

But French diplomacy was shortly to establish a new gain. In August 1629 Charnacé had done much to further the progress of the proposed agreement between Poland and Sweden, and a month later he was able to report to his sovereign that on September 25, 1629, thanks to the mediation of Louis XIII of France, Charles I of England and the Elector of Brandenburg, a six-year truce had been concluded in Altmark between Poland and Sweden. At the same time Charnacé wrote to Father Joseph to say that, although there were certain details which it was inadvisable to commit to paper, he felt compelled to mention one important point: he had been obliged to protest in the strongest possible terms the claims made by the English envoy, who, when he came to sign the treaty on behalf of Charles I, had included among his monarch's titles "King of France."

The elector of Brandenburg expressed his particular gratitude to Charnacé for having defended the Hohenzollern rights to the fortress of Marienburg in the course of the negotiations. Charnacé had of course done his utmost to bring about a close understanding between Brandenburg and Sweden.

And so Charnacé had played his part in extricating Gustavus Adolphus from a conflict that could have brought no possible advantage to French interests. The successful negotiator was then given his next task, which was to ensure that the Swedish forces, no longer needed for Poland, were deployed against the house of Austria.

True to Richelieu's general instructions, whereby all envoys were required to proceed as secretly as possible, Charnacé had sent one of his colleagues, Melchior de Sabran, to the Imperial Court to give assurances of France's loyal intentions and to emphasize that the only subject discussed by the French mediator in Sweden was the Mantuan affair.

Charnacé's most difficult task was to persuade the Swedes to recognize and guarantee the neutrality of the Catholic League, especially Bavaria. This was an objective that France had pursued with great consistency and one that was to occupy her for many years to come.

We possess a memorandum drafted by Richelieu in 1630

that provides an excellent survey of German affairs between 1628 and 1630. In it the Cardinal referred to the peace treaty concluded between the Emperor and the King of Denmark and to the armistice negotiated with his help between Poland and Sweden, which permitted Gustavus Adolphus to intervene on the Continent. He then reported on the outcome of Monsieur de Charnacé's missions to various Electors, chief among them the Duke of Bavaria, and also to the King of Sweden. We are told that in July Monsieur de Sabran was sent to the Emperor with the object of persuading him to approve the investiture of the Duke of Nevers in Mantua, for the usurpation of the hereditary rights of this prince, whose cause was espoused by France, constituted one of the principal threats to the peace of Europe at that time. Sabran, we are told, failed to achieve his objective, as also did Charnacé, who followed him to Vienna on an identical mission. But this was no more than Richelieu had expected, for he stated that the real purpose of sending these diplomats to Vienna was to encourage certain of the German princes in their desire for freedom and to persuade them to throw off the Imperial yoke. In point of fact, the German princes, who had been embittered by the ruthless behaviour of the Imperial armies within the Empire, were particularly susceptible to French influence at that time.

Remarkably, it was the four Catholic Electors who decided to send a joint declaration to the Emperor, in which among other things they demanded justice for the Duke of Nevers, saying that any matters that might "cause dissatisfaction to the Most Christian King" should be disposed of. They expressed themselves in a very authoritarian manner, and the Elector of Trier went so far as to say to the Count of Marcheville that things might well reach a point where they would invoke the rights vested in them by the constitution of the Empire to depose the Emperor and elect another in his place. Richelieu treated this statement in some detail in his Memoirs.

It was at this point that Marcheville was authorized to pay

out a pension granted by the King of France to the Elector of Trier and to assure him for the hundredth time that it was Louis's earnest desire to emancipate both Italy and Germany from the oppression of the house of Austria, to which end a powerful army under the command of Cardinal Richelieu would be sent to Italy, while a further army group, then encamped on the borders of Champagne, was ready to fight for France's good neighbours and ancient allies in Germany with the object of restoring the German Liberties. His Majesty had decided to lead this force himself, which "would fight only for the common good." They would never again have such a good chance to end the evils afflicting the Empire. They must act without delay, as soon as that foreigner Wallenstein had been forced out of the Empire and peace had been restored in Italy and the Imperial army driven from Italian soil.

Then Marcheville was to ask whether, in the event of the Emperor's rejecting the Electors' just demand, the princes of the Catholic League would be prepared to take up arms against Wallenstein or whether they considered it more expedient to drive the Spanish from Germany. In either case the King undertook to raise a powerful army at his own expense and to use it in Germany or elsewhere in order to create a diversion. The King was being very liberal with his promises, none of which he could have honoured at that time. Having proffered the bait, Marcheville was to suggest that it would be in the interests of the German Electors to join the alliance that Louis XIII had concluded with the Italian princes. And finally Marcheville was told: "Both the King and the Electors will keep all this as secret as possible, but Marcheville is to ask the Elector of Trier to inform the Catholic estates about all the issues involved and is to discover their precise intentions, in order that His Majesty may take appropriate measures."

Both before and during the Italian campaign, for as long as he was separated from the King, the Cardinal took particular care to ensure that in his written statements his actions and thoughts were set down as accurately as possible. We are able to sense the constant need to defend himself against Court intrigue. It must be remembered that at the end of the Italian campaign Richelieu again found himself on the brink of political disaster and in peril of his life, that at this time the Day of the Dupes was yet to come.

In his Memoirs the Cardinal wrote that in 1630 the German Electors had looked to the King of France with a view to offering him the Imperial crown. We are told: "They revered the justice, the great courage, the boldness of his enterprises and the incomparable wisdom of his counsel, which bore the constant blessing of God."

Richelieu then went on to say that, since the King of France had no children, the German Princes were confident that he would not try to bequeath the office of Emperor to his successors (strange grounds for confidence), and that if the Imperial crown were to be taken from the house of Austria, power such as the French monarchy's would certainly be needed; a lesser power would not suffice.

It was at this time that the German Electors presented Louis XIII with a copy of "*De statu religionis et rei publicae Carolo V Caesare commentarii,*" a book regarded as the source for the history of the Reformation until the end of the eighteenth century, and one that will always remain a valuable work. Its author was Johannes Sleidanus, who once entered the service of Francis I of France in order to promote the interests of the League of Schmalkalden.

From other instructions sent to Marcheville it is evident that France was trying very hard to win over not only the German Electors but also the Hanseatic cities. These cities had appealed to the Duke of Saxony to accept the leadership of the Protestant Union and command of its army, which was then able to put 60,000 men into the field, in order to free one and all from the "intolerable persecution" inflicted by the Emperor. Marcheville was expressly instructed to use his *dextérité* to turn the Elector of Saxony against the Emperor.

What was meant by "intolerable persecution" was of course the presence of Wallenstein's army, then an army of occupation of more than 100,000 men living off the land. Wallenstein had driven the forces of the Catholic League from the Swabian Circle in order to take over their lush quarters for his own men. He had collected heavy contributions from the Hanseatic cities:

"One has to go à la desperata and take what one can get."

And Wallenstein was insatiable. Properties, offices and titles were heaped upon him. His pay was increased to 6,000 guldens a month, this increase to be retroactive from July 1625. In addition to all this, he was appointed commander of the whole of the Imperial fleet in both the open sea and the Baltic. Apart from the armies in Germany he also commanded the troops in Upper Alsace and Italy. The Emperor had sold him the Silesian principality of Sagan in partial settlement for the money he had advanced in pay to the army. But the most dangerous move—and the one that did most to enhance Wallenstein's prestige and increase his self-esteem and sense of power—was the Emperor's decision to place the Dukes of Mecklenburg under the ban of the Empire in order that he might transfer their lands to Wallenstein in the form of guaranties. He did this on January 26, 1628, and by June 16th of the same year these guaranties had been transformed into fiefs, which meant that Wallenstein had been made an immediate prince of the Empire without the approval of the Electors. From that moment on he considered himself to be independent of the Emperor and to have the same right to pursue his own policies and conclude his own alliances as an Elector of Saxony or Brandenburg. His exaggerated sense of his own importance at that time is clearly illustrated by his insistence on outward show, represented by the splendour of his five princely households: Güstrow, Sagan, Gitschin, Prague and his army camp. Hans de Witte, the financier, advanced any ready money Wallenstein needed. By comparison, the life of the Imperial Court was simple.

From 1625 on Wallenstein had gone from victory to victory. Although he had failed at sea and had been forced to abandon the siege of Stralsund, which was to have crucial consequences, he had imposed a crushing defeat on the Danes, he had stood his ground against Bethlen Gabor, he had pursued Mansfeld as far as the March River, he had reconquered Upper Silesia.

Serious differences of opinion arose between Wallenstein and the Emperor and his advisers when, on March 6, 1629, Ferdinand proclaimed the Edict of Restitution, by which the Protestants were required to restore to the Church the archbishroprics of Magdeburg and Bremen together with twelve bishoprics and five hundred abbeys and monasteries, which had been secularized since the treaty of Passau of 1552 and the Religious Peace of Augsburg of 1555. Restitution was to be effected by 1631. The Protestant Elector of Saxony, who until then had been unwavering in his allegiance to the Emperor, was hit particularly hard by this measure. The edict also authorized the Catholic estates to bring their subjects back to Catholicism.

Wallenstein rejected the Edict of Restitution most emphatically. In speaking of it, he too would sometimes insist on the "Liberties" of the German Electors. But until 1630 he also continued to press for the Emperor's absolute dominion, which meant of course that Wallenstein's inner conflict was already beginning to show.

We have dealt with the three meetings between Wallenstein and Father Joseph in the camp at Memmingen in Volume I. At the time, Father Joseph was struck by the general's unbridled ambition. Wallenstein had told him that the Bohemian crown should be worn by a Bohemian, and Father Joseph had understood him to be referring to himself.

The Electoral Diet at Regensburg in 1630 was one of the high points in the career of Duke Maximilian I of Bavaria. The envoy from the Count Palatine, Rusdorf, reported that the Bavarian Elector was the most powerful man at the assembly. And indeed, the position Maximilian then occupied,

M

in which he was wooed by both the Emperor and the French, brought him a number of triumphs, nearly all of them at the expense of the house of Hapsburg.

It was undoubtedly owing to Wallenstein's great military prestige that in the course of the late twenties Maximilian had lost the effective leadership of Catholic Germany. But various other circumstances had combined to oppose the further progress of the great general. In the first place, as we have already seen, there was an unreasoning and uncritical tendency to hold him responsible for all the distress and afflictions of the war. Then there was his personal manner, his lack of consideration for others, his sudden shifting from cunning and prevarication to uninhibited expression of his most intimate thoughts. In one such pronouncement, which gained wide currency, he said: "The Electors must be taught manners. The Imperial succession belongs by right to the Emperor's son and has no need of electoral ratification." Or again: both the Electors and the German princes were superfluous and that the Emperor must hold absolute power within his territory, like the Kings of France and Spain. Statements like these were hardly calculated to win him the sympathy of the German princes. But his chief opponents were Maximilian of Bavaria, who had been robbed of the fruits of his own great achievements by Wallenstein's intervention, and the French, who regarded him as the most powerful element in the Imperial camp and were determined to remove him at all costs. It goes without saying that Wallenstein's towering personality had relentless opponents at the Viennese Court. In the latter years of their association, the Emperor himself came to regard him as a sinister figure. The outcome of the Electoral Diet at Regensburg was Wallenstein's dismissal. It was a fateful decision.

Sweden

Gustavus Adolphus of the house of Vasa was born in

Stockholm in 1594. His right to rule was disputed, for his father, Charles IX, had deposed his own nephew, Sigismund, the Roman Catholic King of Poland, from the Swedish throne. The great Catholic powers backed Sigismund in this dispute, and he was also able to count on the support of a not insignificant Catholic party within Sweden itself.

In the war between Sweden and Poland, the young Protestant King quickly demonstrated his quite outstanding political and military gifts. In the year of his accession, when he was only seventeen years old, he ended the war with the Danes and in the following year made peace with the Russians. In 1628 he defeated his Polish cousin. He was able to test his modern tactical methods, which called for a high degree of mobility, and his light equipment both in the warfare against Michael Romanov and against Sigismund of Poland, who was still claiming the Swedish throne.

Gustavus Adolphus immediately intervened in the confused labyrinth of European politics. He sent money to the insurgent Bohemians. The Winter King's Chancellor, Camerarius, wrote: "The Swedish King is taking our part as if he were our next of kin, and promises everything to our advantage."

In Paris and London great hopes had been placed in Gustavus Adolphus, but until the war between Sweden and Poland had been brought to a conclusion there could be no question of his attacking the Emperor in Germany. Moreover, Sweden was justifiably asking a very high price for her intervention; consequently France and England had first relied on Christian of Denmark.

The presence of the Imperial and League armies on the Baltic offered a serious threat to Sweden. The Swedish King also had family ties with the Protestant princes of North Germany, for his mother, Christina, was a daughter of the Duke of Holstein-Gottorps, and the Elector of Brandenburg was his brother-in-law.

By 1626, when Gustavus Adolphus took Pillau in the course of his Polish campaign, his main design was already clear to him. It was generally assumed that the principal objective of this campaign was the rich Polish port of Danzig. This, however, was not the case, for by then Gustavus Adolphus was already intent on opening up a route to Silesia and the Emperor's hereditary domains. In May 1627 he concluded a treaty with the Elector of Brandenburg, who was bound to the King of Poland by an oath of fealty. When the Elector ceded the city of Pillau he also informed Sigismund of his neutrality. At that time Gustavus Adolphus received the envoys of the United Provinces in his camp at Dirschau and told them quite openly: "The whole purpose of my military operations is to bring profit and relief to all those who are making common cause against the house of Austria and Spain."

The Swedish King spoke repeatedly of marching on Austria through Poland and Silesia or alternatively through Pomerania and along the Oder. He urgently asked for Dutch support, stating that without an army of 20,000 foot soldiers and 8,000 horse he could not launch the great venture.

On December 8, 1629, Charnacé received a letter in Stockholm signed by Louis XIII, instructing him to conclude the Franco-Swedish alliance with all possible speed and to repeat the ritual French assurance that 40,000 men were waiting in Champagne and could be deployed against the house of Austria. Finally, Charnacé was told that he must try to reduce the amount of the French subsidies to seven or if possible six hundred thousand livres per year. But in January 1630 Gustavus Adolphus sent a representative to Paris who insisted on a considerable increase in French financial aid.

At the end of the same month we find Charnacé in Uppsala, where the King had taken up residence to avoid an outbreak of the plague. The Paris negotiations had gone well for the Swedes, and Richelieu's representative was received in the university town with high honours. By then he was able to promise a payment of 1,200,000 livres and the dispatch of six warships. But only twenty-four hours after he had been received in audience by Gustavus Adolphus Charnacé met with a set-back. To his complete surprise the Swedish King went to visit Wallenstein in his camp; thirteen days later he returned and informed the French negotiator that he would sooner enter into discussions with the Emperor than with the King of France, for he feared that, since Louis XIII was far too occupied in Lorraine and Italy to be able to afford him effective help, he might well suffer the same fate as the Duke of Mantua (whose capital city was then beleaguered—it was plundered and laid waste in the most fearful fashion on July 12, 1630). Charnacé, ignoring these remarks, asked the King how much he really wanted in order to take part in the common struggle against the Emperor. He then reported to Paris through his nephew, Miré, that Gustavus Adolphus' visit to Wallenstein had been a tactical move to force up the French subsidies. This interpretation was borne out by the Swedes, who immediately presented fresh demands. Charnacé accepted them quite impassively and undertook to submit them to his superiors. To this end he dispatched a certain Lignière to Paris, who quickly returned to Sweden again, bearing the necessary authorizations and thus making it possible for the negotiations to be continued. Charnacé was granted a second audience.

At this point we must deal briefly with the petty but obdurate resistance afforded to Charnacé throughout the course of his negotiations in Sweden. Courmenin Deshayes, who had been accredited as French envoy to Denmark and then, from 1624 on, to Sweden, was jealous of Charnacé's special missions, which brought him into personal contact with the Kings of Denmark and Sweden, and he reacted to them with displays of pique. Courmenin Deshayes was yet another of the chameleon-like figures employed in the foreign service. His allegiance to Richelieu had always been in doubt, and he later became known as a follower of Gaston d'Orléans. Richelieu's usual practice with such people was to give them a free rein for a while before pulling them up short.

Where Deshayes was concerned, Charnacé had long kept his council, but then, as was customary in his era, he quickly disposed of his adversary, undeterred by his own official position or by professional loyalty to a colleague. Charnacé suffered from gallstones, and in the summer of 1632 he took the cure in Wiesbaden. On August 14th he was told by his army chaplain that Deshayes had arrived in Mainz, whereupon Charnacé immediately took to the saddle and set out for Mainz, accompanied by a dozen cavalrymen. Once there, he and his companions secreted themselves in a mill outside the walls of the town. When Deshayes left the town in the morning, accompanied by five Swedish noblemen, Charnacé and his men overpowered him, took him prisoner and put him on board a waiting ship. The next morning Charnacé delivered up his victim to the French garrison at Ehrenbreitstein. From there Deshayes was sent with an escort of light cavalry to Trier, which was occupied by Marshal d'Estrées, and thence to Béziers, where Louis XIII had set up his camp. No sooner had he arrived than he was given a summary trial, condemned to death and immediately executed.

Gustavus Adolphus was angered by this event and said so in no uncertain terms; but the King of France sent Charnacé a letter by special courier, in which he expressed his appreciation and gratitude for what he had done. Bouthillier also wrote to Charnacé: "I am sending you the pre-dated order which you have requested and everything of course is perfectly in order."

Richelieu described this incident in his Memoirs:

At the time Gaston d'Orléans was putting forward Deshayes, a member of his household. He was a gifted young man who was brought low by his own ambition. After the King had employed him in Sweden and Russia, he found it intolerable that another should have been chosen to conduct the negotiations with Gustavus Adolphus, which were far more important than the business with which he had been entrusted. He seized the opportunity presented by the flight of the Queen-Mother and the heir-apparent to leave Montargis, where he had succeeded his father as Governor, and proceeded to Brussels. Marie de' Medici and Orléans employed him to conduct talks on their behalf both in Germany and with the King of Sweden; his instructions were to create tension between the German Protestants and the Swedes, in return for which the two expatriates were to receive troops from the Emperor, which they could have used against Louis XIII. They had also hoped to receive money. But thanks to Charnacé's dexterity and courage, Deshayes was arrested on his second mission to Germany. Orléans demanded his release but was told that in deference to His Majesty this was impossible.

The questions put to Deshayes during his interrogation were reproduced in a memorandum addressed to Monsieur de Moriq dated August 25, 1632. Here they are:

1. Why did you leave the country and desert the King's service?

2. Who persuaded you to break your oath by serving the Duke of Orléans and the Queen-Mother?

3. Where had you come from and where were you going?

4. What is your commission, what are the negotiations which you were supposed to conduct and who has sent you?

5. Have you conducted negotiations with the Emperor and the Duke of Friedland in order to obtain troops for the Duke of Orléans which could be used to mount an invasion of French territory?

6. Did you not try to arrange for Orléans's forces, which are at present in Burgundy, to find quarters in Austrian-controlled Alsace?

7. Did you not try to influence the King of Sweden against the King of France?

8. Do you support Orléans's plans? Etc.

Richelieu had already decided that Deshayes must die before the judges had even begun his trial.

This incident further illustrates not only the extent to which the policies pursued by the French opposition vitiated official planning, but also the extent to which the Queen-Mother, Orléans and—as we shall see—even Anne of Austria, both individually and collectively, formed a natural centre for the cabal, which was ready to commit high treason without a moment's hesitation. Secret and sometimes even open opponents of Richelieu's policies, especially concerning his Protestant alliances, were to be found at every level of the King's service.

Swedish Power

Swedish power was much sought after. What was its basis?

At the beginning of Gustavus Adolphus' reign, Sweden had a population of some 900,000 or, if the Finns are included, about 1,300,000. Since the middle of the sixteenth century the country had been constantly at war. The Swedish peasant farmers were free, certain forms of serfdom having been abolished as early as 1325. The Crown had acquired large territories in the Middle Ages and, in the course of time, so too had the great nobles. Many of the peasant farmers had become tenants on Crown land or on noble estates, but without forfeiting their freedom in any way. Others had remained completely independent, farming their own land, on which they paid taxes. In 1611 the land-owning nobility comprised about five hundred families. Some of these were descended from men who had distinguished themselves in the service of the State. Unlike the great nobles of England and France in the early seventeenth century, the great nobles of Sweden, who controlled the Council of State, were able to extend their political influence under Gustavus Adolphus. All in all there were some thirty great Swedish families, several of whom, such as the Brahes and the Güldensterns, owned property on both sides of the Sound. They regarded the Vasas as no more than their equals and themselves as the custodians of the

Swedish Liberties. In the course of the seventeenth century the Swedish provincial nobility extended their economic privileges. The early Vasas had ruled through officials, all of whom had been educated in German schools and many of whom were foreigners. It was almost impossible for a wealthy Swedish merchant to become accepted as a member of the provincial nobility. If he bought property, he simply became a tax-paying farmer. But between 1611 and 1632, when Gustavus Adolphus ruled Sweden, great changes took place both in this stable social structure and in the economic life of the community.

In 1611 Sweden was primarily an agricultural country. The mining industry had not yet been built up, although copper and steel were already Sweden's most important exports. But under Gustavus Adolphus these two commodities were rapidly exploited. If Sweden had not forged so many of her own weapons, it is unlikely that she could have held out in the Thirty Years War. The King transformed the copper trade into a monopoly by granting exclusive rights to a single company with comparatively high capital reserves. This company was created by a royal ordinance of July 24, 1619.

Despite constant increases in taxation at home, despite the speedy change-over from a natural to a money economy and the novel attempt to prepare an accurate budget, despite the financial support of the French, the war that began for Sweden in 1630 was only made financially possible by the exaction of harsh contributions from the occupied territories and by systematic plundering. The cadre of the Swedish army, which was composed of peasant farmers, was financed by the seizure of Church property, while the income provided by the taxes imposed on German territories was invested not only in the army but also in the Swedish economy. The war was the father of many things.

Swedish state revenue for 1623 was estimated at 1,420,000 dalers and total revenue at 2,550,000 dalers, which was the equivalent of 1,569,000 riksdalers. But by 1632 state revenue had risen to 2,200,000 dalers and total revenue to 6,500,000 dalers. In 1632 Sweden spent 156,000 dalers on her navy alone. But by the end of 1630 the cost of the war had already exceeded her total revenue by half a million dalers. The State was running into debt. All the nations taking part in the Thirty Years War suffered a financial crisis, but initially Sweden was least equipped to deal with such a crisis. She did, however, receive considerable help from Louis de Geer, an important entrepreneur who did much to put Sweden's financial and economic affairs on a sound basis.

Louis de Geer

The de Geer family originally came from the bishopric of Liège and moved to Dordrecht at the end of the sixteenth century. Louis de Geer received no formal training, but after serving an apprenticeship in France acquired his knowledge of industry and commerce from practical experience. As a young man he acquired considerable knowledge of the iron industry. Thanks to his father, who was a successful banker, he became equally versed in financial matters. His two sisters married leading financiers, Elias and Jakob Trip. The Trips moved to Amsterdam in 1614 and were followed a year later by the de Geers. At first Louis was also active as a banker, but more especially as an arms merchant. In this second capacity he established contact with Sweden.

In 1618 Gustavus Adolphus suggested to Louis de Geer that he should bring a group of specialist workers to Sweden and settle there. He could then organize the processing of Swedish copper and steel. At the beginning of the twenties de Geer, who had a keen eye for successful investments, advised Gustavus Adolphus to borrow money to finance the Polish war. He gave great impetus to the Swedish iron industry and was quick to recognize that the Dannemora ore was particularly well suited to the production of steel. At first he was a partner in the firm run by his friend de Besche, for at that time he was not allowed to trade under his own name. But by 1622 he had acquired the monopoly for the manufacture of muskets and from 1627 on had effective control of the whole of the Swedish armaments industry, for which he assumed sole responsibility following de Besche's death in 1629; from then on the King's agents all took their orders from him. He was asked to speed up production and succeeded beyond all expectations. On April 27, 1627, he signed a contract in which he undertook to equip fifteen infantry regiments and 3,000 cavalrymen. In the same year he exported to Holland 400 cannon, which had been manufactured in Finspång, after which he also began to receive orders from France. By 1629 he was able to advise the King to discontinue all further imports of war materials, since Sweden was in a position to supply her own needs. In 1632, 910 cannon were exported from Nyköping. Between November 1629 and December 1630 de Geer delivered 20,000 muskets, 13,670 pikes and 4,700 cavalry harnesses to the Swedish royal army. In 1631 the King placed an order with him for equipment of thirty-two infantry regiments and 8,000 cavalrymen, the whole order to be executed by the summer. This was more than de Geer could manage and the order was cancelled, Gustavus Adolphus having meanwhile more than covered his requirements from the booty he had taken. In order to meet his commitments, de Geer was not always scrupulous. He bribed the officials responsible for inspecting his consignments, and in point of fact the equipment supplied by him was often found to be of inferior quality.

In 1630, following a disagreement with Gustavus Adolphus, de Geer resigned his position as Director of the King's factories at Arboga and Jäder. In 1631 the contract that had been concluded four years before was cancelled and the King again directed the affairs of his factories himself.

De Geer was undoubtedly the most important of the entrepreneurs active within the Swedish economy. But for his achievements, the success of Swedish arms on the Continent would have been inconceivable. His activities were many and varied, but his principal interests were the iron and steel industry, brass and the refining of copper. His brass foundry, opened in 1627 and used as a showpiece for foreign visitors, brought him in nearly 250,000 dalers in the course of a single year (1630–31). But he also invested in shipping and textiles, and he owned his own paper mills and tin foundries. He remained a banker throughout his life and advanced loans to the Swedish nobles. He also did much to alleviate the social needs of the workers and he built shops in Stockholm and Norrköping. He became a Swedish citizen in order to avoid customs duties. With his immense fortune he was able to equip thirty warships in 1644 and place them at the disposal of the Swedish navy. For his newly founded industries he imported capable artisans from abroad. In order to encourage immigration the Swedish authorities exempted these foreign workers from the payment of taxes during their first six years in Sweden. Coal-miners from Flanders, woodcutters from Sedan, smiths from Liège, windmill builders from Amsterdam were the principal artisans involved.

In the course of time de Geer's family came to acquire properties throughout the whole of Sweden, the most important being the estate of Leufsta, which is still in the possession of the de Geer family.

Richelieu and Gustavus Adolphus

Richelieu called Gustavus Adolphus "the Goth" and "the Nordic Pensioner of the King of France." For his part, the Swedish King had always found it extremely repugnant to be an instrument of French policy, but he had no choice in the matter, since he lacked the essential—funds. It was for this reason that he was obliged to sign the treaty of Bärwalde on January 23, 1631, which assured him of an annual subsidy in return for a pledge to place 30,000 foot and 6,000 horse in the field in Germany; these forces, however, were not to be used against the Catholic League. But there was never any real trust between the man who gave the money and the man who took it.

Father Joseph distrusted the Swedish undertaking from the outset, although he agreed that it was unavoidable. He considered that "such things must be treated like poison, for while a small dose might be curative, a large one could be lethal." It seemed to him that the most effective antidote would be a French alliance with the Elector of Bavaria, the "representative of the true faith."

What finally drove Maximilian to seek a rapprochement with the French was his fear of the Spanish, who then occupied the County Palatine. But in the treaty of Fontainebleau, concluded on May 30, 1631, France and Bavaria gave a mutual pledge that they would not support any power hostile to the other. Richelieu had hoped to gain the support of a strengthened and militarily effective Catholic League under Bavarian leadership, to persuade it to treat both the German Protestants and the Swedes as neutrals and then to use it exclusively against the Emperor. At the same time he tried to further an alliance between Sweden and the German Protestants as a first step towards obtaining a guarantee of non-aggression from this powerful group in respect of Bavaria and the Catholic League.

It has already been pointed out that the crucial factor in bringing about Swedish participation in the Thirty Years War was that in 1628 Wallenstein abandoned the siege of Stralsund and La Rochelle fell to Richelieu. This made it possible for the Swedes to advance into Germany.

Axel Oxenstierna was both mentor and trusted friend to Gustavus Adolphus. The King was ten years younger than his Chancellor, who, after studying constitutional law and theology in the German cities Rostock, Wittenberg and Jena, had been appointed Swedish envoy to the Court of Mecklenburg when he was twenty-three years old. In the same year he became a Councillor of State and six years later, at twenty-nine, he was made Chancellor. In the following year he concluded the peace of Knäred with the Danes and four years later the peace of Stolbova with the Russians. In the Polish campaigns Oxenstierna had stood at his master's side, and in 1629 Gustavus Adolphus appointed him Governor-General of Prussia.

Most historians report that the Chancellor tried to dissuade Gustavus Adolphus from landing on the coast of Pomerania and invading Germany. But as early as 1625 Oxenstierna was arguing that before they could invade Germany they must first have a harbour. "If we were to undertake a war against the Emperor in any other way, then we would have only ourselves to blame if our venture should fail; consequently we must have a stronghold on the Baltic and must secure it in every possible way, if we are to proceed sensibly and bring our plans to fruition."

In 1630 Gustavus Adolphus occupied the Oder estuary. He was to have just two years in which to transform the whole of the European situation by his incomparable feats of arms. He set out to conquer Germany with no more than 16,000 men. If Wallenstein's army, some 100,000 men at the time of his recall, had still existed, the Swedish offensive could never have taken place. But at Regensburg the Imperial army had been reduced to 39,000 men; the Catholic League had a further 21,000 men under arms and both of these armies were then commanded by the ageing Tilly. Gustavus Adolphus landed in Usedom on July 6, 1630. On the same day the French army crossed Mont Cenis and on July 10th, owing to the personal intervention of the Duke of Montmorency, the French defeated the Duke of Savoy at the battle of Veillane. On July 12th Mantua, one of the gems of Italy, was betrayed to the Imperialists, who then ruthlessly sacked and laid waste the conquered town. On July 20th the French occupied the city of Saluzzo and on the same day Gustavus Adolphus took Stettin.

The Treaty of Bärwalde

The question of maintenance for the Swedish army in Germany was settled by the Treaty of Bärwalde, signed by France and Sweden on January 23, 1631. The following were its principal provisions:

ARTICLE 1:

"This alliance is designed for the defence of the oppressed friends of the signatories, for the security of trade at sea and for the restitution of all princes and estates of the Empire to the positions held by them at the outbreak of hostilities in Germany, as also for the destruction and razing of the fortified harbours on the Baltic coast.

ARTICLE 2:

"Since our adversaries have rejected all peaceful settlements and have made no attempt to offer equitable reparations for the wrongs they have committed, we find ourselves obliged to restore the general peace by force of arms.

ARTICLE 3:

"To this end Sweden is assembling an army of 30,000 foot and 6,000 horse in Germany, for whose support the King of France undertakes to pay an annual subsidy of 400,000 écus, the first instalment to be payable on each May 15th and the second on each November 15th in either Paris or Amsterdam, whichever is preferred by the King of Sweden.

ARTICLE 4:

"The cost of assembling and equipping the army will be imposed on the enemy.

ARTICLE 5:

"After the conquest of any given territory the inhabitants will have the right to practise the religion they first professed, be it Catholic or Protestant.

ARTICLE 6:

"The alliance is open to the princes and territories of

Germany; in the event of their joining, they must also make a contribution to the war.

ARTICLE 7:

"The question of establishing friendly and neighbourly relations with the Duke of Bavaria and the Catholic League will be considered in certain circumstances."[1]

We know from Richelieu that in the course of earlier negotiations with France the Swedish King had already said: "I know that Tilly has stated on many occasions and in public that the only reason he wished to go on living was that he might give battle to the Swedes and win or die." Gustavus Adolphus also said that the ultimate aim of all his actions was to provide the Protestant estates in Germany with a new leader and next to give the Protestants a new constitution. It is clear that the treaty of Bärwalde contained many seeds of conflict. How could the Emperor tolerate the restitution of Frederick of the County Palatine as King of Bohemia, and what would John George of Saxony have to say about it? What could possibly induce the princes of the Catholic League to waive the Edict of Restitution, or Duke Maximilian I to surrender the Upper Palatinate and the Elector's hat?

Tilly in Magdeburg

When Wallenstein had left the scene, the Emperor's Commander-in-Chief was Tilly, and the Catholic League remained Ferdinand's most effective support; Maximilian's loyalty to him was unshaken.

In January, Tilly and his army were stationed in and about Frankfort on the Oder. His troops were in wretched condition and had not been paid. Tilly described his situation as follows:

"If contrary to my strong hopes the help I have so often requested should not be forthcoming, then I trust that in view

---

[1] Quotation taken from *Vertrags-Ploetz*, Part II, Würzburg, 1958.

of my many loyal and humble requests I shall not be blamed or held responsible. . . . The danger, the need and the impoverishment of both armies [the Imperial and the League] are growing not only with each day but with each hour and each moment that passes. Consequently, exchanges of letters, reminders and entreaties and comforting words do little to help our cause, and the calling of meetings and discussions does even less; immediate action is what is needed. If this does not ensue, then the inevitable and certain consequence will be that the whole avalanche of war will plunge into the lands governed by the princes of the League . . ."

While Tilly was writing his honest and unexaggerated appraisal of the military situation facing the Emperor and the Catholic League, Gustavus Adolphus occupied Wallenstein's Duchy of Mecklenburg. Then in April he took Frankfort on the Oder and moved forward to the line of the Oder and the Warthe, but for the time being he avoided an open confrontation with Tilly. Meanwhile, Tilly had sent Pappenheim to besiege Magdeburg, which controlled the whole of north-west Germany and the Elbe and was the key to Bohemia. Magdeburg was the town of which Gustavus Adolphus had said in a letter to Oxenstierna that it would be the rocket with which Sweden would set fire to the whole of Germany. Shortly after the Swedish King had landed in Germany, the inhabitants of Magdeburg had deposed their council, which had been loyal to the Emperor, and signed a treaty with Gustavus Adolphus. At the time of Tilly's siege, Colonel Falkenberg, the representative of the Swedish army, was within the walls of the town. Gustavus Adolphus had given him his word of honour that he would relieve Magdeburg in time, and Falkenberg rejected all demands for surrender. Finally, however, despite brave resistance, Pappenheim took the town by storm. In the course of the ensuing pillage, fire suddenly broke out, destroying the town and killing nearly twenty thousand people. The Swedes immediately put out a report to the effect that the fire had been started on Tilly's orders, while Tilly blamed the Swedes. Clearly, the destruction of the town spelt disaster for Tilly, since it meant that he had lost his most important base together with abundant supplies of arms and food. In a letter to Maximilian he wrote:

"But then a great calamity occurred. While a gale continued to rage, a great fire broke out, which was caused by deposits of powder in various places. And so the enemy had done this thing on purpose, with the intention, as is fully borne out by the testimony of our prisoners, of ensuring that we should derive no benefit from the town. In the great tumult and the heat there was no possibility of extinguishing the flames."

Most contemporary witnesses, some of them Protestants, stated that when Falkenberg realized the town was lost he gave orders for mines to be laid in various places and for the armoury and a number of other buildings to be set on fire. Falkenberg himself was killed in the battle.

The destruction of this prosperous town made an enormous impression on the whole of the Protestant world and especially in Germany. Lutheran Saxony, although conservative and loyal to the Emperor, was also deeply shocked by the catastrophe, and this contributed to the shift in Saxon policy that followed.

Nonetheless, Gustavus Adolphus was perfectly right when he said: "All that the Protestant princes want from me is my help in opposing the Emperor, after which they will give me no thanks but use their power to drive me out."

In May, Gustavus Adolphus appeared before Berlin and delivered an ultimatum to the Elector of Brandenburg, who quickly agreed to his terms and surrendered Spandau and Küstrin to the Swedish army. Later an alliance was concluded between Sweden and Brandenburg, whereby Brandenburg agreed to place her troops and her fortresses at the disposal of the Swedes and to pay them a monthly subsidy of 30,000 talers. William of Hesse-Cassel, the Emperor's oldest opponent within the Empire, was the first of the German princes to join Gustavus Adolphus of his own free will. But the King of Sweden was not able to count on the support of John George of Saxony, who had said to Charnacé that "he would, if he [the King of Sweden] came to Germany, join forces with the Emperor." At the time of the Danish invasion John George had disseminated an apologetical pamphlet, which closed with the words: "It is necessary for all the Protestant princes of the Empire to gather round their Emperor and to refrain from all alliances both among themselves and with non-German powers."

John George of Saxony and Saxon Policy

John George was known to be a hard drinker. Wallenstein once said of him: "What a brute he is and what a life he leads!" But although it would appear that the Elector's predilection for the bottle was uncommonly strong, it was not the only sphere in which he displayed strength, this being one of his principal character traits. He too had been hard hit by the Edict of Restitution. In February 1631 he informed the Emperor that he had summoned a Protestant convention to Leipzig to discuss the interference. The convention met at the beginning of 1631 and was attended by all the Protestant estates, the Hanseatic cities and also by French and Swedish representatives. The French representative was a certain Melchior de Lisle, a close confidant of Father Joseph's. He was a Protestant nobleman, a doctor of canonical and lay law, a citizen of Basle and a professor at the university there.

The Catholic Electors had proposed that George II, the Landgrave of Hesse-Darmstadt (unlike William of Hesse-Cassel, he was a man of conciliatory disposition), should try to negotiate an agreement between Protestants and Catholics concerning the Edict of Restitution. This was the subject discussed by the members of the Protestant convention in Leipzig, and when they failed to make any headway it was agreed that a second convention should be held in Frankfort to discuss the matter further. At Frankfort the French representative was the Catholic Count of Marcheville.

No mention was made in Leipzig of the Swedish advance, but it was decided that henceforth the Imperial and League armies should be denied transit rights, contributions and quarters. John George then proceeded to raise an army of his own and within a very short time had 20,000 men under arms; the command was given to Wallenstein's former field marshal, Arnim-Boytzenburg, who had been the officer commanding the siege of Stralsund. It was announced that the Saxon forces would be employed only for purposes of defence. Tilly's reaction to this new development was to send an ultimatum to the Elector of Saxony and then to invade his territory. The Duke of Bavaria regarded Tilly's invasion as a political blunder, but from a strategic point of view it is difficult to see how it could have been avoided. The immediate consequence of Tilly's advance was the conclusion of an alliance between Sweden and Saxony. This alliance, which had long been pending, was negotiated by Arnim and signed on September 11th. And so the 23,000 Swedes were joined by 20,000 Saxons, which meant that Gustavus Adolphus was strong enough to risk a decisive engagement. Meanwhile Tilly had moved into Leipzig.

Maximilian I of Bavaria called for Catholic unity, but he called in vain. He then approached Pope Urban VIII and informed him of the desperate situation of the German Catholics. But Urban's response was negative; he insisted that the Edict of Restitution must be upheld and advised Maximilian to come to an agreement with the Protestants.

We have already encountered Urban VIII (see Vol. I, p. 174), but at this point we must again consider this Prince of the Church whose interests were so temporal, and compare his activities with those of his predecessor, Pope Gregory XV.

Two Popes: Gregory XV and Urban VIII

Gregory XV, a Ludovisi and a native of Bologna, was a serious scholar and a man of conciliatory nature. It was owing principally to his influence that Maximilian I of Bavaria was given the electorship of the County Palatine, and in the Valtelline dispute between France, Spain and Austria he constantly tried to intervene in the interest of a genuine peace. It was Richelieu who, by pursuing his own plans with such consistency, frustrated Gregory's endeavours.

When Gregory died the favourites of his predecessor, Paul V (Camillo Borghese), still had the upper hand in Rome. The pro-Spanish and pro-Austrian Cardinals formed a minority group. Against this background, Richelieu offered a piece of advice to the pro-French Florentine Maffeo Barberini, who had received both his Cardinal's hat and the bishopric of Spoleto from Paul V while serving as papal nuncio to France. Richelieu's advice was both cheap and, unfortunately, typical of one side of his character, which was imbued with both cynicism and disdain; he was quite prepared to use extremely cunning and petty tricks in order to gain his ends. Richelieu advised Barberini to approach the two rival groups in the College of Cardinals and intimate to each that he was opposed to the other. Out of mutual antagonism both would then support him to their utmost ability.

Barberini had acquired a reputation as an outspoken advocate of the jurisdictional claims of the Roman Curia, and this had won him the favour of the majority of the Cardinals. He was duly elected Pope on August 6, 1623, when he was fifty-five years of age. Until 1644, throughout virtually the whole of the Thirty Years War and certainly during its most important phases, Urban VIII pursued a pro-French policy. Gregory XV had been an eminent theologian, but Urban VIII was interested only in Curial territorial policy, in contemporary history, strategy, tactics, fortification theory and the science of arms. His aim was to transform the Papal States into a military power. He built Castelfranco as a stronghold with which to threaten the Bolognese, who showed pro-Austrian tendencies. In Rome he fortified Castel Sant' Angelo and even stocked it with ammunition and provisions, as if war were expected to break out at any moment. During his childhood the Papal States had been threatened by the power of Spain, and this had doubtless made an impression on him. He destroyed magnificent works of antiquity by surrounding the papal gardens with fortification works; the Vatican Library became an arsenal and the Pope an arms manufacturer. Civitavecchia was developed as a free port. Urban was an absolutist ruler. He was in every respect a child of his time and the spiritual concerns of the pontificate were not for him. Consistories were seldom convened and when they were nobody dared to express an opinion. Like all dictators, Urban silenced those who thought differently and those who represented foreign interests. He alone was allowed to speak his mind. He symbolized the emergence of Italian patriotism, for patriotism was his driving force. He placed all his hopes in the restoration and renewal of a Catholic France, which would act as a counterbalance to the power of Spain. He was the chief contributor to the success of Richelieu's policies.

The Venetian representatives, always acute observers, gave a convincing description of Urban VIII: A moody man who loved to contradict; and they recommended to all who wished to persuade him that they proceed by arguing as strongly as possible against their own case—which was also a favourite precept of Richelieu's.

Pope Urban VIII had no sense of history, and even in his days as papal nuncio to France the only thing that interested him, apart from practical affairs, was fashionable literature. He composed poetry and studied metrics. He even translated Biblical texts into Horatian metrics. Immensely self-assured, he replied, when reminded of a decree of the Roman people prohibiting the erection of any monument to a living Pope, that to a Pope of his stature this did not apply. Urban VIII had this in common with Philip II, that he was jealous of the personal success of his subordinates; whenever a papal nuncio was praised for distinguished service in the interests of the papacy, Urban would declare that he had merely acted in accordance with his instructions. Anything that might be to someone's credit was always due to his influence, but failures were laid at the door of his subordinates.

Cardinal Borgia complained that the King of Spain was unable to obtain even the smallest favour from the Pope and that all requests from Madrid were turned down out of hand. Urban had not even tried to settle the Valtelline affair. It is also quite evident that he did his utmost to prevent a reconciliation between the house of Austria and the Stuarts. When the possibility of a marriage between Charles of England and the Infanta Maria was being mooted, he made it a condition of his approval that Catholic churches should be built in every English county. In fact, he did all he could to prevent the consolidation of Spanish political power that would have resulted from this union with England. He also worked against a marriage between the Elector Palatine and one of the Archduchesses and instead advanced a Bavarian union. And he passionately supported the marriage between the young Princess of Mantua and the son of the Duke of Nevers, who was entirely dependent on France and one of her staunchest advocates.

Pope Urban VIII further encouraged Louis XIII to go to war over the Mantuan succession. He wrote him that this war would be as pleasing to God as Louis's siege of the great Huguenot fortress. Time and again he urged the King of France to espouse the cause of Italian freedom and undertook to put an army of his own into the field to fight the Spanish. But Richelieu abided by the rule of taking one step at a time. He took every possible advantage of the Pope's outspoken aversion for Spain, but never allowed himself to be distracted from his own policies by Urban's political passions.

Richelieu's collaboration with the Curia would not have

had such far-reaching consequences if Ferdinand II, unlike the French, had not been so tied to Rome. Even at the time of his greatest power Ferdinand was bound by ultramontane considerations. All his undertakings, even the most harmless requests—as for example that St Stephen and St Wenceslaus should be included in the Church Calendar—met with resistance from the Curia. On the other hand, it was Urban VIII who insisted on the most rigid application of the Edict of Restitution, which finally dispelled all hope of a détente between Austria and the German Protestant princes and protracted the war in Germany for many years.

This then was the man to whom Maximilian I turned for help in his distress. At the same time, however, since he had no illusions about the Pope, he wrote to the Archbishop of Cologne:

"Contrary to all expectations it has been learnt from Rome that in response to a further request by the Catholic League not only can the League expect no *help and assistance* from His Holiness but that he is perfectly content that the war in Germany should be continued, simply because he does not wish to see the *potentia domus austriacae* too greatly extended by the advent of peace and the war subsequently transferred to Italy. From this it is quite clear that, given these intentions, His Holiness will be less than zealous and less than fervent in drawing the attention of the French and the other Catholic powers to the danger that exists in Germany. But if the Catholics are left helpless by His Holiness even *in negotio religionis*, these same Catholics can scarcely be blamed if they no longer hesitate to enter into an agreement with the Protestants, since they have indeed been forced and coerced into doing so; for the Catholics would be better advised to hold what they already have in peace and contentment than to lose all and thus incur the complete extirpation of the Catholic religion within the Empire."

By his support of Barberini's election to the papacy,

Richelieu had made a masterful move for the advancement of his own policies.

The Triumph of Swedish Arms and the Wrath of Wallenstein

Meanwhile the Swedes continued their triumphal march. On September 17, 1631, Tilly had occupied a strong position on high ground at Breitenfeld, near Leipzig. His army was below its effective strength and he had no intention of giving battle. But Pappenheim's hot-headed cuirassiers became embroiled with the Swedes and were unable to extricate themselves; unless the army were thrown in they would be lost. Tilly was forced to intervene. Battle was not joined until about mid-day and the whole encounter lasted no more than four hours. Tilly's cavalry succeeded in penetrating the enemy's left flank, where the Saxons were drawn up, but the Swedish forces repulsed all subsequent attacks before going over to the offensive themselves and forcing the Imperialists to flee.

Gustavus Adolphus had said to his troops: "If you show your valour you will be rewarded not only in heaven but here on earth. The enemy camp shall be your prize and, what is more, Priest Alley will be opened up to you with one stroke." [1]

Tilly had been wounded in the battle and was taken to Halle; scarcely had he recovered than he proceeded to Alfeld near Göttingen, where he marshalled the shattered remains of his forces. There was still life in him.

At this point the Emperor's other general, still the same fateful, unpredictable and mighty person, emerged from seclusion, casting his great shadow before him. Ever since the capture of Frankfort on the Oder, Wallenstein's followers in Vienna, especially Questenberg, had been pressing the Emperor to recall their fallen leader. And Ferdinand II himself had more than once regretted having dismissed his great commander. It is quite clear that Wallenstein, acting in

---

[1] Name for the territory along the Rhine embracing the bishoprics Chur, Constance, Basel, Strassburg, Speyer, Worms, and the archbishoprics Mainz and Cologne.

accordance with his own deep designs, was playing hard to get. At first he pleaded that his impaired health would not permit him to undertake the taxing office of Commander-in-Chief at such a desperate juncture.

"Even if God himself were to make such a proposal to me I would refuse," he exclaimed. But Ferdinand sent Questenberg, then Werdenberg and finally Eggenberg[1] to Znaim to persuade him to put aside his rancour.

Wallenstein then stipulated conditions that were outrageous, but in the extreme danger of the hour every one of his demands was granted.

Since the Electoral Diet at Regensburg his bitterness had grown more and more intense. His arrogant rebuffs, his mistrust and hatred were relieved only by a characteristic and often tragically misguided capacity for blind trust in particular individuals. But woe to those who disappointed him. They were traitors, and as such engulfed by the same malevolent fury that day and sleepless night raged against the incompetent blunderers who had thought they could do without him. With what a miserable yardstick political ignorance and princely arrogance had measured him! But now they were calling him back, back to the foremost position—now they would see! Once more he was a free agent and could use his freedom as he saw fit, and now of course—how he despised them—they came running, outdoing one another in the obsequiousness of their petitions. And indeed, even Maximilian I of Bavaria, Wallenstein's oldest and most hated antagonist, wrote to him now:

"I would entreat your honour not only to have the goodness to grant the bearer, von Töring, a friendly audience and to place complete confidence in his report, but also to state your own intentions in this matter, as is required by the great urgency of the situation and would accord with my own

---

[1] There was a saying at this time that Austria rested on three hills (*"Bergs"*).—Trans.

particular trust in your honour, to whom I am at all times willing to render friendly and agreeable service.

"Written this day in my fortress of Ingolstadt, April 8, 1632.

"P.S. [In Maximilian's own hand]: The enemy grows daily stronger and is far superior to us in numbers. If your honour does not make speed and force a change, he will break through. He now lusts after the Danube and Austria.

"Your honour's most well-disposed uncle.

"MAXIMILIAN."

But in the summer and autumn of 1631 Wallenstein had approached the King of Sweden through the Bohemian émigré, Rašin,[1] and had made him propositions. Laurens Nikolai (Nilson), the Swedish *résident* at the Saxon Court from the end of 1631, provided Colonel Philip Sadler, private secretary to Gustavus Adolphus, and subsequently Oxenstierna with information regarding Wallenstein's intentions. In December 1631 he wrote to Sadler informing him that Wallenstein had seriously considered coming to terms with Gustavus Adolphus, but had been obliged to abandon the project when Count Thurn had recklessly committed it to writing in a letter to a lady of the Trčka family, which had been intercepted by the Imperialists. Wallenstein had told Arnim that he would "so arrange and direct things that the Emperor, together with his whole house, should be made to see and to feel that he had affronted a gentleman."

Wallenstein had proposed that his communications with Gustavus Adolphus should always be made verbally through a confidant. Laurens Nikolai commented on this proposal in a letter to Gustavus Adolphus: "Just what is to be thought of this offer and just how far the oft-mentioned Wallstein [*sic*] is to be trusted is a matter which your Royal Highness . . . will

---

[1] Jaroslav Sezyma Rašin was appointed by Wallenstein's brother-in-law, Adam Trčka. Leopold von Ranke and Pekař are agreed that Rašin's *gründlicher wahrhaftiger Bericht* (detailed and true report) is for the most part reliable.

doubtless know how to judge for yourself. I was given to understand that I was simply to submit the offer to you."

The letters written by Count Heinrich Matthias Thurn to Gustavus Adolphus contain statements that bear out Rašin's reports. Gustavus Adolphus received the proposals brought to him by Wallenstein's go-betweens with extreme reserve. Wallenstein wanted the King of Sweden to send him 12,000 men and eighteen "pieces" and also to approve his appointment as Viceroy of Bohemia. In return he would attack the Emperor's Silesian army and advance to the walls of Vienna.

Thurn is said to have tried to allay the King of Sweden's suspicions and to persuade him to send the troops and arms requested by Wallenstein. In this he failed. But whether he genuinely and consistently tried and whether Arnim, who was in such close contact with him, ever planned anything other than Wallenstein's downfall, is not entirely clear from the contradictory evidence of the documents, many of which were written with the intent to discredit Wallenstein.

Wallenstein's attempts to establish a rapprochement with the King of Sweden equally aroused the suspicions of the Saxons. This may well explain Arnim's sudden decision to comply with Gustavus Adolphus' wishes and march straight for Bohemia. On the other hand, this move would have been made at enormous risk had not Wallenstein given explicit indications that he welcomed it. Wallenstein was after all the greatest landowner in Bohemia, and the whole of his property was at stake. To the Imperial generals Tiefenbach and Marratas he said that Bohemia and its capital city of Prague must be defended; yet not only did he do nothing to organise resistance within the city, he even intimated to its inhabitants that immediate capitulation would be advisable. On November 20, 1631, just five days after the capture of Prague, when he was negotiating with Arnim in the castle of Kaunitz, he complained of Thurn's indiscretion and said he would have to clear himself and must therefore go to the Emperor and accept the generalship.

Wallenstein's secret negotiations with the Swedes, the Saxons and the French were begun in 1631; we shall be considering later the further course of their development.

In Gustavus Adolphus' eyes, Wallenstein was always suspect—a man of great ability no doubt, but an upstart and an adventurer who was quite capable of wrecking the world order in which he as a Christian ruler had his being. For this reason also, Wallenstein had no other choice in 1631 but to accept the Emperor's offer, insisting however on every one of his exorbitant demands. He was given absolute command, the right to participate with the Emperor in all peace negotiations, and the right to confiscate and to pardon as he saw fit. He was confirmed as a prince of the Empire in Mecklenburg, the Duchy of Grossglogau was transferred to him as a guaranty, and it is said that even the possibility of an electorship—presumably Saxony—was hinted at.

In return for all this, the much-wooed general undertook to raise an army of 40,000 men within three months and to increase its strength to 100,000 within six months. His appointment as Commander-in-Chief of the Imperial forces was made on December 15, 1631, and met with the full approval of the estates of the Catholic League and of the Elector of Bavaria. Tilly wrote at the time: "I was happy to hear it, and all the more so since it relieved me of a great burden and task." Soon he would be able to lay down his burden, but for the present the old commander's sense of duty was still strong. At Miltenberg he joined a force of 12,000 men provided at the urgent request of Maximilian of Bavaria by the Duke of Lorraine, who was himself extremely hard pressed by the French.

The Consequences of the Swedish Victory of Breitenfeld

Breitenfeld was one of the four decisive battles of the Thirty Years War, the others being the battle of the White Hill, the battle of Lützen and the battle of Nördlingen. After their victory at Breitenfeld, the Elector of Saxony tried to persuade the Swedes to invade Austria at once. But Gustavus Adolphus was first determined to have done with Maximilian and the Catholic League and was not to be deterred out of consideration for his French allies, who were of course intent on preserving Bavarian neutrality. Arnim was eager to fall upon Silesia and Bohemia with his Saxon troops and was in fact ordered to do so by Gustavus Adolphus. Count Thurn, who had meanwhile recruited a new force, was to join him. But the Swedish army turned southwards and made for Franconia by forced marches.

Bavaria had long been in a desperate plight. Where was she to turn for help? To France? We have already seen that from the very outset Richelieu had regarded Bavaria as one of the most important elements of his German policy. In negotiating the treaty of Bärwalde he had tried to keep Bavaria and the other members of the Catholic League at one remove from the actual conflict, and by thus ensuring their neutrality to bind them to France. Richelieu needed these territories, not only for the military contribution they were able to make in Germany, but above all as a means of combating the powerful forces opposed to his policies in France. Richelieu's plan was to maintain constant links with all of the Catholic powers of Central Europe except the Hapsburgs. In this way he would be able to justify his whole system of alliances to the French Catholic party by arguing that they were based on purely political and not on religious considerations. Father Joseph said at the time: "For God's sake, let us avoid a religious war; let us treat our King's sensitive conscience with the greatest caution, so that he may without scruple ally himself with the Protestants and break with the house of Hapsburg."

The diplomatic policy Richelieu pursued in Germany, the Netherlands and Scandinavia under the supervision of Father Joseph (who, for all his visionary qualities, soundly assessed and brilliantly handled people) had clear-cut objectives and was based on arguments so traditionally French as to be almost a stereotype.

Richelieu's greatest diplomatic successes were without doubt the establishment of the Swedish alliance and the truces with Poland and Russia that secured the Swedish rear and freed Gustavus Adolphus to undertake his German offensive. Initially France had paid out large sums of money to subsidize this offensive, but the situation was soon changed by a development that nobody at the French Court had foreseen: Gustavus Adolphus stormed his way through the Empire, and the contributions he extracted from the conquered territories soon made him largely independent of France. The Swedish King reached the Rhine and threatened the territories on its western bank; he carried Protestant Germany with him and prepared for the destruction of the German Catholic princes. He was on the point of establishing a great Protestant power in Central Europe, which would then have combined with the Scandinavian countries and, in the opinion of his French contemporaries, he himself might well have exercised absolute control over it.

At the beginning of the Swedish offensive the German Protestant princes, with the exception of the Calvinists, were determined not to enter into any agreement with Gustavus Adolphus against the Emperor. John George of Saxony regarded the Swedes as foreigners who had forced their way into the Empire and with whom no German prince should enter into an alliance. The Elector of Brandenburg adopted a similar view. But the promulgation of the Edict of Restitution changed their attitude. And then there was Tilly's invasion of Saxony. Fearing lest the new Saxon army, raised to defend Saxon neutrality, should join forces with the Swedes, Tilly, acting against the advice of Maximilian of Bavaria, had crossed the Saxon border and occupied Leipzig. John George now concluded his alliance with Gustavus Adolphus, to be followed shortly afterwards by the Elector of Brandenburg.

This development constituted a reversal for French policy, for now the force of circumstance had made the German conflict, which Richelieu had hoped to direct from Paris, again a religious war. It was the one thing he would find difficult to justify to the French opposition. There was also the further fact that Catholic Germany, especially Bavaria, was so completely at the mercy of Swedish arms that its only hope of salvation appeared to lie in a renewal of its links with the Emperor.

The trends revealed at the Protestant convention in Leipzig in 1631 had been viewed with displeasure in Vienna, as an attempt to keep Protestant Germany as independent as possible, not only of Gustavus Adolphus but also of the Emperor. Certainly it appeared at first that the outcome of the convention would be a Protestant initiative to enter into talks with both the Catholic League and Ferdinand II, in order to come to terms with the German Catholics and to discuss the withdrawal of the Edict of Restitution with the Emperor. This would have fitted in perfectly with French wishes, which were clearly demonstrated following the battle of Breitenfeld; but at the time of the convention, the French Court had not yet realized that the one sure means of separating the German Protestants from the Hapsburgs was the strictest possible enforcement of the Edict of Restitution.

The Situation in Bavaria

After the battle of Breitenfeld it seemed that German Protestantism, long the focal point of French political initiatives against the Hapsburgs, would be engulfed by the great torrent of Swedish victories. The situation had already changed to such an extent that France was obliged, for the first time since the reign of Henry IV, to deploy strong military forces along her eastern frontier.

The plight of the German Catholic League seemed quite hopeless. Maximilian I of Bavaria appealed to the Pope, to the Emperor and even, as we have just seen, to his arch enemy Wallenstein. France was his last hope—a faint hope weakened further by mistrust. The Franco-Bavarian alliance and defence treaty had been signed in Munich on May 8th and in Fontainebleau on May 30, 1631. Under its terms Louis XIII and Maximilian each undertook not to give help to the other's enemies and to defend the other's original territories, together with all recent acquisitions. Louis also undertook to support the electorship newly vested in the house of Bavaria. And then there was the important provision that Maximilian reserved his right, as a prince and Elector of the Holy Roman Empire, to fulfil his obligations to the Emperor at all times.

When this alliance was signed, the Franco-Swedish treaty had been in force for four months.

The political vision underlying Richelieu's unwavering approach to German affairs corresponded to a concept developed in the aftermath of the miseries of the French religious wars, which gave birth to the party of the *politiques*. This party advocated that it should be possible for German Protestants and Catholics to unite on purely political grounds in order to oppose the power of the house of Hapsburg on the one hand and the threat now offered by the victorious Swedes on the other—in other words, to dispel the French nightmare of a German Protestant *imperium* pregnant with unpredictable actions and repercussions. But the reality of German political life was not yet ready for the secularization of politics, for the reduction of political problems to their objective contents, as Richelieu saw them.

Where practical matters were concerned, the differences between the individual German states were of a highly complex order: the approach of the various German principalities to any question was so diverse and so contradictory, often being determined by purely local considerations, that general agreement seemed unattainable. But where questions of faith were concerned, we should not underestimate the genuine passions that had survived undiminished into the first half of the seventeenth century.

If we compare the agreement France negotiated with Bavaria with the treaty she concluded with Sweden at Bärwalde, it is noticeable that France did not offer Sweden guaranties of her hereditary territories or of her conquests. The Franco-Swedish treaty dealt solely with subsidies.

The conditions Gustavus Adolphus was prepared to grant to the Catholic League following the battle of Breitenfeld were tantamount to an ultimatum and proved unacceptable.

On October 2, 1631, Gustavus Adolphus took Erfurt. On October 14th Würzburg capitulated after a four-day siege and the town paid a contribution of 100,000 reichstalers. On October 27th Hercule de Charnacé was instructed to enter into negotiations with Gustavus Adolphus. On November 11th Aschaffenburg fell to the Swedes, and on November 15th the Saxons occupied Prague. On November 27th Gustavus Adolphus entered Frankfort on the Main. Mainz fell shortly before Christmas and on St Stephen's Day Louis XIII and Richelieu travelled to Metz, where on December 31st they signed a peace treaty with the Duke of Lorraine.

On January 3, 1632, the Bavarian envoys Kütner and Fenf also arrived in Metz, bearing the draft of a treaty, agreed to in Munich during Christmas, that was to guarantee Bavarian neutrality and protect her against Sweden. The Bavarian envoys insisted that France should require the Swedes to respect Bavarian neutrality and restore all the territories they had annexed from members of the Catholic League. Failing this, France must openly break with Sweden. To gain time, Richelieu asked that the Catholic League first sever its connection with the Emperor, for this, he suggested, would automatically pave the way for friendly relations with Sweden. The severance of his own alliance with Gustavus Adolphus was out of the question. Understandably enough, the Catholic League was not prepared to break with the Emperor without reliable pledges from Sweden and without genuine guarantees, for to have done so could only have led to its complete isolation. France was threatened with the loss of both her allies, the Swedes and the Catholic League; this threat was to be repeated.

Just how complicated things were at that time is evident

from the fact that in Nuremberg, for example, while the population was jubilant at the news of the Swedish victory, the city council, which had not long since assured the Emperor of its steadfast allegiance, was loath to surrender the city to the Swedes and offered their neutrality instead. This, however, Gustavus Adolphus refused to accept. The following letter was sent to the city council at his command:

"Since, in response to his exhortation, you have resolved not to abide by his will but rather to remain loyal to the Emperor or, failing this, to remain neutral, and since he is not prepared to accept neutrality but intends rather to treat all who protest in the name of neutrality as he treats his enemies, and their lands and cities as if he had taken them from his enemies at the point of the sword, he is therefore resolved to consider both you and your city, unless you should come to a different and a better decision, as his declared enemies and to bring fire and sword and death upon you and your subjects as upon his worst enemies, and is likewise resolved to overwhelm and seize each and every one of the citizens, inhabitants and subjects of the city and to confiscate their goods and expose them to wrack and ruin."

The councillors avoided giving a binding reply to this letter. They had conferred with representatives of the towns of Ansbach and Bayreuth in the monastery of Heilbronn, and it was decided to offer the King of Sweden large sums of money but not to enter into an alliance with him. This failed to satisfy the King, however, who demanded a contingent of troops for his army and threatened to lay siege to the walls. On October 14, 1631, the council agreed to his conditions and on October 23rd, five days after a delegation from Nuremberg, Bayreuth and Ansbach had arrived in Würzburg, a treaty was signed between these three towns and the King of Sweden. The towns undertook to pay the King 72 *römermonate*[1] in instal-

---

[1] *Römermonate.* Literally, Roman months. One *römermonat* was the amount of money required to maintain the Imperial army for one month as calculated at Worms in 1521.—Trans.

ments by June 6, 1632; in the case of Nuremberg alone this amounted to an indemnity of 105,560 guldens.

Despite the agreement they had concluded with Gustavus Adolphus, the members of the city council of Nuremberg sent the Emperor—who was well informed of these events— new if vague assurances of their unswerving loyalty. In November, Tilly advanced towards Nuremberg, but he was obliged to turn back before he could lay siege to that rich city and take his weak force with all possible speed to Bohemia, where the Imperial troops were being hard pressed.

On April 15, 1632, the Swedes succeeded in crossing the Lech at Rain. In the course of this engagement, the aged Tilly was severely wounded and died in Ingolstadt five days later, at the age of seventy-three. He had never once deviated from the strict path of allegiance.

Now there was nothing to stop the King of Sweden from advancing via Landshut to Munich and laying siege to Maximilian's capital. Apart from Ingolstadt and Regensburg, the whole of Bavaria was in his hands.

Richelieu meanwhile had used every diplomatic means available in order to avoid breaking with Bavaria and the Catholic League.

On January 16, 1632, his brother-in-law, Urbain de Maillé-Brézé, accompanied by Baron de Saludie, had arrived in Mainz to negotiate with Gustavus Adolphus. Brézé, acting in concert with Charnacé, advocated neutrality between the Catholic League and Sweden based on reciprocal restitutions. Gustavus Adolphus refused to listen. On January 19th, before the Cardinal had been informed of Sweden's refusal, Brézé received fresh instructions advising him that, if it should prove impossible to obtain reciprocal restitution, he was to give way step by step and if necessary to recognize the existing frontiers. He was to suggest that any disputed territories should be safeguarded by France until such time as their rightful ownership could be established. In this way Richelieu hoped to reduce the Swedish threat against the territories on the west bank of the Rhine.

Brézé's mission was unsuccessful. On January 19th, the day the new instructions arrived, Gustavus Adolphus himself submitted fifteen articles as a basis for neutrality: Maximilian and the Catholic League were to desist from all further hostility towards the Swedes and their allies, and to accept no further assistance from the Emperor. The Catholic League was to be allowed an army of ten to twelve thousand men, but it was not to be concentrated in one place. All Protestant territories conquered by the League were to be restored and the Lower Saxony boundaries of 1618 reinstated; this would have cancelled out all the Imperialist victories since the engagement at the White Hill. Cologne and Trier were to have their bishoprics restored to them, but the Elector Maximilian was to retain only those parts of the County Palatine that had always been Bavarian and only until such time as an agreement was reached with Frederick V, this agreement to be negotiated by France and England. All other territories then occupied by the Swedes were to remain in their hands until the conclusion of a general peace. The King for his part undertook to attack no other territories belonging to the members of the Catholic League, with the exception of the bishopric of Bamberg. Louis XIII was to guarantee that Bavaria and the Catholic League would observe the conditions imposed upon them, by force of arms if necessary.

Charnacé and Brézé reluctantly gave their signatures, which meant that the French government would have to approach the princes of the Catholic League and try to persuade them to accept these provisions. The signing of this document amounted to a diplomatic defeat for Richelieu.

Maximilian I rejected the Swedish provisions as too severe. On February 27, 1632, he wrote to his brother in Cologne and said that the chief reason he had refused to accept these conditions was that they were "far too prejudicial to His Imperial Majesty." He knew that Gustavus Adolphus would now attack Bavaria, but he was convinced that, even if he had accepted the Swedish proposals, the Swedes would not abide by the treaty, would not restore the occupied Catholic territories. On the contrary, "when they had finished with His Imperial Majesty, they would have attacked the Catholic Electors and estates, who would have gained from their neutrality at best no more than a bad respite and the *beneficium ordinis*."

And so the proposals Charnacé had brought to Munich were rejected by Maximilian, who was more concerned that Charnacé should persuade Louis XIII to use his influence with the Swedes on Bavaria's behalf. At the same time he instructed his representative Kütner, who was still in Metz, to try to obtain implementation of the articles guaranteeing Bavarian neutrality, which had been negotiated with Charnacé in December in accordance with the terms of the treaty of Fontainebleau. Failing this, he was to press the French to break with the Swedes. Before Kütner was able to discharge his task, however, the Bishop of Würzburg, who had come to Metz on January 24th as the representative of the Electors of Mainz and Cologne, had already made a skilful and eloquent appeal to the French to intervene with Gustavus Adolphus.

Brézé's fruitless mission had made it perfectly clear, however, that at the time there was nothing at all France could do to bring pressure to bear on Gustavus Adolphus, who had the overwhelming advantage of his unparalleled military success.

Bavaria's principal demand was that France should obtain from Gustavus Adolphus the restitution of the Catholic territories occupied by the Swedes, and Richelieu undertook to have this matter raised by Charnacé, although he held out little hope of success.

What could France have done for Maximilian? Despite all the troubles Gustavus Adolphus caused the French, he was still the strongest card they had to play against the Emperor. French military aid for Bavaria and the Catholic League was unthinkable. And yet, against his own better judgement and despite his customary objectivity and detachment, Maximilian continued to clamour for the help the French had been promising him for more than ten years.

Even when he was desperately hard pressed, Maximilian always adamantly refused to turn against the Emperor. It was not until Munich was occupied that the French succeeded in having the clause recognizing Maximilian's loyalty to the Emperor removed from the Franco-Bavarian treaty.

Maillé-Brézé's reports from Mainz were brief and distinctly anecdotal, but they appear to have been straightforward and honest. Brézé, warrior, hedonist and grand seigneur, never tried to boast to his superiors, as did the other French agents, who always wished to appear in a favourable light. Charnacé was also an exception to this general rule. Intelligent and impartial, he was highly esteemed on this account by the Bavarian officials, one of whom described him as "a serious and scholarly gentleman."

Charnacé's reports give the best clue to Gustavus Adolphus' own assessment of his situation in the period between Breitenfeld and Lützen.

On one occasion, when Charnacé observed that the Swedes had broken the treaty of Bärwalde by encroaching on the west bank of the Rhine, Gustavus Adolphus replied: "If your master had conducted his affairs properly, as I have done, then we would have abided by the agreement. But since, in contravention of the Bärwalde agreement, your master has made no contribution to our present victory, but on the contrary has left me to shoulder the whole burden, I have had to do what the situation demanded and pursue my enemies as best I could." And when the Frenchman countered that Louis XIII was on his way at the head of an army of 40,000 men, Gustavus Adolphus declared: "Your master does not need so many men in order to defeat me; for if it had been a question of the numbers and the relative strength of the armies, it is not I who would have defeated the Emperor but he who would have defeated me. But your King may go where he pleases, only let him take care not to come too close to my army, for then he must be prepared for a rencontre with me." When he first came to Mainz, Brézé found the tenor of the Swedish King's remarks distinctly threatening. He reported that during his audience the King's attitude was so cold and abrupt that it would have been easier to break with him and declare war than to negotiate the neutrality of the Catholic League. He went on to say: "He regarded all our statements as completely useless, he insisted that what was needed now were ratifications and not debates, and said that the King of France had allowed himself to be deceived and tricked by Maximilian of Bavaria, whose sole object was to gain time in order to join forces with the Emperor."

Brézé had to wait for fresh instructions and Richelieu was obliged to yield, slowly at first, but eventually to the point of recognizing the status quo. Gustavus Adolphus, well aware that Richelieu was negotiating from a position of weakness, made his demands correspondingly heavy; the army of the Catholic League was to be reduced and broken up into small units; the League was to accept no further help from the Emperor, either directly or indirectly, and was to evacuate all Protestant territories; by contrast, the only Catholic territories to be restored by the Swedes were the bishoprics of Cologne and Trier (but not Speyer) and certain parts of the Rhenish Palatinate. The Catholic League was at the mercy of Swedish power. Both Brézé and Charnacé regarded acceptance of the Swedish conditions as capitulation. When Gustavus Adolphus asked if they had been authorized to conclude an agreement and was told that they had not, he exclaimed: "You can either sign or go and tell your King that he must seek another route into Germany." At this they signed and by doing so appeared to have isolated Bavaria and the Catholic League, sealed the fate of the Catholic territories occupied by Gustavus Adolphus, and placed the Emperor in an extremely precarious military position.

The final word, however, had yet to be spoken, and when Maximilian refused to give his signature everything was again made dependent on the power of the sword. In the desperate situation in which he then found himself, Maximilian as always displayed great courage and determination.

On May 17th Gustavus Adolphus entered the capital city of Bavaria. The Burgomaster was waiting on his knees at Gasteig to hand him the keys of the city gates. Munich was required to pay a contribution of 300,000 reichstalers, which amounted to half the annual sum paid by the whole of Sweden in the form of taxes and duties. The prosperity of Munich was destroyed for years to come, the majority of its citizens were impoverished and its commercial life was completely disrupted.

From a chronicle preserved in the Franciscan archives we learn that

"many uncovered the treasure that they had long been amassing; from the churches several chalices, women's silver belts and also golden cups and goblets together with gold coin were carried to the Burgomaster's house. But even after these donations the citizens were often warned that the city would suffer the dire fate of Magdeburg if the required sum was not delivered up. And so many citizens gave money for a third and a fourth time; and so too, after much asking, even the poor widows, manservants and housemaids brought money, that the city might be rid of its enemies."

Meanwhile Maximilian I had fled to Regensburg to organize the resistance there.

During the three weeks of Swedish occupation, the great majority of the troops observed strict military discipline. But numerous works of art and craftsmanship, manuscripts and books were carried off to Sweden. The King is said to have regretted that he was unable "to put the whole palace on wheels and pack it off to Stockholm."

The following extracts from contemporary chronicles give

some indication of the atmosphere and life of Munich under Swedish rule:

"When His Majesty the King of Sweden had occupied Augsburg by agreement, he did not remain long in that town but marched to the fortress of Ingolstadt with the object of provoking the enemy to come out and give battle, but he was loath to do this, and to his own great advantage remained within the walls.

"His Majesty the King of Sweden, not wishing to incur a loss of time or an unnecessary loss of life before the walls of Ingolstadt, made for Landshut, Moosburg and Freising, which places he conquered and occupied by agreement, and he spent several days within their walls.

"Since it was now readily apparent to the citizens of Munich that their turn was next, they acted betimes and sent a delegation of their citizens to Freising to treat with His Majesty the King. Although at first the delegates were reluctant to accept the proposed conditions, when they saw the stern treatment meted out to farmers who had murdered Swedish soldiers without mercy, whereby over two hundred villages were fired and burnt to ashes, they quickly concluded and approved the agreement on May 5th according to the old calendar.

"Thereupon His Majesty the King of Sweden, Frederick the Count Palatine, the Duke of Weimar, the Palsgrave Augustus of Sulzbach, together with various Counts and gentlemen and many noble officers of high rank, rode into Munich and took up their quarters in the 'New Fortress.'

"His Majesty the King of Sweden inspected the arsenal himself but found very few pieces therein, whereupon he questioned the head armourer, to discover how it could be that so few pieces were present. The man replied that most of them had been distributed to the various bailiwicks, an explanation which His Majesty, in view of the fact that the wheels and carriages were there and only the barrels were missing, was not prepared to accept. And when it was discovered from a farmer that the barrels had been buried, men were immediately sent to search and dig for them, whereupon one hundred whole and demi cannon were dug up, bearing the arms of Denmark, Brunswick, Durlach and the County Palatine. A further twelve whole cannon were also found on which the Apostles were represented. His Majesty the King will have them all transported elsewhere. . . .

"On Ascension Day, His Majesty the King celebrated divine service in the most beautiful of the rooms in the 'New Fortress' and the hymn of thanksgiving, '*Nun freuet Euch, lieben Christen gemein*' (And now rejoice, dear Christians all), was sung. . . .

"Whatever the soldiers bought in the way of beer, bread, etc., they conscientiously paid for. They twice moved camp from the meadows of Schwabing to those in front of the Neuhauser Gate, which was burnt down after their departure. But neither pillows nor bolsters nor any other articles of bedding were left in the city. Often victuals had to be carried out to the camp. A number of Swedish sutlers carried out the March ale casked by the farmers and sold it to the soldiers, ten kreutzers the field measure, which is the equivalent of one and a half standard measures.

"In the daytime the Swedish soldiers brought all manner of things into the city and sold them, large numbers of oxen, many horses, many more pigs, women's veils, all sorts of linen, flax and yarn, oats, tin plates and jugs, a great number of copper saucepans, stolen goblets, wax tapers and many other things for use in the kitchen; they even brought the iron hoops from cart wheels, they brought whole carts, locks taken from doors, coats, women's skirts; all of which things were bought up by the inhabitants of this city at an extremely low price. In those days you really could buy an ox for a gulden and pay the same for a pound of drippings. . . .

"His Majesty the King gave orders that the many curios and pieces of armour found in the Elector's palace, many of which had been hidden, were all to be taken to Augsburg, and the carpenters of Munich had to go with them. The King also released for sale many thousand cakes of salt that had lain here in the storerooms, selling them to the Bavarians themselves, first at two guldens and then at one reichstaler, and sometimes distributing small quantities to the poor.

"All citizens had soldiers quartered on them according to their wealth and income, and provided them with food and drink for up to ten days. But as soon as the Swedes entered the city, a *salvaguardia* was granted to the monasteries and other noble houses, and two or three soldiers, who had to be richly furnished with food and drink, were lodged in each to protect them. Where the owners were absent, the soldiers cleaned out the houses, took corn from the bins and sold it. . . .

"On May 19th, the day before Ascension, when the King was riding out to the camp followed by all of his generals, he halted in front of the Jesuit church, dismounted and entered the church with his head uncovered. The Father Rector, who had been informed, hurried with all of his priests to receive the King, who straightway enquired who had built the church and where was the the mausoleum of Duke William, whose humility he considered to have been excessive. Since it was the hour of vespers, which were said each Wednesday for the successful outcome of the war, and since large numbers of people were flocking to the church for the benediction, the King asked what this signified. The rector replied that the people had come to be sprinkled with holy water, at which the King, whose curiosity was roused, came so close that he too was sprinkled. He then demanded an explanation of the properties of holy water and, after this had been furnished by the Father Rector, he asked if Catholics were required to believe this. The Rector, who had no desire to annoy a victor by indulging in unnecessary speculation, replied that holy water could scarcely be expected to take effect with the same degree of certainty as one of the Holy Sacraments. . . .

"Later at table the King said: 'If I were a Catholic, I would give preference to the Jesuits.'

"After the Swedish withdrawal the citizens were amazed to find that in the meadows outside the city and even in the moat lay all kinds of dead animals, that all the cabbage fields were ruined, all the houses and gardens in a terrible condition. Now all who belong to the town are again permitted to enter and leave at will; the citizens, aided by twenty-five Swedish soldiers who have remained in Munich as an occupation force, have resumed their guard. But where the terror struck, it caused serious illness and killed very many people. . . .

"And so we in Munich have lain for three whole weeks under the enemy's yoke and bondage. May Almighty God grant that we may find joy to compensate for this great harm we have suffered, and may He gladden our hearts with an enduring peace, and protect us as a father from such ravages of war, and constantly confer on us his peace and his blessing."

Wallenstein's Intervention and the Battle of Lützen

At this point Wallenstein returned—an event that gave the war a wholly new aspect. He completed his military preparations with surprising speed and was soon able to confront the Swedes. Gustavus Adolphus had moved into a strongly fortified camp near Nuremberg, where he had mounted some three hundred cannon. On July 16th Wallenstein occupied positions between Stein and Fürth near Zirndorf, which were soon strongly defended.

For seven weeks the two armies were encamped opposite each other with scarcely a shot being fired. Both armies suffered from hunger and disease. Gustavus Adolphus wanted battle, but Wallenstein, despite pressure brought to bear on him by the Emperor and Maximilian I, was reluctant to risk so much at such an early stage. In the end Gustavus Adolphus grew impatient and attacked, but although his army then numbered some 48,000 men, he was repulsed for the first time since his entry into Germany. Wallenstein was able to report to the Emperor that the King had "blunted his horns on this impresa."

After this initial reversal Gustavus Adolphus was prepared to negotiate. True, he still insisted on the rescission of the Edict of Restitution, he demanded the tenure of the Imperial Duchy of Pomerania for himself, and suggested that Wallenstein should accept the Duchy of Franconia in exchange for Mecklenburg. But Wallenstein rejected these proposals, explaining that he "did not possess full powers" and could not negotiate.

At this the Swedes marched out of their camp on September 18th and made for the rich territories bordering the Lake of Constance. Wallenstein let them go and wrote to the Emperor to say that he hoped the King of Sweden would soon be "finished." Then, on September 23rd, he too left his camp, and accompanied by Generals Gallas, Holk and Pappenheim, he proceeded via Coburg into Saxony, taking Leipzig on November 1st. His troops were given full licence to plunder and rob in every corner of the land. Wallenstein was carrying out a punitive expedition against John George.

He was also forcing the Swedes to follow his initiative, for Gustavus Adolphus had to come with all possible speed to the help of his ally, turning away from the Swiss border and making his way back by forced marches.

On November 16th the opposing armies met at Lützen.

Richelieu describes the death of Gustavus Adolphus in this battle as follows:

"When the King saw that the enemy was beginning to yield he took only the Swedish Steinbar [Stenbock] cavalry regiment with him, exhorting the men to follow him and bear themselves honourably. He advanced across the two ditches, captured an Imperial battery, and then, passing beyond the battery, raised his hat and thanked God for the victory that He was granting him.

"But two regiments of enemy cuirassiers were approaching

to give battle, whereupon the King charged the nearer of the two and pressed so far forward that in the mêlée his horse was hit in the neck by a pistol shot; the next shot struck the King himself and shattered his left arm; . . . realizing that he was seriously wounded, he withdrew from the engagement, accompanied only by Duke Francis Albert of Saxe-Lauenburg, who had freely elected to join the King after leaving the Emperor's service only two months before. . . . He was conducting the King to safety and led him along the front between the two armies, when a horseman, a lieutenant colonel in one of the Imperial cavalry regiments whom nobody had recognized as one of the enemy, charged straight at the King and fired at him with his pistol from ten yards range, hitting him in the back and throwing him from his horse; Duke Francis' equerry instantly chased after the horseman and struck him with his sword. Lasbelfin [Läubelfing], his page, who was then emerging from the skirmish with the enemy, found the King lying on the ground and, seeing that the enemy was approaching, offered him his horse, so that he might escape; but the King could no longer speak, and at that point three Imperial horsemen rode up and asked the name of the wounded man; Lasbelfin, not wishing to reveal his identity, said that he appeared to be an officer: angered by this reply, they struck him twice with their swords and shot him, stripped him, took his horse and left him for dead––as he himself reported before he died five days later. One of the horsemen then discharged his pistol into the King's temple, which killed him, struck him several times with his sword and then stripped his corpse, leaving him only his shirt.

"At the same time, about two o'clock in the afternoon, General Pappenheim was killed by a musket shot."

In his excellent biography of Gustavus Adolphus, Michael Roberts states that in the course of the battle the King received news that the Swedish left wing, where Bernhard of Saxe-Weimar was in command, was in great trouble and hurried to his help shortly before Pappenheim arrived on the field. He goes on to say:

". . . taking the Småland regiment with him, he moved over towards the left. He found the Green Brigade of his left centre struggling desperately against odds; and at once he led his cavalry to their assistance. Almost immediately, the King was hit: a ball from a musket shattered his left arm. His horse carried him away from most of his escort, and soon he was caught up helplessly in the mêlée. An Imperialist horseman fired a pistol into his back; he fell heavily from the saddle and with one foot still caught in a stirrup was dragged for some distance along the ground before he disengaged himself. As he lay there face downwards in the mud a final shot through the head ended his life. The body lay where it fell . . . at last,

Fig. 5. H. U. Franckh: A Scuffle among Soldiers

stripped to the shirt, the corpse lay half naked and unregarded, while the King's horse careered riderless about the battlefield."

From this excerpt it is evident that the modern historian, who had access to all the research material amassed since 1632, scarcely diverges from the account given by Richelieu in his Memoirs.

Whether Lützen was a Swedish or an Imperial victory is of no consequence, since both sides failed to exploit the outcome of the battle. Pappenheim was dead. Piccolomini, who had five horses killed beneath him in the course of the engagement, was wounded six times by Swedish musketry. Wallenstein was also wounded, but only superficially. Thanks to the mist, which had greatly influenced the course of the action, he was able to disengage his forces before darkness and lead them to Leipzig. The Swedes were left in possession of the field but

Fig. 6. H. U. Franckh: Death of a Trooper

unable to give pursuit. Not until the next day did they leave the plain, where nine thousand men lay dead.

Whatever the military outcome of the battle, Lützen was the great turning point of the Thirty Years War. The death of Gustavus Adolphus brought amazing possibilities to a sudden end; his disappearance from the scene made November 16, 1632, one of the days of decision.

In his Memoirs Richelieu wrote:

"The death of the King of Sweden provides a memorable example of the frailty of mortal men. Of the many provinces he had conquered from his neighbours and the great wealth he had acquired in Germany, not even a shirt remained to cover his nakedness. The pride of birth and his fame as a soldier, which had raised him above many great monarchs, had been brought so low that he was trampled underfoot by the horses of friend and foe. His corpse now lay among those of the meanest soldiers, bruised and stained with blood and so like the others that even his closest friends found it hard to identify him, that they might accord him the honour of Christian burial. Such was the end of all his glory."

Just one month after the battle of Lützen, on December 15, 1632, Richelieu had written to his King on this same subject, with a detachment very different from the reverberating tone he reserved for his Memoirs. Part of his letter reads as follows:

"It would seem that if the King of Sweden had postponed his death for six months Your Majesty's position would have been more assured. However, if speedy action is taken to prevent any secession on the part of the [Protestant] princes, who might well split up as a result of this accident, I do not think that Your Majesty need fear your enemies in Germany. One of the things I consider necessary in the initial stages of the new situation created by the death of the King of Sweden is that Monsieur de Charnacé should be sent a letter of credit to the value of 30,000 écus, payable in Frankfort or some other

German city, for distribution to those influential persons who will scorn mere promises and who will not take your money without binding themselves to you. The important thing is that this money should be made available quickly . . . I have been emboldened to write to Your Majesty in this matter since I know that you, who are foremost in counsel, are also the most conscientious in execution. I hope that the diplomatic missions which Your Majesty will be sending to the various German princes will produce good results, and provided there is no armistice in Holland, of which I see little indication, I do not see why Your Majesty should have to fear the consequences [of Lützen], which vulgar opinion will predict."

And so Richelieu's first concern was that money should be provided for bribes. But then he always sought out people in high places who were prepared to sell themselves. They were called pensioners and there were many of them, not only in Germany, but also in England, Rome and Switzerland. Their pensions were paid out regularly and in full, while they behaved like importunate creditors.

Immediately after the battle of Lützen a rumour was circulated to the effect that one of the people bought by the Cardinal in this way was Francis Albert of Saxe-Lauenburg and that he had murdered Gustavus Adolphus. According to Avenel, Richelieu was even accused of having been directly responsible for the death of the King of Sweden; he added that such rumours were so ignoble as to be unworthy even of contradiction. Michael Roberts writes: "But there were obstinate stories of treachery: Francis Albert of Lauenburg was long suspected of having murdered him [Gustavus Adolphus] in the heat of battle."

After Lützen

It is by no means easy to give a clear picture of the confusion that reigned in Germany after the battle of Lützen. Conditions appear to have been completely chaotic in the Rhine territories, which at that time made up four of the ten Districts of the Empire: Westphalia in the north; to the south-west the three archbishoprics of Mainz, Trier and Cologne; the Upper Rhine with the Rhenish Palatinate; the Duchy of Lorraine and a large part of Alsace, where one of the Archdukes administered the Hapsburg lands as governor. In every one of these territories there were more marauding bands than regular troops. Imperialists, Swedes, Spaniards, Frenchmen, and mercenaries from Lorraine lived off the inhabitants, whom they daily threatened with torture and death. The Elector of Trier, Archbishop Philip von Sötern, placed himself under the protection of the King of France at the end of 1632 and authorized French troops to occupy the bridgeheads of Philippsburg and Ehrenbreitstein opposite Coblenz. But the Governor of Philippsburg refused to open the gates to the French, and a Spanish unit established itself in Coblenz. Spanish and French troops then faced one another across the Rhine. The Spanish occupied Trier but were driven out again by the French. Richelieu informed Madrid that the French troops were there simply to guarantee the religious freedom of the Catholic population. In Alsace the confusion was even greater. There everything was in a state of flux. In December Rhinegrave Salm, who administered the bishopric of Strassburg and the district of Hagenau for Archduke Leopold, placed these territories under the protection of Charles IV of Lorraine; an Imperial garrison defended the most important strategic point, the fortress of Breisach, which was one of the two key positions on the route linking Italy with the Netherlands. The Sundgau was occupied by Spanish troops.

While all this was happening strong pressure had been brought to bear in Vienna to make the Emperor adopt a more flexible attitude to the question of a general peace. One of Ferdinand II's former ministers who had fallen from favour, Gundakar von Liechtenstein, had drafted an important memorandum, which, since he himself was *a consiliis absens*, was presented to the Emperor by Count Maximilian Trauttmannsdorf. According to Liechtenstein, his own views were identical with those held by Wallenstein, who had "personally acquainted him" with his opinions. It should be mentioned, however, that Liechtenstein, a serious and responsible Austrian statesman, placed little confidence in Wallenstein, for he too considered that in the final analysis the latter's permutations were prompted by self-interest.

In his memorandum Liechtenstein suggested that the Emperor should offer his hand in peace and friendship and renounce all further territorial ambitions on behalf of the Catholic Church and his own house. He argued that Louis XIII, who had not yet entered the war, would welcome a settlement between the opposing forces within the Empire that would create neither victors nor vanquished, for if the war continued and the Emperor gained the upper hand, Hapsburg power would increase to a degree that must appear intolerable to France; while if the Protestants were the victors, the King of France would have to fear a fresh outbreak of the Huguenot revolt, which he had only recently suppressed; moreover, French subsidies to Sweden were extremely costly. A compromise settlement within the Empire, which would restore a balance between the two grievously depleted adversaries, would offer the emerging Bourbon kingdom more certain prospects of acquiring power than could be expected from French intervention in the war and grandiose plans for the election of Louis XIII as King of the Romans. These arguments could be pressed with the French through Bavaria and Lorraine. Turning to the Swedes, Liechtenstein pointed out that their great leader was dead and for the time being they would be fully occupied in trying to replace their losses. But Gustavus Adolphus had also been the leader of the German Protestants, which meant that the Protestant Electors now had a chance to extricate themselves from the dangerous situation of having a foreign power permanently entrenched on German soil. His death would also give free rein to the traditional rivalries between the more powerful estates in the

Empire and must finally convince them, especially Brandenburg and Saxony, that they had nothing to gain and a great
deal to lose from a costly internal war. Nor would they be
able to turn a completely blind eye to universal Christian
interests or to the safety of the Empire. But the Emperor
would have to offer reasonable peace conditions. And there
were the most urgent reasons why he should do so: it should
be impressed upon Ferdinand that the war was being waged by
Christians against Christians, that it was enervating Germany,
placing the territory of the Empire at the mercy of the hereditary enemy and of foreign nations in general and inflicting
the greatest harm on the house of Hapsburg itself. The result
of fifteen years of war was that the Emperor and the Hapsburgs
were now hated in the Holy Roman Empire, and their hereditary domains, which had been cut off from trade and could no
longer pay their contributions, had been laid waste and impoverished. The Emperor's subjects, goaded by the heavy
burdens, religious coercion and the expulsion of their local
authorities (many of whom were biding their time at the
frontiers), were now embittered and in the event of an enemy
attack would go over to Ferdinand's adversaries. The
Spanish enterprise in the Netherlands was going badly; the
house of Hapsburg had no money for fresh levies, no money
even for Ferdinand's household; the Imperial troops had not
been paid for nearly a year and were threatening to mutiny.
Army leaders and commanders were expecting to be paid from
confiscations, since contributions could no longer be raised in
the poverty-stricken Empire or the hereditary domains; if they
were disappointed in their expectations, then it was to be feared
that they would desert, especially since so many of them were
not of the Catholic faith. Apart from the victory at the White
Hill, Ferdinand had had nothing but losses. He was not able
to rely on the Catholic Electors, some of whom were hostile,
some neutral and some ruined; if he were to gain decisive
victories over the enemy, then England and France, Denmark
and Sweden, Poland and Russia, Turkey, Venice, even the

Pope and many other powers besides would move against him; they would never allow the house of Austria to become predominant and would not only deny the Emperor new acquisitions but would take from him much of what he already had. The power of those Imperial cities that were either openly or secretly hostile on account of the religious issue was not easily assessed. The estuaries of Germany's four main rivers were in the hands of the enemy, who was able to send in reserves of troops and materials at will, while the Emperor and the King of Spain lacked both soldiers and money. Meanwhile the Turkish threat was constantly growing, and help in combating this threat could be obtained from the states of the Empire only on extremely harsh conditions; there was also a growing danger that, in the event of the Emperor's military defeat, the Catholic Estates would also form foreign alliances, which would mean that the future election of a Hapsburg as King of the Romans would be rendered difficult, if not impossible.

"A wealth of arguments, which all point to the fact that the Emperor should at long last decide 'to make a compromise peace as soon as possible.' " A wealth of arguments indeed and a wealth of accurate and statesmanlike observations. The only errors were in regard to France. It was not true that an agreement between opposing forces within the Empire, which would create neither victors nor vanquished, would have been welcomed by Louis XIII. In the first half of the seventeenth century the French government wanted to weaken the house of Hapsburg and so was intent on protracting the war. The idea that a new Huguenot uprising could take place was also mistaken. After the fall of La Rochelle and the fearful punitive expeditions in the South of France, in Provence and the Cévennes, the Huguenots no longer existed as an effective political force. In Liechtenstein's assessment of the "hereditary enemy"—i.e., the "emerging Bourbon kingdom" which was aspiring to the Imperial Crown—memories of Francis I must have been at work.

In stating that his views were the same as Wallenstein's, Liechtenstein confirmed a rumour long current in the Holy Roman Empire and the Courts of Europe. In a letter to his brother of October 24, 1632, Duke Bernhard of Saxe-Weimar mentioned that Wallenstein had tried to enter into contact with Gustavus Adolphus; Duke Bernhard expressed his surprise that Wallenstein should have failed to consider that the King of Sweden was an extremely jealous man and could never have tolerated a rival. Since Bernhard's letter was dictated shortly before the death of Gustavus Adolphus, his comments have a retrospective significance. But we also possess a memorandum composed by a French diplomat seven months after Lützen, which describes the relations between Wallenstein and the King of Sweden in far greater detail and which we shall be considering later.

In 1633 the French agents in Germany were particularly active. Isaac Manassès de Pas, Marquis de Feuquières, played a leading role. He greatly strengthened the alliance between France, Sweden and the German Protestant princes. His work in Germany began in Mainz and was continued in Frankfort; wherever he passed he distributed letters from Louis XIII to the German principalities and cities that lay on his route. In Frankfort he learnt that Oxenstierna was expected in Würzburg. (On April 23, 1633, the Protestant estates of Swabia and Franconia and the North German princes were to discuss the question of their alliances with Sweden in Heilbronn. As a result of this meeting the Franco-Swedish alliance was extended and France undertook to continue to pay Sweden an annual subsidy of a million livres. The restitution of the Rhenish Palatinate was again guaranteed to the heirs of Frederick V, the thoughtless and unfortunate Winter King; he had died in Mainz on November 29, 1632, just thirteen days after the battle of Lützen. The League of Heilbronn remained in existence until May 1635—i.e., until the peace of Prague.) On his way to Heilbronn, Feuquières passed near Würzburg, and he made a detour and spoke with the Swedish Chancellor before the assembly convened. Originally it had been intended to hold this meeting in Ulm, but following Lützen the Imperial armies had drawn too close to Ulm for safety, so Heilbronn was chosen instead.

In their Würzburg talks Oxenstierna and Feuquières concentrated primarily on Saxony, on her need for peace, the alleged indecisiveness of her Elector and the influence his Imperialist brother-in-law, the Landgrave of Hesse, was exerting on him. They agreed that pressure must be brought to bear on John George.

As a result of these initial talks, the terms of a memorandum were worked out and on May 5, 1633, it was agreed that Schlettstadt, Hagenau, Zabern, Breisach and Kreuznach were to serve as pawns and to receive French garrisons.

Oxenstierna advised Feuquières not to go to Dresden immediately and also to postpone his proposed visit to Brandenburg, and for the time being to attend the meeting at Heilbronn. This Feuquières agreed to. Representatives from the districts of the Upper Rhine, Swabia and Franconia, the Elector of Brandenburg, the Dukes of Württemberg, the Margrave Frederick of Baden, the Counts of Nassau, Solms and Hagenau, the Margrave of Ansbach, the Margrave of Kulmbach and delegates from the cities of Nuremberg, Ulm, Frankfort and Strassburg all met in Heilbronn. Feuquières entered the Imperial city on March 13, 1633, followed on the 15th by Oxenstierna and the representatives of England and Holland. The English ambassador was negotiating on behalf of the children of Frederick V and their mother Elizabeth, the daughter of James I. He insisted that the County Palatine be restored to these heirs. Paw, the envoy from the United Provinces, who was concerned that the Imperial forces should be tied down as much as possible and thus prevented from combining with the Spanish armies, urged the continuance of the war in Germany.

On March 19th the assembly was opened. In reporting Chancellor Oxenstierna's speech, the *Mercure François* said that he had called for Protestant unity until the territories confiscated under the Edict of Restitution were restored and the old laws of the Empire reintroduced. He asked that every member of the assembly be required to give an undertaking not to sign a separate peace and suggested that they ought to discuss whether the Emperor and the princes of the Catholic League should be proclaimed public enemies. He also called for accurate records so as to establish the precise strength of the army and the means available for its maintenance and for further recruiting. Then he turned to the chief problem confronting the delegates, which concerned the further conduct of their general affairs; in this connection he made the remarkable proposal that they should consider how best to restore discipline among the troops and prevent further atrocities. Finally, with great wisdom and foresight the Chancellor asked the assembly to consider to what extent Sweden should continue to participate in the war and what help she could expect from her German allies if she were attacked elsewhere.

Copies of his speech were distributed to the members of the congress and within a very short time the answers to his questions began to come in.

It was decided to renew the alliance between the Kings of France and England, the Swedes, the German Protestants and the Dutch. Oxenstierna was entrusted with the conduct of general policy but was to be aided by four advisers elected by the four Protestant districts and three advisers elected by the Swedish Crown. This decision displeased the Elector of Saxony and he instructed his representative to oppose the measure. In this he was supported by those members of the assembly who secretly were loyal to the Emperor. Certain points raised by the Swedish Chancellor were deferred for consideration at a later session. Oxenstierna asked Feuquières to do his utmost to promote unity, a request that was in complete accord with the French envoy's instructions from Paris. Feuquières thereupon informed the individual delegates that he had an important communication to make on behalf of his King and was told that his statement would be welcomed.

He delivered his big speech on April 1st. He explained that, although he had already informed most of the delegates individually of his sovereign's intentions, he now wished to address them collectively. His first recommendation was that they should raise the troops needed to combat the common enemy. (It is a remarkable fact that even in Heilbronn, out of respect for his office, the Emperor was never referred to either by name or title. It was considered more fitting to speak or write of him as the "common enemy.") Next Feuquières stressed the necessity for continued collaboration with Sweden, the necessity for all to show their loyalty to the agreement King Gustavus Adolphus had sealed with his blood. He added that his master, the King of France, had actually wished him to avoid all mention of this matter, since in his view it went without saying that all present would keep faith out of a sense of gratitude; if they failed to do so they would be condemned by posterity and would lose the respect of their neighbours for ever. At this point Feuquières warned of the hidden snares in every peace initiative coming from Vienna or Madrid. He urged the delegates to take military action as quickly as possible, for the season favoured an offensive.

The assembly allowed itself to be impressed by this address. Feuquières was promised an answer and very shortly the Protestant estates sent him a note in which they thanked him above all for the interest the King of France was taking in the German Liberties. They then promised a great deal: to carry on the war, to renew the alliance with Sweden, to leave the general conduct of affairs to Oxenstierna, and not to respond to any peace overtures, whether they came from Vienna, from the Catholic League or from Spain. And lastly they asked the French for money.

It was not long before they regretted having promised so much. They tried to defer both the question of the Swedish alliance and that of Oxenstierna's mandate for consideration at a general diet. This view was most strongly held by the representatives of the Swabian estates. There were many differences of opinion within the majority group. A number of delegates wanted to see Sweden's authority weakened and a director appointed for each of the Imperial Districts. Oxenstierna was understandably indignant at this proposal, but for tactical reasons he made concessions and tried to win the Protestants over by promising to restore to the children of Frederick V all the territories Sweden had occupied in the Upper Palatinate and the County Palatine in the course of the war. He also promised them all Church lands to which they laid claim. In this connection he himself was eager to acquire the archbishopric of Mainz, in order to be in a position to bestow this, the foremost of the Imperial electorships, at his wish. But at this point Feuquières suddenly raised a vehement protest. Mainz was too close to the French border.

While these duels were being fought at the negotiating table, the King of Denmark was again trying to intercede as a peacemaker. He acted in concert with the Emperor and particularly with the Elector of Saxony, who was doing his utmost to frustrate the resolutions made at Heilbronn. Oxenstierna had to deal gently with the Danes, so he asked the French envoy and also the representative of the United Provinces to act for him. But their intervention seemed no less suspect to the Emperor than the Danish initiative to Oxenstierna. In this way every single peace move was thwarted before it was able to develop. Oxenstierna none the less did not wish to appear as an outright opponent of peace. He therefore proposed to the Protestant estates that they should pass a resolution granting him, as the person responsible for the conduct of Protestant affairs, full powers to seek out and appoint mediators to negotiate a lasting peace and to conclude a temporary armistice meanwhile. The estates told him that they had no authority to pass a resolution of this kind and asked that the matter be deferred for consideration at a later session. However, a majority voted for the continuation of the war; in actual fact Oxenstierna agreed with them.

The Swedish Chancellor was demanding absolute authority, while Feuquières was doing his best to restrict his powers. Finally—on the last day of the Heilbronn assembly—Oxenstierna was forced to agree to the setting up of an advisory council. The final resolutions expressed the determination of the Protestant estates to restore the Liberties of the Holy Roman Empire and to create a lasting peace within its borders. The princes, the delegates from the Imperial cities and the envoys of the allied powers pledged themselves to a closer union in order that all might procure restitution of their former privileges. To this end the members of the League renewed their joint alliance with the Swedish Crown and gave mutual assurances of help among themselves. They also declared that in accordance with the advice offered by His Most Christian Majesty and in recognition of the services rendered to Germany by the King of Sweden, Axel Oxenstierna would be asked to supervise the conduct of their affairs in the further course of the war. But in order that His Excellency might be relieved of some part of this great burden, a committee had been appointed to assist him in dealing with all issues. This measure, Oxenstierna was told, was not intended to restrict his freedom of action in any way and certainly not where crucial decisions had to be made on the conduct of the war. No member of the League was to enter into negotiations with the "common enemy" without the consent of his fellow members, no member was to declare himself neutral and any member who did so would be regarded as an enemy. The allies all undertook to contribute to the upkeep of the troops. Officers and men were to swear an oath both to the Swedish Crown and to the princes and estates of the Protestant League. These resolutions were contained in nine articles. The last of these stated that the allied princes and estates would do all within their power to preserve for Sweden until the end of the war all the strongholds she had occupied within the Empire.

At the same time a new Franco-Swedish alliance was concluded by Oxenstierna and Feuquières. The Swedish Chancellor hesitated to commit himself, but in the situation confronting him in Germany and with Sweden under a regency, he knew that without help he could not assert the authority vested in him against the Elector of Saxony and his followers. He also knew that this authority of his would be gravely endangered if France took steps to reduce it.

Meanwhile the English envoy had repeatedly plied Oxenstierna with the argument that the German Protestants should on no account place their faith in Catholics and had impressed on him that Sweden would always receive more real help from England and Holland than from France. The Englishman's comments might conceivably have prevented the conclusion of the Franco-Swedish alliance, but Charles I's insecurity at home, his failure to intervene over the Palatinate question or to afford any help at all to his brother-in-law, the Count Palatine, combined with Feuquières' powers of persuasion and Richelieu's ability to pay, persuaded Oxenstierna that in the final analysis a further alliance with France was desirable. And so the treaty of Bärwalde was renewed.

An important point, and one that may be regarded as a tactical victory for the French negotiator, was that the Catholic League and above all Maximilian of Bavaria were to be allowed to remain neutral, which was what Richelieu had long been working for.

Finally it was stipulated that, in the event of a general peace, the two allied powers, Sweden and France, should guarantee the principles embodied in the peace treaty. As soon as this last point had been agreed on, Feuquières asked Louis XIII to ratify the resolutions. Then, at the end of April, he set out to visit the Electors of Saxony and Brandenburg, hoping to obtain from them their unqualified approval of the Heilbronn agreements.

Feuquières was well aware of the difficulties awaiting him in Saxony. He was concerned above all with one particularly pressing issue: he knew that through the agency of his son-in-law, the Landgrave of Hesse, the Elector of Saxony had been negotiating with two of the Emperor's ministers. He knew that they were said to have considered the possibility of concluding a peace from which France would be excluded. He also knew that this project was linked with the King of Denmark's proposal that a peace assembly be convened in Breslau. Feuquières realized at once that if France were to be excluded from a general peace, the Emperor would supply both the Duke of Lorraine and the Duke of Orléans with troops, since these two princes wished for nothing better than to march into France, the former in order to regain the territories annexed by France and the latter for reasons that are only too well known to us.

Feuquières arrived in Dresden on May 19th. John George granted him an audience the very next day. He was treated with great deference but little sign of Saxon confidence. His first object was to probe the Elector's mind, but John George remained extremely reserved and merely told Feuquières at the end of their conversation that he would let him know his intentions through his ministers. Feuquières had proposed that the Elector should ratify the treaty of Heilbronn and accept France's offer of mediation; he should also support French participation in any peace talks that might be held and at the same time press for the exclusion of the King of Denmark. Finally, Feuquières asked the Saxon ruler to abide by the agreements that had been reached on the occasion of the founding of the Protestant Union in Leipzig.

In the reply he received from the Saxon ministers, Feuquières was told that the Elector did not recognize the resolutions passed at Heilbronn and that he would give no assurances and make no decisions until he had learnt the outcome of the peace congress proposed by the King of Denmark. John George did, however, confirm that he still regarded the original agreements reached in Leipzig as binding and that he would not lay down his arms until peace had been restored in the Empire. Feuquières did not conceal his annoyance. He said that he was extremely surprised that the Elector should attach such importance to the Danish peace moves. To his mind this was neither prudent nor sensible, especially in view of the fact that he was being offered both the alliance and the mediation of such a powerful monarch as Louis XIII. He then issued a veiled threat to the effect that the King of France would not forget this lack of confidence and added that he himself was quite amazed to find that an Elector who had been so badly treated by the Emperor should still be so subservient to him, especially at a time when it was still conceivable that "the King of Sweden might return from the grave" to occupy Saxony once more. Feuquières concluded by predicting that John George would incur the hatred of all his allies. His threats were not without effect. After informing the Elector of Feuquières's reaction, the two ministers Miltitz and Tymaeus returned the next day to advise Feuquières that the Elector had been impressed by his comments. The circumstances obtaining at the time, they said, had furnished the Elector with material reasons for accepting the King of Denmark's proposals. But if the King of France was prepared to afford him financial help he could withdraw that acceptance, and since he had no wish to haggle he would say quite openly that he wanted 100,000 reichstalers. Feuquières was delighted and gave immediate assurances of financial help, although he was not able to commit himself as to the exact amount.

Before leaving Dresden to make his way to Berlin, Feuquières was told by the English envoy that in his opinion Saxony would soon be ready to approve the Heilbronn agreements. This diplomat, who had once been in the service of the Danish Crown, was England's accredited representative to the Leipzig Court. He was a man who was well able to hold his liquor, a fact which had recommended him to the hard-drinking John George. When Feuquières first met his colleague, the latter had just come from a carousal that had gone on for seven hours. The Englishman, who was in an animated and expansive mood, claimed great influence with the Elector and assured Feuquières that John George would ratify the Heilbronn agreements and would soon be turning his back on the King of Denmark and his Breslau plan. He then broached the difficult question of the County Palatine, arguing that Maximilian of Bavaria should never have been given the electorship. But Feuquières evaded this issue and returned to the subject of Breslau, insisting that the Danish project must be frustrated and Saxony prevailed upon to endorse the Heilbronn resolutions, adding that he had received no instructions regarding the affairs of the Count Palatine. Feuquières was disturbed by the influence the Englishman evidently had. He asked Miltitz for a further interview and requested him to ensure that, if his master ratified the Heilbronn resolutions, the credit for this would go to the King of France and not to England. The Elector, who had already tendered his financial demands, replied with extreme courtesy that for him the King of France would always take precedence.

Feuquières was on the point of leaving for Berlin when the Elector sent an officer to him with the astounding news that Arnim, who commanded the Saxon troops in Silesia, had concluded a fourteen-day armistice with Wallenstein, beginning June 8th. Feuquières received the messenger coldly and told him to inform the Elector that, by concluding such an armistice and by continuing to negotiate with the King of Denmark while creating so many difficulties over recognizing the Heilbronn agreement, he would incur the displeasure of every member of the Protestant Union and that this could be extremely dangerous for him. After reporting back to the Elector, the officer returned at once to say that in concluding the armistice General Arnim had acted without the Elector's authority and had been recalled immediately. He then contradicted himself by adding that Arnim had also received strict orders not to extend the period of the armistice. Feuquières demanded that the Elector should inform his allies of this incident without delay, since it was perfectly clear that Wallenstein would not only exploit the armistice for military ends but would also circulate reports to the effect that a genuine agreement between the two opposing groups in Germany was imminent.

Wallenstein's disclosures to Feuquières

What were, viewed from a year's distance, the real reasons for Arnim's armistice? Wallenstein was in Silesia when he learnt of the new storm brewing at the Viennese Court. Feuquières thought that the Imperial commander had every reason to assume that he was being threatened with a second dismissal and was trying to safeguard himself against such an eventuality. To this end, Feuquières reported, he planned to use the troops under his command to gain control of the whole of Silesia and its neighbouring provinces and even to acquire the Bohemian crown for himself. But this grand design could not succeed without the help of the anti-Hapsburg powers, so Wallenstein would be obliged to discuss all further steps with the French representative, in order to be sure of effective support when he turned against the Emperor. First, however, he wished to approach the Electors of Saxony and Brandenburg, and so he marched for Silesia, where their army was then campaigning. Arnim, it was said, had been determined to risk an engagement until he discovered that Wallenstein's entrenchments were so strong as to make the outcome of any attack extremely dubious. Feuquières seems to imply that the Saxons were afraid of Wallenstein and that their fears had grown when they saw his army assume an offensive formation. Skirmishes had already broken out between the two front lines when one of Wallenstein's officers rode forward bearing a flag of truce and asked to be conducted to Arnim. The latter quite rightly informed the general commanding the Brandenburg detachment and the senior Swedish officers of this, all of whom, Feuquières reported, advised him to accept the offer of talks and undertook to accompany him to the Duke of Friedland. In the ensuing discussion, Wallenstein stated quite openly that he wished to conclude a peace with the Swedes and the German Protestants. He made them great promises and is said to have whispered in the ear of one of the Swedish officers: "If the Emperor is not prepared to act in accordance with our wishes, we shall force him to do so." Since Arnim had no authority to enter into negotiations of such consequence, he agreed to the provisional armistice, and within the fortnight covered by the truce the Electors of Saxony and Brandenburg, Oxenstierna and Feuquières were all advised of Wallenstein's far-reaching plans. Feuquières reported that Wallenstein undertook to restore the Electorate to the son of the Count Palatine and to restore all his estates to him. (Wallenstein's enduring hatred of Maximilian I is manifest here.) But he went much further, for he also promised to recall all the Bohemian exiles. And it was at this point that he openly demanded the crown of Bohemia together with the Duchy of Moravia, in return for which he was prepared to restore Mecklenburg to its original ruler.

In considering these astonishing disclosures we must remember that Wallenstein had already tried unsuccessfully to establish contact with Gustavus Adolphus. Not that his later proposals produced the results he had hoped for. Indeed, to begin with he received no answer at all from the Electors. This was not because the great *condottiere's* undertakings appeared improbable to them; they took them very seriously and were certainly tempted by them. But they felt a kind of princely solidarity in the face of this upstart, who proposed to betray his sovereign and stretch out his hand toward a royal crown. Oxenstierna was the one who was most opposed to Wallenstein's project, which he regarded as no more than a military strategem.

Not so Feuquières. Count Kinsky, Wallenstein's friend and confidant who was then in Dresden, visited the French representative and furnished him with a detailed account of Wallenstein's intentions. Feuquières then drafted a memorandum for Kinsky in which he listed all the difficulties the Duke of Friedland was likely to encounter but promised him the full support of the King of France, and—with supreme magnanimity—of the Protestant Union.

In actual fact, however, Feuquières's personal assessment of Wallenstein's chances of success was more sceptical than he was prepared to admit to the General's representatives. His chief criticism was that the plan had been talked about far too much and confided to far too many people.

Richelieu for his part was instantly prepared to exploit the possibilities offered by this "military revolt" and Feuquières was quickly authorized to negotiate with the Imperial Commander-in-Chief. In one set of instructions, which was signed by the King himself, he was even told: "I am much gratified by the information you have sent me regarding Friedland. I will gladly employ the power of my own arms and that of my friends and will use my full authority to procure his election as King of Bohemia and even to a higher office."

Shortly after receiving this letter from the King, Feuquières also received a memorandum from Father Joseph confirming the general policy laid down by Louis but with greater detail. Feuquières himself received high praise and was allowed a considerable measure of freedom for purposes of negotiation.

His negotiations with Wallenstein, of course, protracted his stay in Dresden. Although the Elector of Saxony had accepted the 100,000 reichstalers, Feuquières continued to regard him as an uncertain quantity. In one of his reports he stated that while John George appeared to be waging war against the Emperor, he was also negotiating with him. His lack of patience with what he considered the Elector's unreliable attitude prompted Feuquières to set off, in the midst of his secret negotiations with Wallenstein, to visit the Elector of Brandenburg.

At this point we must interrupt our account of Feuquières's activities in order to give a brief résumé of various factors bearing on Brandenburg.

Brandenburg

The Mark of Brandenburg had been in the possession of the Hohenzollern dynasty since 1415. Frederick I of Hohenzollern was faced with the task of strengthening his borders and creating internal order out of the chaos left by the rulers of the Luxemburg dynasty. He conducted local wars against Mecklenburg and Pomerania and reunited the Uckermark with Brandenburg. He broke the resistance of the rebellious nobles and redeemed the bailiwicks and cities that they and other creditors had received in the form of pledges. He forced the knights of Brandenburg to respect the peace of the land and pay homage to the ducal house, and he subdued the von Puttlitz, Rochow and Quitzow families, leaders of the Brandenburg nobility whose power had grown out of all proportion.

In 1510 Albert, Margrave of Brandenburg-Ansbach, was elected Grand Master of the Teutonic Order. Although he was a vassal of the King of Poland, he refused to swear the oath of allegiance to the Polish Crown and proceeded to institute a constitutional reform advocated by Luther which, though making no essential difference to Brandenburg's relations to Poland, entirely changed the internal structure of the territory. In 1525 Albert dissolved the Teutonic Order and transformed Prussia into a hereditary duchy. The King of Poland agreed and under the terms of the treaty of Cracow, concluded on April 8, 1525, Poland transferred Prussia to Albert as a hereditary secular duchy on condition that he acknowledge his vassalage. The acclaim with which this measure was greeted throughout the duchy by knights and subjects alike was due primarily to the wide dissemination of Reformation ideas in Prussia. Among the first to pay homage were the bishops of Samland and Pomerania, who ceded control of their chapters and transferred the capitular estates to the Duke. He for his part granted both nobility and towns the right of representation at a provincial diet. Although Pope Clement

VII protested against the secularization of the territory, Albert retained full control of the new duchy, where he introduced the Lutheran faith and, in 1544, founded the Lutheran University of Königsberg.

One of Albert's successors, John Sigismund, who became Duke of Prussia in 1618, embraced the Calvinist faith in 1613; it was his weak son, George William, who reigned from 1619 to 1640. The extent to which he too was influenced by Richelieu's political strategy is quite evident from how he fared in the storms unleashed by his Swedish brother-in-law.

The auxiliaries led by Christian of Anhalt to the aid of the French Huguenots had consisted for the most part of Brandenburgers. Brandenburg was strongly opposed to the Pope. Refugees from the Netherlands had passed on the distaste for the papacy they had acquired under Catholic persecution. The Elector, who was determined to keep his lands free from Jesuit influence, paid particular attention to higher education and passed a law that no post in the public service could be given a candidate who had not pursued his studies within the duchy.

Lampert Distelmeyer, who was Chancellor of Brandenburg under Joachim II, did much to strengthen Protestant policy during the wars with Charles V and subsequently in the Religious Peace of Augsburg; to this end he renewed the traditional links with Saxony and Hesse. The arrangement with Poland by which the Elector eventually received the Duchy of Prussia in fief was also his work and it was he who pressed Brandenburg's claim to Cleves and Jülich. By establishing close links with Saxony and by strengthening and organizing the established church, Distelmeyer became one of the founders of the Prussian state.

Unlike Saxony, Brandenburg took an active part in the dispute over the Cleves-Jülich succession. The Emperor and his house had planned to sequester these territories and append them to the Catholic Netherlands, which of course would have meant an increase in Hapsburg power. But both the Elector of Brandenburg and the Count Palatine were favoured by the fact that neither the United Provinces, nor France, nor the King of England, who was then backing the German Protestant Union, wanted Cleves and Jülich to fall into Austrian hands. This was also the chief reason underlying King Henry IV's decision to declare war on Spain and Austria. Subsequently, during the regency in France, all such considerations were abandoned. Philipp Ludwig of Pfalz-Neuburg converted to Catholicism and it was only thanks to the fact that Brandenburg enjoyed the support of the United Provinces that she was not then obliged to renounce her claim. Eventually the Spanish moved into Cleves and Jülich on one side, and the Dutch moved in on the other. It was in these circumstances that Elector John Sigismund joined with the Dutch and converted from the Lutheran to the Calvinist faith. He was convinced that Calvinism offered the German princes a more effective means of combating the growing power of the estates. After his conversion he married a princess from the County Palatine. Through this marriage his dynasty developed close ties with all the leading Protestants of Western Europe.

Brandenburg was hard hit when the Bohemians were defeated. The ascendancy she had expected to assume was postponed far into the future, for with Bohemia firmly under control, Austria could easily put a check to Brandenburg's own expansionist policies. Then came the dissolution of the Protestant Union and with it the loss of Brandenburg's influence in North Germany. The Edict of Restitution had a similar but far stronger effect. Then matters came to a head, for though the application of the principle of *cujus regio, ejus religio* would have ensured a Protestant Empire, the restitutions would have led it back to Catholicism.

George William, the son of Elector John Sigismund and the father of the Great Elector, was a man of thirty-eight when Feuquières visited him. For some time, under the influence of his chief minister, Count Adam Schwarzenberg, a Catholic, he had followed a policy favourable to the Emperor.

Wallenstein's army had nevertheless ravaged the Mark. Although at first George William had rejected an alliance with Gustavus Adolphus, being justifiably suspicious of his brother-in-law's far-reaching political aims in Germany, in 1631 he was cowed into acceptance and from then onwards participated, although insignificantly, in the war. But, as we shall see, his fundamental loyalty to the Emperor was clearly shown in 1635 on the occasion of the peace of Prague. The Swedes then took their revenge by occupying the whole of Brandenburg and turning it into a wilderness, whereupon the Elector withdrew to Königsberg in Prussia, where he died on December 1, 1640.

In 1633—when the pressure put on him was beginning to take effect—George William informed Feuquières that he was prepared to join the Franco-Swedish alliance. He promised that he would sign no further treaties save those negotiated by the King of France and gave an undertaking that he would send only observers and no plenipotentiaries to the assembly called by the King of Denmark in Breslau. Feuquières promised that in return France would protect Brandenburg's interests in Cleves and Jülich. He asked the Elector to acknowledge the alliance openly, but George William replied that, in view of his long and close association with the Elector of Saxony, he would first like to discuss the matter with him. When Feuquières informed him that he himself was immediately returning to Dresden, George William delegated one of his ministers to be present at the negotiations between France and Saxony.

Feuquières's Mission to Saxony and His Journey to Frankfort

On his way back to Dresden, Feuquières visited the Prince of Anhalt and various other rulers in the Upper Saxon District and reported that they all approved of recent French initiatives and were of good will.

On July 23rd Feuquières returned to Dresden. The

armistice between Arnim and Wallenstein had meanwhile expired, and two thousand Imperial horse had invaded Saxony and advanced to within cannon range of the walls of Dresden. This Imperial advance had taken place shortly before the Duke of Holstein, the Elector's son-in-law, was due to arrive in the Saxon capital. He and his family were to enter the city on July 24th and the Elector had been preoccupied with the preparations for their reception. When Feuquières appeared virtually at the same time, it is understandable that in the circumstances he found the Saxon administration in a state of confusion. At all events, the Marquis de Feuquières, His Most Christian Majesty's special ambassador, was not accorded the ceremonial reception he considered his due. But that was not all. He and his retinue could find no accommodation within the city and were obliged to go to an outlying district. The next day Feuquières sent an official messenger to advise the Saxon Ministry of his arrival and to state that he required accommodation at once in keeping with his rank. At first his request elicited no response whatsoever, and in a century that was to produce *le roi soleil*, a time when rank counted for everything, that was an extremely serious matter. Eventually the Saxon quartermaster sought him out and was forced to confess that nothing had been prepared for him; together with some of Feuquières's retinue, the quartermaster went out into the streets of the city to look for suitable lodgings, which he was able to find only in houses whose occupants had died of the plague. These he then recommended to Feuquières without himself having set foot into them. The next day the French ambassador sent a messenger to inform the Ministry that he would leave the city without presenting himself to the Elector unless his requirements were met immediately. The minister responsible then offered his apologies. He explained that the difficulties had been occasioned by the sudden advance of the Imperialist troops, which had caused great numbers of people to flee the countryside and seek safety in the capital. And then there had been the arrival of the Duke of Holstein. Feuquières accepted these excuses with very bad grace, declaring that the rank held by a special ambassador of the King of France was superior to that of such petty princes. The minister then promised to do his utmost to help find a suitable house. Feuquières for his part insisted that not a single man of his retinue was to show himself on the streets. The fact that they had been seen there on the previous day was already tantamount to an insult. The whole matter was settled by the evening of the same day, but a further three days passed before Feuquières was granted an audience. By that time both he and the Elector were openly annoyed, and this was reflected in their conversation. Feuquières tried to exert pressure on John George, and after informing him of the Elector of Brandenburg's decisions he insisted that the time had come for Saxony to state her intentions unequivocally.

Later that same day several Saxon representatives called on Feuquières, though not to state the Elector's intentions. On the contrary, they said that they had come to learn the precise nature of the proposals Feuquières wished to make to their master. The French ambassador replied caustically that he had no further proposals to make and that the only reason for his presence was to receive an immediate reply from the Elector of Saxony. He had already expressed himself with such clarity on the occasion of his first visit that His Highness must be well aware of the issues involved. He must, moreover, have been fully informed meanwhile by the Minister from Brandenburg, who had arrived on the same day as himself.

A further two days elapsed. Then, on the evening of the second day, Feuquières received a visit from Doctor von Hoenegg, Herr von Lungwitz and Gönssdorf, a Lutheran pastor who had originally come to Saxony to preach before John George. He then became spiritual adviser and senior preacher to the Elector, and finally one of the leading Saxon ministers. At one time von Hoenegg, acting on behalf of the Elector of Saxony and the Landgrave of Hesse-Darmstadt, had concluded an alliance between them and the Emperor against the Swedish Crown. Feuquières learnt no more from him than from the others. Extremely annoyed, he left Dresden and travelled to Erfurt to meet Duke William of Saxe-Weimar and thence to Cassel to visit the Landgrave of Hesse-Cassel. His object, as always, was to bind the German princes one by one to the League of Heilbronn and so make them dependent on French policy.

We have already seen that, although the Elector of Brandenburg was full of good intentions where Feuquières was concerned, he would make no final decisions without the concurrence of his friend and kinsman, the Elector of Saxony. At this point Feuquières sent a certain Baron de Rorté to Berlin to present George William with a written statement of their discussions to date. He also delegated a Monsieur d'Avaucourt to the princes and towns of Lower Saxony. He himself meanwhile proceeded to Frankfort, where he had the satisfaction of seeing the princes and rulers of the four North German Districts join the Heilbronn League. For the rest of that year and a large part of the following year he made Frankfort his headquarters.

He kept up close ties with all the German Courts and pursued his duties with exemplary diligence. Saxony and Brandenburg remained his principal concern. It was evident that for very good reasons, including his territorial ambitions, John George did not wish to break with the Emperor. Above all, he was opposed to a further alliance with the Swedes. According to Feuquières's reports, the Elector of Brandenburg was far more compliant; but although he promised much, he did nothing.

France and Wallenstein

Both Richelieu and Father Joseph had put their highest hopes on Feuquières's negotiations with Wallenstein, who had given formal assurances that he would immediately break with the Emperor. In a letter from Feuquières to Bouthillier we read: "I have received a letter from Count Kinsky, delivered by a nobleman he had sent to me." And from Kinsky's letter we learn that Wallenstein had been unable to negotiate the previous year because he had failed to obtain the backing of all his officers, but things had since changed. Every single officer right down to the subalterns had now given his oath; above all he had the signatures of Gallas and Aldringer and also Piccolomini. In order to secure his position still further he had recruited 100 cornets and 300 infantrymen under his personal command (in other words, a bodyguard). It had of course been impossible to keep all this secret, and Wallenstein was reported to have said that certain officers loyal to the Emperor had handed Ferdinand the Bohemian crown. "Fortunately they are not able to do the same thing with the kingdom, and I have enough gold and jewels to have an identical crown made."

Continuing his report, Feuquières said, "As soon as the treaty has been concluded, he intends to proclaim himself King of Bohemia and to inform the Emperor of this in person, to which end he proposes to seek him out with his sword in his hand wherever he may be, whether in hell itself."

Kinsky also told Feuquières that, regardless of Wallenstein's outstanding services, the Emperor was determined to be rid of him and was quite prepared to resort to poisoners and assassins in order to do so.

Feuquières then commented:

"Upon receipt of these disclosures I immediately ordered Monsieur de La Boderie to return with Count Kinsky's emissary, having first given him the necessary powers to conclude the treaty with Wallenstein and detailed instructions as to how to proceed.

"One of the principal reasons why I dispatched this messenger with such haste was that I wished him to arrive before Oxenstierna's representative, since I feared that the latter might introduce into the agreement with Wallenstein matters prejudicial to His Majesty the King of France and to the Catholic religion. I thought it important to send my colleague to Count Kinsky with full powers, without of course intimating that I was aware of his having approached the Swedish Chancellor as well."

Feuquières closed his letter by requesting instructions as to how he was to treat the rebels in the event of an agreement being concluded.

By this time it was quite evident that Wallenstein had no intention of sparing the Emperor's person.

Although Feuquières responded to the Condottiere's openings, Oxenstierna did not. His view remained the same— that Wallenstein merely wished to make use of Sweden in order to gain power in the Empire, and that once he had it he would use it to drive the Swedes from Imperial soil. The French, on the other hand, hoped to derive great benefit from Wallenstein's desertion, for not only would the Austrian Hapsburgs be greatly embarrassed by this event, but a general disorder would inevitably follow which would give the advantage to France. Wallenstein's initial approach to his officers proved successful. Trčka, Kinsky and Ilow had undertaken to win over the corps of officers and on January 12, 1634, Wallenstein's leading officers, including Octavio Piccolomini, the Knight of Malta, signed the "oath of Pilsen." But before the day was out Piccolomini had called on the Emperor's nephews, Francis and Matthias de' Medici, who were then in Pilsen, and informed them of all that had happened. The deep loyalty his officers felt for the person of their commander was a fact to be reckoned with.

Piccolomini and Wallenstein

Octavio Piccolomini was one of those younger sons of great Italian families who in the seventeenth century could seek their fortune only in military service, and in this field they often reached great heights within a short time. Like most of these men, Piccolomini began by serving in the ranks, first in the Spanish army, then the Tuscan. At the battle of the White Hill he was already fighting for the Emperor.

In assessing Piccolomini's conduct, it is important to realize that this Italian gave some thought to the project once envisioned by Charles V: the Holy Roman Empire was to be extended throughout the whole of Christendom through the collaboration of Spain and Germany. This was one of the great developments that might conceivably have been realized in that era. Under the first Hapsburg ruler in Spain this universal policy had been completely identified with the concept of Imperial power, both strategically and politically.

Naturally Piccolomini's conduct cannot be explained entirely on the basis of such noble and disinterested aspirations: a great deal of personal ambition and resentment was also involved. But his loyalty to the Emperor was a mitigating factor.

Wallenstein's army had long been a state within the State, and his objectives were diametrically opposed to Piccolomini's. Wallenstein wanted a united Germany, a one-nation State, based on religious equality and with strong centralization. This was one of the reasons why he sought to displace the ruling house, which was bound to the twin concepts of the Counter-Reformation and a supra-national federation. Wallenstein's blind faith in Piccolomini, the fact that he constantly employed him on important secret missions and initiated him into every one of his dark plots, was based on his own astrological calculations, which were corroborated by Seni's. It so happens that Wallenstein favoured all the Piccolominis; in the case of Octavio, he went so far as to grant him, wherever he set up his quarters, "double allowances." Since Piccolomini exploited the situation and mercilessly oppressed and bled the population, he was soon involved in unpleasant incidents. The great disappointment of his military career came when his

Danish colleague and rival, Holk, who was of the same age, was given the supreme command and Piccolomini was obliged to serve under him. This kind of thing produced in Piccolomini the hidden canker of hatred that prompted him to report the general's plans to Vienna.

It has been established that most past assessments of the influence exercised by Jesuit Court intrigue in connection with Wallenstein's tragic end were exaggerated. Certainly Father Lamormaini, who was Ferdinand II's confessor, was Wallenstein's opponent. In the light of the latest research, however, he seems to have been a just and moderate man. It has also been established that Father Johann Weingartner, the other representative of the Society of Jesus at the Viennese Court, was not the author of the pamphlet *Alberti Fridlandi perduellionis chaos sive ingrati animi abyssus*. The probable author of this vicious attack on Wallenstein now seems to have been an official of the Bohemian Chamber in Prague, Johann Putz von Adlersthurn.

Both Pekař, the great Czech authority on Wallenstein, and Heinrich von Srbik stress the fact that the first crucial decision to proceed against Wallenstein was made "with the approval of all the principal partisans" of the Duke, while neither the Spanish ambassador nor Ferdinand's Jesuit confessor, Father Lamormaini, had any knowledge of it.

Meanwhile, after negotiating for months with Saxony, Brandenburg and the members of the Heilbronn League, it seemed that Wallenstein had finally opted in favour of France.

The oaths his commanders had taken at Pilsen, however, had not effectively bound them to his person. Piccolomini's reports produced an instantaneous reaction in Vienna. In an Imperial decree of February 22, 1634, Wallenstein was branded as a traitor and orders were given for his capture, dead or alive. As soon as this decree was promulgated, most of the General's troops deserted him. Accompanied by only a few faithful followers, Wallenstein, who had long been ailing and had at first intended to make for Prague, fled towards the territory then occupied by Bernhard of Saxe-Weimar. But in Eger, on February 25th, he was struck down by the Irish Captain Devereux, after his companions Trčka, Ilow and Kinsky, who had remained loyal to the end, had all been murdered at a banquet.

Friedrich Schiller rightly observed that it was Wallenstein's misfortune that his enemies outlived him to write his history.

The news of Wallenstein's death came as a shock to Richelieu, who had set high hopes on his revolt. On this occasion, Louis XIII's reaction differed considerably from that of his First Minister. In the interests of his foreign policy, he had agreed to Richelieu's proposal that France should support the rebels, but as a monarch the whole affair went against his grain, and when Feuquières's courier brought the news of Wallenstein's death, he said in the presence of his Court: "I wish the same fate for all who betray their sovereign."

The Cardinal was in Rueil at the time, so when the news reached him it was accompanied by a report of his master's reaction, which prompted him to exclaim that the King would have done better not to have spoken so openly. He must have thought of his own situation and its dangers.

Richelieu and Oxenstierna

What really disturbed Richelieu, however, was the realization that, in his preoccupation with the Wallenstein conspiracy and its probable consequences he had been neglecting his diplomacy vis-à-vis Sweden. Not that he had given up his policy of using his Scandinavian ally against the house of Hapsburg, but he had hoped that after Wallenstein's seizure of power in Bohemia, he could bring Sweden to a point where she would be obliged to ask for greater French help and so gradually become dependent on France. Oxenstierna, however, had foreseen this danger. He had been convinced that Wallenstein's revolt would prejudice his own position as leader and the King of France and the Bohemian rebel might well settle the fate of the Hapsburgs between them. This prompted him to try to convince his German allies that Wallenstein's proposals were no more than a military stratagem. For Oxenstierna, Wallenstein's death came as a great relief. France and the French diplomats meanwhile endeavoured to erase all signs of their erstwhile negotiations with that sinister figure.

The Elector of Saxony, for his part, had hoped to gain from Wallenstein's desertion, since Wallenstein's success would have undermined Oxenstierna's position. If he had been able to take his place as leader of the Heilbronn League, he would readily have lent his support to the revolt. Brandenburg's greater willingness to enter into an alliance with Sweden seemed to hinge entirely on George William's wish to marry his son to Gustavus Adolphus' daughter, Christina, who was then still a child. And in point of fact, once the Elector had been given the cold shoulder in Sweden, he soon dissociated himself from the Heilbronn group. At this juncture the Kings of Denmark and Poland were also giving Richelieu cause for alarm, for the Emperor's emissaries, who were trying to counteract the pro-French movement within the Empire by raising hopes of a general peace conference, were being aided in their task by these two monarchs. The Imperialist plan was that the King of Denmark should join with the Electors of Saxony and Brandenburg and with the princes and estates of Lower Saxony, thus creating a third force, which could then press for moderation and compromise and eventually prevail upon Sweden and the Heilbronn League to establish a détente with the Emperor. Denmark had not forgotten that in the twenties she had been urged by French emissaries to go to war and had then been abandoned to her fate. Following the Wallenstein episode, Richelieu immediately worked out a new policy based on Feuquières's reports. His representative in Germany would henceforth concern himself primarily with the Scandinavian states.

Feuquières in Frankfort

Feuquières, however, remained in Frankfort. The envoy to the Scandinavian Courts was Claude de Mesmes, Comte d'Avaux, a Secretary of State who had found particular favour with both Richelieu and Father Joseph because of the great skill he had shown in representing French interests in Rome and Venice.

As for Feuquières, he was still intent on getting his charges to act in concord and at the same time restricting Swedish influence. He continued his rounds to the Elector of Saxony, the Districts of Lower Saxony and Westphalia, the Landgrave of Hesse-Cassel, the Duke of Zweibrücken, the Count of Simmern and the rulers of Wetterau. And time and again he wrote to Bouthillier or Father Joseph: "A little ready money would do more good than all our eloquence."

His policy was evidently felt to be very costly, for at that time France had yet to complete her rearmament programme. Feuquières's greatest problem was keeping Oxenstierna within bounds, for the Swedish Chancellor was an extremely accomplished diplomat, skilful, enterprising and wary. Feuquières was never able to catch him off his guard and he never allowed himself to be trapped. His self-assurance had grown with his prestige and he had become far less amenable than in the past. Now that the French, far from having a hold over him, were obliged to seek his co-operation, he dealt with them accordingly. Feuquières wrote of him: "His moods grow daily more arrogant and insulting."

From statements such as this, it would seem that the Chancellor was determined to safeguard both the interests of the Swedish throne and his own personal position. The situation was complex. Without French help the Swedes could not hope to maintain themselves in Germany, but without the Swedes Richelieu would be unable to attain his objectives. If Oxenstierna were to be deposed as leader of the German Protestants, his place would be taken by the Elector of

Saxony, who would instantly seek a settlement with the Emperor.

Richelieu's plans were not restricted to weakening the house of Austria. He also sought to expand into the Netherlands, to strengthen Alsace and take possession of Philippsburg, thus encircling Lorraine and establishing a wider front from which to advance into Germany. If France were to enter the war, she would need to control the strongholds along her eastern frontier, which at that time were nearly all in Swedish hands. The Swedes for their part had no interest whatsoever in allowing France to acquire excessive power in Germany. Richelieu's and consequently Feuquières's primary objective was the acquisition of Philippsburg from the Swedes. Feuquières demanded this stronghold as a just guarantee for the enormous sums France had been giving her ally ever since Bärwalde. The Landgrave of Hesse, who was particularly responsive to French money, supported Feuquières in his demand and eventually succeeded in persuading Oxenstierna to give way on this point, although the latter still stipulated that the decision must be approved by the Assembly of Princes in Frankfort. Once Oxenstierna had acquainted himself with the views of the German princes at the Assembly, he approached Feuquières and tried to settle some of their recent differences. He asked him to use his influence—chiefly with the Assembly—to ensure that the massive recruiting campaigns which had long been discussed were at last put into effect. As for Philippsburg, Oxenstierna gave a half-promise— which was not enough for Feuquières. Still aided by the Landgrave of Hesse, he worked on every single one of the delegates. Then, on June 21st, he appeared before the Assembly in person and openly asked that Philippsburg be entrusted to the King of France as a depositum. He again recalled the many services of the French king to the German Protestants. He gave assurances that his master had no intention of extending his kingdom beyond the Rhine and that he regarded Philippsburg as a purely temporary

435

security. In his reply to Feuquières's speech, Oxenstierna tried to get the Philippsburg issue deferred. The Assembly then asked Feuquières to submit his request in writing, which he did. The German princes, however, gradually became a little uneasy: the King of France was already in possession of Lorraine, Zabern and other strongholds. At this point Oxenstierna suddenly declared that the Germans must also recompense the Swedes for their great achievements on behalf of the German Liberties and he demanded Pomerania and the best harbours on the Baltic. As he claimed these Imperial territories for Sweden, Oxenstierna's hopes that he himself might yet become the Elector of Mainz rose again, just as Richelieu's hopes of being appointed coadjutor of Trier and Speyer had risen when he was establishing French power in Alsace. In this connection Richelieu's plans for having Louis XIII elected Holy Roman Emperor were not to be denied. The Elector of Brandenburg appears to have given them his approval. Feuquières reported:

"The Cardinal was planning to have Louis XIII crowned Emperor in order that he himself might attain his objective in Trier and Speyer. These plans were to have been put into effect in the event of Ferdinand II's failing to obtain his son's election as King of the Romans. Richelieu had already prevented his election at Regensburg through the intervention of Father Joseph. "

Feuquières also reported that George William of Brandenburg had told him he was prepared to guarantee that nobody would be elected King of the Romans during the lifetime of the present Emperor. According to the provisions of the Imperial constitution the election could only be won by a candidate who had the unanimous support of the six Electors, and George William promised to dissent.

The most effective opponent of French policy at Frankfort was the Elector of Saxony. He wanted the delegates first to insist on the reinstatement of the children of the Count

Palatine in all their hereditary rights and privileges, and then to do all within their power to prevent the Imperial Crown from becoming the hereditary privilege of the Hapsburgs. At the same time he continued to seek a settlement with the Emperor. He wanted to see both the French and the Swedes driven from German soil, since he was convinced that all they really aimed at was to divide the German territories between themselves.

Meanwhile, French influence was increasing, partly because of the dissatisfaction felt by the members of the League with their Swedish leader and partly because of their growing need for French money. It was widely held that the acceptance of an annual stipend from the French did nothing to prejudice their alliance with Sweden. Among those accepting such gifts the most important were William, Landgrave of Hesse-Cassel and William, Duke of Saxe-Weimar, but many other League members did the same, including members of the advisory council. Some princes—George, Duke of Lüneburg, for example—opposed Oxenstierna's authority, and others, tired of the whole undertaking, gave up their commissions. The Duke of Weimar's envoy informed the Swedes that if they did not comply with his master's wishes, he would cede the most important positions occupied by his forces to the French and then place himself under French protection. John George, the Elector of Saxony, threatened to join with the Upper and Lower Saxon Districts and form a third force.

On September 8th Feuquières reported to Bouthillier:

"Duke Bernhard of Saxe-Weimar and Marshal Horn, who have been joined by the forces under the command of Count Otto Ludwig and Count Kratz, are now able to offer resistance to the King of Hungary [Ferdinand III]. The latter's troops, reinforced by those of the Cardinal-Infante, are encamped before Nördlingen. The allies are trying to provoke the enemy into giving battle, while he is determined to remain in his strong position, where it is thought he is waiting to learn the terms of the treaty of Pirna. It is to be feared that because of the difficulties over Pomerania, Brandenburg might also join the enemy."

Father Joseph expressed similar fears, drawing special attention to the collaboration between England and Saxony.

Oxenstierna had left Frankfort and gone first to Mainz and then to Wiesbaden to take the cure, while his agents continued to work on both the princes and the estates. Feuquières had not given up in the Philippsburg affair and in the end, despite the covert resistance of Sweden and the open opposition of the Elector of Saxony, he reached his goal. On August 26th a treaty was signed; France had had her way and all that the dissenting minority had managed to do was to have its position recorded in the agreement. The provisions were precise: Philippsburg was to be handed over to France until such time as a general peace was concluded; France was not to erect a fortress for the defence of the town, and the Governor, to be appointed by the King of France, must be a German.

After achieving this tangible success, Feuquières travelled to Speyer to meet Rhinegrave Salm and the Chancellor of Württemberg, Löffler, the two men appointed by the Frankfort Assembly to effect the transfer of Philippsburg. But they were not there. The Rhinegrave had stayed in Strassburg and Löffler was with his master, the Duke of Württemberg. By the time they arrived, a new event had thrown everything into confusion again.

The Battle of Nördlingen

It was now the Imperialists' turn. They had already taken Regensburg from the Swedes and, encouraged by this success, had pressed forward into the Swabian District and besieged Nördlingen, which was held by a small Swedish force. Although the Regensburg garrison had put up a brave defence, the Swedes had failed to relieve it, and they failed again at Nördlingen.

Bernhard of Saxe-Weimar, who had already proved to be difficult in Gustavus Adolphus' day, was greatly angered when he failed to obtain the post of Commander-in-Chief. It was said that Bernhard was out to break the Swedish Chancellor's power. Such was the state of affairs on August 9, 1634, when Bernhard broke camp on the banks of the Danube and, reinforced by the troops of the Margrave of Baden-Durlach and the Duke of Württemberg, marched for Aalen via Heidenheim, burning and laying waste wherever he passed and killing or taking prisoner large numbers of Imperialist soldiers. On August 11th he occupied the heights between Bopfingen and Dinkelsbühl, where he was joined by Marshal Horn, who had crossed the Danube at Günzburg. They quickly fortified their camp, which had been set up around a wooded height and would thus afford them cover for an approach to Nördlingen. But no sooner had the work been completed than Duke Bernhard urged an assault on the enemy camp. Horn opposed this plan and suggested instead that they put reinforcements into Nördlingen. To this Bernhard agreed and, with the whole army covering the operation, two hundred musketeers were successfully transferred to the town, whose commandant was promised that the siege would be raised within six days. This done, Bernhard fought his way back to the heights of Bopfingen, where he remained for ten days, unable to decide whether to change his position or risk everything on an attack. By then conditions in Nördlingen were desperate. The few messengers who succeeded in penetrating the enemy lines reported that unless action were taken at once the town was lost. Then beacons were lit on the towers of Nördlingen, the prearranged signal indicating that without immediate help the garrison would have to yield. Duke Bernhard wanted to attack before the King of Hungary's army was reinforced by the whole of the Cardinal-Infante's force and by von Werth's cavalry. But again Horn deferred the engagement, arguing that they must first await reinforcements from the Rhinegrave, who was on his way from Strassburg, and the troops commanded by Count Kratz. While these debates were going on, Starhemberg, a marshal of the Imperial Court, appeared in Bernhard's camp on behalf of the King of Hungary. He offered peace talks and told Bernhard that Ferdinand himself wished to speak with him. But Bernhard regarded this move as a stratagem designed to gain time and is said to have told Starhemberg that the papists were not to be trusted, since they always acted on the precept of "no faith with heretics." Bernhard then addressed his officers: "We have lost Regensburg, the banks of the Danube are swarming with the enemy, the Rhine and the Main are threatened, and if we do not save the beleaguered town of Nördlingen we shall become suspect in the eyes of the [Protestant] estates and this will be the end of our renown." But Horn and several other officers countered: "The enemy, who was already superior to us, has now received fresh heart from the arrival of the Cardinal-Infante. If we should be defeated, there is no new army to carry on the resistance; we must at least await the arrival of Count Kratz."

On the 25th, when Kratz appeared at the head of his troops together with several regiments belonging to the Rhinegrave, Bernhard was no longer to be restrained. "We must attack," he said, "I have promised help to the beleaguered town and I must keep my word as a prince." Horn still hesitated, but by then most of the officers were on Bernhard's side. According to an eyewitness, the soldiers in Nördlingen had had nothing to eat for the past five days. A compromise solution was agreed upon. The army was to approach Nördlingen along the road from Ulm and to take the Arnsberg, which commanded the approach to the town, and was to hold this until the arrival of the Rhinegrave, who was expected in two days.

The Imperial siege army, commanded by the Emperor's son, the future Ferdinand III, was Wallenstein's old army and was led by his seasoned officers.

In the events leading up to Nördlingen, Maximilian I of Bavaria had again been threatened, but on this occasion Wallenstein was no longer there to block assistance. Young Ferdinand of Hapsburg had come with all speed to join him. He took Regensburg, then Donauwörth and immediately proceeded to lay siege to Nördlingen, where he was joined by Don Fernando, the Cardinal-Infante, who was leading his army from Italy to the Spanish Netherlands, and by the troops of Charles IV, Duke of Lorraine. The combined armies numbered between forty-five and fifty thousand men. Marshal Horn and Bernhard of Saxe-Weimar commanded a force of only thirty-six thousand.

Possibly the best report of the battle of Nördlingen, one of the turning points of the Thirty Years War, is that given by Bernhard Röse in his biography of Bernhard of Saxe-Weimar. The following excerpt is taken from his work, which was written in the eighteen-twenties:

"At daybreak on August 27th prayers were said in the allied army and the battle-cry *'Gott mit uns!'* proclaimed. The engagement began on the right wing under unpropitious auspices. Horn had ridden up the hill to observe the enemy positions, when Lieutenant Colonel von Witzleben, acting against orders, opened the battle with a cavalry charge. This changed the plan of attack. Witzleben, harassed by the enemy's superior forces, was driven between the entrenched positions of the enemy infantry and was exposed to both cannon and musket fire. Despite the fact that the Field Marshal came to his aid with several squadrons of horse, he was forced to withdraw with the loss of two standards to the foot of the hill, where the infantry, which had been hindered by the undergrowth and by a ravine across their path, had at last arrived. The foot soldiers were then led against the enemy earthworks, which had been thrown up in a clover-leaf pattern and were hard to scale. Two brigades were ordered to drive the enemy from the first line of entrenchments. After a fierce and bloody battle they

441

succeeded and captured two standards, two flags and three demicannon. Unfortunately, the advancing troops fell into disorder, which became universal when the enemy's powder store, or a mine, exploded. A thousand men were blown to pieces and the rest broke and fled, while the cavalry, which had roamed too far afield following their first disastrous action, were not at hand to give support. The Spaniards retook their position, against which Major General von Vitzthum unsuccessfully led fresh brigades. Meanwhile on the left flank Bernhard, who was separated from the troops on the right by a wood but had more favourable terrain, was fighting valiantly, and his cavalry, who were led by Taupadell, would not have been driven back had their line not been too greatly extended. But the power of the cannon, which were drawn up in front of the wood, and the courage of the infantry made good this error and sent the enemy back behind their fortifications, so that the Duke was able to send two regiments under the command of young Thurn to help the Field Marshal. But a perverse fortune led these soldiers too far to the left of the Spanish fortifications. There they encountered a superior enemy force, whose attention was now drawn to the higher side of the wood, which had not yet been occupied. Horn was himself obliged to send support regiments, composed of fatigued troops, to prevent the enemy from occupying the wood and thus cutting him off from the Duke. This meant that the massed forces he needed to storm the fortifications were split. And even then Thurn was forced to withdraw after seventeen unsuccessful attacks, leaving his opponents in possession of the wood. Fearful lest he be attacked from both the flank and the rear, Horn then urged that the army should retreat. The Duke, upon being advised of this, wanted to fight on till evening, but was obliged to yield to the repeated requests of his aide.

"It was not yet mid-day when he gave orders for his infantry to occupy the whole of the wood and his cavalry to hold the field until such time as Horn had gained a firm footing on the hill at Hirnheim. But the enemy, observing this new move, threw the major part of their forces into an attack on Saxe-Weimar's men, who were thrown into disarray by the grape-shot from masked batteries. Bernhard seized the standard of his own personal regiment in order to halt his men and call them to order and then sent his adjutant general to attack the enemy's flank with several squadrons of cavalry. After four bloody assaults Johann von Werth, aided by the heavy cannon, drove them back into the valley before the Field Marshal had been able to reach the appointed position. The result was such a frenzied flight that Duke Charles of Lorraine is said to have snatched the standard from the hands of the Duke of Saxe-Weimar. The great throng of fleeing men then converged on the Field Marshal's troops, who were still executing their withdrawal manœuvre. All attempts to restore order at Hirnheim were in vain, and when the Croats made to attack yet again, Bernhard advised his cavalry to make good their escape. In the general mêlée and carnage, his horse was shot from under him, and he would most probably have shared the fate of Horn and Kratz, who were taken prisoner, if a captain of Taupadell's regiment had not given him his horse. With a superficial neck wound he fled for Kannstadt and was so hard pressed by the Croats that there was hardly time for him to eat as much as an egg to appease his hunger. It is a point worth noting that, according to the reports sent to the French Court by the Marquis of Feuquières, even several days after the battle the Duke still refused to believe that Horn had been captured and held that the Field Marshal had fled to Ulm, where he was gathering the scattered troops about him.

"The Duke had sent his adjutant general, Christoph von der Grün, to Neresheim to save the baggage. But he had scarcely arrived when Isolani appeared with his Croats. Grün fought from noon till evening, when he was obliged to make terms and yield. Before doing so, however, he had burnt the Duke's secret papers—an irreplaceable loss—and distributed his master's valuables amongst the most loyal of his officers and servants to prevent them from falling into the enemy's hands. He himself kept two large diamonds. But he was not able to prevent the enemy from taking the gold and silver vessels, twelve new saddles with embroidered trimming and a like number of suits, which had only just arrived from the Netherlands, a gilded sword hilt set in diamonds and an equally valuable sword-belt, a golden chain and a costly hat-band and finally a piece of gold of the size and thickness of a man's hand which was inlaid with precious stones. The Croats also took all the money that was there, so that, apart from the two diamonds which Grün presented to him in Frankfort after his release, nothing was saved for the Duke. Four thousand waggons, three hundred bugles and standards, the whole of the artillery, together with twelve hundred horses and six thousand prisoners, made up the victor's booty. His losses comprised only twelve hundred dead, while the Swedish dead numbered between six and eight thousand. Almost the entire Swedish infantry had been destroyed. The fleeing cavalry met the Rhinegrave at Göppingen, and he drove back their pursuers."

Saxe-Weimar, although wounded, had escaped. But Horn, many high officers and fully three thousand men had been captured, Nördlingen had capitulated, and the Duke of Württemberg had fled to Alsace. Meanwhile, by September 21, 1634, King Ferdinand of Hungary had entered Stuttgart, his cavalry pressing on as far as Frankfort. Würzburg was reconquered, the Electors of Mainz and Cologne placed themselves under the Emperor's protection, and the Swedes were left in possession of only Heidelberg and Mannheim. The real architect of these victories was Gallas. Their most important consequence was that the Elector of Saxony, deeply concerned for the safety of his territories, decided on May 30, 1635, to become a party to the peace of Prague. The following year, at the Electoral Diet at Regensburg, Ferdinand

II succeeded in having his son, the King of Hungary, elected as his successor to the Imperial throne.

Meanwhile the Imperialists were approaching Philippsburg, still under the command of the Swedish Governor Schmitberg. He immediately sent a messenger to Feuquières, requesting speedy help. Feuquières met him at five o'clock the next day on the farther bank of the Rhine, having first ordered a French officer named La Bloquerie to appear with an infantry regiment and a squadron of cavalry three miles from the meeting-place. At the same time he requested La Force to set his army in motion. He also urged Rhinegrave Otto von Salm and Chancellor Löffler to come with all speed. Feuquières then required the Swedish Governor to transfer the stronghold to him in accordance with the Frankfort resolutions. When the Governor told him that he had not been notified of these resolutions and that if he were simply to hand over the town it would cost him his head, Feuquières suggested a compromise solution: French troops under La Bloquerie would take up position in a redoubt between Philippsburg and the Rhine. It was vital that this redoubt be strongly held, for if the Imperialists got control of it, the defence of Philippsburg would be difficult. At this point the auxiliaries called by Feuquières arrived and behind them the advance guard of the French army could be seen approaching.

The impressive bearing of the French force and the desire to avoid an open conflict with France persuaded the victors of Nördlingen to give up their plan to attack Philippsburg. They turned away and marched off into Upper Alsace. Shortly afterwards the Duke of Württemberg, Rhinegrave Otto and finally Chancellor Löffler arrived in Philippsburg, bringing from Frankfort the document authorizing the French to take control of the stronghold. Feuquières entered Philippsburg with the Duke of Württemberg, who, as the new Governor and lieutenant general, took possession of the town and its lands on behalf of Louis XIII. Feuquières administered the oath to the German prince and on the same day received an

oath of loyalty from Arnauld, the commander of the cara-
biniers, whom Louis had appointed commandant of the
fortress under the Duke of Württemberg.

The transfer of Philippsburg was not the only advantage
France derived from the events following Nördlingen.
Shortly thereafter Louis XIII also took possession of Kolmar
and Schlettstadt and other strongholds that had previously
been held by the allied armies.

Like the battle of the White Hill, the battle of Nördlingen
had great and far-reaching consequences. Thanks partly to
Spanish help, the Emperor seemed once again to occupy an
unassailable position.

Sweden's defeat had caused great consternation among her
Protestant allies. They found themselves faced with the choice
of capitulating or clinging to the untried power of France.
A peace treaty between the Emperor and Sweden had become
a genuine possibility, and the whole system of alliances
created by Richelieu was threatening to disintegrate. For a
while Chancellor Oxenstierna became a humble petitioner.
In a letter to d'Avaux, Feuquières said that Oxenstierna had
told him he was obliged to place his entire trust in the King
of France. Had the Emperor and his son, had His Catholic
Majesty's brother the Cardinal-Infante, had Gaston d'Orléans,
had Gallas laboured to give France the victory?

For Richelieu the Swedish threat no longer existed and the
action he had considered taking against Oxenstierna in the
Chancellor's own country was no longer necessary. The
German Protestants were already thinking of replacing
Oxenstierna in the supreme command. In the end it was
Feuquières who took Oxenstierna's part.

In his despondency Oxenstierna was unable to conceal his
annoyance that France should have occupied a large part of
Alsace, a fact we shall discuss in Volume III in connection
with Charles IV of Lorraine and Bernhard of Saxe-Weimar.

On September 19, 1634, Feuquières reported that the

German allies were urgently demanding France's entry into the war, although they were by no means united among themselves and actually took pleasure in the Swedes' discomfiture. To all enquiries concerning French participation in the war, Feuquières replied that he was not authorized to deal with such matters.

In an attempt to get a tighter grip on the allies, Feuquières sought to persuade them to form a new alliance, one that would be open to all the lands of the Empire. The ostensible purpose would be to work out favourable conditions for a general peace. Oxenstierna was also urging those North German Protestants who were not members of the Heilbronn League to join their co-religionists. His task was not made easier by the fact that the members of the League themselves were none too enthusiastic about their Swedish alliance. And Saxony, which was still the leading Protestant power in Germany, remained independent.

The Peace of Prague

The goal of the peace moves of both the Emperor and the King of Denmark was an agreement between the opposing factions within the Empire, which would make it possible to approach Sweden and France with a united front. It goes without saying that for the Swedes and the French it was imperative that any such unity in the Empire be undermined. Saxony had long been negotiating with Vienna. Brandenburg, on the other hand, had at first been strongly opposed to Saxon policy and was quite prepared to accept still closer ties with Sweden. Subsequently, however, she insisted that Sweden state her ultimate aims in the German war, and when it became apparent that Oxenstierna intended to claim Pomerania, Brandenburg also abandoned the Protestant cause, followed by a large number of her dependencies. From that moment she too regarded Sweden as an intruder in the Empire and a transgressor of its rights.

Even before the battle of Nördlingen there had been indications of a revival of national feeling in the German territories. This trend was strengthened by the Imperialist victory, which gave the Hapsburgs control of the whole of southern Germany, and also by the preparatory negotiations conducted by the Saxons at Leitmeritz and later at Pirna. In fact, the Saxons had been so thorough in their endeavours for German unity that John George was obliged to withdraw his original stipulation that Sweden be invited to the peace conference. By November 24, 1634, a peace treaty had been drafted at Pirna and the negotiators had separated to obtain final instructions from their principals. In April 1635 they met again—this time in Prague, a choice previously eschewed in deference to Sweden. The provisional nature of the resolutions agreed upon at Prague, with their many built-in safeguards, were indicative of the extremely difficult negotiations. Vienna tried in every possible way to force Saxony to conclude a separate peace, but Saxony was determined to keep her position as leader of the German Protestants, and it proved beyond the powers of Imperial diplomacy to make the Elector abandon his role of mediator; so the outcome of the negotiations in Prague was a general agreement between the German territories.

The Emperor and the Elector of Saxony were the main negotiators and the principal signatories to the peace of Prague, which was concluded on May 30, 1635. Lower and Upper Lusatia, together with a number of bailiwicks taken from Magdeburg, were transferred to the Elector. Prince August of Saxony received the archbishopric of Magdeburg and Archduke Leopold William the principality of Halberstadt. The affairs of Bohemia and the County Palatine were not dealt with in the treaty but were left to the decision of the Emperor. No general amnesty was granted. Württemberg, Baden and the North German estates that were allied to Sweden were excluded from the peace. The remaining estates of the Empire, however, were invited to participate. The peace of Passau and the Religious Peace of Augsburg were ratified. The Edict of Restitution was suspended for forty years, at the end of which time the two sides were to try to reach an amicable agreement. The Swedes were offered three and a half million talers to withdraw from Germany. In the event of their rejecting this offer, it was agreed that the Emperor and the Elector of Saxony should join forces to drive both the Swedes and the French from the Empire.

On July 12th all the German estates not expressly excluded by the provisions of the treaty were invited to join the peace. Despite the annoyance shown by the Protestant estates at the Elector of Saxony's arbitrary action, Brandenburg, Brunswick-Lüneburg, Mecklenburg, Anhalt and many Imperial cities decided to accept, although their decision was largely prompted by the provision stipulating that all who refused to join would be regarded as enemies of the Empire.

The Elector of Saxony was able to obtain one concession— a small one—from the Emperor: he was authorized to approach the Swedes before the outbreak of further hostilities in an attempt to reach a settlement with them. And in point of fact, despite the undertaking he had given the French that he would not conclude a separate peace, Oxenstierna responded to the Saxon initiative. But he played for time, for he had no wish to negotiate at a time when he could expect only the most unfavourable terms. The possibility of a financial settlement, with mortgages as security on the Baltic coast, was discussed. Oxenstierna had said in 1634 that he intended to keep Pomerania for Sweden, and on this he refused to yield. He demanded compensation for Sweden's contribution to the war and also insisted that an amnesty be granted to the German estates excluded from the peace of Prague.

In September the armistice between Sweden and Poland was renewed in Stuhmsdorf, and this, together with the Swedish victory at Dömitz, strengthened Oxenstierna's hand. By November, when talks between Sweden and Saxony were renewed through the agency of Duke Adolph Frederick of

P   449

Mecklenburg-Schwerin, it was agreed that a separate peace should be concluded between Sweden and the Emperor. But, as we shall see, this thread soon broke.

In his desire to transform the Holy Roman Empire into a united nation, Wallenstein stood for one of the fundamental trends of his age. The same goal was pursued, if in a very different manner, by the Austrian branch of the house of Hapsburg. After the Imperialist victory at Nördlingen it seemed the moment had come when, despite religious differences, the creation of a German nation under a single monarch might be possible. But this development was opposed not only by the French, but also by the Germans themselves, whose deeper instincts were still opting for separatist issues and whose age-old sense of autonomy had not yet been exhausted. Soon it would be too late, for within thirteen years regional organization based on provincial diets, a structure carefully and tenaciously advocated by Richelieu, was officially adopted, and Germany was divided up into innumerable principalities for a long time to come.

BIBLIOGRAPHY

CHAPTER I: A GOVERNMENT PROGRAMME

Lettres, instructions diplomatiques et papiers d'état du Cardinal de Richelieu, recueillis et publiés par M. Avenel, 8 vols. Paris, 1853–1877.

Collection de documents inédits sur l'histoire de France, publiés par les soins du Ministère de l'Instruction Publique. Mélanges Historiques. Choix de Documents. Vol. 3: *Maximes d'Etat et fragments politiques du Cardinal de Richelieu,* Paris, 1880.

Testament Politique du Cardinal de Richelieu, published by Louis André, Paris, 1947.

Mémoires du Cardinal de Richelieu, Edition Petitot, 11 vols. Paris, 1821–1823.

Mémoires du Cardinal de Richelieu, published by the Société de l'Histoire de France, 10 vols. Paris, 1908–1931.

NOTE: The above are all basic sources referred to throughout the text.

CHAPTER II: THE NAVY AND NAVAL HARBOURS

d'Avenel, Vicomte G.: *Richelieu et la monarchie absolue*, Vol. 3, Paris, 1887.

Boiteux, L.-A.: *Richelieu—grand maître de la navigation et du commerce de France*, Paris, 1955.

Caillet, J.: *L'administration en France sous le ministère du Cardinal de Richelieu*, Paris, 1863.

Charliat, P.: *Trois siècles d'économie maritime*, Paris, 1931.

de Chastenet, J.: *Histoire de l'Amirauté de France* (thesis), Paris, 1906.

Clamageran, J.-J.: *Histoire de l'impôt en France*, 2 vols. Paris, 1868.

David, Jean-Marc: *L'Amirauté de Provence et des mers du levant* (thesis), Marseille, 1942.

Gouron, Marcel: *L'Amirauté de Guienne depuis le premier amiral anglais en Guienne jusqu'à la Révolution* (thesis), Paris, 1938.

Hanotaux, Gabriel and le Duc de La Force: *Histoire du Cardinal de Richelieu*, Vol. 4, Paris, 1935.

Hauser, Henri: *La pensée et l'action économique du Cardinal de Richelieu*, Paris, 1944.

Jouan, René: *Histoire de la marine française*, Paris, 1950.

La Bruyère, René: *Maillé-Brézé Général des Galères*, Paris, 1945.

La Clère, Julien: *Glossaire des termes de marine*, Paris, 1960.

Lacour-Gayet, G.: *La marine militaire française sous les règnes de Louis XIII et de Louis XIV*, Paris, 1911.

Laird Cloves, W.: *The Royal Navy—A History*, Vols. 1 and 2, Boston and London, 1897, 1898.

Le Hénaff, Armand: *Etude sur l'organisation de la marine* (thesis), Paris, 1913.

Masson, M. P.: *"Les galères de France"* in: *Annales de la Faculté des lettres d'Aix*, Vol. 20, 1937, Fascicles 1 and 2, Aix-en-Provence, 1938.

Mémoires de Henry, dernier Duc de Mont-Morency, Paris, 1666.

Morini-Comby, Jean: *Mercantilisme et protectionnisme* (thesis), Paris, 1930.

Recueil de pièces concernant la compétence de l'amirauté de France, Paris, 1759.

de La Roncière, Charles: *Histoire de la marine française*, Vols. 4 and 5, Paris, 1923, 1934.

Tramond, Joannès: *Manuel d'Histoire Maritime de la France*, Paris, 1916.

CHAPTER III: THE MONTMORENCYS

d'Avenel, Vicomte G.: *Richelieu et la monarchie absolue*, Vol. 2, Paris, 1884.

Bailly, Auguste: *Richelieu*, Paris, 1934.

Barozzi, Nicolò and Guglielmo Berchet: *Relazioni degli Stati Europei*, Series 2: *Francia*, Vol. 1, Venice, 1857.

Batiffol, Louis: *Richelieu et le Roi Louis XIII*, Paris, 1934.

Burckhardt, Jacob: *Historische Fragmente*, from the posthumous papers, edited by Emil Dürr, with a preface by Werner Kaegi, Stuttgart, 1957. *Judgments on History and Historians*, tr. by Harry Zohn, Boston and Toronto, 1958; London, 1959.

Canu, Jean: *Louis XIII et Richelieu*, Paris, 1944.

du Cros, Simon: *Histoire de la vie de Henry, dernier duc de Montmorency*, Paris, 1643.

Dethan, Gaston: *Gaston d'Orléans conspirateur et prince charmant*, Paris, 1959.

Hanotaux, Gabriel and le Duc de La Force: *Histoire du Cardinal de Richelieu*, Vols. 3 and 4, Paris, 1933, 1935.

de La Roncière, Charles: *Histoire de la marine française sous Louis XIII et de Richelieu*, Vol. 4, Paris, 1923.

Mémoires de Henry, dernier Duc de Mont-Morency, Paris, 1666.

Mercure François, 1606.

Motteville, Madame de: *Mémoires pour servir à l'histoire d'Anne d'Autriche épouse de Louis XIII roi de France*, Vol. 1, Amsterdam, 1783.

Pagès, G.: *La guerre de trente ans 1618–1648*, Paris, 1949.

Pontis, Sieur de: *Mémoires*, Vol. 2, Paris, 1676.

Tapié, Victor-L.: *La France sous Louis XIII et de Richelieu*, Paris, 1952.

Vaissette, Dom Joseph: *Histoire générale du Languedoc avec des notes et pièces justificatives*, 5 vols. Paris, 1730–1745.

Vaunois, Louis: *Vie de Louis XIII*, Paris, 1944.

CHAPTER IV: THE REPERCUSSIONS OF THE EXECUTION OF MONTMORENCY

Batiffol, Louis: *La duchesse de Chevreuse*, Paris, 1913.

Canu, Jean: *Louis XIII et Richelieu*, Paris, 1944.

Fontenay-Mareuil (François-Duval, Marquis de): *Mémoires 1609–1647*, Paris, 1886.

Hanotaux, Gabriel and le Duc de La Force: *Histoire du Cardinal de Richelieu*, Vols. 3 and 4, Paris, 1933, 1935.

de La Porte, Pierre: *Mémoires*, Geneva, 1756.

Le Vassor, Michel: *Histoire de Louis XIII*, 3 vols. Amsterdam, 1757.

Motteville, Madame de: *Mémoires* . . ., Vol. 1, Amsterdam, 1783.

Tallement des Réaux, Gédéon: *Les Historiettes*, Vols. 1 and 2, Paris, 1932.

Tapié, Victor-L.: *La France de Louis XIII et de Richelieu*, Paris, 1952.

Vaunois, Louis: *Vie de Louis XIII*, Paris, 1944.

CHAPTER V: THE CIRCUMSTANCES OF RICHELIEU'S PERSONAL LIFE

Albertini R. von: *Das politische Denken in Frankreich zur Zeit Richelieus*, Marburg, 1951.

Andreas, Willy: *"Pater Joseph"* in: *Geist und Staat*, Göttingen, Berlin and Frankfurt, 1960.

Aubéry, Antoine: *Histoire du Cardinal de Richelieu*, Paris, 1660.

d'Avenel, Vicomte G.: *Découvertes d'Histoire sociale*, Paris, 1910.

—— *Histoire économique de la propriété des salaires*, 5 vols., Paris, 1913.

—— *La noblesse française sous Richelieu*, Paris, 1914.

—— *Richelieu et la monarchie absolue*, Vol. 1, Paris, 1884.

Bailly, Auguste: *Richelieu*, Paris, 1934.

Batiffol, Louis: *Autour de Richelieu*, Paris, 1937.

—— *Richelieu et le Roi Louis XIII*, Paris, 1934.

de Beaupoil de Saint-Aulaire, Auguste-Félix-Charles: *Richelieu*, Paris, 1932.

Belloc, Hilaire: *Richelieu*, London, 1930.

Boiteux, L.-A.: *Richelieu—grand maître de la navigation et du commerce de France*, Paris, 1955.

Bossebœuf, L.-A.: *Histoire de Richelieu et des environs*, Tours, 1890.

Briquet, M.: *De l'origine et du progrès des charges de secrétaires d'état*, The Hague, 1747.

Cabanès, Docteur: *Légendes et curiosités de l'histoire*, 3rd Series, Paris, 1914.

—— *Les Condé*, Vol. 1, Paris, 1932.

Caillet, J.: *L'administration en France sous le ministère du Cardinal de Richelieu*, Paris, 1863.

Canu, Jean: *Louis XIII et Richelieu*, Paris, 1944.

Carré, Henri: *La jeunesse et la marche au pouvoir de Richelieu*, Paris, 1944.

Chénon, E.: *Histoire générale du droit français public et privé des origines à 1815*, Paris, 1929.

Chéruel, A.: *Histoire de l'administration monarchique*, Paris, 1855.

Clamageran, J.-J.: *Histoire de l'impôt en France*, Vol. 2, Paris, 1868.

Dedouvres, L.: *Politique et apôtre: Le Père Joseph de Paris*, 2 vols. Paris, 1932.

Deloche, Maximin: *La maison du Cardinal de Richelieu*, Paris, 1912.

—— *Le père du Cardinal*, Paris, 1923.

—— *Un frère de Richelieu, le cardinal Alphonse de Richelieu*, Paris, 1936.

Duchesne, A.: *Histoire des chanceliers et gardes des sceaux de France*, Paris, 1680.

Ellul, J.: *Histoire des institutions*, Paris, 1956.

Eysinga, W. J. M.: *Hugo Grotius*, with a preface by Werner Kaegi, Basel, 1952.

Fagniez, G.: *Le père Joseph et Richelieu*, 2 vols. Paris, 1894.

Fauvelet-du-Toc, A.: *Histoire des secrétaires d'Etat*, Paris, 1668.

Fay, Bernard: *Naissance d'un monstre—L'Opinion publique*, Paris, n.d. (1965).

Fidao Justiniani, J.-E.: *Richelieu précepteur de la nation française*, Paris, 1936.

Griffet, le Père: *Histoire du règne de Louis XIII, Roi de France et de Navarre*, 3 vols. Paris, 1758.

Hanotaux, Gabriel and le Duc de La Force: *Histoire du Cardinal de Richelieu*, 6 vols. Paris, 1893–1947.

Hauser, Henri: *La pensée et l'action économique du Cardinal de Richelieu*, Paris, 1944.

Holzmann, Robert: *Französische Verfassungsgeschichte von der Mitte des neunten Jahrhunderts bis zur Revolution*, Munich and Berlin, 1910.

Huxley, Aldous: *Grey Eminence*, London, 1941 and 1949.

La Bruyère, René: *Maillé-Brézé—Général des galères grand-amiral 1619–1646*, Paris, 1945.

Lafue, P.: *Le Père Joseph diplomate et capucin*, Paris, 1946.

La Valette (Louis de Nogaret, Cardinal de La Valette): *Mémoires*, Paris, 1771.

Le Clert, L.: *Notice généalogique sur les Bouthillier de Chavigny, seigneurs de Ponts-sur-Seine, de Rance et de Beaujeu*, Troyes, 1907.

Le Vassor, Michel: *Histoire du règne de Louis XIII*, 3 vols., Amsterdam, 1757.

Luçay, Comte: *Les Secrétaires d'Etat depuis leur institution jusqu'à la mort de Louis XV*, Paris, 1881.

Minot, Pierre: *Sur quelques cas de psychopathie dans la famille du Cardinal de Richelieu*, Paris, 1929.

de Morgues, Mathieu, Monsieur de St Germain: *Abrégé de la Vie du Cardinal de Richelieu*, Paris, 1643.

——— *Charitable Remonstrance de Caton Chrestien au Cardinal de Richelieu*, Antwerp, 1643.

——— *L'Ambassadeur Chimérique*, Paris, 1643.

——— *Très humble, très véritable et très importante Remonstrance au Roy*, Antwerp, 1643.

Mousnier, Roland: "*Les Règlements du Conseil du Roi*," in: *Annuaire-Bulletin de la Société de l'Histoire de France*, Paris, 1948.

Pagès, G.: *La monarchie d'ancien régime en France*, Paris, 1932.

——— "*Le Conseil du roi sous Louis XIII*," *Revue d'Histoire moderne*, Vol. 12, Paris, 1937.

——— *Les institutions monarchiques sous Louis XIII et Louis XIV*, Paris, 1937.

Pontis, Sieur de: *Mémoires*, 2 vols. Paris, 1676.

Ranum, Orest: *Richelieu and the Councillors of Louis XIII*, Oxford, 1963.

Robin, P.: *La Compagnie des secrétaires du roi*, Paris, 1933.

Rogues de Fursac, M.-J.: "*La Pathologie dans l'histoire*," *Annales Médico-psychologiques. Revue psychiatrique*, 1935, Vol. 2.

de Silhon: *Le Ministère d'Estat*, Paris, 1639.

Tallemant des Réaux, Gédéon: *Le Cardinal de Richelieu, sa famille, son favori Bois-Robert*, Paris, 1920.

——— *Les Historiettes*, 8 vols. Paris, 1932–1934.

Tapié, Victor-L.: *La France de Louis XIII et de Richelieu*, Paris, 1952.

de Vaissière, P.: *Gentilhommes campagnards de l'ancienne France*, Paris, 1904.

Zeller, G.: *Les institutions de la France au XVIe siècle*, Paris, 1948.

CHAPTER VI: FRANCE AND ENGLAND

Aytona, William E.: *The Life and Times of Richard the First*, London, 1840.

Bailly, Auguste: *Louis XI*, Paris, 1936.

Below, Georg von: *Der deutsche Staat des Mittelalters*, Vol. 1, Leipzig, 1914.

—— *Die italienische Kaiserpolitik des deutschen Mittelalters*, Munich and Berlin, 1927.

Bernard, Jacques: *Recueil des traitez de paix, de trêve, de neutralité, de suspension d'armes, de confédération, d'alliance, de commerce, de garantie, et d'autres actes publics . . .*, 4 vols. Amsterdam, 1700.

Beumelburg, Werner: *Friedrich II von Hohenstaufen*, Oldenburg, 1934.

Bezzola, Reto: *Les origines et la formation de la littérature courtoise en Occident (500–1200)*, Part 2, Paris, 1960.

Black, John: *The Reign of Elizabeth, 1558–1603*, Oxford, 1959.

Bordeaux, Henry: *Un précurseur: Vie, mort et survie de Saint Louis, roi de France*, Paris, 1949.

Bougeant, Le P. Guillaume-Hyacinthe, S. J.: *Histoire des guerres et des négotiations qui précédèrent le traité de Westphalie*, 3 vols, Paris, 1744.

Boussard, Jacques: *Le gouvernement d'Henri II Plantagenet*, Abbeville, 1956.

Brandi, Karl: *Deutschland und Italien*, Munich, 1941.

Braubach, Max: *"Zur Beurteilung der mittelalterlichen Kaiserpolitik"* in: *Vergangenheit und Gegenwart*, XVth year, 1925.

Brentano, Lujo: *Eine Geschichte der wirtschaftlichen Entwicklung Englands*, 3 vols. Jena, 1927/29.

Bühler, Johannes: *Deutsche Geschichte*, Vol. 2, Berlin and Leipzig, 1935.

—— *Die Hohenstaufen*, Leipzig, 1925.

Büttner, Heinrich: *Staufer und Zähringer im politischen Kräftespiel zwischen Bodensee und Genfer See während des 12. Jahrhunderts*, Zürich, 1961.

Burckhardt, Carl J.: *Vier historische Betrachtungen*, Zürich, 1953.

Calmette, Joseph: *Chute et relèvement de la France sous Charles VI et Charles VII*, Paris, 1945.

—— *Les Grands Ducs de Bourgogne*, Paris, 1949.

—— *Louis XI*, Paris, 1937.

—— and Georges Périnelle: *Louis XI et l'Angleterre (1461–1483)*, Paris, 1930.

Capes, William Wolfe: "The English Church in the Fourteenth and Fifteenth Centuries" in *History of the English Church*, Vol. 3. London, 1900.

Cartellieri, Alexander: *"Die staufischen Kaiser, die Auffassung ihrer allgemeinen Politik"* in: *Neue Heidelberger Jahrbücher* XIII, 1904.

—— *Philipp II. August*, 4 vols. Leipzig, 1899–1921.

Daimann, Hermann: *Die Doktrin vom göttlichen Rechte der Könige bei Jakob I von England in ihrem Einfluss auf die Anfänge der Soziologie in England im 17. Jahrhundert*, Marienberg, 1957.

Diederichs, Arthur: *Staufer und Welfen*, Jena, 1943.

Doernberg, Erwin: *Henry VIII and Luther*, London, 1961.

Dumont, Jean: *Recueil de divers traite̜ de paix, de confédération, d'alliance, de commerce, etc., faits depuis soixante ans, entre les Etats souverains de l'Europe*, The Hague, 1707.

Foreville, Raymonde: *L'église et la royauté en Angleterre sous Henri II Plantagenet*, Paris, 1943.

Gaxotte, Pierre: *Histoire des Français*, Vol. 1, Paris, 1951.

Gronen, Editha: *Die Machtpolitik Heinrichs des Löwen und sein Gegensat̜ gegen das Kaisertum*, Berlin, 1919.

Grundmann, Herbert: *"Das hohe Mittelalter und die deutsche Kaiser̜eit"* in: *Die Neue Propyläen-Weltgeschichte*, Vol. 2, Berlin, 1940.

Gubler, Friedrich T.: *"Besteht in der Schwei̜ ein Bedürfnis nach Einführung des Instituts der angelsächsischen Treuhand (trust)?"* in: *Zeitschrift für schwei̜erisches Recht*, Basle, 1954.

Güterbock, Ferdinand: *"Barbarossa und Heinrich der Löwe"* in: *Vergangenheit und Gegenwart*, 23rd year, 1933.

Hackett, Francis: *Henry the Eighth*, London and New York, 1929.

Hampe, Karl: *Das Hochmittelalter. Geschichte des Abendlandes von 900 bis 1250*, Berlin, 1932.

———— *Deutsche Kaisergeschichte in der Zeit der Salier und Staufer*, Leipzig, 1945.

———— *Kaiser Friedrich II. der Hohenstaufe*, Lübeck, 1935.

Heimpel, Hermann: *Deutsches Mittelalter*, Leipzig, 1941.

———— *Kaiser Friedrich Barbarossa und die Wende der Staufischen Zeit*, Strassburg, 1942.

Höpfl, Heinz: *Kleine Geschichte Englands*, Frankfurt a. M., 1955.

Holtzmann, Walther: *"Friedrich Barbarossa und Heinrich der Löwe"* in: *Gestalten deutscher Vergangenheit*, Potsdam, 1938.

Jäger, Oscar: *John Wycliffe und seine Bedeutung für die Reformation*, Halle, 1854.

Joinville, Jean de: *Histoire de Saint Louis*, Paris, 1883.

Kantorowicz, Ernst: *Kaiser Friedrich der Zweite*, 2 vols. Berlin, 1927/31.

Kendall, Paul Murray: *Richard the Third*, London, 1955.

Kern, Fritz: *Gottesgnadentum und Widerstandsrecht im frühen Mittelalter*, Münster and Cologne, 1954.

Kirfel, Hans Joachim: *"Weltherrschaftsidee und Bündnispolitik—Untersuchungen ̜ur Auswärtigen Politik der Staufer"* in: *Bonner Historische Forschungen*, Vol. 12, Bonn, 1959.

Koschaker, Paul: *Europa und das römische Recht*, Munich, 1947.

Lacombe, Charles de: *Henri IV et sa politique*, Paris, 1860.

La Ferrière, Hector de: *Les deux cours de France et d'Angleterre*, Paris, 1895.

Landon, Lionel: *The Itinerary of King Richard I*, London, 1935.

Lann, Justus Ferdinand: *Die Prädestination bei Wyclif und Bradwardein*, Giessen, 1932.

Loserth, Johann: *Hus und Wiclif*, 2nd edition, Munich, 1925.

———— *Über Wiclifs erstes Auftreten als Kirchenpolitiker*, Graz, 1895.

Magna Carta Libertatum von 1215 lateinisch—deutsch—englisch, mit ergän̜enden Aktenstücken, edited by Hans Wagner, Berne, n.d. (1951).

Man, Hendrik de: *Jacques Cœur*, Berne, 1950.

Marbault: *Remarques sur les mémoires des sages et royales œconomies d'Estat, domestiques, politiques et unitaires de Henry le Grand . . . , de Maximilian de Béthune, duc de Sully*, Paris, 1837.

Marcham, Frederick George: *James I of England and the "Little Beagle" Letters*, New York, 1931.

Martin, Charles: *John Wyclif. Les Lollards*, Lausanne, 1919.

Maschke, Erich: *"Der Kampf zwischen Kaisertum und Papsttum"* in: *Handbuch der deutschen Geschichte*, Vol. 1, Stuttgart, 1936.

Michaux, Theodor: *Die Hauptentscheidungen des Kreuzzugs Ludwigs IX. in ihrer politischen Bedingtheit*, Cologne, 1954.

Mikoletzky, Hanns Leo: *Kaiser Heinrich II und die Kirche*, Vienna, 1946.

Mitteis, Heinrich: *Der Staat des hohen Mittelalters*, Weimar, 1940.

———— *"Politische Prozesse des frühen Mittelalters in Deutschland und Frankreich"* in: *Sitzungsberichte der Heidelberger Akademie der Wissenschaften*, 1926/27.

de Morgues, Mathieu: *Histoire de la mort déplorable de Henri IV, Epître dédicatoire à Marie de Médicis*, Paris, 1612.

Neale, John Ernest: *Elizabeth I and Her Parliaments. 1559–1581*, London, 1953.

———— *Queen Elizabeth*, London, 1934.

Olivier, Martin-L.: *Saint Louis*, Paris, 1937.

Oman, Sir Charles William Chadwick: *The History of England from the Accession of Richard II to the Death of Richard III, 1377–1485*, London, 1906.

Painter, Sidney: *The Reign of King John*, Baltimore, 1949.

Patmore, Katherine Alexandra: *The Seven Edwards of England*, London, 1911.

Peterson, Earl Herman: *Early English Chronicle and Biographical Antecedents of Henry VI*, Urbana, Ill., 1940.

Pfister, Christian: *Les "Economies royales" de Sully et le grand dessein de Henry IV.*, Nogent-le-Rotrou, 1894.

Poirson, Auguste-Simon-Jean-Chrysostome: *Histoire du règne de Henri IV. Atlas pour la guerre, les travaux publics, les beaux-arts, pendant ce règne, publié sous la direction des M. A. Poirson, avec les textes et les légendes des auteurs contemporains . . .* , Paris, 1865.

Poole, Austin Lane: *From Domesday Book to Magna Charta (1087–1216)*, Oxford, 1951.

Ranke, Leopold von: *Englische Geschichte*, Vol. I, Berlin, 1859.

Read, Conyers: *Lord Burghley and Queen Elizabeth*, London, 1960.

———— *The Tudors*, New York, 1936.

Riess, Ludwig: *Englische Verfassungsurkunden des 12. und 13. Jahrhunderts*, Bonn and Berlin, 1926.

Riggenbach, Christoph: *Johann von Wiclif, der englische Reformator vor der Reformation*, Basle, 1874.

Ritter, Moritz: *"Die Memoiren Sullys und der grosse Plan Heinrichs IV."* in: *Abhandlungen der königlich bayerischen Akademie der Wissenschaften*, Cl. 3, Vol. 11, Sect. 3, Munich, 1871.

BIBLIOGRAPHY

Robson, John Adam: *Wiclif and the Oxford Schools*, Cambridge, 1961.

Runciman, Steven: *The Sicilian Vespers*. Cambridge and New York, 1958.

Schramm, Percy Ernst: "*Die Geschichte des mittelalterlichen Herrschertums in Lichte des Herrschaftsbereiches*" in: *Historische Zeitschrift*, 178, Munich 1954.

────── *Geschichte des englischen Königtums*, Weimar, 1937.

Stählin, Carl: *Die inneren Verhältnisse Englands um das zweite Jahrzehnt Elisabeths*, Leipzig, 1920.

Strachey, Lytton: *Elizabeth and Essex*, London, 1929.

Thieme, Hans: *Die Ehescheidung Heinrichs VIII. als europäischer Rechtsfall*, Lindau and Konstanz, 1956.

Towne, Frank: *Wiclif and Chaucer on the Contemplative Life*, Berkeley and Los Angeles, 1950.

Trevelyan, George Macaulay: *England in the Age of Wycliffe*, London, 1899.

────── *History of England*, London, 1926.

Vogt, Hans Joachim: *Konrad II im Vergleich zu Heinrich II und Heinrich III*, Frankfurt a. M., 1957.

Walsh, Joseph-Alexis: *Saint Louis et son siècle*, Tours, 1851.

Warren, Wilfred Lewis: *King John*, London, 1961.

Workman, Herbert B.: *John Wyclif. A Study of the English Medieval Church*, Oxford, 1926.

CHAPTER VII: GERMANY

Acta pacis westphalicae, Series 1: *Instruktionen* Vol. 1: *"Frankreich— Schweden—Kaiser,"* edited by Franz Dickmann, Kriemhild Goronzy, Emil Schieche, Hans Wagner and Ernst Manfred Wermter, Münster, 1962.

Acta SC de Propaganda Fide Germaniam Spectantia. Die Protokolle der Propagandakongregation zu deutschen Angelegenheiten: 1622–1649, Paderborn, 1962.

Asplund, Nils: *Gustav Adolf,* German edition, Berlin, 1938.

Aubéry, Antoine: *Mémoires pour l'histoire du Cardinal de Richelieu,* 3 vols. Paris, 1660.

Albrecht, Dieter: *Die auswärtige Politik Maximilians von Bayern 1618–1635,* Göttingen, 1962.

——— *Richelieu, Gustav Adolf und das Reich,* Munich and Vienna, 1959.

——— *"Zur Finanzierung des Dreissigjährigen Krieges"* in: *Zeitschrift für bayerische Landesgeschichte,* 19 (1956), pp. 534–567.

Andreas, Willy: *"Richelieu"* in: *Persönlichkeit und Geschichte,* Göttingen, 1958.

Aretin, K. M. von: *Bayerns auswärtige Verhältnisse seit dem Anfang des 16. Jahrhunderts,* Passau, 1839.

——— *Wallenstein. Beiträge zur näheren Kenntnis seines Charakters, seiner Pläne, seines Verhältnisses zu Bayern,* Regensburg, 1846.

Babinger, Franz: *Mehmed der Eroberer und seine Zeit,* Munich, 1953.

——— *"Mehmud II, der Eroberer und Italien"* in: *Byzantion XXI,* Brussels, 1951, pp. 127–170.

Baron, Hans: *Calvins Staatsanschauung und das konfessionelle Zeitalter,* Berlin and Munich, 1924.

Batiffol, Louis: *Au temps de Louis XIII,* Paris, 1904.

——— *La Duchesse de Chevreuse,* Paris, 1913.

——— *Le Roi Louis XIII à vingt ans,* Paris, 1910.

——— *Richelieu et le roi Louis XIII,* Paris, 1934.

Baustaedt, Berthold: *"Richelieu und Deutschland. Von der Schlacht bei Breitenfeld bis zum Tode Bernhards von Weimar"* in: *Histor. Studien,* No. 295, Berlin, 1936.

Bergl, Josef: *"Wallenstein und Friedland: Der Anteil der Herrschaft Friedland an der Ausrüstung des Wallensteinschen Heeres im Jahre 1628"* in: *Mitteilungen des Vereines für Heimatkunde des Jeschken-Iser-Gaues,* 28th year, No. 1, Reichenberg, 1934.

Bernard, Jacques: *Recueil des traitez de paix, de trêve, de neutralité, de suspension d'armes, de confédération, d'alliance, de commerce, de garantie, et d'autres actes publics . . .* 4 vols., Amsterdam, 1700.

Bezzel, I.: *Kurfürst Maximilian I. von Bayern als Reichsfürst in den Jahren 1623–1627* (thesis), Munich, 1957.

Blet, P.: *"Richelieu et les débuts de Mazarin,"* in: *Revue d'histoire moderne et contemporaine,* 6 (1959), pp. 241–268.

Boehn, Max von: *Wallenstein,* Vienna and Leipzig, 1926.

Bougeant, Guillaume-Hyacinthe: *Histoire des guerres et negotiations* . . . , 3 vols. Paris, 1744.

Brandi, Karl: *Deutsche Geschichte im Zeitalter der Reformation und Gegenreformation*, Leipzig, 1941.

––––––– *Kaiser Karl V*, 2 vols. Munich, 1937/41.

Braubach, Max: *Der Aufstieg Brandenburg-Preussens 1640–1815*, Freiburg i. Br., 1933.

Braun, Maximilian: *Die Slawen auf dem Balkan*, Leipzig, 1941.

Braunsberger, Otto: *Peter Canisius. Ein Lebensbild*, Freiburg i. Br., 1921.

Brezzi, P.: *Il Papato*, Rome, 1952.

Briefe und Akten zur Geschichte des Dreissigjährigen Krieges in den Zeiten des vorwaltenden Einflusses der Wittelsbacher, Vols. 4–8, ed. by F. Stieve, K. Mayr, and A. Chroust, Munich, 1878–1909.

Briefe und Akten zur Geschichte des Dreissigjährigen Krieges. New Series: *Die Politik Maximilians I. von Bayern und seiner Verbündeten 1618 bis 1651*. Part 2, Vol. 1–4, ed. by W. Goetz, Leipzig and Munich, 1907–1948.

Bruchmüller, Ernst Joachim: *Die Folgen der Reformation und des 30 jährigen Krieges für die ländliche Verfassung und die Lage des Bauernstandes im östl. Deutschland besonders in Brandenburg und Pommern*, Crossen, 1897.

Brünink, Wolfgang: *Der Graf von Mansfeld in Ostfriesland (1622–1624)* (thesis), Aurich, 1957.

Burckhardt, Carl J.: *"Ein unveröffentlichter Brief Montecucculis an den Fürsten Piccolomini"* in: *Mélanges offerts à M. Paul-E. Martin*, Geneva, 1961.

––––––– *"Kalter Krieg im 17. Jahrhundert"* in: *Betrachtungen und Berichte*, Zürich, 1964.

Callot, Jacques: *Die grossen Schrecken des Krieges*, Bremen, 1936.

Canu, Jean: *Louis XIII et Richelieu*, Paris, 1944.

Capefigue, M.: *Histoire de la Réforme de la Ligue et du règne de Henri IV*, 8 vols. Paris, 1834.

––––––– *Richelieu, Mazarin, la fronde et le règne de Louis XIV*, 6 vols. Paris, 1835.

de Charnacé, Guy: *"Un ambassadeur de Louis XIII"* in: *La nouvelle revue*, Vol. 23, Paris, 1903.

Danstrup, John: *A History of Denmark*, Copenhagen, 1948.

Dickmann, Fritz: *Der Westfälische Friede*, Münster, 1959.

Doerberl, Michael: *Bayern und Frankreich*, 2 vols. Munich, 1900–03.

Dotterweich, Helmut: *Der junge Maximilian. Jugend und Erziehung des bayerischen Herzogs und späteren Kurfürsten Maximilian I. von 1573 bis 1593*, Munich, 1962.

Droysen, Gustav (the younger): *Gustav Adolf*, 2 vols. Leipzig, 1869/70.

Mémoires et correspondance de Duplessis-Mornay, 12 vols. Paris, 1824–1825.

Ebeling, Gerhard: *Luther, Einführung in sein Denken*, Tübingen, 1964.

Eder, K.: *Glaubensspaltung und Landstände in Österreich ob der Enns 1525–1602*, Linz, 1963.

Elementa ad fontium editiones VIII—Documenta polonica ex archivo generali Hispaniae in Simancas, Part I, ed. by Valerianus Meysztowicz, Rome, 1963.

Elementa ad fontium editiones IX—Res polonicae ex archivo regni Daniae, Part I (1526–1572), coll. by Leon Koczy, Rome, 1964.

Elementa ad fontium editiones XI—Documenta polonica ex archivo generali Hispaniae in Simancas, Part I, ed. by Valerianus Meysztowicz, Rome, 1964.

Ernstberger, Anton: *"Albrecht von Wallenstein"* in: *Mitteilungen des Vereines für Heimatkunde des Jeschken-Iser-Gaues*, 28th year, No. 1, Reichenberg, 1934.

—— *"Aus den Tagen Wallensteins," ibid.*

—— *Franken—Böhmen—Europa*, 2 vols. Lassleben, 1959.

—— *Hans de Witte. Finanzmann Wallensteins*, Wiesbaden, 1954.

—— *Wallenstein als Volkswirt im Herzogtum Friedland*, Reichenberg, 1929.

—— *"Wallensteins Heeressabotage und die Breitenfelder Schlacht 1631"* in: *Historische Zeitschrift*, Vol. 142, Munich, 1930.

Essen, Alfred van der: *Le Cardinal-Infant et la politique européenne de l'Espagne 1609–1641*, Vol. 1: *1609–1634*, Brussels, 1944.

Fagniez, G.: *Le père Joseph et Richelieu*, 2 vols. Paris, 1894.

Lettres et négotiations du marquis de Feuquières, 3 vols. Amsterdam, 1753.

Förster, Friedrich: *Albrecht Wallensteins Briefe und amtliche Schreiben*, Berlin, 1828.

Gardiner, Samuel Ranson: *The Thirty Years' War, 1618–1648*, London, 1874.

Gindely, Anton: *Böhmen und Mähren im Zeitalter der Reformation*, 2 vols. Prague, 1857/58.

—— *Die Entwicklung des böhmischen Adels und der Inkolatsverhältnisse seit dem 16. Jahrhundert*, Prague, 1886.

—— *"Die Gegenreformation und der Aufstand in Oberösterreich im Jahre 1626"* in: *Sitzungsberichte der kaiserl. Akademie der Wissenschaften*, Vol. 118, Vienna, 1849.

—— *"Die maritimen Pläne der Hapsburger und die Antheilnahme Kaisers Ferdinand II. am polnisch-schwedischen Kriege während der Jahre 1627 bis 1629"* in: *Denkschrift der kaiserl. Akademie der Wissenschaften*, Vol. 39, Vienna, 1850.

—— *Geschichte der Ertheilung des böhmischen Majestätsbriefes von 1609*, Prague, 1858.

—— *Geschichte des Dreissigjährigen Krieges*, 4 vols. Prague, 1869–1880.

—— *Rudolph II und seine Zeit. 1600–1612*, 2 vols. Prague, 1863/65.

—— *"Waldsteins Vertrag mit dem Kaiser bei der Übernahme des zweiten Generalats"* in: *Abhandlung der Böhmischen Gesellschaft der Wissenschaften*, 2nd Series, Vol. 3, Prague, 1889.

—— *Waldstein während seines ersten Generalats im Lichte der gleichzeitigen Quellen 1625–1630*, 2 vols., Prague and Leipzig, 1886.

Goetz, Walter: *"Das Zeitalter der religiösen Umwälzung—Die Gegenreformation in Deutschland"* in: *"Reformation und Gegenreformation 1500–1660," Propyläen-Weltgeschichte*, Berlin, 1930.

Gogarten, Friedrich: *"Martin Luther und die deutsche Reformation"* in: *Die Grossen Deutschen*, Berlin, 1935.

Gragger, Robert: *"Türkisch-ungarische Kulturbeziehungen"* in: Franz Babinger, Robert Gragger, Eugen Mittwoch and J. Mordtmann: *Literaturdenkmäler aus Ungarns Türkenzeit,* Berlin and Leipzig, 1927.

Gregorovius, Ferdinand: *Urban VIII. im Widerspruch zu Spanien und dem Kaiser. Eine Episode aus dem Dreissigjährigen Krieg,* Stuttgart, 1879.

Günter, Heinrich: *Die Hapsburgerliga 1625–1635,* Berlin, 1908.

Hämmerle, Albert: *Die Radierungen des Hanns Ulrich Franckh, Malers aus Kaufbeuren 1603/1675,* Augsburg, 1923.

Hallwich, Hermann: *Briefe und Akten zur Geschichte Wallensteins 1630 bis 1634,* 2 vols. Vienna, 1904/12.

———— *Fünf Bücher Geschichte Wallensteins,* 2 vols. Leipzig, 1910.

———— *Wallensteins Ende,* 2 vols. Leipzig, 1879.

Hanotaux, Gabriel and le Duc de La Force: *Histoire du Cardinal de Richelieu,* 6 vols. Paris, 1893–1944.

Hantsch, Hugo: *Die Geschichte Österreichs,* Vol. 1, Graz, 1947.

Hartmann, Richard: *"Die neue Türkei"* in: *Der Vordere Orient, Auslandstudien,* Vol. 4, Königsberg, 1929, pp. 88–115.

———— *Die Welt des Islam einst und heute,* Leipzig, 1927.

Hassinger, Erich: *Das Werden des neuzeitlichen Europa, 1300–1600,* Braunschweig, 1959.

Hauser, Henri: *La pensée et l'action économiques du Cardinal de Richelieu,* Paris, 1944.

Helbig, Karl Gustav: *Der Kaiser Ferdinand und der Herzog von Friedland während des Winters 1633–1634,* Dresden, 1852.

Heyne, Otto: *Der Kurfürstentag von Regensburg von 1630,* Berlin, 1866.

Hubatsch, Walter: *Das Zeitalter des Absolutismus, 1600–1789,* Braunschweig, 1962.

Huch, Ricarda: *Der Dreissigjährige Krieg,* Wiesbaden, 1958.

Hurter, F.: *Beiträge zur Geschichte Wallensteins,* Schaffhausen, 1855.

———— *Französische Feindseligkeiten gegen das Haus Österreich zur Zeit Kaiser Ferdinands des Zweiten,* Vienna, 1859.

Irmer, Georg: *"Die Verhandlungen Schwedens und seiner Verbündeten mit Wallenstein und dem Kaiser von 1631 bis 1634,"* Part 1: 1631 und 1632, *Publikationen aus den preussischen Staatsarchiven* 35, 1, Leipzig, 1888.

———— *Hans Georg von Arnim,* Leipzig, 1894.

Jäger, Oscar: *John Wycliffe und seine Bedeutung für die Reformation,* Halle, 1854.

Janssen, Johannes: *Gustav Adolf in Deutschland,* Frankfurt a. M., 1865.

Jessen, Hans: *Der Dreissigjährige Krieg in Augenzeugenberichten,* Fribourg, 1963.

Juritsch, Georg: *Beiträge zur böhmischen Geschichte zur Zeit der Přemysliden,* Prague, 1928.

Khevenhüller, F. Chr. von: *Annales Ferdinandei,* Vol. 9 and 11, Leipzig, 1724/26.

Klopp, Onno: *Tilly im Dreissigjährigen Krieg,* 2 vols. Stuttgart, 1861.

Köhler, Ludwig: *Johannes Hus und seine Zeit,* Leipzig, 1846.

464

Köhler, Walther: *Martin Luther und die deutsche Reformation*, Berlin, 1917.

Krabbe, Ludvig: *Histoire de Danemark*, Copenhagen, 1950.

Krones von Marchland, F. X.: *"Tschernembl"* in: *Allgemeine deutsche Biographie*, Leipzig, 1894.

Krügel, Gerhard: *Aus dem Dreissigjährigen Kriege. Schilderungen und Berichte von Augenzeugen*, Leipzig, 1911.

Krüner, F.: *Johann von Rusdorf*, Halle, 1876.

Lavisse, Ernest et Raumbaud, Alfred: *Histoire générale du IVe siècle à nos jours*, Vol. 4: *Renaissance et Réforme. Les nouveaux mondes 1492–1559*, Chapter XIX: *"L'empire Ottoman l'apogée—L'alliance française 1481 à 1566,"* Paris, 1894, pp. 699 ff. Vol. 5: *Les Guerres de Religion 1559–1648*, Paris, 1895.

Leman, A.: *Urbain VIII et la rivalité de la France et de la Maison d'Autriche de 1631 à 1635*, Lille and Paris, 1920.

Lemée, Bernard: *Les missions d'Hercule de Charnacé de 1629 à 1635* (thesis), Paris, 1953.

Lochner, George Wolfgang Karl: *Über die Theilnahme der Stadt Nürnberg am Dreissigjährigen Kriege*, Nuremberg, 1832.

Loesche, Georg: *Die böhmischen Exulanten in Sachsen. Ein Beitrag zur Geschichte des 30 jährigen Krieges und der Gegenreformation auf archivalischer Grundlage*, Leipzig and Vienna, 1923.

Mann, Golo: *"Das Zeitalter des Dreissigjährigen Krieges"* in: *Propyläen-Weltgeschichte*, Berlin, 1964, Vol. 7.

Mauvillon, Eléazar: *Histoire de Gustav Adolph roi de Suède. Composée sur tout ce qui a paru des plus curieux sur un grand nombre de Manuscrits & principalement de ceux de Mr. Arkenholtz*, Amsterdam, 1764.

McKnight, J. P.: *The Papacy: A New Appraisal*, New York, 1952.

Meester, B. de: *Correspondance du Nonce G. F. Guide di Bagno 1621–1627*, 2 vols. *Analecta Vaticano-Belgica*, 2nd series: *Nonciature de Flandre V, VI*, Brussels and Rome, 1937/38.

Meinecke, Friedrich: *Die Idee der Staatsraison in der neueren Geschichte*, Munich and Berlin, 1925.

Mercure François, 1633.

Messow, Hans Christoph: *Die Hansastädte und die Habsburgische Ostseepolitik im 30 jährigen Kriege*, Berlin, 1935.

Mommsen, Wilhelm: *"Vier Jahrzehnte europäischer Krieg (1618–1660),"* in: *Propyläen-Weltgeschichte*, Vol. 5, Berlin, 1930.

Noack, Ulrich: *Geschichte der nordischen Völker*, Vol. 1, Munich and Berlin, 1941.

Axel Oxenstierna intill Gustav Adolfs död, Stockholm, 1940.

Pagès, G.: *"Autour du 'Grand Orage' Richelieu et Marillac"* in: *Revue Historique*, 179, Paris, 1937.

———— *La monarchie d'ancien régime en France—de Henri IV à Louis XIII*, Paris, 1932.

———— *"Richelieu et Marillac—deux politiques"* in: *Revue Historique*, Jan.-June, 1937.

———— *La guerre de trente ans 1618–1648*, Paris, 1949.

Q

de Pange, Jean: *Charnacé et l'alliance franco-hollandaise* (*1633–1637*), Paris, 1905.

———— *Le roi très chrétien*, Paris, 1949.

Pastor, Ludwig von: *Geschichte der Päpste seit dem Ausgang des Mittelalters*, 16 vols. Freiburg i. Br., 1886–1933.

Pekař, Josef: *Wallenstein 1630–1634*, German edition, 2 vols. Berlin, 1937.

Pfister, Kurt: *Kurfürst Maximilian von Bayern und sein Jahrhundert*, Munich, 1948.

Pick, Friedel: *Pragensia und Der Prager Fenstersturz i. J. 1618*, Prague, 1918.

Précis de campagnes de Gustave-Adolphe en Allemagne (*1630–1632*), Brussels, 1897.

Préclin, Ed. et Victor-L. Tapié: *Le XVIIe siècle*, Paris, 1943.

Preuss, Hans: *Martin Luther, Seele und Sendung*, Gütersloh, 1947.

Ranke, Leopold von: *Die deutsche Geschichte im Zeitalter der Reformation*, 6 vols. Berlin, 1839–47.

———— *Die römischen Päpste in den letzten vier Jahrhunderten*, 3 vols. Berlin, 1854/57.

———— *Über die Epochen der neueren Geschichte*, Leipzig, 1888.

———— *Wallenstein*, Leipzig, 1869.

———— *Zwölf Bücher preussischer Geschichte*, 3 vols. Munich, 1930.

Rassow, Peter: *"Die Reichstage zu Augsburg in der Reformationszeit"* in: *Augusta 955–1955, Forschungen und Studien zur Kulturgeschichte und Wirtschaftsgeschichte Augsburgs*, Munich, 1955.

Reade, Hubert G.: *Sidelights of the Thirty Years' War*, London, 1924.

Reicke, Emil: *Geschichte der Reichsstadt Nürnberg*, Nuremberg, 1896.

Riezler, Siegmund von: *Geschichte Bayerns*, Vols. 4–5, Gotha, 1899/1906.

Ritter, Gerhard: *"Gustav Adolf, Deutschland und das nordische Luthertum"* in: *Die Weltwirkung der Reformation*, Munich, 1959.

———— *Luther, Gestalt und Tat*, Munich, 1948.

Ritter, Moriz: *Deutsche Geschichte im Zeitalter der Gegenreformation und des Dreissigjährigen Krieges*, Vols. 2 and 3, Stuttgart 1895/1908.

———— *"Untersuchungen zur Geschichte Wallensteins 1625–1629"* in: *Deutsche Zeitschrift für Geschichtswissenschaft 4* (1890), pp. 14–53.

Roberts, Michael: *Gustavus Adolphus: A History of Sweden, 1611–1632*, 2 vols. London, New York and Toronto, 1958.

Roca, Emile: *Le règne de Richelieu 1615–1642*, Paris, 1906.

Röse, Bernhard: *Herzog Bernhard der Grosse von Sachsen-Weimar*, 2 vols. Weimar, 1828/29.

Rohde, Hans-Wilhelm: *Evangelische Bewegung und katholische Restauration im österreichischen Breisgau unter Ferdinand I. und Ferdinand II, 1521–1595. Studien zur Kirchenpolitik der Habsburger in Vorderösterreich im 16. Jahrhundert*, (thesis), Freiburg i. Br., 1957.

Rystad, Göran: *Kriegsnachrichten und Propaganda während des Dreissigjährigen Krieges. Die Schlacht bei Nördlingen in den gleichzeitigen, gedruckten Kriegsberichten*, Lund, 1960.

Sailer, Anton: *Münchner Spectaculum*, Feldafing, 1955.

Schaeder, Hans Heinrich: *"Der osmanische Staat von seiner Entstehung bis zum Ausgang des siebzehnten Jahrhunderts"* in: *"Das Zeitalter der religiösen Umwälzung, Reformation und Gegenreformation. 1500–1660,"* Propyläen-Weltgeschichte, Vol. 5, Berlin, 1930.

Schaefer, A.: *"Interessantes und Amüsantes aus der Finanzgeschichte,"* lecture given in Zürich on April 6, 1960, before the Volkswirtschaftliche Gesellschaft.

Schäfer, Walter: *Petrus Canisius. Kampf eines Jesuiten um die Reform der katholischen Kirche Deutschlands,* Göttingen, 1931.

Schiller, Friedrich: *Geschichte des Dreissigjährigen Krieges,* Insel-Ausgabe, Vol. 5, Leipzig, n.d.

Schmerl, Wilhelm Sebastian: *Gustav Adolf. Ein Lebensbild des grossen Königs dem evangelischen Kirchenvolke dargeboten,* Erlangen, 1939.

Schnitzer, Joseph: *Savonarola,* Vol. 2, Munich, 1924.

Schreiber, F. A. W.: *Maximilian I. der Katholische, Kurfürst von Bayern,* Munich, 1868.

Schubert, Friedrich Hermann: *"Die pfälzische Exilregierung im Dreissigjährigen Krieg"* in: *Zeitschrift für die Geschichte des Oberrheins,* Vol. 102 (new series, Vol. 63).

——— *"Die Reformation in Augsburg"* in: *Augusta 955–1955, Forschungen und Studien zur Kulturgeschichte und Wirtschaftsgeschichte Augsburgs,* Munich, 1955.

——— *Ludwig Camerarius (1573–1651) als Staatsmann in Dreissigjährigen Krieg,* (thesis), Munich, 1952.

Schulz, Hans: *Wallenstein und die Zeit des Dreissigjährigen Krieges,* Bielefeld and Leipzig, 1912.

Schwarzenfeld, Gertrude von: *Rudolf II. Der Saturnische Kaiser,* Munich, 1961.

Seppelt, Franz Xaver: *Geschichte der Päpste,* Vol. 5, Munich, 1959.

——— and Georg Schwaiger: *Geschichte der Päpste von den Anfängen bis zur Gegenwart,* Munich, 1965.

Silberschmidt, Max: *"Das orientalische Problem zur Zeit der Entstehung des türkischen Reiches, nach venezianischen Quellen,"* Beiträge zur Kulturgeschichte, edited by Walter Goetz, Vol. 27, Leipzig and Berlin, 1923.

Spindler, Max: *Die Anfänge des bayerischen Landesfürstentums,* Munich, 1937.

Srbik, Heinrich von: *Wallensteins Ende,* Vienna, 1920.

Stadtmüller, Georg: *Geschichte Osteuropas,* Munich, 1950.

Stieve, Felix: *Das kirchliche Polizeiregiment in Baiern unter Maximilian I. 1595–1651,* Munich, 1876.

Sturmberger, Hans: *Aufstand in Böhmen,* Munich and Vienna, 1959.

——— *Georg Erasmus Tschernembl,* Linz, 1953.

Taeschner, Franz: *"Der Weg des Osmanischen Staates vom Glaubenskämpferbund zum islamischen Weltreich"* in: *Die Welt als Geschichte,* VI, 1940, pp. 206–215.

Tapié, Victor-L.: *La politique étrangère de la France et le début de la Guerre de Trente Ans 1616–1621,* Paris, 1934.

Treitschke, Heinrich von: *Gustav Adolf und Deutschlands Freiheit*, Leipzig, 1895.

Tschudi, Rudolf: *"Das osmanische Reich"* in: *Hesperia*, Vol. 4, No. 10, 1953.

───── *"Die osmanische Geschichte bis zum Ausgang des 17. Jahrhunderts* in: *Die neue Propyläen-Weltgeschichte*, Vol. 3: *Das Zeitalter der Entdeckungen, der Renaissance und Glaubenskämpfe*, Berlin, 1941.

Vertrags-Ploetz: Konferenzen und Verträge, Würzburg, 1958.

Vigier, O.: *"L'influence politique du Père Joseph. Négociations avec les princes d'Allemagne et la Suède"* in: *Revue des questions historiques*, 50 (1891).

Vindiciae Grotianae, ed. by ter Meulen and P. J. J. Diermanse, The Hague, 1950.

Waas, Adolf: *Die Bauern im Kampf um Gerechtigkeit, 1300–1525*, Munich, 1964.

Wagner, Georg: *Wallenstein*, Vienna, 1958.

Weber, Ottocar: *Von Luther zu Bismarck. Zwölf Charakterbilder aus deutscher Geschichte*, Vol. 2, Leipzig, 1906.

Wedgwood, C. V.: *The Thirty Years War*, London, 1938.

Weigel, Helmut: *Franken, Kurpfalz und der Böhmische Aufstand 1618 bis 1620*, Erlangen, 1932.

Westenrieder, Lorenz von: *Beyträge zur vaterländischen Historie*, Munich, 1788–1817, Vol. 7.

Westin, Gunnar: *Negotiations about Church Unity 1628–1634, John Durie, Gustavus Adolphus, Axel Oxenstierna*, Upsala, 1932.

Wiens, Erich: *Fancan und die französische Politik 1624–1627*, Heidelberg, 1908.

Winter, Georg: *Geschichte des Dreissigjährigen Krieges*, Naunhof b. Leipzig, 1934.

de Witt, Pierre: *Louis de Geer*, Paris, 1885.

Wostry, Wilhelm: *"Wallenstein"* in: *Die Grossen Deutschen*, Berlin, 1935.

Zilbermayr, I.: *Noricum, Baiern und Österreich*, Berlin, 1944.

INDEX

469